Creature Comforts

Creature Comforts

New Zealanders and their pets

AN ILLUSTRATED HISTORY

Nancy Swarbrick

Published by Otago University Press
PO Box 56 / Level 1, 398 Cumberland Street
Dunedin, New Zealand
university.press@otago.ac.nz
www.otago.ac.nz

First published in 2013
Copyright © 2013 Nancy Swarbrick

The moral rights of the author have been asserted.
ISBN 978-1-877578-61-8
A catalogue record for this book is available from the
National Library of New Zealand.
This book is copyright. Except for the purpose of fair review, no part
may be stored or transmitted in any form or by any means, electronic or
mechanical, including recording or storage in any information retrieval
system, without permission in writing from the publishers.

Publisher: Rachel Scott
Editor: Anna Rogers
Design/layout: Fiona Moffat
Index: Diane Lowther

Cover image: Sketch of Maori girl and her dog by William Strutt, c. 1855.
Alexander Turnbull Library. Reference: E-452-f-011-1
Back cover image: An unnamed Maori woman plays with her cat and its kittens.
Alexander Turnbull Library, Price Collection.
Reference: G-1534-1/2. Photograph by William Archer Price

Frontispiece: Sam Hunt and Minstrel, c. 1976.
Alexander Turnbull Library, *Dominion Post* Collection.
Reference: EP/1976/0034. Photograph by Ron Fox

Opposite Preface: Gumdigger Mr Gallagher and his cat,
Northland, probably in the 1890s or 1900s.
Alexander Turnbull Library, Northwood Collection.
Reference: G-6270-1/1. Photograph by Northwood Brothers

Printed in China through Asia Pacific Offset Ltd

Contents

	Acknowledgements	6
	Preface	9
Chapter 1	Making introductions	13
Chapter 2	Happy homes	37
Chapter 3	A man's best friends?	61
Chapter 4	The fancy	83
Chapter 5	Learning to be kind	107
Chapter 6	Feels like Calf Club Day	129
Chapter 7	From helpers to heroes	151
Chapter 8	Pets or pests?	175
Chapter 9	Local legends	197
Chapter 10	One of the family	223
	Endnotes	248
	Bibliography	275
	Index	283

Acknowledgements

Many people have helped me with my 'pet project'. Sally Maclean put me up to it in the first place, and offered many insights and much friendship along the way. Jock Phillips made excellent suggestions on structure and provided some of the illustrations. Bob Kerridge of the Royal New Zealand SPCA responded swiftly to my requests and gave invaluable feedback on one of the chapters. Andrea Barnard contributed sensible suggestions and warm support. I am especially indebted to Alison Parr, who not only read and commented on the text, but also gave wise counsel and urged me to keep going at a difficult time.

I spent many hours researching at the National Library, the Alexander Turnbull Library and Archives New Zealand. Thanks to all the staff who helped, especially Joan McCracken, Barbara Lyon, Peter Attwell, Marian Minson, Heather Mathie, Ann O'Rorke, David Colquhoun, David Retter, Denise Roughan, Natalie Marshall and Jenni Chrisstoffels at National Library, and Rachael Manson, Lillie Le Dorré, Vernon Wybrow and Greg Goulding at National Archives. I also appreciated the assistance of Rose Young, Martin Collett, Christina Tuitubou and Zoe Richardson at Auckland Museum; Melanie Brebner at the Davis Law Library, Auckland University; Lucy Macfarlane and Charlotte Stace at Puke Ariki, New Plymouth; Nicholas Wotton and Nicola Frean at the J.C. Beaglehole Room, Victoria University; Lucy Broadbent and Jeanette de Montalk at the Massey University Library, Wellington; Kirstie Ross and Rebecca Loud at Te Papa Tongarewa; Helen Pannett at the Nelson Provincial Museum; Michelle Lambert at the Canterbury Museum; Lyn Gifford and Amanda Brown at Christchurch City Libraries; Tony Rippin at the South Canterbury Museum; Chloe Searle at the North Otago Museum; Victoria France and Richard Munro at the Hocken Collections, Dunedin; Geoff Marsh at the Museum of Sydney, and Jovita Callueng, Martin Mintz and Chris Rawlings at the British Library.

Christine Burbush provided publications relating to the history of the Auckland SPCA and Amy Ewles arranged access to the society's annual reports. Julie Sleep of Wellington City Council located information on 'pooper scooper' regulations, Rob Dickson of Euromonitor supplied statistics on pet ownership and David Thomas of Massey University Institute of Food, Nutrition and Human Health and Matthew Jones of Nestle Purina Petcare gave me material on the history of pet food. Frederick S. Milton of Newcastle University sent me extracts from his PhD thesis on British children's societies for the prevention of cruelty to birds and animals. Annie Potts of the New Zealand Centre for Human-Animal Studies was generously collegial. I received useful research advice and information from Paul Diamond, Malcolm McKinnon, Bronwyn Labrum, Richard Brake, Shona Jones, Louise Burnside, Redmer Yska, Odette Rowe, Noel Smith, Emily Stott, Tony

Sillars, Janine Cook and the late Jeannette Ward. Trena Marshall, Alex McEwing, Keith McEwing, Julia Brighouse, Anna Smith, Margaret O'Connor, Susan Harper, Philip Rowe, Mark Smith, Narelle Pollock, Claudia Tasker, Fiona McKergow and Christine Potter kindly shared their recollections of calf and lamb-rearing clubs.

A number of people assisted me with my image research: locating, supplying and giving permission to reproduce photographs and other visual material. As well as those already named, sincere thanks to Peter Shaw, Paul Tapsell, Paul van Herpt, Annette Taylor, Kim White, Codie White, Julie Pirie, Grant Pascoe, Amy Symes, Charlotte Hood, Graeme Wright, Margaret Aish, Frances Faulkner, Pete Huggins, Melissa Reid, Karen Arnold, Richard Gill, Natalie Souness, Malcolm Evans, Derek Hughes, Tom Scott, Jude Tewnion, Jo Hurford, Danny Hodgson, Joann Ransom, Iain Torrance, Andrea Collins and Shirley Williams.

I would like to acknowledge with gratitude an Award in History from the New Zealand History Research Trust Fund.

Colleagues at Manatu Taonga: the Ministry for Culture and Heritage were consistently helpful. In addition to those I have mentioned above, my thanks to Janine Faulknor, Marguerite Hill, Neill Atkinson, Imelda Bargas, Melanie Mills, Ben Schrader, Peter Clayworth, Basil Keane, Margaret Marks, Brodie Stubbs, Julia Vodanovich, Lisa Young, Mark Derby, Caren Wilton, David Green and Andy Palmer for assistance of various kinds. Fran McGowan was always obliging in tracking down books, Kerryn Pollock contributed information on animal rearing and reviewed the chapter on that topic, and Melanie Lovell-Smith answered my many questions about image research, gave much-needed technical aid and provided several of the photographs.

I owe special thanks to Anna Rogers for her expert guidance, advocacy and sensitive editing of the book. I am very grateful to Rachel Scott and her team at Otago University Press, especially Fiona Moffat and Rhian Gallagher, for producing and promoting it. Diane Lowther compiled the excellent index.

Friends tolerated my anti-social ways and cheered me on. In particular, I valued the steadfast encouragement of Helen Wood and the sound advice of Pam Davidson. As always, Murray Grant listened with patience and good humour to my long monologues, and Joan, Helen and Jim Swarbrick gave practical and moral support from the start. Finally, I pay tribute to a feline friend, Guido, who kept me company while I wrote this book – wicked, funny and affectionate – my own creature comfort.

Nancy Swarbrick

Preface

The keeping of pets dates back hundreds of years in many cultures, and in the twenty-first century is more popular than ever before. This is certainly the case in New Zealand. In 2011, according to a Companion Animal Council survey, pets here outnumbered people: there were 5 million pets compared with 4.4 million humans. Sixty-eight per cent of households had at least one pet – a higher percentage than Australia, the United States or Britain.[1] Nearly half had a cat and more than a quarter had a dog. Also well represented in the nation's homes were tame rabbits, birds and fish. Clearly, New Zealanders love their pets.

Yet most New Zealand animals are regarded quite differently – as 'stock', 'game' or 'pests'. Much of the nation's wealth derives from farming of sheep and dairy cows; hunting and fishing are very popular sports. Attitudes towards farm and feral animals can be extremely matter-of-fact, even harsh – a far cry from the way people view their pets, which are named, played with, stroked and groomed, talked to and teased affectionately. Money is lavished on their food, toys and medical treatment. When they die, their owners are often devastated.

Is pet keeping, then, just a pastime for sentimental townies? Not at all. There are plenty of pets in country districts as well: in fact, where there is open space, the range is even wider, including larger animals such as horses and ponies. Farm animals, too, can become pets: many country children have tame lambs and calves.

The existence of a thriving pet culture alongside a deeply pragmatic approach to other animals is a paradox that cannot be simply explained. In a further complication, animals that are usually killed and eaten, or targeted as pests, can also be pets. Essentially, people make pets: they decide, often quite arbitrarily, to befriend certain animals. This book is as much about humans and their contradictory behaviour as it is about pets.

My definition of the word 'pet' is deliberately wide, and I use it together with the more inclusive term 'companion animal'. This allows me to talk about some animals – farm dogs and work horses, for example – that may not have been cosseted like most pets but lived alongside people and played an important part in daily life. For although many New Zealanders believe there is an impassable divide between pets and working animals, and treat them differently, both have long been valued for their company. Another common belief, that pets are or should be restricted to certain species, can be easily dismissed. All kinds of creatures – indigenous and exotic; furry, feathered and finned – have become loved companions. For these and other reasons, it is impossible to discuss pets without considering animals more generally.

Why do we become so attached to individual animals? One reason is that pets have a very important social function. As well as giving unquestioning loyalty and affection, they allow people to express protectiveness and love and to have straightforward fun. They can act as go-betweens in relationships. In a demanding, competitive and often unfriendly world, they offer an outlet for important emotions, and fulfil the human need to relate to other living creatures. This is as true of the past as it is of the present. Countless tales – touching, heart-warming and funny – can be told about the vital but often overlooked everyday connections between pets and people.

New Zealand's pet-keeping history needs to be seen in the context of ideas and movements that originated elsewhere. Beliefs and customs relating to animals, including pets, were brought here by Maori from the thirteenth century, by eighteenth-century European explorers and by British settlers sailing south in the nineteenth century. Later arrivals from elsewhere introduced other views about pets. Animal welfare and rights campaigns that began in other countries, particularly Britain, the United States and Australia, were very influential in New Zealand in the later nineteenth and twentieth centuries, and affected how people saw their animal companions. The explosion in pet ownership and the pet industry in New Zealand after World War II followed an international trend.

But New Zealand pet keeping has some distinctive features. Companion animals helped migrants to overcome homesickness and adjust to a new life:

they are a shadowy presence in our foundation stories. Maori and Pakeha introduced each other to their favourite animals in the eighteenth and nineteenth centuries – with some interesting results. One was the emergence of a unique fauna that included both native and imported animal species, many of which could, in certain circumstances, become pets.

This book explores the main events, issues and movements that have shaped pet keeping here. It considers the different roles companion animals played, and the way people thought about and treated them. The thematic chapters follow a broadly chronological sequence, starting in the late eighteenth century and finishing in the early twenty-first. This reveals how pet keeping in New Zealand has changed.

These days images, film footage, commentary and articles about companion animals are everywhere. A major metropolitan newspaper runs a popular feature based on readers' photographs of their pets. Stories about heroic, clever or unusual animals make the front pages of papers and the final moments of radio and television news bulletins. Reality TV programmes about animal rescue work, service dogs and show animals attract large audiences. The pet-loving New Zealand public dotes on frisky endangered parrots, playful dolphins and confused penguins. Through cable television and the internet these 'honorary pets' become international stars. How did we arrive at this point? Why are pets so popular today? What does the phenomenon say about New Zealanders? By looking at the origins and development of our pet traditions, we can begin to find some answers to these questions.

This unusual painted carving in Tamatekapua meeting house, Ohinemutu, depicts Potaka Tawhiti, the famous kuri of Te Arawa ancestor Houmaitawhiti. The killing of Potaka Tawhiti sparked a war, which led to the migration of Te Arawa from Rangiatea in Hawaiki to Aotearoa (New Zealand). Te Arawa explorer Ihenga later gave the name Potaka Tawhiti to his dog. *Permission of Paul Tapsell. Photograph by Krysztoff Pfeiffer*

Chapter 1

Making *introductions*

It is early morning. Two tall ships float on a crescent of sea rimmed by dark bush. The birds' great overture has faded, to be replaced by other noises: the creaking of timbers and the slap of water. The sun is still warm, but there is a keen edge to the breeze. Winter is coming.

At the rail of one ship leans a young man. He is drawing a fern, his eyes darting from the fronds to his sketch and back again, his fingers deftly tracing an outline. A spaniel curls at his feet. Around him, men prepare the ship for sailing: heaving boxes, nailing down planks, coiling ropes. Shouted commands are punctuated by bursts of laughter.

The dog stirs, his ears pricked to a distant sound. On the horizon, three long shapes appear. Across the water drifts the chant of the paddlers as their sturdy craft draw closer. Nearer still they surge with their freight of goods for trade: gleaming pounamu, feather cloaks, flax kits of kumara. And in the bows are dogs – fox-like dogs of all colours, their tails like plumes, their sharp noses to the wind.

It may not have happened quite like that, but it did happen. In May and June 1773 two English sailing ships, the *Adventure* and the *Resolution*, lay at anchor in Totara-nui (Queen Charlotte Sound) at the top of New Zealand's South Island. They were nearly a year into a scientific voyage to the Pacific led by Captain James Cook, who had first called at New Zealand in 1769–70. While the ships' crews made preparations to set sail for the southeast Pacific and Tahiti, Maori from the Sounds and further afield visited. On 1 June waka (canoes) approached the *Resolution*, and their occupants came on board to trade pounamu (greenstone) tools and ornaments in return for glass bottles and linen shirts.[1] Georg Forster, a young German botanist who travelled with Cook, later wrote:

> *A good many dogs were observed in their canoes, which they seemed very fond of, and kept tied with a string, round their middle; they were of a rough long-haired sort, with pricked ears, and much resembled the common shepherd's cur ... They were of different colours, some spotted, some quite black, and others perfectly white.*[2]

Forster was describing kuri – the descendants of Polynesian dogs brought to New Zealand by Maori in the thirteenth century. The kuri was rather like a fox, with powerful forequarters, upright ears, a long pointed muzzle and bushy tail. Its fur was black, white, combinations of both colours in patches or spots, or, occasionally, yellow. Compared with similar mid-sized European dog breeds, kuri had smaller skulls and much shorter leg bones, especially in the lower leg. They also had a strange cry – more a howl than a bark.[3]

Forster and his contemporaries immediately saw similarities between the kuri of New Zealand and dogs from other Pacific islands. When Europeans began their Pacific explorations from the sixteenth century they encountered indigenous dogs and also contributed to their spread. Pacific peoples often presented their dogs to the visitors, who in return made gifts of both European and Polynesian dogs, introducing or reintroducing them to islands that did not have them or had lost them.[4]

Throughout the Pacific, dogs were often pets – named, caressed and carried around. Owners were grief-stricken when their dogs died, and some animals were given special burial. But dogs were also raised to be eaten, along with the pigs and fowls that were domesticated in Tahiti, Hawaii and other islands. Polynesian peoples generally distinguished between dogs intended for food and those that were pets, but sometimes they sacrificed favourites and offered the meat to the gods as a way of fending off evil or bringing good fortune.[5]

The scientists who travelled with Cook on his voyages acquired kuri specimens while in New Zealand, and watched the dogs interacting with their Maori owners. Kuri were larger than their counterparts elsewhere in the Pacific, weighing between 13 and 15 kg, and they had longer fur, probably an adaptation to New Zealand's cooler climate.[6] Despite these minor physical differences, it was soon evident that kuri had a similar status to other Pacific dogs.

Like these dogs, kuri were eaten. After his first voyage Cook wrote of Maori, 'Land animals they have none, either wild or tame, except dogs, which they breed for food.'[7] Forster confirmed this in 1773: 'The food which these dogs receive is fish, or the same as their masters live on, who afterwards eat their flesh, and employ the fur in various ornaments and dresses.'[8] Both Jean François Marie de Surville, who explored the northern part of New Zealand in 1769, and Marc Joseph Marion du Fresne, who visited in 1772, agreed that kuri were domesticated food animals.[9]

But the Europeans realised that kuri were also pets. Although explorers did not apparently see in New Zealand the overt displays of pet keeping they had observed in other parts of the Pacific, Joseph Banks, a botanist on Cook's first expedition, claimed that kuri were 'the companions of men',[10] and French explorers in 1772 commented that the animals were often quite tame.[11] And, as we have seen, Georg Forster gained the impression that kuri were treated affectionately.

~

A fondness for pets was one thing that Europeans had in common with Polynesians. In Europe, pet keeping was originally the preserve of royalty and the ruling elite, but by the eighteenth century it was entrenched among the middle and lower classes. Many people, if they could afford it, tamed animals — mainly dogs, cats and birds — for amusement and company.[12]

This was certainly true of Cook's men. The gentlemen scientists, tasked with observing and recording the flora and fauna of the new lands, brought with them their faithful dogs. On the first voyage, Banks took his greyhound and a mongrel he laughingly called his 'Bitch Lady'.[13] Young Georg Forster and his father Johann, who was the senior scientist on Cook's second voyage, also travelled with their pet dogs. Some of these animals were reluctantly given as special gifts to Pacific chiefs; for instance the Forsters presented a spaniel to the Tahitian chief, Tu.[14]

Among the sailors, too, there were pet lovers. One midshipman made a favourite of one of the ship's cats, carried to keep rodents in check. She always took him the rats she caught and he divided them, giving her the head and forequarters, and cleaning, roasting and peppering the hindquarters for himself.[15]

The new enthusiasm for discovery, to which Cook's Pacific voyages contributed, encouraged pet keeping. Scientific enquiry led to closer observation of the natural world, and from this often grew curiosity and wonder. As a result, many educated people took a more benign view of animals, and this began to influence religious thought, laws and customs.[16] Looking after pets became intellectually acceptable as well as emotionally rewarding.

Older ideas, however, were also very much in evidence. European thought had been shaped by the Judeo-Christian tradition, in which humans were set apart from all other living things because of the belief that they alone had immortal souls. Most people were convinced that because God had placed animals on earth purely for the use of humans, they were not owed any special consideration. For centuries, certain animals had been farmed for food and for clothing materials, and used for transport and to haul heavy loads. As farming became commercial, and related industries developed, exploitation and abuse of animals increased.[17] Although attitudes were beginning to change, cruelty was rife.

Pets, like other animals, were completely subject to the unpredictable moods of humans, as an incident on Cook's second voyage shows. At Porto Praya in the Cape Verde Islands, the sailors on the *Resolution* acquired some pet monkeys, which ran around the ship, causing the captain increasing annoyance. Finally, on his orders, they were thrown overboard.[18]

~

The Maori society that Europeans now encountered was based on a very different view of creation. And, rather than farming animals, as Europeans did, Maori hunted them.

Arriving in New Zealand from eastern Polynesia, Maori voyagers discovered a much more variable climate, and some important plants they had previously used for food or clothing, such as taro and aute (paper mulberry), did not grow well. They gathered edible plants such as fern root, and cultivated others, especially kumara, but to survive, they needed animal protein in their diet. Aside from bats, there were no indigenous land mammals, and only kuri and kiore (Polynesian rats) had survived the long journey to New Zealand in the migration canoes. However, the flightless moa and kiwi, and other birds such as kaka, tui and kereru (pigeons), were abundant in the forests and were hunted using various ingenious techniques. Fish and crayfish could be trapped in lakes and streams, and hooked or netted in the seas that lapped at the country's long coastline. The ocean also provided seals and other mammals as well as shellfish.

Anthropologists have suggested that in hunting cultures there was a reciprocal relationship between people and animals.[19] Hunters viewed their prey with respect, and even awe. This is borne out by the traditional Maori understanding of nature, in which animals could be powerful spiritual beings. The forest was the realm of the god Tane, who fathered trees and birds with various spirits – the tui with Parauri (Dark), for example. Birds could be hunted only after propitiating Tane through special rituals.[20] In the European view of the world, humans and animals were quite separate beings, but for Maori, the same life force (mauri) gave energy to every living thing. All creation was linked: Tane was the ancestor of humans as well as trees and birds. People likened themselves to other creatures in chants, sayings and songs.[21]

Accounts of ancestors taking the form of animals reinforced the ties between humans and animals. Irawaru was turned into a dog by his brother-in-law, the demigod Maui, and became the guardian deity of kuri. Animals were often described as spiritual guardians or guides; in various traditions whales guided the migratory canoes on their journeys to New Zealand and two birds helped Kupe to survey the South Island.[22] And animals, like humans, could have an afterlife. Maori believed that when kuri died, their spirits travelled to Te Reinga at North Cape just like the spirits of deceased people, though they took a different route.[23] The contrast between this view, and the Christian doctrine that animals lacked souls, could hardly be more extreme.

Companion animals were particularly important in the early Maori world. Kuri assisted their owners in adapting to and mastering a challenging new environment, accompanying explorers and navigators on their travels. Kupe, who explored New Zealand in his waka *Matawhaorua*, brought with him two dogs called Tauaru and Hurunui, and the *Tokomaru* waka was guided to land by the cries of a dog that jumped overboard and swam ahead.[24] Ihenga, of the *Arawa* waka, discovered Lake Rotoiti with the aid of his dog Potaka Tawhiti.[25] Kuri acted as watchdogs for the village, and when its inhabitants ventured along rivers in their waka, the animals were taken so they could scan the banks for signs of enemies and sound a warning.[26]

Kuri also learned new tricks. Unlike other Polynesian dogs, they helped their owners to hunt. In the forest, a kuri would usually be tethered by a rope that gave it enough slack to run ahead and catch unwary birds, especially kiwi, kakapo, weka and pukeko. The kuri might be muzzled, or have rattles attached to its neck to lead the way through dense vegetation.[27]

The exploring and hunting partnership between kuri and humans sometimes developed into an emotional connection. The depiction of kuri in rock art, and the existence of kuri burial sites, suggest that they were highly valued not just as a species but as individual animals.[28] Place names, too, evoke the special bond between some kuri and their owners. Paoa, captain of the *Horouta* canoe, named a famous Poverty Bay headland, later known as Young Nick's Head, Te Kuri-a-Paoa after his lost kuri. A hill at Whakatane is called Te Kuri-a-Taneatua after one of the pet dogs of Taneatua, who explored the area. The Ohau Channel, linking Lakes Rotorua and Rotoiti, was named by Ihenga as a tribute to one of his dogs that drowned crossing it.

Some accounts suggest that kuri were special pets belonging to people of chiefly rank. The wife of Tamatea, captain of the *Takitimu* canoe, had two pet dogs that kept vigil by her when she died. When such favoured dogs were stolen or killed there could be bloodshed between tribes.[29]

Kuri were also an important food at first. Because they lived alongside humans they were a more reliable source of meat than wild birds or fish. In the South Island, some kuri were castrated to fatten them more quickly for eating. Kuri bones were later a common find in middens during archaeological excavations of Maori settlements. But as kuri numbers diminished, their flesh became a rare delicacy reserved for those of high status.[30]

In addition, kuri provided the raw materials for ornaments, tools, weapons and clothing. Their bushy tails were shaved and the hair used to decorate both weapons and a special garment to ward off weapons, their bones were made into awls and necklaces and their teeth were used for fish hooks and ear pendants.[31] Kuri fur was precious in a climate that called for heavier clothing. Women made several different types of dog-skin cloaks. Some were constructed from whole pelts stitched together; others used tufts or strips of dog fur that were attached to a base cloak woven from muka (flax fibre).[32] Weavers and wearers appreciated the decorative qualities of dog fur, and, probably because kuri were increasingly scarce, dog-skin cloaks – kahu kuri – were worn only by chiefs. As a consequence, the animals received greater care and attention; for example, white kuri were given clean mats to sleep on, to protect their fur.

Birds, too, were both killed for food and feathers, and kept as pets. As well as hunting them, Maori captured and tamed birds such as kaka, tui, kakapo, huia, kotuku (white herons), kereru and seagulls. Sometimes they did this in order to harvest the feathers for cloaks and ornamentation: for example, they often confined huia in large cages made of vines and branches and, once the birds had matured, plucked their tail feathers. Tame seagulls, on the other hand, were released among the kumara crops to eat caterpillars on the plants.[33]

Kaka and tui were the most common bird pets. Kaka were useful decoys during bird hunting expeditions: tied to a pole, they scratched around and screeched to attract other birds. The comical antics of kaka, and the fact that they could be taught to speak, also made them amusing companions. The owner used a kaka poria – a leg ring – and a cord to tether his pet bird to a rod, which he would carry on his shoulder. Poria could be made from wood, pounamu, whale bone or human bone, and were often beautifully crafted treasures. Pet kaka lived in a whata kaka (kaka shelter), which consisted of a perch or feeding trough on posts, with a bark roof overhead. Sometimes the perches or troughs were carved. The birds usually had names, and were often called after an ancestor of the owner.[34]

Kaka could say a few words, but pet tui were voluble talkers. They could mimic almost every sound they heard, and were capable of memorising passages of 40 to 50 words or even more. Like pet kaka they had names, and were kept in cages until they were so tame that they would not fly away if released. Maori

Kaka poria (leg rings) were used to tether pet kaka to a stick or perch. Made of a range of materials, they were often finely carved and became treasured heirlooms and items of adornment – sometimes people wore them as pendants.

Museum of New Zealand Te Papa Tongarewa. Reference: MA_I.073457. Photograph by Michael Hall

went to some trouble training tui to recite long ritual speeches and karakia (prayers). Taming the birds and teaching them to speak was a way for people to maintain a link with the realm of spirits. An apprentice tui was often housed by a waterfall, so that it would learn to imitate flowing sounds. Its tongue was split or trimmed of bristles, or its throat stretched with a plug, in order to make its speech deeper and more distinct. When strangers were being received on the marae, a pet tui perched on a rooftop or its owner's shoulder might welcome them with a traditional oration. When this happened, the visitors would be deeply impressed.[35]

There were some similarities between European and Maori pet-keeping practices, but there were also big differences. Perhaps the most significant was that in the Maori world view, animals and humans were seen as spiritually connected. The word 'mokai' – the rough equivalent of 'pet' – illustrates this. It was used to describe not only companion animals but also human captives. Both could be treated either kindly or harshly, depending on circumstances. Maori pragmatically distinguished between those mokai that were to be killed and those that were to be spared: the term 'tauhe mokai' referred to a pet animal – or pet human – that was also destined to be food.[36]

~

In the late eighteenth century, European explorers introduced Maori to a range of new animals. Those on board the *Endeavour* during Cook's first Pacific voyage of 1768–71 included a cat, Joseph Banks's pet dogs, a milk goat, some pigs, sheep, ducks and chickens in pens on the foredeck – and, inevitably, some European rats. On the *Resolution* and *Adventure* during the second voyage of 1772–75 there was a similar complement of domestic animals, and the vessels took on board more, including native dogs, pigs and poultry, at places such as Tahiti. On the third voyage of 1776–80, the *Resolution* and *Discovery* carried sheep and cattle from England, and picked up more cattle, sheep, horses, goats, rabbits and poultry at the Cape of Good Hope on the way to the Pacific.[37] Most of these animals were to supply the crew with milk and meat, but they were also to be used in trade with local people.

By the 1770s, New Zealand was seen as the Pacific country best suited for colonisation, and Cook hoped to prepare the way for this by introducing breeding pairs of farm animals, reasoning that if Maori domesticated these animals, they would be more receptive to the introduction of European farming. This would teach them the 'civilised' virtues of discipline, hard work and thrift, and they would then be able to support colonists with food and labour, and engage in trade.[38] Animals would be the gift that kept on giving. Cook was not

Georg Forster and his father Johann were the scientists on James Cook's second voyage to the Pacific, systematically observing and recording flora and fauna and collecting specimens. The younger Forster was also a talented artist, and later referred to one of his sketches to make this engraving of a tui, described as a 'Poe bird', perched on a native fuchsia branch. It was one of the illustrations in Cook's account of the voyage, published in 1777.

Alexander Turnbull Library. Reference: C-051-028. Engraving by Johann Georg Adam Forster

the only explorer who attempted to introduce farm animals to New Zealand. In 1769 French explorer Surville left pairs of pigs and poultry at Tokerau (Doubtless Bay) at the northern tip of the North Island, and his countryman Marion du Fresne left a pig and a hen at the Bay of Islands in 1772.[39]

Some Maori did seem to appreciate the potential of the new animals, but perhaps not quite in the way the Europeans had expected. In April 1773 an old man and a girl of about 16 accepted an invitation to come aboard the *Resolution* at Tamatea (Dusky Sound). Intrigued and impressed by the geese, sheep and goats, they were less surprised by the dogs, but a little frightened of them. The girl was particularly taken with the ship's cat, stroking its fur the wrong way, possibly to see how long it was.[40] She may have been comparing it to the kuri fur so sought after by weavers.

Most of the animals that Cook gave to Maori or simply liberated in the hope they would multiply appear to have died out.[41] One exception may have been the pig known as the Captain Cooker. A big, fierce animal, it had a very long snout, a razorback and black bristles. Thriving in the New Zealand bush, it was prolific by the mid-nineteenth century in both North and South Islands.[42] It was hunted by Maori and, later, by Pakeha (white) settlers.

After Cook's voyages of exploration, British plans to colonise New Zealand waxed and waned until the early nineteenth century. In 1803 a young Maori man called Teina travelled from Northland to Port Jackson (Sydney) on a whaling ship. The Governor of New South Wales, Philip Gidley King, gave him pigs which he brought home with him. King later sent gifts of pigs to chiefs in the Bay of Islands, as a way of gaining their favour and a foothold in New Zealand.[43] These pigs may have been ancestors of the breed that became known to Maori as kunekune (meaning 'fat and round'). They were short and sturdy, with a blunt, upturned snout and two tassels hanging from the lower jaw, and could be black, tortoiseshell, ginger, smoky blue and other colours. Friendly and intelligent, they were easily tamed, and Maori discovered, as people around the world have since, that they made good pets. They were also an excellent source of food. When the first Pakeha residents arrived, there was plenty of pork available for barter.[44]

European dogs and cats probably became established from the late eighteenth century. They were brought by sealers, who set up shore bases in New Zealand from the 1790s, and flax traders, who were active around the coast. Whalers, who plied their trade in New Zealand waters from the 1790s and had coastal camps from the 1820s, also kept cats and dogs.[45] These animals may have been exchanged for other goods, or may simply have escaped and bred. They were in evidence by the time the missionaries arrived. In January 1815, while he was at the Bay of Islands, Samuel Marsden saw Maori from the Cavalli Islands arriving in waka with their cats.[46] Maori called cats 'puhihi' (a transliteration of 'pussy') or 'ngeru', derived from the word for sleek, suggesting that their fur invited stroking.[47]

More European animals were introduced when Marsden established his mission at the Bay of Islands in late 1814. Like the explorers before them, the missionaries wanted to civilise Maori by teaching them farming skills, so they brought stock from Australia – horses, cattle, sheep, pigs, chickens, goats – and more cats and dogs. These animals endured a stormy crossing of the Tasman, suffering seasickness along with the human passengers. When they were first landed at Rangihoua in the Bay of Islands they caused a sensation. Maori were astonished at the cattle and horses, scattering when a cow ran among them and

Artist George French Angas journeyed through the Waikato region in 1844. His sketch of an evening scene in a Maori settlement on the banks of the Waikato River shows how animals, both newly introduced and long established, were by then part of daily life. On the extreme right are a full-grown kuri and puppy. A cat huddles close to the people around the fire, while two small pigs search for food near the flax kits.
Alexander Turnbull Library. Reference: PUBL-0029-033. Tinted lithograph by George French Angas

watching thunderstruck as Marsden rode a horse along the beach. Apprehension soon turned to desire: on his later travels Marsden met one chief who refused a gift of nails, asking instead for a cat; and a calf and cow were among the treasured possessions that Nga Puhi chief Ruatara, protector of the Rangihoua mission station, gave away before his death in March 1815.[48]

The new animals reached some parts of New Zealand sooner than others. As late as the 1830s and 40s some were still a novelty to more isolated tribes. When Edward Jerningham Wakefield visited a South Taranaki pa on horseback in the early 1840s the inhabitants were fascinated with the horse, calling him 'kuri nui' (big dog) and asking all kinds of questions about his care and feeding. While Wakefield stayed at the pa, the horse was showered with attention. People constantly offered him corn cobs, grass and sow thistles, and kept a wooden bowl near him topped up with water, while 'little knots of curious observers sat around the circle of his tether-rope, remarking, and conjecturing, and disputing, about the meaning and intention of every whisk of his tail or shake of his ears'.[49]

The animal introductions were not all one way. Marsden and his fellow travellers were offered tui in wickerwork cages when they journeyed around

Northland in 1815, and the birds were being sold to Europeans in the 1830s.[50] That decade, William Puckey of the Kaitaia Church Mission had a tame tui that had been taught to give a traditional Maori welcome to visitors. Fellow missionary William Colenso recalled 'when it rattled off its Maori song it would also inflate its body, appear bulky, and ruffle up its glossy feathers, and so make itself look nearly twice its real size, and all the time move up and down on its perch as if with glee. Truly it was a pretty sight to see and hear it.'[51]

~

With the British settlers who arrived from 1840 came many more animals, which often preyed on existing species or competed with them for food. One outcome of this process was highly significant for Maori society: European dogs caused the extinction of kuri by interbreeding with them.[52]

It seems that pure-bred kuri were becoming rare as early as the 1830s. When a Northland woman of high status had her chin tattooed with the moko, about 1830, the tohunga performing the operation was expected, as usual, to eat tapu (sacred) food. To provide this, the only kuri in the district was forcibly taken from its devastated owner.[53] But kuri, or dogs with strong kuri characteristics, survived in some places for decades. There are accounts of feral dogs with kuri features as late as the 1850s and 1860s. In 1858 in Otago W.D. Murison shot wild dogs that were 'low set with short prick ears, broad forehead, sharp snout, and bushy tails'.[54] Taylor White, who had similar memories of killing wild dogs in Canterbury and Otago in 1856 and 1860, noted their unusual colours and markings, sharp noses and tendency to howl rather than bark.[55]

As these recollections show, settlers saw such dogs as pests to be eradicated. Feral dogs, probably including kuri half-breeds, were common throughout New Zealand in the middle of the century, especially in Otago, Canterbury, Marlborough and the central North Island, and sheep farmers detested them because they killed lambs and other farm animals. People imported big, bony kangaroo dogs (a greyhound-deerhound cross) from Australia to help hunt them down. Although very swift and strong, kangaroo dogs had a poor sense of smell, needing to see their prey before they could follow it, so were more useful in open country than dense bush. They also gained a reputation for attacking farm dogs and sheep, and eventually fell out of favour.[56] But if kangaroo dogs were not the final answer, the gun was. Shepherds and farmers shot wild dogs on sight.

The kuri was disappearing at the same time as Maori society was being increasingly exposed to European goods, customs, values and laws. Settler Charles Hursthouse thought the adoption by Maori of European dress, which largely replaced traditional garments such as the dog-skin cloak, may have hastened the kuri's demise. He also suggested that the substitution of pork for dog meat in the Maori diet meant that kuri were given less care.[57] Kuri may no longer have been a preferred food because interbreeding with European dogs had altered the taste of the flesh. As scientist Ernst Dieffenbach wrote in 1843, 'The native dog was formerly considered a dainty, and great numbers of them were eaten; but the breed having undergone an almost complete mixture with the European [dog], their use as an article of food has been discontinued, as the European dogs are said by the natives to be perfectly unpalatable.'[58]

~

As two cultures struggled to comprehend each other, one source of tension was the different views held by Maori and Pakeha on which animals could be killed for food. This had emerged when Cook and his men encountered the practice of dog eating during their Pacific journeys.[59] Although this had been common in Europe during prehistoric times, by the eighteenth century Europeans had a strong cultural aversion to eating animals they now thought of as companions.[60] Maori, who lacked the same range of domesticated animals, could not afford the luxury of exempting an entire species from the oven. Overcoming their qualms, explorers sampled cooked dog at feasts, and in fact when they ran short of other forms of protein, were prepared to eat the dogs they had collected as specimens.[61] This caused a few of them pangs of guilt. Georg Forster attempted to rationalise one such incident by claiming that it was no worse to eat dogs than pigs; and that people avoided doing so only because, through training, dogs had acquired 'those eminent qualities which attach them so much to us'.[62]

Later European arrivals, less likely to face this dilemma, were disapproving when Maori ate and killed animals they regarded as pets. Until the mid-nineteenth century Maori treated cats just like any other edible species, and used their skins for mats and clothing.[63] Visiting New Zealand on the *Dromedary* in an expedition to collect kauri spars in 1820, Richard Cruise was startled when a Maori man offered him a live cat to kill for food.[64] Samuel Marsden, journeying around the Waitemata Harbour the same year, was likewise taken aback at being presented with roast cat during a meal at one village. His hosts were probably even more put out at his refusal, especially after they pointed out that it was a good-quality English cat.[65] Cat eating continued for at least two or three decades. In 1838 trader J.S. Polack wrote sarcastically, 'This animal is looked upon with much affection by these kind-hearted people, for the delicacy of its flesh when cooked, and its skin; it is accounted as very nutritious food.'[66] In 1857 American journalist Charles Nordhoff repeated this claim, adding, 'Residents ten or fifteen years ago complained much of the impossibility of keeping cats.'[67]

The choice of pets and their treatment provided further scope for criticism. Maori had come to value pigs highly, and not just as a source of food. Their treatment of kunekune and other domesticated breeds recalls their earlier attitude to kuri. Although most pigs were raised to be eaten, some were pets. Pakeha observed, often with distaste, how pigs were allowed in houses and even permitted to sleep in the same bed as their owners.[68] On his travels around New Zealand in the 1840s, artist G.F. Angas encountered many tame pigs and noted that it was 'a frequent custom with the Maori females to pet young pigs in the same manner as the European ladies fondle dogs and kittens'.[69]

Another point of difference was how companion animals should be controlled. As kuri became rare, Maori acquired European dogs. In the 1850s Charles Hursthouse commented that these animals were alternately thrashed and petted by Maori girls, who were particularly fond of the puppies.[70] But unrestrained dogs irritated Pakeha living near Maori settlements. These 'mongrel curs', as they were dismissively called, seemed to belong to no one, and hung around in the hope of finding or being given scraps. Settlers suspected such dogs of stealing food and poultry, and occasionally enticed the animals with morsels, then killed and buried them in the early hours of the morning.[71] George Clarke, raised in a missionary family at the Bay of Islands in the 1830s, recalled teaming up with another boy to trap and dispose of troublesome dogs. This was reluctantly allowed by local chiefs, and quietly encouraged by one, who wanted the skins for a cloak. He even offered to kill the dogs. The scheme backfired, however, when one night he killed his own dog, crying out when he realised his mistake, 'Why this is *my* dog.'[72]

This charming portrait of a Maori girl carrying her pet dog was drawn by William Strutt in Taranaki in 1855 or 1856. Strutt, an English-trained artist, lived briefly in New Plymouth and nearby, and made numerous studies of local life and customs that are now considered outstanding for their authenticity and professionalism.

Alexander Turnbull Library. Reference: E-452-f-011-1. Coloured sketch by William Strutt

~

Between the 1840s and late 1860s, wars between Maori and Pakeha over land and political authority changed the balance of power. Many tribes lost their land, were driven into temporary or permanent exile and reduced to poverty. Before the wars, some had successfully adopted European farming, supplying settlers with food and even exporting their produce to Australia and the west coast of America.[73] In many areas armed conflict and its aftermath slowed or halted these enterprises, and Maori were often forced back into a subsistence lifestyle. Even after peace had been established, lingering mutual distrust contributed to heightened racial tensions. Conflicting attitudes to animals increased this bad feeling.

One major source of disagreement was hunting. Following post-war confiscations and forced sales of land, and the spread of Pakeha settlement,

hunting remained vital as a means of survival for Maori. For Pakeha, hunting had other meanings. It was an important source of food, especially in the lean, early years of settlement, but it was also symbolic of new freedoms. Many settlers recalled with bitterness the restrictive game laws of England, and defended their right to hunt in the New Zealand bush. From the 1860s, acclimatisation societies imported game animals solely for recreational hunting. Introduced game birds included species of pheasant, partridge, quail, swans and ducks. Later, the societies successfully established deer and other large game animals.[74] Meanwhile, settlers shot native birds, including tui, kaka and kereru, both for food and for sport.

The Pakeha passion for hunting as a sport led to the passage of numerous 'animal protection' acts from 1861 onwards. These had nothing to do with animal welfare: they aimed to conserve certain species so they could continue to be hunted. They defined hunting seasons, and introduced a licensing system that was eventually administered by local acclimatisation societies.

At first the legislation covered introduced animals. Then from 1867, some indigenous birds, including the kereru, bittern, wild duck, teal, black stilt, curlew, pied stilt and native quail, were designated 'native game', probably because their numbers were likely to be threatened by over-enthusiastic hunters. The seasons in which these birds could be hunted were defined to allow their populations to recover, but a licence was not required to hunt them. During the course of the century various species were added to or removed from the schedule of 'native game', but many were not listed at all, which meant they could be freely hunted at any time. Until 1896, unlisted birds included kokako, kiwi, kakapo, tieke (saddleback), hihi (stitchbird) and korimako (bellbird).[75]

For some years the impact of these laws on Maori hunting was probably not great, especially in areas where there were few Pakeha settlers. By the last couple of decades of the century, however, there was a tightening of the conditions under which native game could be hunted, and greater enforcement of the law. This angered many Maori, as the defined seasons for hunting native game conflicted with their ideas of when certain birds should be harvested in order to conserve their numbers. They particularly resented the growing restrictions on hunting kereru, and made no secret of continuing to kill the birds according to their own timetable.[76]

By the late 1880s and 1890s it was also becoming obvious that native bird numbers had dropped alarmingly. Voracious hunting contributed, as did the killing of birds by collectors of specimens. In addition, the felling of forests for timber and agricultural purposes removed the trees, plants and insects on which the birds fed. But the introduction of predators – including, ironically, cats and

An unnamed Maori woman plays with her cat and its kittens – evidently cherished pets.

Alexander Turnbull Library, Price Collection. Reference: G-1534-1/2. Photograph by William Archer Price

A Christmas card of about 1900 shows a Maori woman feeding a pet kaka. The card presents a romanticised view: the old practice of taming kaka was probably becoming much less common by this time.

Alexander Turnbull Library. Reference: E-279-q-020. Chromolithograph by Kennett Watkins

dogs – was a major reason for the mounting number of extinctions. Some Maori were swift to make this connection. In 1873 Hapurona Tohikura of Taranaki wrote to a government-sponsored Maori newspaper, *Te Waka Maori o Nui Tirani*, 'It was you the Pakeha that introduced the dog and the cat which destroyed the food of this country, the weka, kiwi, kakapo, the piopio [New Zealand thrush] and the many endemic birds.'[77]

To complicate matters, by the later nineteenth century, many Pakeha New Zealanders had developed a sentimental attachment to certain native birds, such as tui, fantails and bellbirds. Encouraged by this, conservationists began to call

Many Pakeha New Zealanders had developed sentimental affection for native birds when this poster was produced in 1901. By then, however, many species it illustrated were critically endangered and some later became extinct. Among the birds depicted here are a kaka (top left) tui (just below) and kakariki or parakeet (top right). *Alexander Turnbull Library. Reference: C-066-008. Artwork by William Shaw Diedrich Schmidt*

for the absolute protection of some indigenous species, so that they could not be hunted at any time.[78] To their surprise, however, they encountered opposition not just from the Pakeha hunting lobby, but from Maori members of parliament, who wanted their people to have control of the birds on their own lands, a right that, as they pointed out, was guaranteed under the Treaty of Waitangi. They argued that traditional hunting seasons and systems of rahui (prohibitions on taking birds at certain times of the year) would protect bird populations.[79] But it is unlikely that hunting restrictions, whether imposed by Pakeha or Maori, were going to save native birds: many species were already in serious jeopardy.

Ultimately, the conservationists prevailed: by 1911 the kereru, teal, grey duck, pukeko, kea and shag were the only native species that were not absolutely protected in New Zealand, and there were strict conditions for hunting kereru, which became completely protected in 1922.[80] These laws, lower bird populations and social and economic changes arising from the spread of European settlement did not just disrupt traditional hunting patterns, they dealt a blow to the close connection of Maori with the forest, its plants and animals.

The custom of keeping native birds as pets was probably affected as a result. Some Maori certainly continued to keep birds in order to harvest their feathers, and tui and kaka were tamed and trained to talk in the old way.[81] Annie Butler, the English author of numerous religious works for children, travelled around New Zealand in the 1880s and later described kaka as 'a red-breasted parrot which the natives teach to talk', adding approvingly, 'We heard of one kaka which could say the Lord's prayer through in Maori.'[82] But, as this story suggests, old practices were being modified by new beliefs.

One man who honoured the knowledge and traditions of the past was Teone Taare Tikao, a late-nineteenth-century Ngai Tahu scholar and leader. He kept a kakariki and a tui, both of which he taught to speak. The tui was a particularly apt pupil and could recite the entire Rarotimu whakapapa (a creation genealogy). 'I became greatly attached to this bird,' Tikao recalled, 'and when it died I felt its loss severely. I covered it with a soft silk handkerchief and buried it with a very sad feeling.'[83] His sadness at the loss of this beloved pet may well have been intensified by recognition that a way of life was under threat.

~

Another cause of ongoing friction between Maori and Pakeha was dog control. According to ethnologist Makereti Papakura, 'The Maori liked the new large dogs. I remember the one which my koroua [elder] Maihi owned. It was a large dog, not unlike an Alsatian, of a dark cream colour. He named it Ngaumu, and it was a very good dog for hunting the pig.'[84] Pig hunting was an important way of supplementing food supplies for many Maori, so they needed packs of dogs. And the traditional value placed by Maori on dogs meant that owning large numbers of them signified prestige.[85]

Hunting dogs were companions, just as kuri had been. James Cowan's humorous short story, 'The Worst Dog in the World', probably based on his experience as a journalist during the 1890s, tells of his trip up the Mokau River in the company of a Pakeha politician and two Maori, Tuke and Panapa.[86] They travel in a dugout canoe, the *Tainui*, named after Panapa's ancestral waka, and in the company of Panapa's pig dog, called Hoturoa after the captain of the *Tainui*. The wily and unprepossessing Hoturoa is distinctly unfriendly towards the Pakeha (or so they believe), but the object of his owner's pride and affection. Panapa explains to his aghast listeners how he listed Hoturoa as his son in a recent census, and enrolled him on the electoral roll for the Western Maori seat, voting several times on his behalf. He assures them the dog is his 'best friend': 'I take Hoturoa everywhere – everywhere.'

Famous Rotorua guide and entrepreneur Makereti Papakura was photographed in 1907 outside her whare Tukiterangi with her dog, one of a long line of pets. Educated in the traditions of both her mother's Tuhourangi hapu and her father's English family, Makereti was familiar with the pet-keeping practices of both cultures, and her posthumously published book, *The Old-time Maori*, commented on traditional Maori customs in relation to animals.

Alexander Turnbull Library, Hislop Collection. Reference: PA1-o-229-26-4. Photograph by Harold Stevens Hislop

Hoturoa proceeds to effectively sabotage the expedition, leaping ashore to chase every wild pig he sees, nearly capsizing the canoe on a rapid and helping himself to the best morsels of food and the most comfortable sleeping places. On one level, the story can be read as a reflection on tense Pakeha–Maori relations; on another, it reveals the close bond that could exist between Maori and their dogs.

Cowan viewed Hoturoa with amused exasperation, but Pakeha sheep farmers had a harder attitude towards Maori-owned dogs, which they believed preyed on their lambs and sheep. 'Maori kuri', or the variant 'goory', was a term of abuse applied to any wild or mongrel dog.[87] Various laws were introduced to deal with the problem. A system of dog registration began with An Ordinance to Abate the Dog Nuisance 1849, passed by the province of New Munster, which included the Wellington region and the South Island.[88] Before 1876 various provinces introduced dog registration laws.[89] In addition, the 1865 Injuries by Dogs Act attempted to prevent both sheep worrying and attacks on people by making owners liable for damages and giving citizens the right to destroy marauding dogs.[90] Finally, in 1880, the Dog Registration Act repealed all these measures, requiring owners throughout New Zealand to license their dogs annually for a fee. All dogs over the age of six months had to be registered and wear a collar with an identifying tag. Any unregistered dog that strayed onto someone else's property could be summarily destroyed, as could any dog, registered or not, seen attacking a person or another animal.[91]

Farmers regarded Maori villages with their numerous dogs as the seat of the problem, and in some districts tax collectors targeted them in an attempt to reduce dog numbers. Because Maori had been only partially integrated into the cash economy, they often simply could not afford to pay. In any case they objected strongly to being taxed for something they considered a right. They correctly perceived that the dog tax was another attempt to control them, and resisting it became a central plank of several Maori separatist movements, including those led by Te Whiti in Parihaka in the early 1890s, Hone Toia in Hokianga later that decade and Rua Kenana in Te Urewera after the turn of the century.[92]

Collecting dog registration fees from Maori owners was not a job for the faint-hearted. Local body-appointed dog registrars sometimes received a higher commission for registering Maori dogs. In 1878, for example, registrars for the Wairoa County Council received 1s commission for registering the dogs of Pakeha, but 2s 6d for the dogs of Maori owners. In other areas, authorities judiciously did not attempt to enforce the law.[93] Pakeha sheep farmers saw this as unfair, and complained bitterly. Maori were occasionally hauled before the courts for having unregistered dogs, and if they escaped prosecution, the farming lobby expressed disgust.[94]

~

Both the game laws and the dog tax sparked what has been called the Dog Tax Rebellion or the Dog Tax War in 1898. A Ngapuhi religious sect with Wesleyan origins, known as Te Huihuinga, developed in Hokianga in the 1890s under the leadership of Hone Riiwi Toia. Members wanted to govern themselves and their lands, and were particularly opposed to seasonal restrictions on hunting and various taxes, including the dog tax. Until the 1890s the resident magistrate at Hokianga had deemed it inadvisable to introduce the dog tax there, but his successor decided to impose penalties on Maori who would not pay. The response was a civil disobedience campaign led by Toia and his followers. Dog tax defaulters were fined and refused to pay; were summonsed and did not appear in court. Maori shot pigeons out of season and offered them to police as a challenge.

In February 1898 Henry Menzies, appointed by the Hokianga County Council to collect dog registration fees, visited Toia's people and issued 40 or more summonses. Toia tried to broker a compromise and set up a meeting in late April, to which he invited police and representatives of the council. However, statements made at this meeting by Maori, and a telegram later sent to the resident magistrate, gave the impression that Toia's followers intended to march on Rawene with their guns to wage war. This sparked panic among Rawene settlers, many of whom fled. The government overreacted, sending a force of over 120 armed men with two field guns in two armed steamers, and a British warship, to Rawene in early May. Troops marched on Waima, where Toia and his followers were living, and following negotiations the Maori surrendered. Sixteen were arrested. Most were fined, but five, including Toia, were sentenced to 18 months' hard labour for 'conspiring to levy war against the Queen in order to force her to change her measures' and 12 months for other charges, including 'conspiring by force to prevent collection of taxes'.[95] That was the end of the so-called Dog Tax Rebellion, but it was by no means the end of Maori resistance to both game laws and dog taxes.

In a short period of time, Maori were forced to accept many changes, including an altered relationship with the animals they thought of as companions and helpers. Although they had been introduced to some new, useful animals, others they valued were lost or threatened, along with the way of life in which they played such significant roles. There were some gains, but the corresponding losses were profound. Tuhoe leader Rua Kenana understood that when he refused to pay the dog tax in 1907.[96] When the local policeman presented him with a summons for failing to register his dogs, he expressed his opinion not in words, but in a simple gesture of defiance. He took the Pakeha's piece of paper, and ripped it into shreds.

This cartoon, published in the *New Zealand Graphic and Ladies Journal* on 14 May 1898, comments on the racial tensions that arose from enforcing dog registration in Maori communities. A Maori man and his dog challenge Premier Dick Seddon, who holds in his hand the dog tax legislation. By this time 16 Maori men involved in the Dog Tax Rebellion at Hokianga had been arrested, and in the following months five were to be convicted and imprisoned.

Alexander Turnbull Library. Reference: PUBL-0163-1898-001. Wood engraving by Ashley John Barsby Hunter

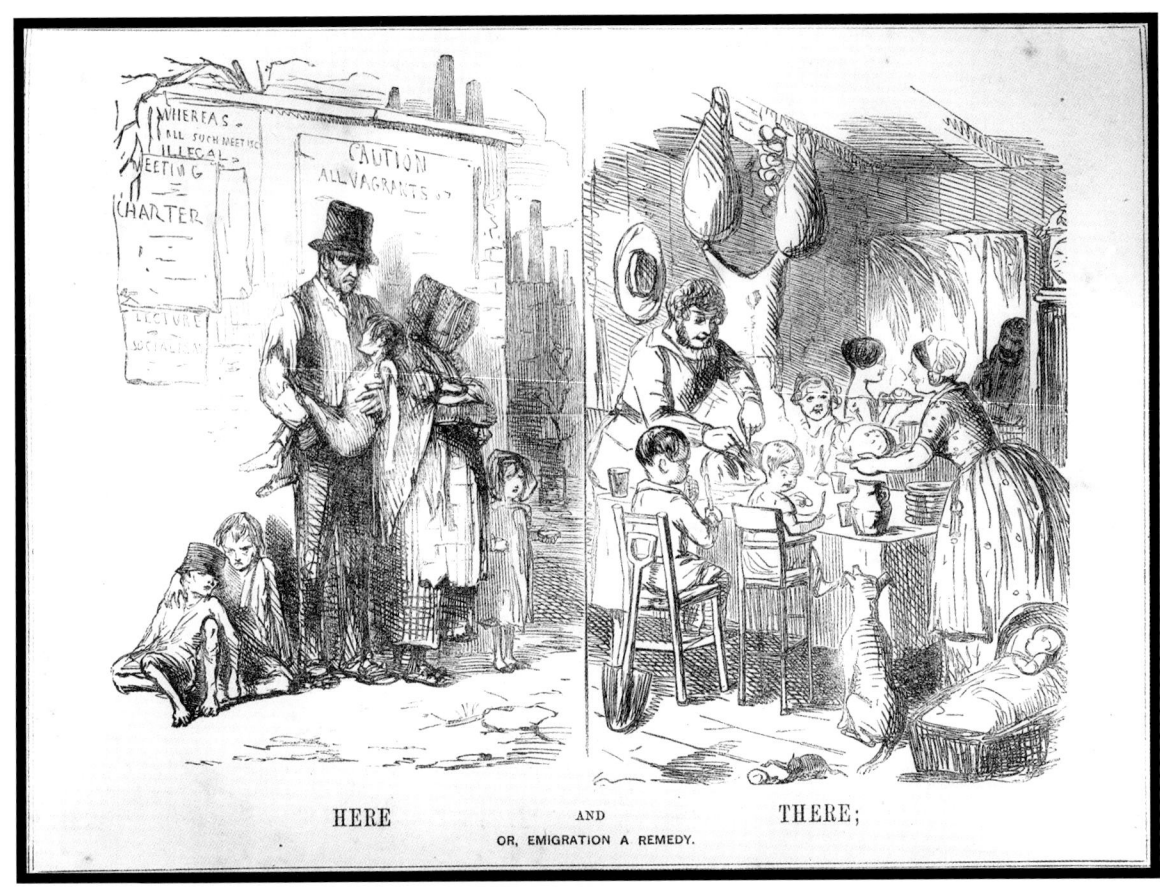

This famous cartoon, 'Here and There; or, emigration a remedy', published in *Punch* in 1848, shows how the starving family will profit by emigrating. In the second frame, the well-fed dog and playful kitten are among the signs of prosperity.

Alexander Turnbull Library. Reference: PUBL-0043-1848-15. Wood engraving by unknown artist

Chapter 2
Happy homes

God help the hardy emigrant who leaves his native land,
With little more in his slight store than willing heart and hand,
'Tis for his children's sake he goes, the forest wild to clear,
And try to win, in some strange land, the bread he can't win here.
May favouring gales swell out the sails that bear him o'er the sea;
May peace and plenty bless his home, where e'er that home may be:
And may new friends make full amends for those he's left behind –
His children, tho' a burden here, a blessing there he'll find.

The nineteenth century was an age of upheaval, when millions of people from Britain and Europe took the gamble of emigrating to a distant country in the hope of bettering their lot.[1] From 1840, New Zealand was the most far-flung of Britain's colonies, and prospective settlers were no doubt encouraged by the thoughts expressed in this poem from *Out at Sea, or, The Emigrant Afloat: Being a hand book of practical information for the use of passengers on a long sea voyage*. It finished, optimistically, 'Then once again God help the men who boldly dare to roam/With willing hands in distant lands to plant a happy HOME.'[2]

Home – leaving one, finding or making another – was a recurring theme in emigration propaganda. It was famously invoked in a cartoon published in *Punch* in 1848, entitled 'Here and There; or, emigration a remedy'. On the 'Here' side of the sketch, a desperate-looking couple with their starving and sick children were pictured against a grim urban backdrop. On the 'There' side, the same family, now healthy and cheerful, were shown gathered around a dinner table, about to tuck into a large meal. A dog waited expectantly by the table for a morsel of food, while a kitten played with a ball of wool nearby. This vision of the 'happy home' included pet animals.

In these years the middle-class home in particular represented a refuge from the harsh realities of the male working world. It was a comforting sanctuary where women, especially mothers, upheld religious values and social standards. Pet animals were important in this private domain. As the lowliest and weakest members of the household, they provided opportunities for children to learn about responsibility and compassion, and for adults to demonstrate these virtues. Contented pets suggested domestic harmony. For those families wanting to proclaim their respectability, or to advance socially, a well-groomed, well-behaved pet was an essential accessory. These beliefs contributed to the rise of pet keeping.[3]

The idealising of home, and the associated rise in the status of the 'domestic pet', gained acceptance throughout Britain, America and Western Europe, and travelled with the settlers to New Zealand. But letters, diaries and memoirs reveal that, in the process of relocation, these values acquired new meaning. Anecdotes, jokes, throwaway comments, postscripts – all show that the bond between people and their pets became particularly important as settlers strove, sometimes against great odds, to make new homes.

~

Animals were essential to the colonising enterprise. Cats and several breeds of dog had been introduced to New Zealand before 1840, and farm animals, including sheep, cattle and horses, were also well established in some places by that date. More were imported from Australia. But their relative scarcity in the early years, and the need to introduce new blood, meant that those emigrants who could afford it brought animals with them from the northern hemisphere.[4] Transporting animals safely to the other side of the world was a major challenge, and people valued them all the more because of that.

Along with their human passengers and cargoes, sailing ships bound for New Zealand carried cows, sheep, pigs and poultry. Some were being taken to the final destination, but often their purpose was to provide fresh food for the cabin (first-class) passengers; subsidised passengers who travelled in steerage had to make do with preserved food for the three to four months at sea. Cabin passengers also took with them horses, farm stock and smaller animals such as

Cabin passengers relax on the poop deck of the *Royal Dane*, an emigrant clipper, on a voyage 'home' to England from New Zealand in 1864. A dog and pet birds are fellow travellers.

Alexander Turnbull Library. Reference: B-064-022. Watercolour by unknown artist

cats and dogs and even caged birds. In his *Handbook for New Zealand*, published in London in 1848, Edward Jerningham Wakefield listed among the birds that had been introduced 'Canaries and Bullfinches, taken over safely by their mistresses from this country'.[5]

For animals as well as humans, this sea voyage from Britain to New Zealand – the longest possible emigration journey – was uncomfortable, potentially dangerous and sometimes frightening. Farm animals were confined in pens and cages on the deck. Often pets, and prize animals too, had to endure the entire passage in boxes and crates on deck, exposed to weather and breaking waves. Henry Petre, who brought two thoroughbred stallions to Wellington in 1842, had to supervise them in rough weather because of the danger of their falling in the horse boxes on the deck.[6] Dogs suffered similar discomforts. In his *Handbook* Wakefield advised that anyone bringing a dog from Britain should have a kennel made for it in or under the long boat, adding, 'You will be able to obtain straw enough for bedding from the casks of bottled liquors, etc, opened during the passage.' If passengers had to put up with a monotonous diet, it was much worse for such dogs fed, according to Wakefield's instructions, on 'oatmeal, or spoilt navy biscuit'.

For much of the journey dogs were confined in their kennels. 'Let your dog have plenty of exercise about the decks,' Wakefield wrote, 'but have his kennel fastened so that you alone can open it, and never let him out when he will be in the way of either passengers or crew.'[7] On the other hand, cats on board ship were usually not caged, and for good reason. When one young emigrant wrote home from Wellington in 1842 describing local conditions, his old nurse sent him 'a splendid rat-catching cat'. This animal proved so useful in controlling rodents during the voyage that the captain begged to keep her.[8]

Emigrants watched anxiously over their animals. Edward Ward, who set out from Plymouth in September 1850 on the *Charlotte Jane*, bound for Lyttelton, kept a shipboard diary in which he regularly reported on the health of the birds, cow and dogs on board. His dog, Bob, started the journey in poor condition: 'looking very wretched in his mange. He can hardly last the voyage.' But Bob began to perk up, thanks to special care that included doses of salts and late-night runs on the deck. In early October, Ward wrote, 'I am obliged to deprive Bob of his nightly run, as during his prowl last night he retrieved a large piece of salt pork – this in addition to the mauling of a dead pig a few nights ago, has been the occasion of his sentence.' After application of a 'macassar' ointment consisting of gunpowder, burnt leather and butter to his bald patches, Bob's fur began to grow back, and Ward was able to record, 'He is getting into handsome form and his hair is crimping into good curl.'[9] Bob not only survived the voyage but outlived his young master, who drowned with one of his brothers in a boating accident on Lyttelton Harbour in 1851.

The rigours of the voyage took a toll on many animals. When ships reached the tropics, any birds on board moulted, and then, as the vessel sailed into chillier latitudes, they succumbed to the cold. Other animals contracted a condition called 'shipping fever' (also known as pasteurellosis), which could be brought on by the stress of living in overcrowded conditions with poor food. This contributed to lowered resistance, and the animal would sicken with such symptoms as swelling of the head, neck, throat or abdomen, and discharge of blood or mucus.[10]

Emigrants could be mystified by an animal's sudden death. When Edward Seager travelled to Canterbury in 1851 on the barque *Cornwall*, a fellow passenger's hound died on the journey. A post mortem was held, with much learned discussion but no recorded verdict, and the dog was given a solemn burial at sea.[11] In some cases, however, there was no doubt about the cause of death. Ellen Shephard Tripp recalled a horrific voyage from England in 1864 on the *Ivanhoe*, which was under the command of a drunken and deranged captain. As soon as the ship left Plymouth a passenger who had paid a pound as fare for his dog discovered that, on the captain's orders, the animal had been thrown overboard. This was just the start of many troubles, which included a typhoid epidemic, near-starvation of the passengers and narrowly averted disaster when the captain threatened to bring the ship ashore on a rocky coast as it approached New Zealand. After arrival in Lyttelton the captain was tried on various charges, including killing the dog, for which offence he was fined £20.[12]

Animals could provide a welcome diversion during the long, tedious journey. Charlotte Godley, wife of Canterbury founder John Robert Godley, who came out to New Zealand on the *Lady Nugent* in 1850, related the amusement passengers and crew had at the expense of Algernon Gray Tollemache, who was travelling with his dog Jack. In a letter to her mother she wrote, 'It is a large white ugly nondescript cur, but he is very fond of it, and made so much fuss with it as to invite some little fun.' First Jack made an entrance with a terrible gash on his front leg which proved to have been painted on, then he started appearing with a kettle tied to his tail. Mr Tollemache became increasingly wound up by these incidents, and matters came to a head one day when he spotted Jack on the forecastle surrounded by sailors. 'His tall, gaunt figure was instantly precipitated down the ladder, and in three strides he was in the forecastle and violently punching one of the ringleaders.'[13] It turned out that the sailors had made Jack a little dress and were in the process of fitting it when they were interrupted by the furious Mr Tollemache. There were no more practical jokes after this, because Jack was kept under lock and key by his touchy owner.

Both pets and farm animals provided entertainment and companionship for all on board the *Alpaca* when it sailed to New Zealand in 1863–64. The ship carried two dogs, four pigs and dozens of chickens and ducks, along with a complement of cats owned by the sailors. An emigrant described in his journal hilarious play-fights between the dogs and one of the pigs, which was called Dennis. Some of the cats had kittens, and were well fed on seabirds and fish caught by the passengers and crew.[14]

~

After the ordeal of the voyage out, there were fresh challenges for the immigrants. For some, New Zealand was not, and never could be, home. Jemima Martin of Tamaki wrote to her sister in England in 1852: 'The change of seasons, Xmas in the middle of summer & winter in August gives one an uncomfortable sensation of being turned upside down & I cannot get over it & don't think I ever shall.'[15] In addition to the reversal in seasons, the wild landscapes and variable climate of New Zealand contrasted sharply with the milder environments of the northern hemisphere. Settlements were few and far spaced, and most of the familiar amenities of civilised life were absent or in short supply. Plants and animals were strange. Maori, who until the 1860s outnumbered Europeans, could seem foreign and sometimes frightening with their unfamiliar customs and attitudes.

For most people there was no way back: they had to make a home in New Zealand. This involved not just building a house or breaking in a block of land, but gradually acquiring a sense of belonging. One way of adjusting was to introduce the habits, laws, flora, fauna and material culture of Europe. As we have seen, from the early 1860s regional acclimatisation societies successfully introduced plants and animals, but individuals, too, attempted to naturalise species. Frances Caverhill, who in 1865 was living with her husband and children on a North Canterbury farm, described in her diary the consignments of English linnets, swans, magpies and other birds they brought from Christchurch for local release.[16] The sight and sound of familiar creatures brought comfort to many a homesick settler. As one journalist put it in 1882, 'The pheasant whirring out from the hedges or the quail running under the roadside weeds, and the lark carolling away everywhere, give an air of civilisation and Old Country reminiscences to the scene.'[17]

Pet animals, too, provided soothing reminders of home and helped their owners to reconcile themselves to life far from family and friends. This was especially the case when the pets accompanied their owners on the voyage out, as they were a living link with loved ones left behind. When Catherine Douglas Fyfe came to New Zealand from Scotland in 1859 to marry George Fyffe, who managed a shore-based whaling station and farm at Kaikoura, she brought with her a dog and a cat. She did not have children, and the animals were a great consolation to her in her rough new surroundings.[18]

This was also true for John Bradshaw, who brought his fox terrier, Wasp, from England to Canterbury. Writing in 1883 about his arrival at Lyttelton many years before, he recalled the dog's delight on reaching land after many months at sea.

It was vastly amusing to see him prick his ears, and sniff the air, evidently in some doubts as to his whereabouts. That he had suspicions of being no longer on board was clear, but it was not until the actual soil was reached, and a patch of grass smelt and eaten, that he seemed fully to realize the pleasant fact. Then his enthusiasm knew no bounds. Every street corner was investigated, and every open door attracted his attention.

Charles Moore Igglesden painted the home of his uncle and aunt, Captain and Mrs Sharp, which was located on The Terrace in Wellington, in 1868. The Sharps were very fond of animals, and had dogs, cats, turkeys and a parrot. A special pet was the monkey, seen here, which the captain brought out from India. It was allowed complete freedom, and at dinner parties used to climb up the back of chairs and play with the ladies' pretty earrings and necklaces.

Permission of The Fletcher Trust Collection

Memories of Wasp were entwined with thoughts of people and places on the other side of the world. 'Dear old dog – now no more! a link that bound us to kind friends at home, and happy times in pleasant places.'[19]

When she travelled from Christchurch in 1866 to her new abode, Orari Gorge Station in South Canterbury, Ellen Tripp made the momentous journey in the company of her husband, four children, their nurse, and 'also the cat'.[20] As this suggests, unobtrusively, familiar pets became associated with the process of home-making in the new country. In a memoir thinly disguised as a 'novel', Sarah Amelia Courage described a similar journey about the same time from Christchurch to join her husband at Waipara Station near Leithfield. Before she left in the coach she was given a handsome grey kitten by a servant, Mary.

'I sat inside with baby, nurse and the kitten, which I was glad to have, for I must confess to a feeling of loneliness, having left Mary behind.' This cat, Kitty, which lived to the age of 16, was a comfort at other lonely times. Sarah spent days by herself while her husband was away, drinking tea, 'the cat meanwhile sitting on the hearthrug purring away with all its might'. On at least one occasion she was so grateful for this calming sound that she gave him 'an extra saucer of milk for his amiability'.[21]

Home-making involved establishing routines and rituals, and of these, food preparation and eating were perhaps the most important. In colonial New Zealand the feeding of pets was closely associated with human meal times. Some prepared pet foods such as dog biscuits and bird seed gradually became available, but people usually gave cats and dogs the scraps left after a meal. Writing to her aunt in 1854, for instance, Jemima Martin noted, 'Dinner over, portioned out the dinner remainder for the dogs and cats.'[22] More than one sketch of the inside of a settler's house showed animals queuing up for food while people were eating. The sight of a waiting dog or cat by the dinner table became a powerful and enduring image of domestic happiness, a reassuring sign of security and contentment.

~

'The Festive Season', published in the *New Zealand Farmer* in January 1888, depicts the family cat and dog lining up for and getting their share of an enormous Christmas dinner. It is an interesting sequel to the emigration cartoon 'Here and There' of 40 years before, in which pets waiting expectantly beside the dinner table symbolised future domestic harmony and prosperity. A couple of generations later the promise has been fulfilled. *Alexander Turnbull Library. Reference: S-L 1040-15*

For some immigrants it was fascination with the animals of the new country, not nostalgia for those of the old, that enabled them to feel more settled. One of New Zealand's attractions was its abundant birdlife. New arrivals were often deeply impressed by the overwhelming chorus of native birds in the still mostly untouched forests. When John and Catherine Orbell and their 12 children sailed into Otago Harbour in 1849 on the *Mariner*, for example, they were greeted by the welcoming song of thousands of birds on both sides of the inlet – a magnificent sound they never forgot.[23] Some settlers made themselves at home by taming native birds. Such pets were available to all, rich or poor.

Handbooks for prospective settlers gave enticing details about the most handsome or melodious native birds, promising that they were 'common round every homestead',[24] and describing them in ways that made them seem familiar – a clever ploy to make New Zealand appear less distant and strange. Kakariki were usually referred to as parrots, parakeets or paroquets – common pet birds in Britain. Tui were dubbed 'parson birds' on account of their white neck feathers, which looked like clerical collars. They were also called 'mocking birds' because of their ability to mimic a range of sounds.

The pleasing song of native birds made them desirable pets. In addition, tui, kakariki and kaka (often called cawcaws) could be tamed and taught to speak – a much admired trait. John Ward, in his 1840 book *Information Relative to New Zealand Compiled for the Use of Colonists*, said of the tui, 'There is not a note of any bird of the woods but what it exactly imitates; and, when confined in a cage, it learns with great ease and correctness to speak long sentences.' The kaka, he noted, was 'a bird of the parrot kind, much larger than any other New Zealand parrot, but possessing all their mischievous qualities, and capable of learning to imitate the human voice to an astonishing degree'.[25]

In an 1845 letter to his father in Scotland, Canterbury settler John Deans recounted how his pet tui could produce all kinds of sounds: 'In the morning before we rose it commenced mocking, at one time coughing as a person would do that had a bad cold, then laughing as if he would have split his sides, and occasionally whistling his native notes; a stranger could not keep from laughing to hear him.'[26] Ellen Hewett, who arrived in Nelson with her family in the mid-1850s, remembered taming a kaka: 'I caught one and tied it on to the branch of a tree quite near the house, and all its bird friends used to visit it and help it to eat its food; and it became so tame and fond of us that when set at liberty it would not leave us.'[27] Mary Hay, growing up at Pigeon Bay on Banks Peninsula in the 1880s, was presented by one of her many admirers with a kakariki that he had trained to talk. Later, when she was being courted by her husband-to-be, this bird caused her great embarrassment. As a joke her brothers taught it to say, 'Oh, Tom, just one kiss! Quick.'[28]

Birds were not the only native species kept as pets. Young Mervyn Stewart, whose parents arrived at the Bay of Plenty settlement of Katikati in 1878, was given a green lizard (probably a common green gecko), which he kept in a mustard tin by his bed and fed on flies. He was delighted when Liz, as he called her, produced babies. But, according to his mother, Adela Stewart, 'in course of time, they had to be liberated, or were eaten by the cat – I forget which!'[29]

~

Those who arrived with little in the way of money or possessions had to work hard to make their way in New Zealand, and rated highly those animals that could assist them to become established. Unlike the wealthy emigrants, they could not afford to bring animals out, so obtaining them in the new country was a priority. Acquiring livestock for a small subsistence farm was a measure of progress, something to be reported with pride to relatives and friends back in England. Cows, horses, pigs and poultry – but also cats, dogs, and other small animals – were listed in letters home. In 1842 Taranaki settler William Henwood boasted to his parents in Cornwall: 'I have got the first cow in the country, which cost me £30. I am sure, if I remained in England, I should not have been the owner of the tail of a cow. But not all yet: I have one nanny goat, which cost me £2.5s; I have got one pig, a dog, and two cats.' He added, apparently without any sense of irony, 'and the best of all, I have got a nice little wife'.[30] Benjamin Wells, also from Taranaki, had tongue firmly in cheek when he reported in 1854: 'Our livestock is as follows: 1 Girl, 1 Boy, 1 Heifer, 1 Sow Pig, 1 Tom cat, and I think Zac [his brother] has some rabbits.'[31]

Most domestic animals were either stock or working animals, providing food, fibre, transport and labour of various kinds. Many were destined to be slaughtered and eaten. But because they were few in number and essential to the family's survival and future prospects, they had status in the settler household and were treated accordingly. They were usually named and received attentive care.

Often settler women were responsible for milking the cow and managing the dairy, and for keeping poultry. Feeding the livestock was another woman's job. Sarah Stephens of Motueka wrote to her mother in 1843: 'Sometimes I find my fowls want food and daily I pick a basket of thistles for them or cabbage leaves; then the goats are crying out for a bush or two from me and then the cows will look out for their share, although they can get plenty elsewhere, and the dog and the cat too is to be cared for to say nothing of those uninteresting animals the pigs – six of them will be poking their noses after me …'[32] Some women may have thought these routines mundane, but others found them a pleasure. Frances Caverhill's diary for 1865 is full of concerned and interested remarks about domestic animals, showing the close relationship with them that could develop. She recorded the regular task of setting hens on clutches of eggs ('Jane put 11 bantam eggs under the hen "Sally" which is sitting in the kitchen'),[33] and rejoiced when young ones were born ('"Tulip" calved this evening, to our great surprise for Mrs Curle milked her up to a few days ago').[34] Adela Stewart also enjoyed the work of looking after farm animals. One day she and her lady companion set off to sow clover seed: 'On our way there we met a tiny pig, so pretty that we called it "Venus", caught it, and put it into a little fenced enclosure at the stables. Then we felt we had really started a farm, and delighted in feeding this pig more than we did as they increased in after years.'[35]

Children, too, could make pets of farm animals. One man who grew up in Wellington in the 1840s recalled: 'We had strange pets … My father bought a little white pig from a Maori woman for sixpence. Adolphus we called him. He was bathed every day, and slept in a little box at the foot of the cubby-house [play room] till he grew too big. He followed us everywhere.'[36] Adolphus became fat, and met 'the usual fate', but not before serving time as a companion animal. For some people, apparently, the boundaries between domestic animals and pets were quite flexible.

~

Horses were the most versatile of domesticated animals. Throughout the nineteenth century and well into the twentieth they were used for such farm jobs as ploughing, pulling loads and powering machinery; they were a source of hauling and motive power for extractive industries such as timber milling and coal mining; they carried freight and pulled trams.[37] They also provided an essential means of transport, particularly in the early years of settlement when roads were bad or non-existent. Many parts of New Zealand were covered in dense bush that had to be negotiated with care by travellers. Often horses could find their way home, a great advantage in unfamiliar or trackless terrain, as Anglican clergyman Vicesimus Lush discovered when he became lost in the Hunua forest south of Auckland in 1867 during one of his many pastoral trips. After trying fruitlessly to find his way out, he clung to the back of his 'first rate bush horse', Zingarie, gave up the reins and allowed her to find her way to the road, which she eventually did.[38] There are many similar accounts of horses

Four little girls of the Jones family sit in order of age on their pony while their brother holds a cow nearby. This photograph, taken in Taranaki in the early 1900s, is similar to many others showing siblings on horseback. New Zealand children of the nineteenth century often learned to ride early and for many, a trusty pet horse or pony was their means of transport to a distant country school. *Alexander Turnbull Library, James McAllister Collection. Reference: G-011732-111. Photograph by James McAllister*

bringing disoriented riders home. When roads improved, horses also pulled passengers in carts, buggies, traps and dogcarts. For a settler on a run or farm, or even living in a small town, being able to ride or drive from place to place was a way of combating isolation.

Horses had an important role in popular sports. Horse races were among the earliest entertainments organised by New Zealand settlers, and Maori soon took up the pastime. Other equestrian sports developed during the course of the nineteenth century. Horses were also central to more leisurely pursuits, providing comfort and companionship. For some settler women, riding offered a rare taste of liberty. As Mary Hobhouse wrote in 1862, 'My comfort has been greatly increased by the purchase of a butcher's pony, on wh[ich] I can ride about quite alone, so that what formerly I could not do without tiring myself for the day I can accomplish without fatigue & with much benefit from fresh air.'[39] Ponies provided a similar outlet for children, giving them great freedom to range widely in play, and allowing them to get to and from distant schools.[40]

Even work horses could be viewed as pets. W.K. Howitt, who grew up on a Taranaki farm in the 1870s and 1880s, remembered the steady, reliable farm horse, Donald, on which he and his brothers and sisters learned to ride. Another farmer in the district was determined to buy Donald, and finally made such a good offer that it was accepted. 'When the day came for Donald to leave the farm many tearful children stood at the front door as they watched their faithful old horse and companion led away by a stranger. It was a great wrench to the young hearts, and after all these years it is not hard to recall our grief and our regrets at the parting.'[41]

~

Settlers also considered cats very useful animals – in fact, they were vital to the smooth running of colonial homes. From the 1840s to the 1860s many parts of New Zealand were plagued by rats.[42] Norway rats, introduced by Captain Cook, had overrun the indigenous rat or kiore, and the ship rat arrived in the 1860s. Worrisome pests, attracted by food and tallow soap and candles, rats would eat anything they could reach, sometimes even stealing from people's plates during meals. Sarah Higgins recalled how they invaded the huts made for immigrants arriving in Nelson in 1842: 'such a lot of great, wild rats; and some of the people got bitten.'[43] In the early 1850s Charlotte Godley, in Lyttelton, commented on how brazen they were – on one occasion a servant left the kitchen door open for a few moments 'and as she returned met three, coming together into the house'.[44] Sarah Courage stayed at a rodent-ridden Christchurch hotel in 1864: 'Our bedroom was infested with mice, which were nightly chased by rats as big as rabbits, if one might judge by the weight of them as they bounded over our bodies in bed. Such a scrimmage and a squeaking as there was at night!'[45]

People desperately sought cats, then in short supply, to deal with the problem. Local entrepreneurs met the need to some extent – Baron Charles von Alzdorf was selling cats for £1 each from his farm at Lower Hutt in the early 1840s[46] – but many cats had to be imported. They faced no easy task: rats were big and aggressive and could put up a good fight. As surveyor John Rochfort noted in 1854, 'I have known six cats turned out of a house by them in a single night.'[47] A cat often earned an honoured place in a household by ridding it of rats and mice – and might gain favour in other ways. 'One day,' wrote Adela Stewart, 'our cat brought in a quail, which I took from it, plucked and myself ate, giving it a bit of mutton in exchange. This became a common practice with succeeding generations of cats.'[48]

Yet such cats could also be pets. Sarah Courage wrote of the welcome she would receive from Kitty on returning home from a visit to Christchurch, 'with much purring and feline talk, his grass-green eyes looking the love he felt'.[49] She fondly described his escapades, such as his interference in her first attempt at making puff pastry:

I gathered together my paraphernalia and began, my cat (which I had brought from Christchurch) sitting on the corner of the table watching the process and occasionally putting out his paw to arrest the motion of the rolling pin ... While rolling out the paste, a piece of wood fell out of the fire and burnt a big hole in the back of my brown Holland dress, but I squeezed it out, burning my thumb badly in the process. Then Kitty walked along the flat paste, leaving his footprints thereon, and coolly licked off, under my very nose as it were, all the little dabs of butter dotted upon it. So ended my first attempt at making puff paste.[50]

~

Dogs, like cats, had various functions: emigration handbooks portrayed them as useful for many colonising tasks. In the 1840s Edward Jerningham Wakefield recommended terriers for killing rats, Newfoundlands or boarhounds as helpers when shooting wild fowl and crossing rivers, bloodhounds as watchdogs, pointers for hunting game and Scotch collies for working sheep.[51] In the 1850s Charles Hursthouse claimed that the three types of dogs worth bringing to New Zealand were Scotch collies, retrievers for flushing out and fetching wild ducks, and any sort of terrier suitable for pig hunting.[52]

In the early days some dogs were used as rat catchers, especially when people had to travel or make a temporary camp while moving from place to place. When Agnes Jameson's parents and a friend camped near Christchurch's Heathcote River in 1850, their dogs guarded the supplies: 'They built two primitive toi toi tents or huts, and another on piles, called the whata, a place for stores. I think Tan, my father's sheep dog, had his sleeping quarters underneath, and helped to keep the rats from getting at the food. Tiny, the little terrier, slept in mother's tent, and, valiant little fellow, many a rat did he kill.'[53]

Watchdogs were also essential in a frontier society, where theft and intimidation by itinerant men was a problem in remote areas. As Wakefield pointed out, 'A good watch-dog or two were no despicable guardians of a house, and were very desirable companions out-of-doors at night.'[54] For women left alone in an isolated house all day, a watchdog was a dependable bodyguard. But some of these animals could be unpredictable and aggressive. Charlotte Godley complained about the ferocious bulldog kept chained in a barrel by the door of James and Fanny FitzGerald's Lyttelton house: 'You are obliged to wait at a distance till your voice, and his barking, can bring out one of the inmates, who sits against the mouth of the barrel while you pass. It will bite anyone but Mr FitzGerald, and I think ought to be shot.'[55] Not all watchdogs – or 'house dogs' as they were also known – were as fearsome as this one. Later in the

Ernest Binns took this photograph of his baby son Oswald in his pram, guarded by Carlo the dog, in 1890. The Binns family of Auckland had several other pets, which often featured in snapshots.

Sir George Grey Special Collections, Auckland Libraries. Reference: 920 BIN (4). Photograph by Ernest Charles Binns

nineteenth century, when newspapers often carried advertisements for people seeking 'a good house dog', the term had come to mean a family companion and faithful protector of the home. The house dog alerted the family to the arrival of visitors, welcome or not, and was often a pet too, well fed and treated.

~

Although animals that were both useful and companionable were especially prized, those that were simply pets had an important place in many settler homes. They provided a necessary antidote to loneliness, homesickness and isolation, and were often pleasing to look at or listen to. They were also a sign that a family had attained one of the important goals of emigration – financial independence. Well-off, respectable folk could afford to keep animals that served no obvious practical function: pets were symbols of success.

Quite a range of pets were kept from early settler days. Caged birds, both native and exotic, were popular with adults, and other small animals such as rabbits were common pets for children. In 1848 Wakefield mentioned, intriguingly, a cage full of white mice which escaped in a store at Wellington, 'and for some time that and the neighbouring houses were infested with their descendants'.[56] By 1868 a Wellington general store was selling goldfish and canaries and, according to an article in the *Wellington Independent*, 'a Belgian canary in excellent plumage and good song especially attracts the attention of passers-by'.[57]

Some of the species brought out by acclimatisation societies did not, or were not intended to, adapt to the wild, but were kept in captivity as curiosities or pets. The guinea pig, for instance, first introduced by the Auckland Acclimatisation Society in 1869, could not survive when released, but soon became a children's pet.[58] Monkeys were another type of exotic pet introduced to New Zealand from the middle of the century – they could be obtained if ships called into South African or South American ports on their way to New Zealand. Young Rose Speedy of Pukekohe had a pet monkey during the 1860s, when Vicesimus Lush regularly called on her family. He often brought treats for the animal and on one occasion shared his cake with it.[59]

In nineteenth-century Europe the gentry sometimes kept menageries of animals, and this led to the development of public zoos. From the beginnings of settlement in New Zealand, too, a few wealthy individuals had collections of prestigious animals. When Henry Petre returned to Wellington from a visit to England with his new wife, Ellen, he brought not only his thoroughbred horses but a number of pheasants and peacocks. At least one of the peacocks seems to have been a special pet of Ellen's. When the Petres shifted from Wellington to

The connection of pets with home and family is clear in this photograph of the Lovell-Smith family on the verandah of a house in Christchurch around 1900. A bird in a cage and a dog are included in the family group. *Alexander Turnbull Library. Reference: F-76261-1/2. Photograph by Hubert Lovell-Smith*

Petone in 1843, Ellen wrote, 'At 1 o'clock a large cavalcade left the house – my piano, a large cart of furniture topped up with chickens, rabbits, Pheasants, Turkies and my dear old Peacock in a large clothes basket with a piece of linen round him like a mummy to preserve his tail.'[60] Perhaps the best example of a private menagerie in New Zealand was that of Governor George Grey, who bought Kawau Island in 1861 and stocked it with a variety of rare species.[61]

~

It was inevitable that in settler New Zealand, as in Britain and the United States, pets would become an important way of socialising children, teaching them empathy, gentleness and patience.[62] One of the traditional ways of learning such values was through stories. Animals had long featured in nursery

The cover of this well-worn children's book by Shirley Hibberd, *Clever Dogs, Horses, etc, with anecdotes of other animals*, illustrates the story of a horse that was able to work a pump to get water when it felt thirsty. The book's flyleaf was inscribed 'Charles Wilkinson Bigge, with Granny's best wishes, Xmas 1870'. Hibberd encouraged children to look for 'the key' to understanding and communicating with domestic and wild animals by explaining their many similarities to humans. One of the underlying moral messages was the importance of treating animals with consideration. Children's animal and pet books such as this one became very popular in the nineteenth century.

Author's collection

rhymes and fables as embodiments of virtues or vices, to illustrate moral lessons. In the eighteenth century, stories about animals, especially those directed at older children, began to take a more realistic turn. True stories about the deeds of animals (often dogs) showed the importance of faithfulness, courage and obedience.[63] Now children were being encouraged to use their imagination to identify with the experiences of animals and think of them as having feelings. By the mid-nineteenth century, pet keeping and its responsibilities became a theme in children's fiction. In addition, books of anecdotes about pets and advice on pet care were published for children in England from the 1850s. They included titles such as *Live Toys; Or anecdotes of our four-legged and other pets* by Emma Davenport, *Domestic Pets; Their habits and management; with illustrative anecdotes* by Mrs Jane Loudon, and *Our Domestic Pets* by the Reverend J.G. Wood. An English author with New Zealand connections, Mrs George Cupples, also wrote children's books about pets.[64] Some of these volumes made their way to New Zealand.[65]

For children without easy access to books, locally published newspapers and magazines provided improving reading matter about animals. There was often a page for children, including stories, jokes and riddles, and advice or homilies on various topics, often syndicated or copied from overseas journals – and animals, notably pets, featured prominently.[66] Some local papers also copied the overseas practice of publishing pages of children's letters. Young readers were encouraged to write to an adult editor who might take on the persona of an aunt or uncle, or even a fairytale creature. Children's correspondence pages became immensely popular in late-nineteenth-century New Zealand, and proliferated in the first half of the twentieth century.[67]

From 1886 the *Otago Witness* published a page called 'Dot's Little Folk', where letters were answered by 'Dot', a role taken by several journalists over the years.[68] The first Dot told her correspondents that she wanted them to write about their pets, among other subjects.[69] In 1888 the *New Zealand Farmer* also started up a 'Children's Post Office'. The editor, the father of young children, explained:

> *We think it would amuse and interest you all to read letters from children your own age, living in different parts of New Zealand, describing their homes and favourite occupations, and generally comparing notes one with another. For instance, the boys could tell one another about any adventures they might have had in the bush, and whether they can swim or ride, or drive a team of horses: and about boating and fishing excursions and what animal pets they have, if any.*[70]

Both boys and girls eagerly accepted this invitation, and were soon writing to 'Uncle Ned', as the editor called himself, and their 'cousins'.

Children's many anecdotes about their animal companions in letters to Dot and Uncle Ned show how widespread pet keeping had become by the 1880s and 1890s, and how central pets were to home life. Often children had several animals, ranging from cats and dogs to guinea pigs, rabbits and birds such as canaries. As well as describing their pets' endearing characteristics and habits, the youngsters were keen to explain their usefulness or versatility – suggesting that settler values were still important. Dogs would often bring the cows in for milking, catch rabbits or find hens' nests. Cats killed mice and rats and at least one worked cooperatively with the family dog, as Elizabeth Lineham recounted: 'Our cat Toby brings home live rats for the dog to kill.'[71] Elizabeth Parr described how the family cats were tethered in the orchard to stop birds from eating the cherries.[72] Sometimes helpfulness could backfire, however, as a letter from 'Totsy' revealed: 'My brother had a little guinea pig for a few days, but the poor little creature came to a very tragic end. I think I spoke of our old blind dog in my last letter who is a very good ratter. On Sunday afternoon he came up to my brother wagging his tail and looking quite delighted at having, as he thought, caught a rat, but it was in reality the poor little guinea pig.'[73]

That children had indeed learnt empathy through observing and caring for pets was shown in a letter-writing fad of the early 1890s when youthful correspondents adopted the guise of an animal. One 'cat' wrote, 'I have got a very good home here. I do like to sit on the hob and warm myself.'[74] 'I was given to my master when I was only a pup,' a 'dog' reminisced, 'and many a race I have had with him, both of us stretching our legs to see which one of us could run the fastest.'[75] And a 'kaka' recalled: 'I must have been taken out of the nest because I do not remember anything further back than when I lived in a cage. When I had grown up I used to live around the place and never fly away.'[76]

~

Native birds, including kaka, kakariki, tui and the flightless kakapo, were still popular household pets at this time. Professor G.S. Sale described how his pet kakapo would show affection by nestling on his hand, ruffling out his feathers, fluttering his wings and shaking his head from side to side. Another kakapo, called Major, belonged to Mr A. Hansen, one of the lighthouse keepers at Puysegur Point in Fiordland. Major's amusing, if disruptive, antics included climbing onto the table and throwing all the dishes and cutlery off it, hopping about on both feet at once, twisting his head in all directions and 'making headlong rushes like a man trying to recover himself after stumbling over an obstacle'. He disliked the cat and terrorised the fowls, but was great friends with the dog, Hector. When Hector was lying in front of the kitchen fire, Major used him as a cushion to sleep on. But as soon as Major had had enough sleep he would pull the dog's ears, nose, tail, toes and hair and run all over his body, 'apparently to Hector's thorough enjoyment'.[77]

In 1891 Oliver Laking Wadsworth of Wai-iti told Uncle Ned about his pet tui, called Joe, who 'tries hard to talk'.[78] The following year Edith David of Stratford in Taranaki wrote, 'We have a nice paroquet [kakariki], and we call him Joe. We brought him all the way from Barry's Bay, Canterbury, with us two years ago, and he talks very nicely.'[79] But some children were aware that native birdlife was on the wane. Ethel, of Fitzherbert East, near Palmerston North, appealed for help in 1892: 'My sister has a young paroquet. Would you please ask some of the cousins if they could tell us how to teach it to talk? My sister bought it in Nelson, as they are so scarce here.'[80]

Imported birds replaced native birds in people's affections. By the 1890s Australian birds such as cockatoos and galahs were in vogue. Lorna Monckton recalled how her mother's galah, Cocky, was allowed to range freely in the

house. Cocky had an extensive vocabulary, which he used to baffle and intimidate visitors. He also had the habit of breaking crockery: he would sidle up to a china cup, drop it on the floor and then celebrate the crash by jumping up and down and shouting, 'Hooray, hooray!'[81] Another galah called Cocky was the pet of the Monro family of Palmerston North in the 1890s. He adored Mrs Monro: the bottom of her navy serge skirt was often fringed with white powder from his feathers as he jumped up repeatedly, trying to make her pick him up. One of his tricks was to roll on his back, waving a cotton reel in his claw like a dumb-bell.[82] In 1894 the Edwin family of Wellington had a cockatoo called Chuckie, who was occasionally let out of his cage after dinner and 'chased the family around the table with great vigour'.[83]

~

Photography helped to trace the emergence of a lively pet culture in New Zealand. Pet portraiture began mid-century and soon grew in popularity. Many studio photographs show a person with a dog, or occasionally a cat or other small animal. Pets may have been included at the photographer's request to make the setting appear more naturalistic, but it is hard to escape the conclusion that in many cases the owner wanted a permanent memento of a beloved animal. Having your photograph taken was a rare and important occasion: a formal portrait might be sent to a relative as a keepsake or treasured within the immediate family as a record of a person at a significant stage of life, such as

The pet dog is wearing someone's cap – perhaps the photographer's? – much to the amusement of the woman holding him. These Greymouth people are having afternoon tea outdoors in the early years of the twentieth century.

Alexander Turnbull Library. Reference: G-96572-1/2

'Poor Mrs Duck was very old'

NINETEENTH-CENTURY pet owners, like their modern counterparts, grieved when a loved pet died. In *Lights and Shadows of Colonial Life*, Sarah Courage vividly remembered her sorrow when her dog, Charkie, was fatally kicked by a horse: 'I went to my room and — shall I confess it? — cried bitterly over the sad fate of my poor little dumb companion.'[86]

One way of coping with the sadness was to ceremonially bury a pet. This practice, which can be traced back for centuries, underwent a revival thanks largely to Queen Victoria. When one of her pets died, she was beside herself with anguish, and buried the animal with proper mourning rites. Elaborate tombstones and monuments marked the graves of all the royal pets, a tradition that continues to the present day.[87] In New Zealand, governors and their families followed suit. For example, when Lady Ranfurly's little dog, Hamish, died in 1897 he was buried in the grounds of Government House in Wellington beneath a large headstone.

Children were also encouraged to follow the royal example, possibly to help them come to terms with the ever-present reality of death. In 1888, 12-year-old Lucy Ford from Christchurch wrote to Uncle Ned of the *New Zealand Farmer*, 'Mother has a flock of beautiful pure Aylesbury ducks. She gave me one a little time ago to start my own poultry yard, but last week she died. I think she died of old age, and I buried her at the bottom of mother's garden and planted daisies all over her grave.'[88]

The editor's reply included condolences and a tongue-in-cheek verse that probably consoled Lucy and made her parents smile:

Poor Mrs Duck was very old,
So old she scarce could quack or waddle,
And now at rest beneath the mould
She lies all snug. To call it twaddle
To write her epitaph is wrong.
For blameless she has walked life's mazes.
And done her duty all along
As well as those who earn great praises:
So, shrouded in her plumage white,
Sound may she sleep beneath the daisies.

Another way to remember a loved pet was to have it stuffed so that it could remain a household presence after its death. This custom, strange to modern eyes, was not thought odd by grieving Victorian pet owners; rather, it showed their affection and esteem for the dead animal. Again, there were royal precedents. In 1898 the *Bruce Herald* reported that 'Domestic pets which have endeared themselves by long years of association to the Prince or Princess of Wales are always stuffed immediately after death, and find a permanent resting-place in a corridor at Sandringham or in Marlborough House.'[89]

Taxidermists located in various towns around New Zealand offered this service. For instance, in 1883 Mr G. Lambert, a taxidermist and chemist at Pleasant Point in South Canterbury, advertised: 'Birds, animals, fishes, and domestic pets set up and stuffed with the greatest skill.'[90] In some cases, just the skin was preserved. The *Otago Witness* of 23 June 1909 published detailed instructions for readers on preserving the skins of pets to make a rug mat.[91] Stuffing deceased pets or preserving their skins continued until well into the twentieth century.

Hamish, the beloved pet dog of Lady Ranfurly, was buried in the grounds of the old Government House in Wellington, near where the Beehive now stands, in 1897. A large headstone bearing his name marked the grave. Vice-regal examples such as this made the ceremonial burial of pets more generally acceptable.

Alexander Turnbull Library, Ranfurly Collection. Reference: PA1-f-194-17

Everyone looks thoroughly relaxed and at home in this photograph of Elizabeth Wilford on her front porch with her cat and dog in March 1904.

Alexander Turnbull Library, George Moore Collection. Reference: G-65342-1/2. Photograph by George Moore

childhood or young adulthood. Immortalising an animal in a studio photograph was a measure of strong attachment.

Pets also featured incidentally in photographs of houses. Plain dwellings on stark, treeless sections were enhanced by the presence of cats and dogs on the verandah or front door step, and horses or ponies nearby.[84] The inclusion of animals in these photographs seems deliberate. They helped to create an impression of domesticity and, like the early letters listing livestock, were evidence of success — of having established not just a house, but a home.

From the 1890s, when the advent of hand-held cameras made photography easier and cheaper, people started to take their own candid photographs or 'snapshots',[85] which reveal that animals were a focus for family games and jokes. Outdoor morning and afternoon teas and picnics often included the family pets — cats, dogs and sometimes even a bird in a cage. For a laugh, pet owners dressed animals, usually dogs, in human clothing and posed them for snaps. Photographs of pet animals appeared not just in the family album but in popular magazines, often with sentimental captions that underlined the connection of pets with home and family.

Such images bear witness not just to pet-keeping trends, but to the greater prosperity and ease often enjoyed by Pakeha settlers. The emigration propaganda of 50 years before had promised future abundance: now the dream was being realised. And for many people in this land of plenty, a house without a pet was simply not a happy home.

A dejected-looking dog shares the discomforts of his human companions in this painting of an Otago high-country surveyors' camp in bleak weather, about 1847. Enduring hardships together could help to forge bonds between men and their animals.

Alexander Turnbull Library. Reference: B-155-010. Watercolour by Edward Immyns Abbot

Chapter 3

A man's best friends?

In 1851, 17-year-old Percy Whitehead set out from London for Nelson, intent on improving his prospects in New Zealand. After finding employment as a shepherd on a Marlborough sheep run, he was soon impressed at how his new dog, Bluff, helped to keep the flock grazing on the high ridges. In a letter to family members in England he explained:

> I say to my dog, 'Bluff, my boy, go on up,' and away he goes. At some distance he stops, and looks round. I wave my hand, and cry 'Go on!' and he takes the sheep up. And when far enough, I cry out, 'Steady! That'll do. Come in, my boy;' and down he comes, and I pat him.

In Percy's estimation, Bluff was a real treasure:

> He is such a handsome dog – not one of those bob-tailed ugly sheep-dogs you see with drovers in England, but a fine, compact, strong dog, with a long shiny black coat, a white breast, and a spot on his neck and tail – a tail like an ostrich feather, and a capital head; he is so willing to work, he will go anywhere if he can see sheep and I give him the word. You would easily understand how I love him if you knew what a blessing he is, both as a companion and assistant, and how much trouble he saves me.[1]

Similar expressions of affection and gratitude can be found in other stories men told about their working dogs and horses. These were unmistakeably companion animals.

~

In colonial New Zealand there were many back-breaking jobs to be done – establishing farms, clearing forests, building settlements and creating transport links. This heavy manual labour fell to men, and as a consequence, until late in the century, society was male-dominated. Some men, like Whitehead, worked alone, while many belonged to teams. All looked to other men for friendship, comfort and help, and mateship – a support system based on shared attitudes and values – developed. Mates respected hard work, physical strength and versatility and a readiness to 'rough it' and face dangers. They appreciated the importance of joint effort in overcoming difficulties, and expected and offered loyalty.[2] Animals, especially dogs and horses, could obviously perform some of the functions of mates. Their strength, speed and willingness could mean the difference between success and failure, and sometimes life and death. These attributes explain the close relationship that often developed between them and the men they worked alongside.

From the 1840s Scottish shepherds arrived in New Zealand to work on large sheep runs, bringing with them Border collies. These dogs, highly strung but renowned for their intelligence, were invaluable in the early days of settlement. One of their first tasks was to help move sheep from the docks at Lyttelton and Dunedin into the vast tussock country of the South Island. They were also used to drive sheep from the port of Wellington to the North Island pastoral region of Wairarapa and on to Hawke's Bay.[3] The collie was essential to the shepherd, guarding the flock against wild dogs and pigs, stopping sheep from straying and gathering them together when necessary. Initially such dogs were few in number and difficult to replace, so they were especially precious. In their absence, sometimes young trainee farmers or cadets were sent alone to herd sheep on the hills – a frustrating and exhausting job without a dog.[4] Percy Whitehead was among the fortunate ones.

As sheep farming developed, so did the sheep dog, with two separate types – the heading dog and the huntaway – being bred specifically for New Zealand conditions. Other kinds of dogs were used for different purposes on pastoral runs and dairy farms. Cattle dogs, larger and heavier than sheep dogs, helped to muster cows and bulls, nipping cattle on the heel or nose to stop or turn them. Handy dogs, as the name suggests, were versatile and did a range of jobs on the farm. Before rail and motorised transport, teams of drover's dogs shifted mobs of stock over long distances.[5] Without obedient, energetic dogs, many farming jobs would have been exceptionally difficult or impossible. It is no wonder, then, that the loss of a skilled dog was seen as a calamity. When in 1851 Canterbury colonist Edward Ward heard that Lass, the dog of a fellow settler, had been accidentally poisoned he wrote, 'I can easily believe what he says, that he cried like a child when she died.'[6]

~

In 1846 Thomas Brunner and Charles Heaphy, with Maori guides Kehu and Tau, ventured down the West Coast of the South Island as far as the Arahura River in a search for land suitable for settlement. Heaphy sketched an incident when the party had to ascend the sheer Te Miko Cliff north of Punakaiki on a rotting ladder made of rata vines. The dog accompanying them was hoisted up on a flax rope. This poor animal had already put up with being fed sea urchin ('not a favourite food of Scotch terriers', remarked Heaphy), being thrown overboard to swim when the party was crossing a river on a sinking raft, and being nearly swept out to sea during another perilous river crossing.

© The British Library Board. Reference: Add.19954f.50. Pencil and wash drawing by Charles Heaphy

Early explorers and surveyors also depended on the assistance of dogs. Although most of the coastline of New Zealand had been mapped by 1840, large parts of the interior remained uncharted by Europeans. A few daring individuals set out to explore the rugged new environment, but it was extremely challenging for those used to more forgiving northern hemisphere landscapes. Some travelled in bands or with Maori guides, while a brave few went without human company. Both solo explorers and groups almost always took a dog or two with them. During lengthy journeys into remote areas, the ability of dogs to hunt and catch birds for food enabled their owners to survive.

Gerhard Mueller, a pioneer surveyor on the West Coast, wrote repeatedly to his wife Bannie in 1865 and 1866 begging her to send his dog Topsy to the Survey Office at Hokitika: 'Without a dog it is practically impossible to catch either kiwi or green-bird [kakapo] … I am glad I had the chance of a gun and ammunition, but if I had Topsy, I would not require it – she would keep me in woodhens [weka] and kiwis, of which I hear there are plenty in the Ranges.' A short time after, Topsy arrived and on 26 April 1866 Mueller was able to report from a camp at the Arahura River: 'Topsy is enjoying herself well. While I was unwell (ie convalescent) and we had no gun, she supplied me with woodhens and ducks, which latter she used to catch in small creeks in the bush.'[7]

Andreas Reischek, an Austrian naturalist and collector who lived in New Zealand for 12 years from 1877 and made numerous expeditions in search of rare birds, credited his dog Caesar with saving his life on several occasions. Highly intelligent, Caesar could not only hunt and kill birds, but catch them live if necessary. He could also retrieve lost items, warn of dangers such as floods and quicksand near rivers and fetch help in an emergency. On one occasion Reischek set off in a canoe to explore Dusky Sound in Fiordland. 'After we had got away a distance Caesar sat up and growled. I told him to lie down, but he would not, keeping on growling and looking at me, and then down into the canoe, so I scrambled up to where he was and found the canoe half full of water.' Bailing frantically, Reischek managed to make it to shore: 'Had it not been for Caesar I should more likely have been drowned.'[8]

In an 11-year partnership, Reischek and Caesar developed a strong affinity. As Reischek observed, 'Being always my companion he understood every word I said, and also could read my face. If I was annoyed, pleased, or unwell, he would make his sympathy manifest.'[9] Forced to leave Caesar behind in New Zealand when he returned to Austria, Reischek clearly felt that he had lost a true friend. His 1889 published memoir of Caesar, *The Story of a Wonderful Dog*, was a heartfelt tribute: 'It has been a labour of love to place on record the unselfish services that have been rendered me by a creature, which, though usually classed as far beneath the rank of humanity, exhibited throughout its life virtues which, in any human being, would command our highest admiration.'[10]

Other lone explorers relied heavily on their dogs. Charlie Douglas, who explored and mapped much of the West Coast for the Department of Lands and Survey between the late 1860s and late 1880s, usually worked with only a dog. He kept diaries in which he often recorded the help of Betsey Jane (he had at least two dogs by this name) and other dogs he travelled with. These animals shared Douglas's hardships on his journeys of exploration. The last Betsey Jane, for example, went short of food, injured herself hunting and endured being hauled across rivers at the end of a rope. She remained faithful to the end, meeting her death in the bush, probably by falling down a cliff. When Douglas reported this to a friend, some of his sadness was conveyed in a poignant comment: 'peace to her ashes'.[11]

~

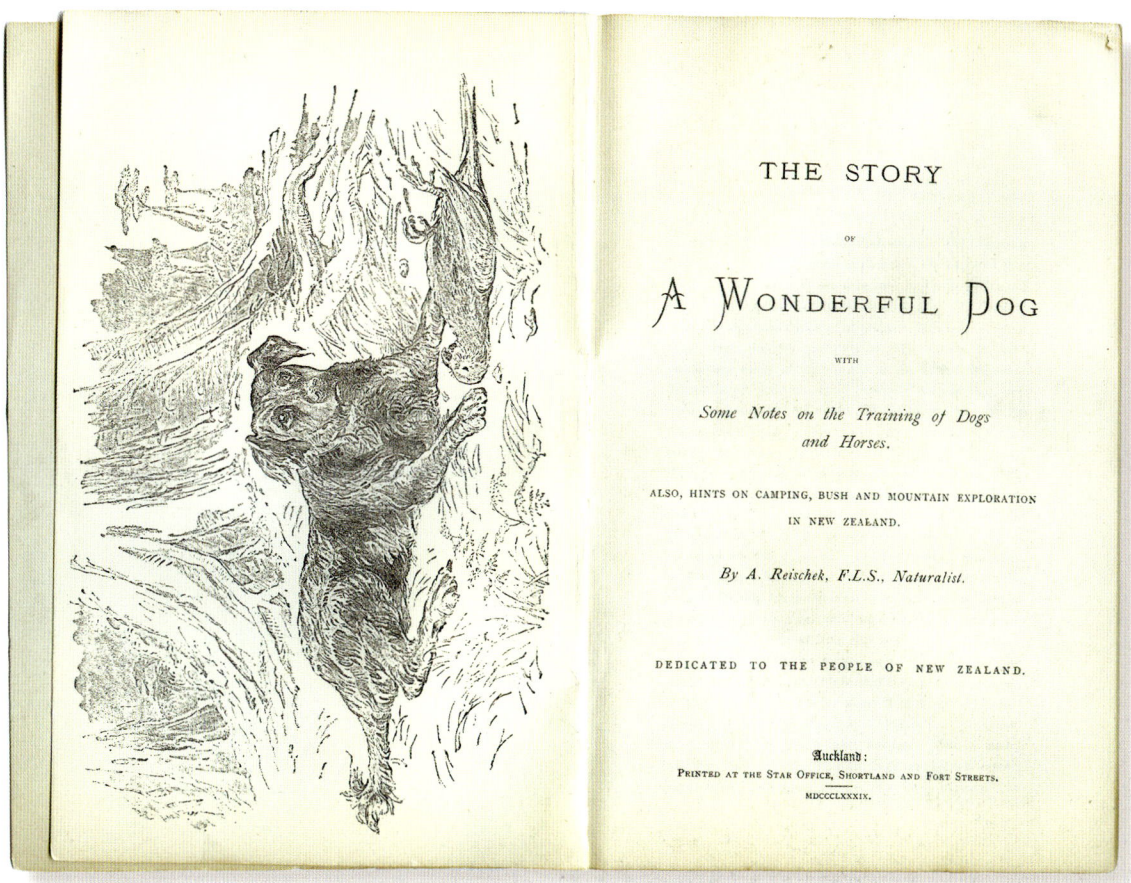

A sketch of Caesar in his prime, alongside a dead kaka that he has retrieved, illustrates the title page of *The Story of a Wonderful Dog*. Caesar's father was a thoroughbred Newfoundland and his mother a well-bred retriever, but as a puppy he was 'as ugly as could be. His legs and tail were long, his head big and his body small.' But what he lacked in looks he made up for in intelligence and faithfulness. A. Reischek (1889), The Story of a Wonderful Dog, with some notes on the training of dogs and horses, Star, Auckland

A man's best friends? **65**

Horses, too, were essential in many types of endeavour. Faster and more versatile than bullocks, the other main draught animal, they provided transport as well as helping with the heavy labour of hauling goods, ploughing and harvesting crops. Later they supplied the motive power for agricultural machinery such as threshing mills.[12] In the South Island packhorses made it possible to shift large loads across treacherous rivers where there were no bridges. Horses skilled in making these crossings were sometimes referred to as 'river horses'.[13] Other horses were capable of mustering and yarding cattle, and apparently they were 'wonderfully eager and clever at it, – cutting out and dodging single beasts with extraordinary sagacity and spirit'.[14]

Good work horses could be regarded with deep affection. The poem 'Old Nugget' by balladeer David McKee Wright, which celebrates a veteran packhorse, veers between humour as it dwells on the animal's highly individual

LAST DAY IN HARNESS.

'Last Day in Harness', depicting the death of Wild Dayrell, faces the title page of *Crusts*, by Laurence Kennaway, who gave a poetic and touching account of the old horse's last days: 'We proposed to give him a retiring pension of oats and shelter, and merely used him now and then as he grew old, to get in the broken-in bullock teams; but one day the bullock driver, being anxious to make an early start to get over a rising river, pushed him a little hard in bringing in the team; coming back, Wild Dayrell did what he had never done before, – he lagged at the spur, – and a little farther on he bore his head heavily upon the reins, and within sight of home slowly stopped, – kneeled quietly down under the rider, – and sank upon the ground, trembling to his hoofs. The driver raised his heavy head and tried to rouse him, but the old fellow had seen his last morning, and still bridled, and saddled, and at his post, stretched out his head, and died there among the dew-laden ferns.'

Alexander Turnbull Library. Reference: B-K-1004

quirks and faults, and respect when talking about his longevity and hard work. Grateful regard underlies its final gruff judgement of Old Nugget as having done 'a fairish day's work when it comes to the saying goodbye'.[15] A similar sense of gratitude underlies an account of the death in harness of a faithful old stockhorse called Wild Dayrell, in Laurence Kennaway's 1874 reminiscences *Crusts: A settler's fare due south*. 'It is a hard thing to think that the faithful life of our time-tried, four-footed friends makes no record in the future, and I know that when he died, all the men believed that if there were for horses a hereafter of happy feeding-grounds, there would be there a sheltered and sunny paddock, watered with sweet water, – for old Wild Dayrell.'[16]

The horse's usefulness was not, of course, limited to farming activities. Once roads had been made, horse-drawn carts and coaches carried people and supplies from place to place, and the introduction of Cobb and Co. coaches in the South Island from the early 1860s ensured a reliable and speedy service. In forestry work, horses hauled felled logs to timber mills. Pit ponies pulled trucks in gold and coal mines.[17] They, too, gained the admiration of those who worked alongside them. Les Morgan, for instance, fondly remembered a pit pony called Dolly, who pulled trucks of quartz in the Martha gold mine at Waihi, south of the Coromandel Peninsula, early in the twentieth century. Like other such ponies, Dolly spent almost all her life underground, with just a three-week break at the surface over Christmas. She was treated as a pet by the miners, who took her sugar bags of grass to supplement her hard food, offered her bread crusts and indulged her when she stole their lunches from their crib tins. 'Whenever the talk goes to the time I was underground I remember old Dolly, the almost human pony, and am thankful for having worked with her.'[18]

~

As this suggests, animals were valued not just for their working abilities: they were company, and very amusing company at that. On a journey of exploration in Westland in 1891, Charlie Douglas and Betsey Jane were joined by another dog, Poker, who was adept at playing on Douglas's sympathies. His diary told of a stormy night in the bush:

> Betsey Jane generally lies at my feet & the weather was so bad that poor Poker determined to try & get under the Tent also. He couldn't lie before the fire, there was no room so he commenced a piece of Generalship, to try & get Betsey out & himself in, but she knew too much for him & wouldn't budge.
>
> Then he made an appeal to my feelings, he shivered & looked at me, then he craned his neck over, & evidently thought there was room for him between me & the back of the Tent; he looked with eyes that plainly told me so. He takes up as much room as a two

A relaxed-looking cat keeps Mr Gallagher company as he scrapes kauri gum, a job that was usually done at the end of a hard day's digging. The photograph was taken in Northland, probably in the 1890s or 1900s.

Alexander Turnbull Library, Northwood Collection. Reference: G-6270-1/1. Photograph by Northwood Brothers

year old Donkey, but the weather outside was certainly miserable, & his cute hints were too much for me & I let him in, & there he now is jammed behind & giving vent to his happiness, in occaisional [sic] groans of satisfaction.[19]

Other men who were isolated by the nature of their work relied on the companionship of animals. Shepherds and boundary watchers had to spend long periods working in the hills, alone except for horses, dogs and sometimes other animals. Writer Lady Mary Anne Barker, who spent some years on a Canterbury sheep run, remarked on the importance of pets to 'pastoral hermits'.

'Are you not very lonely here?' was often my first instinctive question, as I have dismounted at the door of a shepherd's hut in the back country, and listened to the eternal roar of the river which formed his boundary, or the still more oppressive silence which seemed to have reigned ever since the creation. 'Well, mum, it aint very lively; but I've got Topsy (producing a black kitten from his pocket), and there's the dogs, and I shall have some fowls next year, p'raps.'[20]

Men were still living in these circumstances late in the century. In 1890 an Irish journalist travelling around New Zealand spoke to a number of such shepherds: 'It is a lonely life, as may be imagined, with only horses and dogs as companions, but they are more companionable than some people imagine, especially the latter.'[21]

Rabbiters, who used teams of dogs to control plagues of rabbits that destroyed pasture, also worked alone. These men were often back-country shepherds or fencers who had given up their previous employment so they could be free to come and go as they pleased. The dogs, collectively referred to as 'the rabbit pack', included terriers, spaniels, foxhounds, greyhounds and Labradors, united by a strong hunting instinct. Once they had scented a rabbit, they would pursue and kill it. Rabbiters often had a favourite dog that was treated as a pet. For one man it was a black cocker spaniel, which always sat beside him in front of the fire when he was enjoying a pipe and a cup of tea. The dog would consent to having a hat put on its head and a pipe in its mouth.[22]

Some men actually preferred to live by themselves, with animals as their only company. Seclusion was more bearable if there was another beating heart under the same roof. A few gold prospectors chose to work alone, becoming known to other men as 'hatters' – apparently from the phrase 'mad as a hatter'. In *New Zealand After Fifty Years*, published in 1889, journalist Edward Wakefield commented, 'The hatter's life seems, indeed, almost intolerable, for he often sees not a human face from week's end to week's end, and has absolutely no companionship save that of a dog, a cat, or a bird.'[23] There were other such solitary men, for whom pet animals were psychologically important. W.K. Howitt remembered an old poacher who lived with his pack of gun dogs near the family farm in Taranaki in the 1880s: 'He shared his small, rough, boarded whare with its earthen floor with his faithful "old setters" which he had trained so well, as they were the only real companions he ever knew.' These dogs had a special corner near his bunk and he relied on them to alert him to anyone approaching his hut.[24]

Swaggers, men down on their luck who walked from job to job with their possessions tied to their backs, were a common sight on rural roads, especially during and after the Long Depression of the 1880s, and some of them had animal companions. Famous swagger Edmond (Ned) Slattery, 'The Shiner', tramped the roads of Southland, Otago and Canterbury from the 1870s, often accompanied by a pair of greyhounds.[25] Another eccentric swagger was Barney Winters, better known as 'Barney Whiterats', who shuffled along South Island highways until his death in 1911, aged 90. His nickname referred to the white mice he carried with him, which he taught to perform tricks. Stopping at towns along his route, he would set up a screen with light behind it and throw shadowgraphs of birds and animals onto it, or show magic lantern slides, or stage a Punch and Judy show. The main attraction, however, was the performing mice, and many children begged their parents for a penny to see his shows.[26]

The gender imbalance in the population – women were significantly in the minority until after World War I – meant that a number of

Swagger Ned Slattery, better known as 'The Shiner', was famed for his story-telling and his inventive money-making ploys. Very fond of dogs, he was photographed with this canine companion when he was still tramping the roads in his old age. *Alexander Turnbull Library. Reference: F-50133-1/2*

colonial men never married. Among them was James Cox, who moved from job to job around the lower North Island in the 1880s and 1890s. In a biographical study of Cox, *Nearly Out of Heart and Hope*, Miles Fairburn mentions his important relationships with two horses and a dog, which distracted him from his harsh existence. With very little money and no permanent abode, Cox was not able to keep pets. While living in Carterton in the 1890s, however, he formed a strong attachment to animals belonging to his employers. In his diary he commented affectionately on the daily activities of Major, the dog, and Gassy and Prince, the cart horses. He watched out for their welfare, particularly that of the horses, noting

> *their every visit to the blacksmith, their every escape from the paddock, which of them went out on which harvesting and chaff-cutting run, all the rest periods they needed, all the ailments that afflicted them, and the name of every human who borrowed them, shod them, unharnessed them, worked them, took them to the blacksmith, or retrieved them from the pound.*[27]

Major was accidentally poisoned in 1895, and as was common when such animals became too feeble to work, Gassy and Prince were sent to the knacker's yard – where old horses were slaughtered and turned into dog food, fertiliser, glue and other products – in 1895 and 1898 respectively. Although their deaths grieved Cox greatly, his association with them was a consolation in a lonely, hardscrabble life.

~

For both loners and groups of men living in rough, primitive conditions the presence of cats and dogs could summon up a cosy, home-like setting. Sketches of the interiors of men's huts often show animals around the table or hearth.[28] Such domestic associations may have been one reason for Samuel Butler's remark, 'I do not know how it is, but men here are much fonder of cats than they are at home.'[29] Another likely reason was the need for rodent control. In 1860 Butler brought a cat from Christchurch especially to deal with the rats in the communal living quarters at his sheep run, Mesopotamia, in the Canterbury high country. Obliged to ford the flooded Rangitata River with the cat in a bag on the pommel of his saddle, he was very relieved to hear her purr after her soaking.

This cat became a favourite at the simple hut, which featured what is possibly the first recorded cat door in New Zealand. 'Having made it [the hut] neat we kept it so,' wrote Butler, 'and of a night it wore an aspect of comfort quite domestic, even to the cat, which would come in through a hole left in the thatched door for her especial benefit, and purr a regular hurricane.' She proved to be both an excellent ratter and a diversion for the men: 'We blessed her both by day and by night, for we saw no rats after she came; and great excitement prevailed when, three weeks after her arrival, she added a litter of kittens to our establishment.'[30]

Brothers John and Charles Enys, who from the early 1860s ran another Canterbury sheep station, Castle Hill, rivalled Butler and his men in their fondness for cats. When they took their meals in the kitchen, Charles's cat would lie around his shoulders and help himself off the fork, while John's would sit on his knee. At one stage there were five cats in the household. Like Butler's cat, they used a special door, too small for the dogs, made from the verandah into the living room. When John Enys finally sold Castle Hill and returned to England in 1890, he took his favourite cat, Taipo, along with his special chair and sheepskin, to a friend's house and stayed there a fortnight to settle the animal into his new surroundings.[31]

Working or companion animals could act as go-betweens in groups of men, easing social interactions. They could also be a focus for play and practical joking, rather like family pets. For example, Andreas Reischek once got Caesar to quietly retrieve all the pigeons that a companion shot during a hunting expedition on Mt Pirongia in the Waikato region. When this man complained at the end of the day that he had missed nearly every bird, he was stunned to be shown all the pigeons that Caesar had secretly recovered.[32] Animals also allowed men to express tender feelings they might not otherwise admit to. Laurence Kennaway recalled the reaction of his companions when a faithful stockhorse drowned crossing a river: 'We looked at him and thought of the years of work we had had together, – of long day's journeys, and cold night-campings, and river crossings without number which the faithful old fellow had done with us, – and we lifted his cold forefoot in farewell, and left him there, and rode away, sorrowfully remembering him as a tried old friend who could stand by us no more.'[33]

The yarning associated with mateship often centred on animals. As Lady Barker noticed, shepherds took great pride in their dogs: 'A New Zealand shepherd will always consider it a point of honour to cap his neighbour's anecdote of his dog's sagacity, by a yet stronger proof of canine intelligence.'[34] Exaggerated though these stories may have been, they were always entertaining. As another writer commented, 'Sometimes a neighbouring shepherd will drop in for a chat, dogs being the great subject of conversation. Wonderful, and occasionally doubtful, are the yarns spun about favourite dogs.'[35]

Often, animals appear to have accompanied working men mainly to provide company. Many photographs of bushmen, railway labourers and other workers show them with a dog which seems to be just along for the ride. From this habit may have emerged the popular custom of adopting animal mascots. Later in the century a range of urban and rural men's groups, including firemen, brass bands and sports teams, had such mascots. These special animals, which represented the pride or prestige of the group, were usually dogs, though there were some exceptions: for instance, in 1884 the Christchurch Fire Brigade had a cat mascot named Marco Polo.[36] To underline its status, an animal mascot was sometimes given a uniform coat or an identifying collar.

~

Animals were integral to many of the games men played: contests, trials of strength and sports that often involved gambling. Horse and later dog races were extremely popular.[37] Informal sheep dog trials, which started as early as 1860, pitted shepherds and their dogs against each other in a test of skill.[38] Hare-coursing, in which greyhounds pursued live hares, was a favourite recreation of working men[39] – and a target of animal welfare campaigns until well into the twentieth century.

Even more gory and violent types of competition included organised animal fights and animal baiting. During the 1860s on the Otago gold fields, miners trained roosters to fight and bet on specially staged dog, rat and mice fights. Gamblers also went along to 'rat pits', where dogs were put in an escape-proof enclosure with rats and encouraged to kill them. The dog that killed the most rats within a set time won money for his backers. Illegal cockfights were held on the West Coast regularly from the 1860s to the 1880s, and occasionally as late as the 1930s. The birds had curved steel spurs attached to their claws that inflicted terrible injuries. Fights were usually to the death, unless the owner of the bird conceded defeat, but seriously injured birds often had to be destroyed anyway.[40] Working-class men were not the only participants in such activities: cockfights were held for the entertainment of all the male passengers and crew on the *Hydaspes* during its voyage from London to Lyttelton in 1869.[41]

One of the most popular male leisure pursuits in nineteenth-century New Zealand was pig hunting.[42] The Captain Cookers introduced in the eighteenth century had become wild and multiplied. Because they posed a threat to sheep flocks they had to be culled, but they also provided meat

This painting of the Enys brothers' abode at Castle Hill, around 1868, shows how familiar domestic pets could help make a hut a home. Charles Enys chats to a visitor while stroking a dog on his knee. Nearby, a cat wanders under a table, possibly looking for scraps of food.

Private collection, copy supplied by Alexander Turnbull Library. Reference: NON-ATL-P-0089. Watercolour by William Packe

to supplement an otherwise restricted diet. Numerous early accounts of colonial life describe the pig hunt, where men, usually armed only with knives (although some carried guns), would go out with a pack of dogs, which would pursue the pig and bail it up. Various breeds were used as pig dogs, including ordinary sheep dogs. Whalers had bred dogs for fighting, and the descendants of these animals, too, made useful pig dogs.[43] Usually a very powerful dog such as a bulldog was sent to hold on to the pig's ear once it had been run to ground. When the men arrived, one of them would finish off the pig with a knife – the ultimate test of manliness.[44]

In pig hunting, as in other animal sports, the dog became the extension of his owner's ego. Winning was a triumph; defeat was a disaster. The animal's feats or failings reflected on the man. George Chamier's novel, *Philosopher Dick*, explains the shame of one man, Sailor Jack, when his prize pig dog Caesar balked at the sight of a fierce boar:

> *Confusion and disgrace! At such an inconceivable breakdown; at conduct so unbecoming a bulldog; so irretrievably currish, Sailor Jack was seized with fury and despair. He spurned from him the unworthy minion which hitherto had been his boasted pride, and hurled upon the crestfallen brute all the thunder of an enraged bushman's vocabulary, emphasised with the choicest sea oaths most suitable for the occasion. Yet through all the gamut of vituperation, through the rolling accompaniment of awful blasphemy, there sounded a plaintive expression of reproach and disappointment, that seemed to say, if in less elegant language – 'Nevermore be officer of mine'. Caesar had ratted, and Jack felt humbled in what touched his heart most keenly –* his bulldog.[45]

According to the hunters, pig dogs enjoyed the chase just as much as the men.[46] But dogs were regularly killed or seriously wounded in pig hunts, ripped by the boar's tusks. W.H. Koebel, an English journalist who worked in rural New Zealand in the early twentieth century, deplored the poor judgement of pig hunters who sent lightweight dogs after pigs, only to see them torn apart.[47]

~

Animals may have acted like mates, but they were clearly not always treated as such. Men appear to have had an ambivalent relationship with their animal offsiders, seeing them alternately as co-workers, friends, playthings or slaves.

One apparent reason for this was the need for self-preservation. For example, a starving explorer would consider eating his dog, even if the animal was a loyal companion. Around 1883 Charlie Douglas went on a journey with Betsey Jane and three men, including Gerhard Mueller. They ran short of food, and Betsey Jane was unable to catch any birds. One of the men recalled:

Men and dogs pursue fleeing pigs through realistically dense New Zealand bush in this engraving of a pig hunt on the West Coast, published in the *Illustrated New Zealand Herald* in June 1868. From 1865, men flocked to the region's gold fields, and, when not prospecting, turned to hunting for both food and sport. 'The hardy settlers, or rather diggers of our West Coast,' claimed the paper, 'have joined this pastime, and there is every probability while so engaged many of them have discovered fresh auriferous ground.'

Alexander Turnbull Library. Reference: PUBL-0047-1868-04-01

One night, as we sat round the fire, Betsy [sic] was lying on one side of Mr. Mueller, and I was on the other. Mr M. pointed to her and said 'I'm afraid we will have to –' – and I knew what he meant. Of course Mr. Douglas couldn't kill her, so I said I'd do it, and I stretched across and put my hand under her. But she was skin and bone, poor Betsy, and to use her would not help much, and we didn't want to do it, so nothing more was said.[48]

Fortunately, the next day Betsey Jane helped to catch a kakapo, saving the party from starvation and herself from an untimely death.

Not so lucky was Rover, the dog of Thomas Brunner, who made some epic journeys of exploration in Nelson and the West Coast between 1846 and 1848. In late 1846 Brunner set off with two Maori guides, Kehu and Pikewati, and their wives, to trace the Buller River to the sea, traverse the West Coast and find a pass across the Southern Alps. Birds were scarce, and their food began to run out. Brunner was pressured to kill Rover, and eventually he gave in. Although he may have regretted having to do this, he did remark rather heartlessly in his diary, 'The flesh of a dog is very palatable, tasting something between mutton and pork.'[49] When Rover's fate became more widely known, Brunner was the target of some criticism, particularly from the man who claimed to have lent him the dog. He was also known thereafter to Maori as 'Kai Kuri' (dog eater).[50]

One possibly apocryphal story relates how an explorer got around the dilemma of whether or not to eat his dog. Some distance from his destination he found himself completely without food. Apparently 'having withstood the pangs of hunger as long as he could, he cut off the dog's tail, broiled it, ate it, *and gave the bone to the dog.* Thus sustained, the pair marched gaily into the camp they were making for, on the day following their ingenious meal.'[51] But there was not always such a happy ending.

~

The imperative of economic survival was another likely reason for the harsh treatment often meted out to animals, especially in farming, where they were usually seen simply as a resource to be used. Lady Barker observed that farmers and farm workers universally regarded sheep as stupid:

I never heard of them spoken of with affection, nor do I consider that they were the objects of any special humanity even on their owners' part. This must surely rise from their enormous numbers. 'How can you be fond of thousands of anything?' said a shepherd once to me, in answer to some sentimental inquiry of mine respecting his feelings towards his flock.[52]

Predictably, the hand-rearing of appealing baby farm animals such as lambs and calves was usually delegated to women and children.

Not just stock, but working animals too – mainly horses and dogs – were regarded as money-making machines, especially as they became more numerous and therefore more dispensable later in the century. They were often disciplined and driven relentlessly. Working dogs were frequently thrashed if they failed to carry out commands, and horses were whipped and struck to make them move faster or haul heavy loads. Sheep dogs sometimes had their eye teeth cut or fencing wire inserted in their noses to prevent them from biting sheep. They were usually not fed until the end of the day, because of a theory that they would work better if they were hungry.[53]

If a working animal did not perform adequately, its days were numbered. Sheep dogs that had reached the end of their working lives were generally shot. Before fences became common, some old dogs escaped this sentence, only to be chained to kennels along boundaries to deter sheep from straying.[54] This was a much worse fate. Because boundary dogs were no longer considered to be genuine working animals they were not fed very often, and the enforced isolation was a particularly refined form of torture for a social animal.

Traditional farming practices could be cruel. In his autobiography, *A Canterbury Tale*, F.O. Bennett explained his decision not to take over the family farm after World War I.

> As my responsibilities on the farm had broadened so had my conviction that farming was not for me. Something repelled me. I did not know then what it was but I know now. It was the unremitting involvement with farm animals, the wretched piteous dumb animals. I have seen a horse zigzagging up a hill with a fat man sitting on the shaft, lambs dying in a blizzard, thirsty horses denied a minute for drinking in mid-stream, kittens tied in a sugar bag with stones and tossed into the dam, a horse-collar strapping down a shoulder ulcer, dogs tied up for three days without food.[55]

~

The underlying reason for exploitation of animals was the ancient conviction that men should have mastery over them. This had a religious basis: in the often-quoted Genesis 9:2, for example, God told Noah: 'The fear and dread of you shall fall upon all wild animals on earth, on all birds of heaven, on everything that moves upon the ground and all fish in the sea; they are given into your hands.' This widespread belief in man's right to dominate animals had a more profound meaning in the colonial setting. Men who could control and subdue animals were looked up to by other men. Mastery of animals was one sign of competence in the male working world, a passport to approval and acceptance.

Some men who were experts at managing animals became legendary. Sir William Fraser, who later became Minister of Mines and a member of the

Legislative Council (New Zealand's upper house of parliament), emigrated to New Zealand from Scotland as a youth to work on an Otago sheep run. There 'he astonished the other hands by his remarkable power of driving and directing teams of horses, which, in those days of lack of roads, was an extremely useful qualification'.[56] The admiration for this outstanding ability may well have been a factor in his rise to political power.

Many farming jobs called for expert animal handling skills. Travelling from farm to farm, Laurence Kennaway expressed his awe at the 'pluck' of men who worked with wild cattle in stockyards, and this esteem for experienced stockmen was echoed by E.W. Elkington, who worked on a Hawke's Bay cattle station later in the century, and W.H. Koebel, who was briefly a farm cadet.[57] Good 'dogmen' – those proficient at handling working dogs – were also highly regarded, and men judged one other by the obedience and aptitude of their dogs.[58] The ability to control a horse was taken for granted, but the knack of breaking horses involved a higher level of mastery, and young Maori men who were adept at this were readily welcomed as station hands. Good shearers were also sought after. This arduous job involved a range of abilities, not the least of which was holding down a struggling sheep. Shearing gangs had their own hierarchy based on skill, topped by the 'ringer', the fastest shearer in the shed, with 'gun' or fast shearers close behind, and others ranked below them according to speed and expertise.[59]

Being a good judge of animals was another measure of a man in rural society. One agricultural expert, addressing the Taieri Agricultural Society in July 1881, asserted that it was an essential prerequisite for becoming a successful farmer in New Zealand.[60] It was certainly respected. Edward Wakefield listed the different classes of rural working men and praised their skill at evaluating animals. Permanent hands on a sheep station often did 'a little trade on their own account in horseflesh, of which they are often excellent judges'. Shepherds were 'first-rate men, nearly all Scotchmen, and usually Highlanders, with an extraordinary knowledge of sheep and of country and weather'.[61]

Training dogs and horses to perform tasks on command was the key to getting many jobs done efficiently. Working men debated theories about the best methods for training animals, and experts in the field acquired status. Some counselled against the use of force. An old Scottish shepherd who told Sarah Courage that 'a collie once beaten is a collie spoilt for ever' claimed that threats and a stick thrown between the dog and the sheep to keep him wide of them were enough to ensure compliance.[62] Others advised owners to use tone of voice and only the threat of physical punishment. A 1907 article counselled dog owners to keep a whip, but not to use it: 'The continual thrashing of a

Nelson artist Benjamin Aylett Branfill painted this idealised scene, *After a Long Day on the Run*, in 1884. Waiting for the kettle to boil for his tea, the runholder reads a book by the fire, with his sheep dog and a cat also enjoying the warmth. By this time the reality was probably rather different, with many working dogs banned from coming into the house.

Alexander Turnbull Library, Reference: G-007. Oil painting by Benjamin Aylett Branfill

dog breaks his spirit, sours his nature, and cows him.'[63] In the influential 1886 manual *Our Horses: or the best muscles controlled by the best brains*, Alfred Saunders advocated kindness and good management rather than traditional cruel methods in training horses.[64]

Often, however, training and disciplining of animals involved inflicting pain or withholding food. Andreas Reischek, who otherwise advocated kindness in training dogs and horses, cured his dog Caesar of his fear of water by starving him and then throwing bread in the river for him to fetch. He also taught him to retrieve birds without damaging them by throwing him a ball stuck with sharp pins.[65] A.M. Paterson, author of *The Colonial Horse Doctor*, published in

These tough-looking blokes – Maori and Pakeha – were photographed at a Taumarunui sawmill in the early twentieth century. Two of them have brought their dogs to work, a practice harking back to the nineteenth century when groups of men laboured alongside animals. In this setting, however, such dogs would have been companions rather than fellow workers. *Alexander Turnbull Library, A.W. Bathgate Collection. Reference: PAColl-3001-01-14. Photograph by Alexander William Bathgate*

1906, advised giving horses less food on wet days and Sundays to ensure that they did not become overfed and therefore work-shy.[66] An animal that could not or would not learn was a liability and an embarrassment, and could be summarily shot – if not by its owner, then by another man appointed to do so. When a retriever owned by Reischek persisted in killing birds rather than bringing them back live, he asked a friend to take her away and shoot her.[67]

Killing an animal was the ultimate expression of mastery over it. Most nineteenth-century rural workers had to kill and butcher an animal at some stage, and anyone venturing into the bush had to be prepared to hunt birds and pigs to survive.[68] This fostered a pragmatic attitude. Describing the bloody and protracted business of slaughtering cattle, E.W. Elkington commented, 'I did not care for this part of the job, but one grows callous and takes things as they come when one has been a little while in the colony.' His account also reveals a grudging respect for the slaughterman, who was both repellent and curiously fascinating: 'That man could use the most peculiar oaths I ever heard, and he had the most evil-looking face I ever saw, but he was an excellent man at his trade, and there was nothing he relished more than "pithing" [killing by knifing the head behind the horns] a fighting beast.'[69]

In colonial New Zealand, animals provided labour, loyalty and companionship and most men would have acknowledged their reliance on them. A dog, horse, cat or other creature could be a man's best friend. But men also believed they were entitled to exercise ruthless control over all animals. This contradiction lay beneath the popular image of the tough frontier man. Perhaps it still does?

A poultry fancier poses his prize bird, a Silver Laced Wyandotte, for a photograph. It appears to have been taken at a poultry show, probably in the late nineteenth or early twentieth century. *Alexander Turnbull Library, Adam MacLay Collection. Reference: G-23434-1/1. Photograph by Adam Henry Pearson Maclay*

Chapter 4
The fancy

'Fifty years a fancier! How many people can apply that to themselves? What a time to look back on. The changes – the advancement – the regrets – the triumphs – what a lot of circumstances go to make up a half-century.'[1] So wrote the editor of the *New Zealand Poultry Journal* in 1908 in praise of veteran bird fancier Alfred Walker, president of the Christchurch Poultry Club. Walker was born in Tasmania in the 1840s, and started breeding poultry, pigeons and game birds as a schoolboy, exhibiting his birds at shows around Australia. After moving to New Zealand in 1875 he joined the Christchurch club and later judged at poultry shows throughout the country.

'The fancy' was a term used to describe the breeding and showing of small animals, ranging from poultry and pigeons through to cats and dogs, guinea pigs, rabbits and other pets. 'Fanciers' were the people who took up this challenging, highly competitive and at times combative hobby. There were associations of fanciers not just in Britain and its colonies, but also in Europe and the United States. When this tribute to Walker appeared, the fancy, and in particular the hobby of poultry, pigeon and cage bird breeding, had reached a peak of popularity in New Zealand.

Were animals bred for competition really pets? Accounts of shows sometimes used that word to describe them, but usually in the sense of something viewed with special admiration rather than fondness. Many serious breeders of animals were motivated by money – pedigree pet animals began to command high prices during the nineteenth century.[2] Often these fanciers advertised their animals

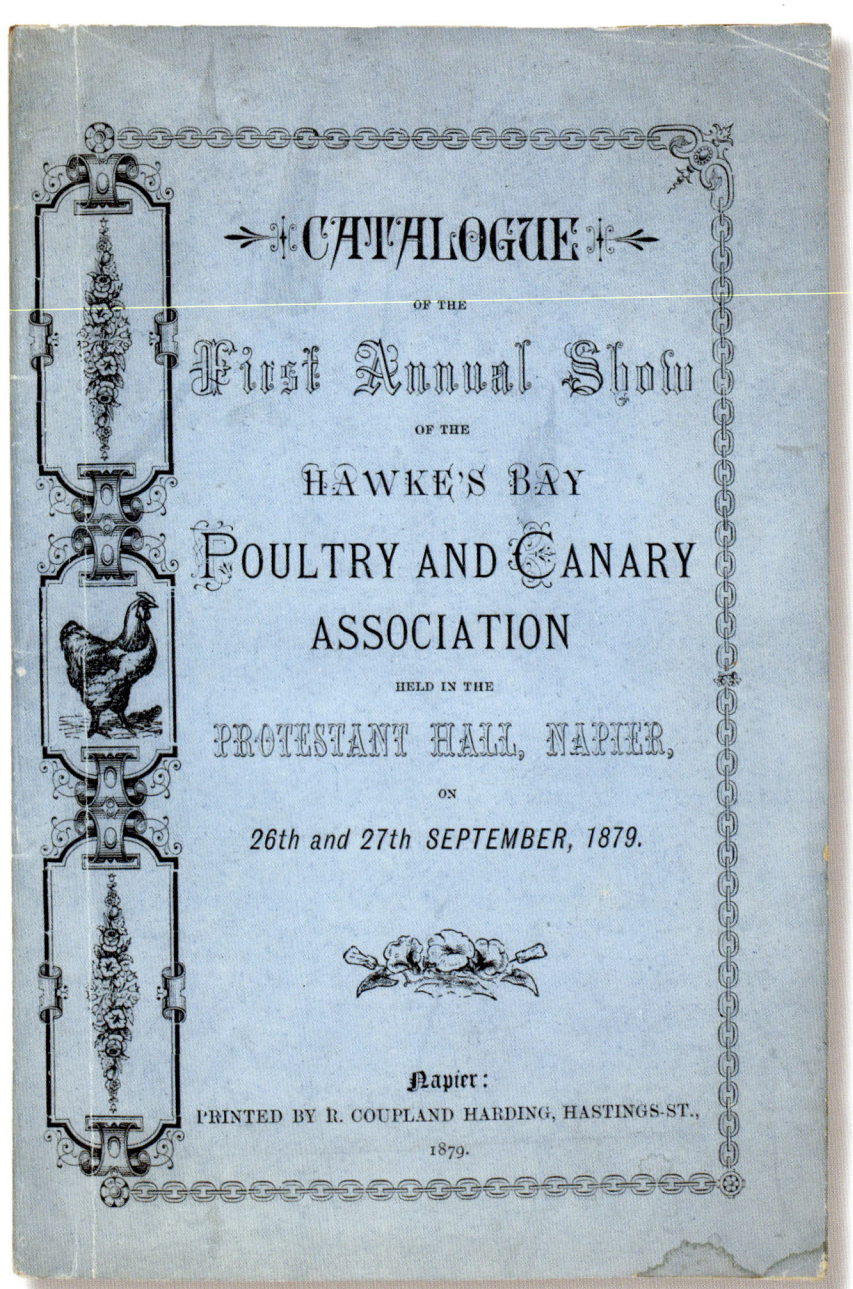

The Hawke's Bay Poultry and Canary Association was one of the earliest societies for bird fanciers established in New Zealand. This is the elaborate cover of the catalogue for its first annual show in Napier in 1879.

Alexander Turnbull Library. Reference: B-K 929-COVER

for sale, and some went into business: by 1900 there were a number of shops for poultry and cage birds in New Zealand towns and cities.[3] Although these enthusiasts looked after their animals carefully, they were quite objective about them.

But for others who bred and exhibited animals, fancying was an extension of pet owning. The rewards of winning were great, but so too were the pleasures of grooming and training an animal, and competing and socialising with like-minded people. For these fanciers, the secret conviction that their animal was indeed the best, regardless of judges' opinions, sustained them through setbacks.[4] They often refused to part with their prized bird, cat or dog, viewing it not just with pride but with affection.

~

Throughout the western world, the fancy had wide appeal for a number of reasons. For a start, it focused on the concept of improvement, which was high on the scale of Victorian values. The goal of fanciers was to improve the quality of a species through selective breeding. By identifying desirable characteristics, known as 'standards of perfection', and then mating those animals that had them, fanciers could modify breeds over generations. Most nineteenth-century animal breeders relied on chance and guesswork, but the hobby became popular during a period when significant scientific discoveries were being made, notably by geneticist Gregor Johann Mendel and evolutionary biologist Charles Darwin. In fact Darwin drew on the findings of poultry breeders to help formulate his theories on the variation of animal species under domestication.[5] As the century wore on it became increasingly possible, therefore, to employ scientific principles – another great Victorian interest. The fancy also had an attractive moral dimension: as an educational and productive use of leisure time it was a means of self-improvement. In New Zealand the popularity of the fancy owed much to Anglophilia. Settlers of British stock looked to the mother country for ideas, fashions and standards, and New Zealand fanciers' societies were inspired by 'home' examples.

The underlying allure of the fancy was its class associations. Different animals were categorised into groups, and then ranks. The all-important pedigree, written in the stud book, recorded these decisions. The fancy was also traditionally associated with the social elite, and the British royal family were enthusiastic followers of it during and after the reign of Queen Victoria. Increasingly the middle class and even the 'lower orders' took it up. For many people there was almost certainly an element of social aspiration in becoming a fancier.

But at the same time the fancy subtly undermined rigid notions of social class. Any fancier, high-born or humble, could, in theory, breed a champion, and an elite animal shed glory on its owner.[6] For people striving to better their lot in life – people like New Zealand's nineteenth-century settlers – the fancy confirmed that, with energy and hard work, and a bit of luck, advancement was possible.

In Britain the fancy began to flourish when two separate interests converged around the middle of the nineteenth century. One was the enthusiasm for breeding prize livestock; the other was the popularity of pet owning. By the 1850s a 'cult of pets' was well established, particularly among the middle classes. From this grew an interest in new breeds, and exotic animals were imported and crossed with indigenous breeds. Unlike cattle and horse rearing, breeding of small animals was a hobby in which many people could take part. The fancy was open to town dwellers as well as country folk, those of modest means as well as the rich and powerful.[7]

In colonial New Zealand the fancy developed hand in hand with the craze for acclimatisation. Of all the acclimatisation societies established throughout the world from 1863, more than half were in New Zealand. Although they concentrated on introducing species to naturalise them in the wild, they also imported birds and animals destined for domestication or captivity, including cage birds and poultry. One goal of many acclimatisation societies echoed the ideals of the fancy: 'The perfection, propagation and hybridization of races newly introduced or already domesticated.'[8]

Interest in agriculture played a part too. From the earliest days of settlement, farming was seen as the industry on which the country's future wealth would be based. To support its development, from the 1860s groups of community-minded landowners around the country formed Agricultural and Pastoral Associations, which began to hold annual shows.[9] As well as parades and competitions for different classes of farm stock, there were horse and pony riding and 'leaping' events, displays of produce and domestic crafts, musical entertainments and sideshows. Both rural and urban families attended these shows, which were typically held at grounds in or near the town at the centre of a farming area. An A&P show was often a district's most important annual event, offering something for everyone.

The breeding of larger farm animals and horses of course concerned farmers, but smaller animals also found a place at A&P shows and probably interested a wider group of visitors. There were usually poultry and working dog sections at shows in the early days, and by the 1880s there were classes for 'fancy' birds and dogs.[10] A&P shows therefore supported the fancy from the outset, and continued to do so. After separate fanciers' clubs became established, they would sometimes collaborate with their local A&P associations to stage joint shows. In the early 1900s, for instance, the Ashburton A&P Association and the Ashburton Poultry, Pigeon and Canary Society held an annual combined winter show.[11]

~

Of all branches of the fancy, poultry and cage bird breeding seems to have been the first established and the most widespread in New Zealand. The centuries-old hobby soared in popularity in Britain after cock pits were banned in 1835 and cockfighting was outlawed in 1849. It also caught on in the United States and other parts of the new world.[12] In New Zealand it had a few followers from the 1860s, but the 1880s witnessed a boom. Bird fanciers' clubs were formed in the main centres of Dunedin, Christchurch, Wellington and Auckland, and also in smaller towns and rural areas like Oamaru and Wairarapa. There were even suburban clubs in larger places, for example the Sydenham Poultry, Pigeon and Canary Society in Christchurch and the Newton Pigeon, Canary and Cage Bird Association in Auckland. The annual shows of these clubs allowed members to enter their best birds in various categories, with cash prizes for the winners. More clubs emerged in the 1890s and the early years of the twentieth century. They began to diversify, with new clubs specialising in particular breeds. When a national organisation set up in 1893 disintegrated, South Island and later North Island associations, to which clubs affiliated, were formed.[13]

The growth of the Christchurch Poultry Club, the longest-established association of poultry fanciers, illustrates the surge of support for the hobby. At the club's 1868 show, held in the town hall, there were 163 entries, and categories included Dorkings, Game, Spanish, Cochins, Brahmas, Hamburghs, Polands, French Fowls, Malay, Barndoor and Bantams. In addition, there were classes for turkeys, geese, ducks, pigeons, canaries and, curiously, rabbits.[14] Over time, classes for other birds were added. By 1876 the number of entries had grown to 267; by 1883 there were 481, and by 1890, 843. In 1906 there were a record 1655 entries.[15]

The huge following for poultry fancying in particular seems to have had practical origins. In the early days of Pakeha settlement it was customary – in fact necessary – for households to produce at least some of their own food by growing vegetables and keeping hens, pigs and cows, and this continued on a smaller scale in later decades. Even in cities, sections were often large enough to accommodate a few chickens, soon universally known as 'chooks', and a vegetable garden. A young Englishwoman visiting Christchurch in the 1880s wrote, 'The greater number of people keep fowls, all lodging houses, boarding houses, and private families also.'[16] It was relatively cheap to buy hens and eggs, and they could be sold to make a little extra money. From poultry raising it was a small step to poultry breeding. Poultry clubs aimed to lift the standard of birds being kept. As one person put it, 'Shows are of great value in rousing public interest in the breeding of good fowls, and in leading all poultry owners to invest in the best kinds ... It is not as if these birds were good for show only; the best birds are the best layers and the best for eating.'[17] This pragmatic approach eventually led to the emergence of a poultry farming industry in the early twentieth century.[18]

The local poultry and cage bird club's show was a big day out in nineteenth-century New Zealand. Aside from providing the opportunity to compete and win prizes, shows allowed fanciers to sell their birds – in fact it was usually a condition of entry that a price be displayed on the cage or pen.[19] The exchange of birds allowed fanciers to improve their breeding stock, and gave interested members of the public a chance to take up the hobby. A proportion of the price was payable to the show organisers, so sales and entrance fees were a major source of revenue for clubs. But fanciers could choose not to sell: the Christchurch show regulations for 1868 stated 'Persons not willing to sell their birds can avoid doing so by affixing a fancy price',[20] and later catalogues specified that some entries were for exhibition only.

A distinctive feature of New Zealand shows was the inclusion of classes for native birds kept as caged birds. For example, at the third Wellington Poultry Show in 1886, prizes were awarded for the best specimens of 'New Zealand Parroquet' (kakariki). Not in the competition, but exhibited at the Nelson Poultry, Bird and Dog Show of 1889 were two kiwi owned by Mr P. Adams. At the 1890 Wanganui Poultry and Dog Show there was a cage bird class for 'New Zealand Native Birds', with kakariki winning both first and second prize. J. Walker's tui took first prize in a class for both native and foreign cage birds at the Newton Pigeon and Canary Club Show in 1892.[21]

Poultry and cage bird fancying seems to have been a Pakeha pastime. That aside, it was an accessible hobby, open to people of both sexes, all ages and from every walk of life. Whereas in Britain pigeon fanciers in particular tended to be working-class men, in New Zealand the fancy crossed social boundaries. Men of all occupational groups, from railway workers to company managers, were fanciers.[22] Women, too, were encouraged to participate as a way of 'not only learning the nature of the fowls and what is needed to bring the best results, but learning to love them and feel the satisfaction of being able to minister to the wants of God's creatures'. Rearing ducks and chickens especially was praised as 'homely and womanly' and the 'ideal home employment'.[23] Women were among the exhibitors at the first Christchurch Poultry Show in 1868, and although some poultry fanciers' societies evolved into all-male clubs, women continued to enter competitions.

Adults believed that poultry rearing was a wholesome and morally improving occupation for children. 'It is hard to imagine a boy who loves little chicks becoming a criminal later in life. And where we see girls so kind to their feathered pets that the chicks fly all over them at feeding time we are not afraid that they will leave their own offspring to the care of ignorant nursemaids while they daudle [sic] their time away in fashionable society.'[24] Pigeon raising was considered a particularly suitable hobby for boys, and from 1913 the *New Zealand Poultry Journal* encouraged them with a special 'junior' column.

Pigeon fancying gave rise to the sport of pigeon racing. In 1877 the Christchurch Poultry Club held the first major pigeon race in New Zealand, from Christchurch to Timaru, offering a silver medal to the year's winner and a challenge cup to anyone winning three times. Although this event seems to have lapsed, soon more pigeon flying clubs were set up, their spread influenced by the popularity of pigeon races in England and Europe in the 1880s.[25] The triumphs and tragedies of these events were reported in detail in the press. When the Dunedin Homing Pigeon Club flew a race from Cape Campbell to Dunedin in November 1906, a distance of 345½ miles (556 km), only 17 out of 81 birds reached home 'because of south-west wind, rain and fog'.[26] In these dire conditions the winning bird, called Après Moi, made it back to Dunedin in 10 hours and 36 minutes.

The ability of homing pigeons to carry messages and mail swiftly was of great interest in a country where transport and communication networks were still rudimentary. Pigeons were soon put to work in New Zealand, taking mail to and from areas inaccessible to the telegraph. Some newspapers, such as the *Auckland Star* and the Christchurch *Press*, maintained flocks of well-trained homing pigeons that were used to get sports results quickly from events held in distant places, and carrier pigeons also brought bulletins from mountainous areas and offshore islands.

In 1903 William Phipps set up a pigeon post service between the Mountain House on Mt Taranaki (Egmont) and New Plymouth. By the following year, for the price of 1s, visitors to the mountain could send messages to his home at New Plymouth and receive a reply. Phipps was a butcher and pigeon fancier: he won show prizes for his pigeons and was a keen member of the New Plymouth Homing Pigeon Club. Here, he stands alongside the pigeon aviary at the Mountain House; the woman with him is possibly his wife.

Alexander Turnbull Library. Reference: PAColl-6208-48

However, bad weather could affect services. In 1897 the *Evening Post* reported: 'In the Awarua election the return from Stewart Island of the polling there was brought across by pigeon post. Owing to a heavy fog hanging over the land, the bird took four hours to do an hour's journey.'[27] Pigeon postal services flourished for a few years, but the spread of telegraph, telephones, and later aviation, led to their demise.

~

New Zealand poultry and cage bird associations and shows provided a springboard for fanciers of other animals, particularly cats and dogs. Some of the bird clubs incorporated these fancies: for a time in the 1880s the Christchurch

Poultry Club was known, incongruously, as the Christchurch Poultry, Pigeon, Canary and Cat Society. Around the same time there were clubs in Invercargill, Dunedin, Auckland, Wanganui and Nelson for both poultry and dogs. Other poultry and cage bird club shows included classes for cats, dogs or children's pets in a calculated, and successful, move to boost attendance. On the second day of the Napier Poultry and Canary Association's 1885 show, for example, 'a novelty was introduced in the shape of a Cat Show, and the felines exhibited were very much criticised and admired'.[28] Encouraged by this, the following year the association included a class for guinea pigs, and both adults and children showed these animals.

By 1888 the Christchurch Poultry Club was opening its show to all kinds of pets. It gave notice that 'An alteration in the usual programme is the addition of classes for pets, which it is hoped will make the Show more popular with the general public', and made an appeal 'to the proud possessors of such favourites to come forward and make this department of the Show as interesting and attractive as possible by numerous entries. The classes for pets include prizes for cockatoos, parrots, magpies, small birds, cats, dogs, rabbits, guinea pigs, and even monkeys.'[29] Occasionally more exotic animals were shown: for instance at the Nelson Poultry, Bird and Dog Show in 1889, Mr F. Trask's 'Madagascar cat' – actually a lemur with a black banded tail – attracted much attention.[30] Children's pet shows became a popular feature of many poultry shows, and in 1896 a Hokitika club introduced a competition for pet photography.[31]

~

A young woman sits for a studio portrait with her tabby cat. By the early 1900s, when this photograph was taken, the cat fancy was well established in New Zealand and more exotic types were being imported.

Alexander Turnbull Library, H.N. Whitehead Collection. Reference: G-24801-1/2. Photograph by Henry Norford Whitehead

The cat fancy most obviously grew out of pet owning, though the purpose of breeding and showing cats was not initially self-evident. Whereas the range of possible dog breeds was vast, cats differed from each other mainly in the colour and texture of their coats. They were not easily trained, were not a source of food, had no role in popular sports and for centuries had been associated with witchcraft and dark superstitions. Their negative image, along with their allegedly secretive ways and love of independence, meant they were often thought of by men, and not fondly, as 'the natural allies of womankind'.[32] By the nineteenth century, however, cats were becoming more favoured as pets. Queen Victoria contributed to their growing popularity, both by keeping them and by advocating kindness to them.[33] Seeking to share their appreciation of the feline's sinuous beauty and gracefulness, some cat lovers became cat fanciers, defining breeds and standards. The first cat show took place at the Crystal Palace in London in 1871.[34]

The cat fancy in New Zealand developed from shows run in conjunction with poultry exhibitions from the 1880s. The initially limited range of classes reveals the difficulties early breeders had in formally differentiating cats. The main basis of comparison was colour – tortoiseshell, black, white, silver or blue, and 'sandy'. The most commonly defined type was the tabby, but some shows had classes for Manx, Angora, Persian and 'French' cats.[35] A crowd-pleasing feature of these shows was the contest for 'heaviest cat'. At the Christchurch Poultry, Pigeon, Canary and Cat Society Show in 1886, Miss Hibbard's champion black tom tipped the scales at 15 lb 12 oz (7.1 kg), while at the Nelson Poultry Show in 1889, Mr Bird's black and white tom was placed first, weighing in at a relatively light 12 lb 12 oz (5.8 kg). A 16 lb 13 oz (7.6 kg) cat was awarded the prize at the Christchurch show in 1888, and at the 1891 show of the Napier Poultry and Canary Association, the winning cat was a hefty 19 lb (8.6 kg).[36]

Some observers of these events were quick to suggest that only women were interested in cats; for instance, a reporter at Christchurch in 1886 commented: 'The Cat Show opened on the afternoon of the second day and attracted many lady visitors.'[37] Prize lists, however, reveal that both men and women entered their cats in the competitions. Some cat owners copied the poultry fanciers by advertising sale prices on the cages of the cats they exhibited, and there was sometimes a 'selling class for kittens'.[38] But the exorbitant prices asked for many cats make it clear that their proud owners were not interested in selling. At the 1884 Christchurch show Mrs F. Adams put a price of £1000 on Tim, a 13-year-old brown tabby – and evidently much loved.[39]

Persians emerged as the elite cat breed after Queen Victoria acquired one.[40] In 1904 the *Otago Witness* ran an article about a Mr Kerr of Mornington in Dunedin, who was breeding silver Persians using imported English champions. The reporter marvelled at their cattery, obviously a great novelty at that time:

> *Cats! Such cats, and such palatial cat homes! Surely cats – even such furry beauties as Mr Kerr's – were never housed in such glory and comfort in New Zealand before. Fancy! five handsomely-built two roomed cottages, each and all designed to ensure luxurious care and health. The rooms are lofty and commodious, well raised from the ground, properly ventilated, opened to the sun, and guarded from wind and wet.*[41]

An auction of pedigree cats in Auckland in 1909 made the news because of the high prices obtained for Persians.[42] Although consignments of Siamese and other 'Oriental' cats arrived in the first decade of the twentieth century, long-haired cats dominated the world of pedigree cats in New Zealand until World War II, and remained popular thereafter.[43]

Cat shows were an additional event at poultry shows through the 1890s, but after the turn of the century some cat fanciers aspired to autonomy. In 1909 a group of them, including fanciers from Auckland and Dunedin, formed the Christchurch Cat Club, which aimed to improve the breeds of cats, organise cat classes for shows and raise funds for prizes.[44] Within a few years independent cat clubs had been established in Auckland and Wellington, but until World War II several cat groups maintained their links with poultry and dog clubs.[45]

~

Dog breeding became established more easily, and was unquestionably the most prestigious branch of the fancy. New Zealanders readily appreciated the dog for both its companionship and its usefulness, and saw value in developing and improving breeds. The New Zealand Kennel Club began in Christchurch in 1886, little more than a decade after the establishment of the English Kennel Club in 1873.[46] Even so, dog shows had been held in connection with A&P shows for years before the New Zealand Kennel Club came into existence, and a number of poultry clubs incorporated the dog fancy.

In New Zealand, as in England, owning pedigree dogs had status because of its association with royalty. Queen Victoria doted on all animals, but especially dogs. Her childhood pet had been a King Charles spaniel; her later favourites were Skye terriers, dachshunds and collies, but she also loved fox terriers and Pomeranians. In the 1840s she had around 30 dogs, and by the end of her reign in 1901 there were more than 80 in the royal kennels. That her example was influential can be gauged by the vogue for keeping spaniels as pets – by 1841 there were allegedly 5000 of the breed in London alone.[47]

Members of the royal family were dog breeders and exhibitors as well as dog lovers. The first patron of the English Kennel Club was Edward, Prince of Wales. He and the Princess of Wales had entered their dogs in shows from 1864.[48] The Kennel Club's links with royalty were maintained in the colonies. When the New Zealand Kennel Club was established, the Queen's representative, Governor Sir William Jervois, was the first patron. He was the first of a succession of New Zealand governors and governors-general who held this office.[49]

One of the main concerns of the English Kennel Club was to discourage the breeding of mongrels, and to keep a register of pedigree dogs.[50] The New Zealand Kennel Club followed suit, and also set the rules for shows. Because of the wide range of clubs and associations that incorporated the dog fancy, after a few years the Kennel Club gave up organising shows on its own account and instead offered affiliation to regional clubs. By 1893 there were five affiliated societies: the Dunedin Fanciers' Club, the Christchurch Dog Society, the Nelson Poultry and Dog Society, the Wellington Kennel Club and the Auckland Kennel Club. The system for holding shows and awarding prizes was complex, and the finer details changed many times over the years. Dogs participating in shows had to be registered with the Kennel Club, which decided on standards against which the various breeds would be judged.[51] Any shows held by affiliated clubs had to conform to Kennel Club rules.

In 1896 the headquarters of the Kennel Club shifted to Wellington, and in 1901 it applied for and was granted affiliation with the Kennel Club of England. From this time its influence increased. By 1907 the list of affiliated clubs had grown to 16 – they were mainly A&P associations and all-breeds clubs. Specialist clubs, for instance toy dog clubs for breeds such as poodles, were initially affiliated to the Kennel Club but later had the status of associated clubs, allowed to hold field trials and parades but not championship shows.[52] The first championship shows were held by regional clubs from the late 1880s.

In order to become a champion, a dog had to collect a certain number of challenge certificates (later points) in different competitions. Fanciers therefore had to transport their dogs to shows around the country. This was no easy undertaking. Train and steamer travel could be particularly gruelling for dogs. They were barred from passenger carriages, and so had to travel in the guard's van, either in a special crate provided by the owner and paid for at a higher rate, or in the infamous 'dog box'. This small enclosed kennel might contain several dogs, which often fought during the journey. One fancier from Marton took his bulldog to and from the Auckland show in 1917. According to an SPCA official, on being taken out of the box back in Marton, the dog 'was found to be in a

The proud owner of this greyhound can be glimpsed at the edge of the frame. This is one of a series of photographs of pedigree dogs probably taken at a dog show in the Nelson district in the early twentieth century.

Alexander Turnbull Library, F.N. Jones Collection. Reference: G-26067-1/2. Photograph by Frederick Nelson Jones

An appropriately decorated certificate was produced for a dog show held in Christchurch in 1885, the year before the New Zealand Kennel Club was established.

Alexander Turnbull Library. Reference: Eph-B-DOG-1885-01

very bad way, bleeding and showing signs of having received a severe mauling from another large dog, which had been put in the same box, and had evidently fought till both were exhausted'.[53]

Dog shows – a highlight on the calendar for fanciers – were not always popular with the general public. One Wellington resident, using the nom de plume 'Sing me to sleep', wrote to the editor of the *Evening Post* in 1911, complaining about the howling and barking emanating from a dog show held in the skating rink in Vivian Street. 'May I ask,' he concluded, 'that the promoters [either] supply their canine pets … with muzzles, or the whole suffering neighbourhood with sleeping draughts.'[54]

Not surprisingly, working and sporting dogs were popular breeds for nineteenth-century New Zealand dog fanciers. In the 1880s the most numerous entries in dog shows were for rough-coated collies, fox terriers and other types of terriers.[55] Dog fanciers imported these and other dogs from Australia and further afield. An idea of the range of breeds that had been introduced around this time is given in a report of an 1888 dog show in Auckland. Prizes were won by mastiffs, Newfoundlands, Saint Bernards, greyhounds, pointers, English setters, Irish setters, Gordon setters, retrievers, Sussex spaniels, cocker spaniels, collies, cattle dogs, bull terriers, fox terriers, Scotch terriers, Skye terriers, black and tan terriers, bulldogs and toy terriers.[56]

This cartoon, 'Overheard at the Dog Show', published in the Wellington *Free Lance* in 1906, takes a light-hearted view of an exchange between a proud dog owner and her gentleman admirer at a fanciers' show.

Free Lance, 22 September 1906, p. 13

Quarantine, imposed to prevent the introduction of animal diseases, slowed but did not stop the arrival of new breeds. By the 1890s dog fanciers were urging the government to make quarantine stations more central so owners could visit their pets, and to allow private quarantine.[57] Breeds fashionable in England and Europe were imported: a January 1907 report told of the steamer *Kaipara* arriving in Lyttelton with a pair of black schipperke terriers, two Pomeranian poodles and a King Charles spaniel, varieties 'in great demand in England and on the Continent as pets for the ladies, the Pomeranians being in very high favour at present'.[58] Around the same time a Wellington fancier imported a Russian wolfhound or borzoi, then a favourite breed of Queen Alexandra.

~

Considerable controversy surrounded the introduction of one breed. The Alsatian, often known as the Alsatian wolf-hound (and later as the German Shepherd), first arrived in New Zealand in the 1920s, when a few dogs were imported from Australia and England.[59] In these two countries the Alsatian had gained a reputation for mauling sheep and attacking people. Former High Commissioner to London, Sir Thomas Mackenzie, drew attention to this in 1929 after returning from a trip to England. He warned that the importation of Alsatians into New Zealand represented a danger both to stock and citizens

96 *Creature Comforts*

and announced his intention to introduce into the Legislative Council a bill, modelled on recent Australian legislation, to prevent the importing and breeding of Alsatians.[60]

Some owners and breeders of Alsatians immediately sprang to the dog's defence, but many sided with Mackenzie, including farmers' associations and, later, municipal authorities. Even some dog fanciers were opposed to Alsatians.[61] Articles in the press were mostly negative, with headlines such as 'The Alsatian dog: dangerous and savage animal'. Debate raged during the 1930s, with the Auckland-based New Zealand Alsatian Club and a short-lived National Council for Alsatian Shepherd Dog Control mounting a public relations campaign for the breed.[62]

Mackenzie introduced a notice of motion in the Legislative Council in 1929, but he died the following year.[63] The cause was then taken up by C.J. Carrington, who introduced a private member's bill which passed in the Legislative Council in 1934, but lapsed in the House of Representatives. The same fate befell bills that he introduced in 1935, 1936, 1937, 1938 and 1939. Finally, his term of office was not renewed and there were no further attempts to get the bill through.[64]

The Kennel Club claimed credit for the failure of these attempts to ban the Alsatian breed. Some of its executive members had made representations to the Legislative Council and had managed to limit the severity of some of the provisions in the proposed legislation.[65] There is no doubt that the Kennel Club had influence in high places, but there were other, more straightforward reasons for the bills' lack of success. One was that the powers of the Legislative Council were waning; it was to be abolished within a few decades. By the twentieth century it was no longer expected to introduce legislation, and if it did, such bills were unlikely to pass in the House of Representatives. Also, the departments of Agriculture and Internal Affairs had concluded that preventing the import of Alsatians was pointless, since the dogs were already in New Zealand and had produced litters. Public servants believed that other restrictive measures, such as sterilising the dogs and making it compulsory to muzzle them in public, were impractical.[66] And the Alsatian had become popular both as a guard dog and a family pet.

The near-banning of the Alsatian breed is a chapter in New Zealand's history that had a later parallel. A similar public controversy occurred in the late twentieth century over American pit bull terriers, but the outcome was different the second time around.

~

While the Kennel Club took its lead from standards and rules set in England, another group of dog enthusiasts established a movement that became indelibly associated with the New Zealand way of life. Farmers, particularly sheep farmers, were reliant on dogs, and bred them not for looks but for their working abilities.

Because flocks were much larger and grazing areas more extensive than in Britain, New Zealand shepherds had to learn to control their dogs from a distance, using verbal and whistle commands, and sheep dogs soon had to do more than just gathering sheep and stopping them from straying.[67] Gradually, through both breeding and training, two distinct types of New Zealand sheep dog evolved. One, the heading dog, worked silently around a flock of sheep, intimidating them into moving in a certain direction by its almost hypnotic gaze. Often described as 'strong-eyed', the heading dog could eyeball and stalk individual sheep or groups of sheep to hold them or separate them from the flock. The other type of sheep dog, bred specially for New Zealand conditions, was the huntaway. Loud and boisterous, it would bark steadily, 'hunting' and forcing the sheep in the desired direction. It could also be used for controlling sheep in yards and woolsheds.[68]

The respect and even affection farmers had for a good sheep dog is suggested in this photograph of E.A.J. Elliot of Waipukurau and Trump, taken in 1907.
Alexander Turnbull Library, Watt Collection. Reference: F-80512-1/2

Heading dogs owed much of their ancestry to the Border collies that arrived in the early days of settlement. The New Zealand dog, however, evolved into a much leaner, longer and more upright animal. Instead of being black and white, it was often tri-coloured, with tan markings, and had a smoother coat. This physical difference was the result of matings, sometimes deliberate and sometimes accidental, with other breeds. But the heading dog's ability to 'eye' sheep was the result of highly selective breeding. One influential breeder, James Lilico, who arrived in Southland in 1893, imported and bred from Border collies that showed particular aptitude, and 'Lilico dogs' became much sought after.[69]

The huntaway, on the other hand, was bred in New Zealand to shift flocks over long distances and difficult terrain. Farmers identified noise as the desirable characteristic in these dogs – they had to be able to bark continuously and hurry the sheep along without frightening them. A really clever huntaway could be trained to head as well as hunt. The genes of Border collies and bearded collies were vital in the development of the huntaway, but other contributing breeds included Gordon setters, bloodhounds, fox hounds, Great Danes and Labradors. Huntaways could vary quite widely in appearance, but the one characteristic they had in common was noise.[70]

Sheep dog trials developed in the British Isles as a way of testing and comparing the skills of working dogs in a sporting contest. In New Zealand,

trials began informally in the 1860s, and were soon eagerly anticipated events in country areas. The oldest New Zealand sheep dog trial club, Waitaki, was established in 1885, and many more, sometimes called 'collie clubs', were set up in farming districts of both North and South islands.[71] A&P shows often included sheep dog trials. Regional trial associations were formed, followed by a North Island Sheep Dog Trial Association in 1910 and a South Island Association in 1932.[72] Groups of clubs organised championship trials: the first New Zealand championship was held at Hawera in Taranaki in 1936. Finally in 1957, after resolving regional differences in rules and procedures, the North and South Island associations amalgamated to form the New Zealand Sheep Dog Trial Association.[73]

There were four main events at a sheep dog trial, two for heading dogs and two for huntaways. The heading events – the long head, and the short head and yard – both began with the dog being sent out to head sheep from a hill and pull them down toward the handler. In the shorter event, the dog had to steer the sheep through a set of hurdles and into a small pen. The huntaway events – the zig-zag hunt and the straight hunt – involved sending the dog to drive the sheep away, up a hill. On the zig-zag course the sheep had to be taken through a set of markers, forcing them to change direction twice. There was a time limit for all events, and judges subtracted points for any errors made by both dog and man.[74] Many factors contributed to the outcome: the sympathy between dog and master, the skill and obedience of the dog and its ability to anticipate and deal with unpredictable ovine behaviour, the stubbornness or otherwise of the sheep, and luck on the day.

Although sheep dogs were working animals, not pets, this did not mean that the relationship between them and their masters was not close. It had different facets, illustrated by two stories in the history of the Methven Collie Club, *Whistles in the Wind*. One tells of Monty Lewin, a cultured man with a military background, who joined the club in 1908. At a local sheep dog trial, Lewin was running a huntaway that was not performing to his expectations. He turned to the onlookers and suggested that if the ladies would like to put their fingers in their ears, he would show them how good the animal really was. He then addressed his dog in very earthy and colourful language. Apparently it understood perfectly, because it went on to win the event.

Another story in the same book reveals that though handlers might talk to their dogs harshly in public, in private they could be more demonstrative. The elderly man who recounted it had a clear boyhood memory of going to look at the dogs during a trial about the time of World War I. Coming around the corner of a tent, he witnessed one of the competitors petting his dog affectionately with the words: 'You're a one eyed old hua, but I love you.'[75]

Sheep dog trials were not just sporting contests: they had a very important practical purpose. Because winning dogs were much sought after for their stud services, trialling helped to improve sheep dog breeds. In the 1930s a sheep dog 'stud book', later known as the sheep dog register, was established. Although the dogs recorded were not 'pedigrees' in the usual sense of the word, they set standards for subsequent breeders to build on. It became a requirement for all winners of an open event in a sheep dog trial to be registered.[76]

In some ways the concerns of farmers and fanciers were very similar – they wanted to breed the ideal dog. But the departure of sheep dog breeders from the rigid standards and rules set by the Kennel Club caused a rift between the two groups. There were serious attempts to bridge the divide: in 1927 representatives of the Kennel Club and the North Island Sheep Dog Trial Association got together to define and publish a standard for working dogs, and for a time the association was affiliated to the club.[77] Inevitably, though, the two movements developed separately because of their different attitudes to breed purity.

~

Breeding and competing with animals may have been a hobby for most fanciers, but they took it very seriously indeed. 'Poultrymen are usually considered a most antagonistic crowd of fellows on clubs, competitions, or any movement requiring co-operation. We must be finely strung,' remarked the editor of the *New Zealand Poultry Journal* in 1910.[78] In the highly charged atmosphere of poultry shows, procedures and judging were frequently questioned. Typical of such quarrels was a letter from Mr T. Strong of Doyleston to the editor of the *New Zealand Poultry Journal* in 1908. He had sent several pens of ducks by rail to the Christchurch show, indicating the classes he wanted to enter them in. To his dismay, he found when he arrived at the hall that two pens had been placed in the wrong class. 'I have been breeding Indian Runner Ducks for a number of years and reckoned these two pens were the best I had ever bred, so I did not have a chance of being beaten,' he complained, adding, 'I am sorry to rush into print but had no alternative as I saw the officials at the show, but received no satisfaction and since I have written to the society but received no answer.'[79]

The sometimes bitter politics of fanciers' organisations was illustrated in the emergence of two national cat organisations. By 1930 there was a New Zealand Cat Club, which registered pedigree animals. That year another organisation based on and affiliated to an English society, the New Zealand Governing

Council of the Cat Fancy, was established in Auckland to provide centralised standards for breeding and showing cats. It proceeded to set up affiliated cat clubs in other cities, and began to register cats, making it a rule that cats not on its register could not enter its shows. A power struggle between the two associations ensued, with the NZGCCF emerging as the victor. However, there were ongoing arguments, with various clubs, notably the Christchurch Cat Club, refusing to accept the authority of the NZGCCF. There were also heated squabbles within the council. Mrs Baggott, an unpopular president in 1931, was deposed by a motion of no confidence after just a few months in office. Her successor, Mr Jones, seems also to have had a rocky ride, because he eventually tendered his resignation, according to the minutes, owing to his 'severance with the Cat Fancy'.[80]

Similarly, the Kennel Club's rigid authority over the dog fancy in New Zealand was occasionally challenged. In 1930 a group of Auckland Pekingese owners broke away from the local Toy Dog Club and joined cat owners to form the New Zealand Pekingese and Persian Cat Club. They applied for Kennel Club affiliation, but were turned down because by then the organisation had resolved not to affiliate single-breed clubs – and officials, not surprisingly, frowned on the inclusion of cats. Following this dispute, an Onehunga all-breeds club was denied affiliation. As a result, disaffected Auckland dog owners, led by Robert Marshall, a well-known breeder of Pekingese, poodles and schipperkes, set up the New Zealand Kennel Council in direct opposition to the Kennel Club. The latter fought back, drawing on the strategic skills of its new secretary, Stan Rastall, a journalist who was clearly as determined as the bulldogs he bred. First the Kennel Club sought and obtained English Kennel Club endorsement. It then proceeded to disqualify any judges who had officiated at Kennel Council shows, drafted new disciplinary rules and regained supremacy.[81]

Confrontations between individual fanciers could get personal, even insulting. In 1907 Clifford Braham, a former secretary and vice-president of the New Zealand Kennel Club, was suspended for three months from the Wellington Kennel Club for telling a fellow member, Ernesto Bernasconi, that he was 'not a Gentleman', and that the last club show had been run by 'three Bloody Foreigners'. Braham was later expelled from the club because he wrote to the *Otago Witness* repeating the accusation, only this time using the expression 'two bloody foreigners and a Yid'.[82]

Another such dispute between two members of the Christchurch Toy Dog and Cat Club ended up in court in March 1935. Mrs Mary Priest, secretary of the club, alleged that Mrs F. Vincent had called her one of the 'scum of the earth': 'I know all about your character, and if I told people what I know of your

Officials of the Wellington Kennel Club and the New Zealand Kennel Club were photographed together in 1896, the year that national headquarters moved to Wellington. It all seems very brotherly here, but competitiveness could lead to some aggressive exchanges between fanciers.

Alexander Turnbull Library, A.P. Ferguson Collection. Reference: PAColl-0045-03

character they would never come back to this hall again.' She apparently added injury to insult by flicking Mrs Priest in the face with a pair of gloves. The judge found in Mrs Priest's favour, fining Mrs Vincent £7 and costs.[83]

~

The fancy could be divisive, but it also brought people together. New Zealand fanciers shared ideas and insights through magazines and newspaper columns devoted to their interests. One of the best known was 'The Kennel', a long-running column written for the *Otago Witness* by fancier H.P. Harvey under the pen-name 'Terror'.[84] The urge to compete also forged bonds. In 1887 the *New Zealand Farmer* was 'pleased to note that the several Colonial Societies

'Devotedly fond of animals'

The elegant Lady Ranfurly was photographed in a Christchurch garden with a cockatoo, sometime between 1897 and 1904. The Ranfurlys were very fond of pets, which feature in a number of photographs of the family during their time in New Zealand. Like other vice-regal families before and after them, they were involved with fanciers' societies and the Society for the Prevention of Cruelty to Animals.

Alexander Turnbull Library, Ranfurly Collection. Reference: PAColl-5745-1-23

BEST KNOWN for donating the famous Ranfurly Shield to the New Zealand Rugby Football Union in 1902, the affable Earl of Ranfurly, governor from August 1897 to June 1904, was also a figurehead for fanciers' clubs.[91] Before he arrived in New Zealand with his wife, Constance, Countess of Ranfurly, and their three children, word had spread that the family were 'devotedly fond of animals, especially dogs'.[92] In the late nineteenth century most New Zealanders were ardent royalists, and the arrival of a new governor was an important event. The name Ranfurly became popular for babies, commercial products and services – and, of course, dogs. As a newspaper gossip column remarked, 'On Lambton Quay, dogs by the name Ranfurly are thick as flies in treacle time. The Wellington people simply dote on Governors, you know.'[93]

Within a few weeks of his arrival it was announced that the new governor was willing to accept the position of patron to the Wellington Kennel Club and the New Zealand Collie Club, and the following year he became patron of the Canterbury Kennel Club.[94] He regularly performed the opening ceremony at the Wellington Kennel Club's annual show, and took a close interest in proceedings. In August 1900 the *Evening Post* reported: 'His Excellency the Governor (who was accompanied by his daughters, Ladies Constance and Eileen Knox), after declaring the show open in the afternoon, went round the benches under the guidance of Dr Newman, President of the Club, and other officials, and also watched the judging for Messrs Hill and Son's trophy for the best dog in the show.'[95] The governor may have had mixed feelings when he learned that one of the four contenders for this title was a greyhound bitch called Lady Ranfurly. Although she missed out on this occasion, she won top honours at other shows.[96]

The Ranfurlys also extended vice-regal support to the Wellington Society for the Prevention of Cruelty to Animals. The governor presided over at least one annual meeting and delivered speeches on the topic of humane treatment of animals. He and his wife were patrons of the society.[97]

Lady Ranfurly brought her Skye terrier, Hamish, with her to New Zealand, and during their term of office the Ranfurly family acquired several dogs. Sadly for them, they had to leave behind the last of these – a Scottish terrier named Jock – when they departed in 1904.

are working together in a thoroughly friendly spirit in the interests of the poultry breeding industry'.[85] By then, New Zealand poultry breeders were competing at shows in Sydney and Melbourne. There was also friendly rivalry between New Zealand societies, in particular Auckland and Wellington.

In order to compete at shows, fanciers had to overcome major transport difficulties. In the nineteenth century, Christchurch participants in Auckland dog shows faced a journey by sea that took over a week.[86] As late as 1916, members of the Marlborough Poultry Pigeon and Cage Bird Association had to travel from Blenheim to Picton by road and then by sea to Nelson to attend a show there.[87] Transporting animals was also expensive, but in the mid-1930s the Kennel Club secured shipping and rail concessions to convey dogs for stud and shows.[88] The barrier of distance was gradually broken down in pursuit of the fancy.

Cooperation between fanciers' groups included exchanges of judges. In 1897, for example, Mr R. Wark, a noted collie expert, went to Australia to judge Kennel Club events there and Mr Court Rice from Sydney came to New Zealand to judge at shows in both islands. The practice continued.[89] From the nineteenth century, New Zealand fanciers' associations communicated with similar organisations in Australia, the United States, England and other countries, and prize animals were both imported and sent overseas. Consignments of poultry were being sent by New Zealand breeders to Sydney in the 1880s, at least one cat had been exported to England in the early 1930s, and by 1936 pedigree dogs were being sent to the United States as well as the existing market of Australia.[90] For fanciers, new and exciting opportunities were opening up. What a time to look back on indeed.

A brother and sister, members of the Dickson family, carefully hold kittens outside their father's Te Aroha workshop around 1906. By this time many people believed that looking after pets was the best way for children to learn kindness to animals.

Alexander Turnbull Library, R. McIndoe Collection. Reference: G-23878-1/4

Chapter 5
Learning to be kind

New Zealand's British settlers imported to this country both animals and ideas about them. One of the most radical of the ideas was that humans should be kind to other living creatures. For centuries the British, like most Europeans, considered animals a lower form of life, existing solely for their use and entertainment. Seen as nothing more than property, they could be worked, beaten, played with, neglected and disposed of as convenient. Many Christian thinkers endorsed this belief, quoting biblical texts to support it. But others began to suggest that humans ought to be merciful, claiming that cruelty to animals would lead to cruelty to people. Kindness to animals, they claimed, was the mark of an enlightened individual. On the other hand, taking pleasure in cruelty, for instance by watching staged animal fights, was a sign of depravity.[1]

By the eighteenth century more people – especially the growing numbers of Quakers, Methodists and evangelical Christians – accepted there was a Christian duty to care for animals because they were a gift from God. Some went further, insisting that animals deserved respect because God had made them for their own sakes, not just for human use. The revelation that people might not, after all, be central to creation was consistent with recent scientific discoveries. Explorers of distant lands were coming across many new, strange animals that were apparently of no use for food or labour.

There was a growing awareness, too, that humans and animals, as sentient creatures, had much in common physically. Some philosophers began to argue for the claim of animals to kindly treatment on these grounds: in 1789 Jeremy

Bentham pointed out that although they could not talk or reason, animals, like people, could suffer pain.² These ideas flourished in a warmer emotional climate. The Romantic poets praised the human capacity to feel as well as reason, glorifying the natural world and all the creatures in it. And growing sympathy for animal life was almost certainly affected by the spread of pet ownership.³ People who developed a strong sentimental attachment to their pets could become more inclined to show tenderness towards other animals.

In spite of these developments, the British had a reputation for being crueller to animals than other nations.⁴ Abuses were widespread and appalling – horses and oxen were often overloaded and flogged viciously if they tired; baiting bulls and bears with dogs was thought hugely entertaining; and wild animals and birds were hunted and killed simply for sport. But supporters of animal protection began to speak out more forcefully.

After several unsuccessful attempts to introduce legislation, in 1822 a member of parliament, Richard Martin, later dubbed 'Humanity Dick', successfully argued for an act to prevent the ill-treatment of cattle, sheep and horses. Two years later the Society for the Prevention of Cruelty to Animals was set up in London to help enforce the law. Its members included evangelical Christians and anti-oppression activists, notably William Wilberforce, leader of the campaign against the slave trade. Women soon became involved, and in 1829 a 'ladies' committee' was established. The society published anti-cruelty tracts, and its male members patrolled the streets and markets of London, but it struggled because of insufficient funds.

In 1835, SPCA committee member Joseph Pease managed to usher through another act, outlawing the baiting of bulls, bears and other animals, and extending protection to domestic pets.⁵ The same year, in an inspired move, the SPCA persuaded the Duchess of Kent and her daughter Princess Victoria to become patronesses. After Victoria became Queen in 1837, the society's reputation was further enhanced, and in 1840 she allowed it to adopt the prefix 'Royal'. Throughout her life she was keenly sympathetic to the suffering of animals and supportive of the work of the RSPCA. She corresponded with the society, donated money, attended the annual meeting in 1887 (the year of her fiftieth jubilee), and instigated the Victoria Medal, to be presented on her behalf to members who had performed distinguished service.⁶

~

When New Zealand was proclaimed a colony in 1840 the English law protecting animals became applicable, and some of its offences and penalties were also echoed in a Prevention of Cruelty to Animals Ordinance passed by

Settler hopes for the future are evoked in this idyllic scene of a couple and their child, accompanied by the family dog, surveying the new town of Dunedin in 1849. Dunedin became the seat of the Otago Provincial Council, which in 1861 passed New Zealand's first indigenous anti-cruelty law. It was also home to the country's second Society for the Prevention of Cruelty to Animals, established in July 1882.

Hocken Collections, Uare Taoka o Hakena, University of Otago. Reference: 14,414. Watercolour by Edward Immyns Abbot

the Otago Provincial Council in 1861.[7] The principle that it was wrong to mistreat animals increasingly influenced public opinion: in the 1860s and 1870s newspapers regularly reported and commented on cases of cruelty, most of them related to horses. Because horses were used to transport people and goods, they were often roughly handled in public, in front of witnesses. And as more people regarded horses not just as beasts of burden but as faithful family friends, they were distressed by the abuse they saw.

   This could be stomach-turning. Some carters thought nothing of working a horse that was lame or suffering from injured shoulders, or had sores caused by the friction of an ill-fitting harness. One man appeared before the Raglan Magistrate's Court charged with riding a horse with an open wound on its back; when he was arrested, his trousers were stained with the animal's blood.[8] Merciless kicking or beating of horses was not uncommon. In a typical case, an Auckland workman tried to make a horse pull a cart out of an incline into which it had fallen, and when the animal could not, he thrashed it savagely

> **CRUELTY TO ANIMALS.**
> TO THE EDITOR.
>
> Sir,—I was glad to find that in your issue of the 21st instant you brought under public notice a case of flagrant cruelty to a horse drawing a load of scoria, as I think that those so employed—having mostly to deliver their loads in the bad places around Auckland—are generally treated with great brutality. Last week I noticed a man delivering scoria on the reclaimed land between Hardinge and Nelson-streets strike a horse, which he had beaten and driven to a standstill, a violent blow on the head with a pickaxe, and again to day the same man (whom I can point out to the police) lashed a horse most furiously and in too disgusting a manner to describe, merely because it stopped to obey a call of nature, and then wound up by kicking it violently on the mouth with his heavy nailed boots. I noticed, in the last papers from home, that a man of fortune there had lately been committed to prison for two months, without option of a fine, for gross cruelty in over-driving two horses, and I think that some such salutary lesson should be inflicted here, instead of imposing paltry fines which the drivers only laugh at, such things being a mere bagatelle to men with large contracts, and have no deterrent effect whatever.—I am, &c.,
> EYE-WITNESS.

The revulsion and horror felt by people witnessing cruelty to horses is apparent in this 1877 letter to the editor of the *New Zealand Herald*, which gives graphic details of the brutal beating of an Auckland cart horse by its owner. The Cruelty to Animals Act, passed the following year, allowed for stiffer penalties, including significant prison terms for such offences. *New Zealand Herald, 1 September 1877, p. 5*

about the body and hit it on the head with the handle of the whip.[9] Sticks, doubled stock whips, pickaxe handles and spades were also used in frenzied assaults on animals that shied, jibbed or fell. A Thames man using a pair of horses to haul a cart of quartz belaboured one with a sledgehammer, beating it first on the belly and then on the back until another man intervened.[10] These cases were bad enough, but some suggested an even more disturbing element of sadism. In what was described by the *Nelson Examiner* as 'a piece of gross and disgusting cruelty', a driver cut off the tip of his horse's tongue when it failed to obey him.[11] And another man, whose horse stumbled on the road from Bulls to Marton, removed its saddle and bridle and slashed at its throat with a pocket knife for 20 minutes. He then led the animal to the side of the road, pushed it over on its side and left it to die.[12]

People were often outraged at the small fines that were imposed for these offences – never more than £5 and sometimes only a few shillings. In 1874 the Nelson Provincial Council passed the Cruelty to Animals Act, which raised the maximum penalty to £20 or six months' imprisonment for offences committed in that region.[13] This provision carried over to the first national anti-cruelty law, the Cruelty to Animals Act of 1878, which applied to 'any beast or bird of any kind or species whatever, and whether of domestic or wild nature, and whether indigenous or imported into the colony'. It was succeeded, in 1880, by the Cruelty to Animals Act, containing similar penalties.[14] Legislating against cruelty gained wide acceptance in New Zealand – and not just among Pakeha. For instance, when the second Maori King, Tawhiao, established his Kauhanganui (parliament) in the Waikato region in the 1890s, forbidding cruelty to animals was one of the measures it considered.[15]

~

Introducing law was one thing, making it work was another. There were practical limits on what police could do. Both the 1878 and 1880 acts empowered constables to arrest offenders on their own initiative or on the basis of information provided by the public, but a police force reduced during the 1880s depression had many other concerns aside from animal cruelty cases.[16] Obtaining a conviction usually depended on a witness being prepared to lay a complaint and give evidence in court – not always an easy thing for people to do in small communities. It is safe to assume that only a tiny minority of cruelty cases made it as far as the magistrate's court. It was soon evident that New Zealand needed its own SPCA to help uphold the law.

On 8 June 1882 concerned citizens met in Christchurch to inaugurate the New Zealand Society for the Prevention of Cruelty to Animals (later renamed the Canterbury SPCA). The mayor of Christchurch chaired the meeting, which attracted a large audience of men and some women. Speakers, including clergymen, a politician and an educationalist, agreed that cruelty to animals was a problem in the colony. The Reverend John Elmslie expressed his disgust at the callous abuse of working and farm animals – he claimed never to have witnessed as much cruelty to horses in Europe as he had seen inflicted in New Zealand – and deplored 'the wretched treatment of cows here'. The Reverend H.O.M. Watson denounced the popular sports of hare-coursing and captive pigeon shooting. He hoped that it would soon 'become impossible for man or woman to be a spectator of poor dumb animals being torn to pieces'.[17]

The new society announced two main aims: to educate people, especially children, in humane principles, and to promote anti-cruelty legislation. It also expressed the hope that other societies would be set up around the country. This challenge was soon accepted. Just a month later, on 13 July 1882, the Otago SPCA was set up. The following year, on 10 October 1883, the Auckland SPCA was established, and almost exactly a year after that, on 6 October 1884, a Wellington SPCA.[18]

Recognition of the need to enforce the anti-cruelty law had obviously triggered the formation of SPCAs. There was also the fear, voiced at the Christchurch meeting, of New Zealand being left behind other British colonies, and once the Canterbury society was formed, Dunedin, Auckland and Wellington did not want to be seen as backward in comparison. But a crucial factor was the changing nature of New Zealand's urban environment: by the end of the 1870s, Dunedin, Christchurch, Wellington and Auckland had all been designated cities and their transport networks were expanding. Horse-drawn hansom cabs, the forerunners of taxis, had been operating since the 1860s, and in the early 1880s horse-drawn trams appeared.[19] The numbers of starving, injured or overworked animals in the streets were growing and were impossible to ignore. In addition, all four centres had major railway stations and ports, so the driving, loading and transport of farm animals took place under the gaze of city dwellers.

Just as the RSPCA attracted the support of the high and mighty, the first leaders of the New Zealand SPCAs included the elite of colonial society. Lawyers, politicians, administrators and local worthies packed the committees. Both Christian and Jewish leaders were prominent in the first four SPCAs, as were women of social standing: within a short time, 'ladies' auxiliaries' were formed.[20] Names of early officials included current or future national leaders such as Sir John Hall, first president of the Canterbury SPCA; G.M. Waterhouse, first president of the Wellington SPCA; and Robert (later Sir Robert) Stout, an honorary solicitor in the Otago SPCA and later involved in the Wellington SPCA. There were also royal connections: the Queen's representative in New Zealand, Governor Sir William Jervois, was first patron of the Wellington SPCA, and Lady Jervois became patroness of the Ladies' Branch. Although the New Zealand SPCAs took advice from their Australian counterparts, they deferred to the English RSPCA, and the Canterbury society adopted its rules.[21]

The respectable, well-to-do members of New Zealand SPCAs, like their British counterparts, monitored the behaviour of the working classes: those who farmed animals or used them to carry out manual jobs. Some campaigns – notably that to prevent cruelty by cab drivers to their horses – copied RSPCA initiatives.[22] The idea that cruelty was a characteristic of the 'lower orders' was sometimes hinted at in the press. In 1886, for example, the *New Zealand Farmer* reprinted a lecture on 'Kindness to animals' delivered in London by a Professor Woodroffe Hill, prefacing it with the comment, 'There is nothing to our mind more surely betrays a low grade of human being, mentally and morally, than any exhibition of cruelty to domestic animals, or even of disregard for their comfort and well-being.'[23]

As most early SPCA members were apparently well-heeled town dwellers, it is likely that their sympathy for animals arose mainly from love for pets, and indeed, some used their companion animals to help raise funds. In 1893 'Clio' (Mrs C. L. Innes), who edited the Wellington *Evening Post*'s 'Ladies' Column', recalled the early days of the Canterbury SPCA.

> *On one occasion my handsome Pomeranian dog Punch – alas! now dead – sat at the door with a plate before him and a placard round his neck, on which was printed in large letters "Please Help our Cause." A good sum was collected by his help, and at the last meeting I attended Punch had a silver medal presented to him for his efforts at the cause of humanity.*[24]

~

In their first few years most of the societies threw considerable energy into policing the 1880 act. They soon recognised the importance of appointing inspectors to identify cases of cruelty, and solicitors to take prosecutions. The Christchurch society promptly appointed three honorary inspectors and an honorary veterinarian, and within a few months had honorary solicitors.[25] The Otago Society also had honorary veterinary surgeons and solicitors but decided, following RSPCA practice, to employ an inspector, Robert Aitken. He was sworn in as a special constable, which gave him a policeman's power to deal with offenders. The Christchurch and Auckland societies soon took up the idea.[26]

New Zealand SPCA inspectors often had a background in enforcement, either as policemen or soldiers. Their efforts were critical to the success of the societies in the early years. The Wellington SPCA's first inspector lasted only a month, and members were unable to raise enough money to employ another. Failing to make a public impact by securing prosecutions for cruelty, the society faded away and was not revived until 1893.[27]

The SPCAs also wanted to repeal the law which, among other things, was too vague in its definitions. After societies had conferred with each other and the Tasmanian SPCA, two new bills were put forward in October 1884,[28] and by the end of the year most of their provisions had been incorporated in the Police Offences Act. This listed some offences that were in previous acts, such as being a party to the baiting or fighting of animals, and slaughtering, branding or conveying animals in such a way as to cause unnecessary suffering. It added overloading to the catalogue of cruelties, which already included beating, ill-treating, overdriving, abusing or torturing; and identified inadequate provision of food, water and shelter as an offence. Magistrates were allowed to order the destruction of any disabled or suffering animal.

But the most innovative clause allowed for the appointment of SPCA officers as special constables, making official an arrangement that had already been tried and found workable. Special constables had the power to enter and inspect saleyards. They could also take people committing animal cruelty offences into custody and bring them before magistrates. This was a great advance on the English situation, where RSPCA inspectors did not have any legal status beyond that of private citizens.[29] With a few amendments, the law remained in force for the next 76 years.

~

The high-powered members of early SPCAs were able to achieve significant law reform within a short time, but they preferred not to become involved in

This early 1900s postcard of Queen Street, Auckland, shows a new electric tram, but most of the traffic was still horse-drawn. The constant presence of horses on city streets made them the main focus of anti-cruelty campaigning in New Zealand in the nineteenth and early twentieth centuries.

Author's collection

the day-to-day grind of identifying instances of animal cruelty and bringing offenders to justice, leaving this largely to the paid inspectors. The societies soon found that this work was expensive, and obtaining sufficient money was a problem. As early as December 1882 the Christchurch SPCA noted that 'Unless the funds of the Society are considerably augmented with the assistance of the public, even the present very moderate expenditure cannot be maintained'.[30]

Nor was there financial assistance from central or local government, although in the 1890s the Auckland and Wellington societies achieved such concessions as free railway and tram passes for inspectors. The Auckland SPCA was in serious financial difficulty by the mid-1890s and folded temporarily in 1897. By early 1899 the Wellington SPCA was again so short of money that it came close to winding up.[31] After the turn of the century there were occasional local body grants, but several societies relied on 'lady collectors' to follow up overdue subscriptions, obtain donations and enlist new members.[32] A 1924 amendment to the act gave magistrates the option of awarding local SPCAs the revenue from fines for cruelty offences, but this did not generate much money. The depressions of the 1920s and 1930s had a further negative impact on revenue.[33] Financial concerns were to plague SPCAs regularly over the years.

Also discouraging was the difficulty of obtaining convictions for cruelty: a significant number of cases were dismissed. The SPCAs found the law insufficiently precise in some of its wording, and many magistrates were unsympathetic to the societies' ideals, insisting that cruel intent had to be proved. Sometimes people successfully used the defence that it was necessary to beat a working animal severely in order to make it obey commands.[34] For decades the SPCAs made repeated but unsuccessful attempts to persuade politicians to introduce more robust anti-cruelty legislation.

Another problem was the size of the task. For many years only the four main centres had SPCAs,[35] and their few energetic inspectors visited saleyards, docks, railway stations and race meetings and made forays into adjacent country areas. In the 1910–11 year, for example, Auckland's sole inspector, Henry Alder, issued 860 cautions and took 40 successful prosecutions.[36] The society was aware, however, that he was merely scratching the surface of the problem: 'It is unpleasant to reflect on the hundreds of cases which must occur in the remoter districts where the unfortunate animals have to suffer until released by death; here we could do much more if the public would show their interest by providing the means.'[37]

Although more SPCAs were formed in the 1890s and early 1900s, they were still few and far between, especially in rural areas, until after World War II. Some sympathetic country people became local SPCA 'agents' in places such as Eketahuna and Waipukurau, but generally it was difficult to get the anti-cruelty message across to farmers. This limited the effectiveness of SPCA campaigns against common farming practices: invasive surgical procedures such as castration and dehorning without anaesthetic, overcrowding and neglect of animals being transported, and inhumane slaughter.[38]

For 20 years until his sudden death in 1921, Henry Alder was the public face of the SPCA in Auckland and adjacent rural areas. Like most of the early SPCA inspectors he worked alone, and had the daunting task of protecting all the region's animals from cruelty and bringing offenders to justice. In the process he checked sales and auction rooms, walked city streets and the waterfront and made long journeys into the surrounding countryside. In a 1922 tribute to him, a granite horse trough was placed at the corner of Sturdee Street and Market Lane, where it still stands. *Alexander Turnbull Library. Reference: S-L 1028 FRONTIS*

Even in towns and cities there were some signs that support for SPCAs was limited. Newspapers generally paid lip service to the importance of preventing cruelty to animals, but there was the occasional outspoken detractor. Some people were clearly annoyed that concern for animals might get in the way of such popular New Zealand pastimes as hunting and fishing. 'The passing show', an article published in the family magazine *The Budget* in 1910, ridiculed the SPCA and proposed the establishment of a Sport Protection Society.[39] At the 1915 annual general meeting of the Wellington SPCA, William Watson conceded, 'We are regarded by many people as a lot of amiable, harmless faddists.'[40]

~

The SPCAs looked to other reform movements for much-needed support. Overseas, concern for animal welfare infiltrated many Christian denominations, and the temperance movement and SPCAs developed a close connection during the nineteenth century. Prevention of cruelty to animals also became associated with combating child abuse. Neither children nor animals had many legal protections, and both were subject to neglect and cruelty. Those intervening on behalf of abused animals could not help but notice the similar treatment often suffered by children.

Not surprisingly, bonds between animal and child protection organisations developed. In the United States wealthy social reformer Henry Bergh initiated both the American Society for the Prevention of Cruelty to Animals, in 1866, and the New York Society for the Prevention of Cruelty to Children, in 1874. The RSPCA lobbied for the establishment of a similar organisation for children in England, and cooperated with the London (later National) Society for the Prevention of Cruelty to Children after its establishment in 1884. Meanwhile, from 1877 the American Humane Association was the umbrella organisation for local societies that often worked to eliminate abuse of both children and animals.[41]

The link between violence to women and children and cruelty to animals was all too clear to some New Zealanders. One indignant man wrote to the *Auckland Star* in 1873, threatening to name and shame his neighbour, a doctor, who was in the habit of brutally whipping his wife and children. 'Their cries, to those who have any merciful feelings, are very painful to hear, and the sound of the scourging rope on their backs and shoulders, coupled with the tyrant's voice, obscenely cursing and shouting "I will be master in my own house" are enough to make the blood curdle and rouse the feelings of the most apathetic.' But this was not all: 'At other times, by way of changing the amusement, he will tie up his little dog midway between two posts, and flagellate the poor animal till it can hardly stand.'[42] In opposing such abuses, the temperance cause was often a rallying point. Alcohol consumption was very high in nineteenth-century New Zealand, and many people saw it as a threat to the ideal of the happy home. Drunken men could waste household money and ill-treat their wives and children – and often domestic animals as well.

Often, therefore, the same individuals and organisations promoted women's and children's rights, temperance and humane treatment of animals as part of a broad agenda of social reform.[43] Sometimes the connections between crusades were personal as well as political. For example, in the late 1890s Arthur Richmond Atkinson, a leading member of the New Zealand Alliance, a temperance organisation, was also a prominent member of the Wellington

SPCA. His fiancée, Lily Kirk, a feminist and a vice-president of the New Zealand Alliance, was involved in the Wellington Society for the Protection of Women and Children. Their love story may help to explain why the SPWC and the SPCA branches in Wellington undertook joint fund-raising.[44]

A passion for justice was the common thread that drew together New Zealand temperance activists, feminists and animal welfare advocates. But these groups shared another concern: most had very limited funds. This led some SPCAs to consider amalgamating with kindred societies. The Auckland SPCA, which had collapsed for financial reasons in 1897, joined forces with the Auckland Society for the Protection of Women and Children in 1898.[45] The bizarrely named Society for the Protection of Women and Children and Prevention of Cruelty to Animals operated until 1926, when the two branches split. In the late 1890s there was also a suggestion, not taken up, that the Wellington SPCA might amalgamate with the local Society for the Protection of Women and Children.[46]

~

Attempts to attract more adult supporters were often unsuccessful, but SPCAs had better luck with their children's education initiatives – which were much needed. The popular romantic belief that children had a special affinity with animals, and could even communicate with them, was undermined by the reality that, if allowed to, children could be very cruel.[47] Newspapers periodically condemned instances of children stoning birds and domestic animals or shooting them with pea guns. It seems that alongside pet keeping, many young New Zealanders enjoyed pastimes involving cruelty to animals – bird nesting, snaring, hunting, and inventive tormenting of both wild and domestic creatures: inflating frogs until they burst, for example, or tying firecrackers to dogs' tails.[48]

Many adults feared that such cruelty was a sign of moral delinquency and loss of innocence. An article in the *Wanganui Chronicle* in November 1888 lamented that children in Australasian colonies were not as tender and considerate to pets and other animals as English children, suggesting that they were therefore harder and less 'childlike'.[49] Boys were thought to be particularly at risk of developing vicious behaviour, and some believed that this could lead to abuse of women and children. In August 1897 the *Clutha Leader* issued a stern, if slightly odd, warning:

> *If you see a horse or a cow quietly edging away when a certain boy enters the paddock, keep a watch on that boy. He is of a cruel disposition and unless placed under discipline he will likely follow the occupation of a butcher and may be heard of charged with cruelty to his wife and children. If checked at the outset his cruel propensity may be overcome.'*[50]

The view that children needed to learn moral lessons the hard way is evident in this cartoon, 'A Change of Opinion', published in the *New Zealand Farmer* in January 1887. Tommy, who torments a kitten by picking it up by its skin, is treated similarly by Dobbin the horse. The accompanying homily concludes, 'Perhaps it will make him think, when he is playing with kittens and puppies, that what is fun to him is perhaps not fun to them a bit.'

Alexander Turnbull Library. Reference: S-L 1039-30

'Checking' signs of violent or cruel behaviour in children could, ironically, involve adult violence. In March 1897 young Alfred Pratt of Christchurch appeared in court for ill-treating a kitten by striking it with a stick and stamping on its head. Mr Galloway, the SPCA representative, said he would not press for a penalty because he had been assured that the boy 'had been severely flogged by his parents'. Satisfied with this explanation, the judge 'admonished the lad and discharged him'.[51]

There had to be a better way. New Zealand SPCAs adopted the strategy of teaching children to empathise with animals rather than punishing cruelty. It was an approach already well established in children's literature. Imported children's books about animals, and magazine articles copied from overseas newspapers and journals, often used tips on caring for pets as a way of introducing the subject of kindness. In 1885, for example, the *New Zealand Farmer* published a pet care article for children that concluded:

> *Try to win the affections of all pets by love and gentleness, never by harsh means, and always talk to them as if they really were thinking creatures. You have a duty to perform to whatever pet you possess, if you neglect that duty you are committing a great sin, and do not deserve to possess anything that lives and breathes. Always feed and tend your pets before you sit down to your own meals; if you do so your conscience will be easy, and I think your appetite will be good.*[52]

Some primary schools, too, tried to educate children to recognise and respect the needs of animals. In October 1881 the *New Zealand Schoolmaster*, a teachers' journal, published a detailed science lesson for young children on the anatomy and habits of the cat, which advocated the use of an animal as a teaching aid: 'I have found that good results follow from allowing a Cat to be a regular inmate of the Schoolroom. By taking care that she is not ill-treated, the principle of kindness to dumb animals will be better inculcated than in any other way.'[53]

The following year the *Schoolmaster* welcomed the formation of the Canterbury SPCA, and suggested that the best way to promote its aims was through teaching children in public schools:

> *Like most things having a direct bearing upon the welfare of a country, the teaching of kindness, to be effective, must begin at an early period in the life of an individual, when the susceptibilities are great and the sympathies can be readily won … We sincerely hope that the teachers throughout the country will readily join in the promotion of such a laudable object.*[54]

SPCAs seized on cooperation with schools as an ideal way of promoting humane ideals among children. In the 1880s most societies established junior branches, and much of the recruitment was carried out with the assistance of teachers.[55] Several months after its formation the Canterbury SPCA had 190 adult members, and boasted a Young Persons' Branch with no fewer than 600 members. The following year adult numbers had dropped to just over 100, but the junior membership had ballooned to 820.[56] Teachers were asked to tell their pupils about the SPCA's aims, and the society's secretary gave talks to the children, inviting them to join, which they apparently did 'in great numbers'.[57] SPCAs evidently found enlisting children easier than trying to get the moral and financial support of adults. This must have given them some sense of achievement when the task of preventing cruelty seemed overwhelmingly difficult.

~

Promoting special children's organisations known as Bands of Mercy was one of the SPCAs' most influential nineteenth-century educational initiatives. The concept originated in England, where Catharine Smithies, an RSPCA member and temperance advocate, established the first Band of Mercy in 1875. These groups were similar to the children's Bands of Hope started by the temperance movement in 1847, and in fact were often run by Band of Hope workers. Like Band of Hope adherents, Band of Mercy members had to sign a pledge – in this case a solemn promise to be kind to animals and birds and protect them from cruel treatment. Bands of Mercy first operated independently of the RSPCA, but came under its wing in 1883.[58]

The bands soon spread to the United States and to other British colonies. In New Zealand, some SPCA Young Persons' Branches were supplemented or replaced by Bands of Mercy. Occasionally Band of Mercy members were recruited from the Band of Hope, which had been active in New Zealand since the late 1850s. When Canterbury SPCA secretary W.H. Shaw spoke to the St Matthew's Band of Hope in St Albans, Christchurch in May 1885, for instance, several members joined the Band of Mercy at the conclusion of the meeting.[59] In

New Zealand, some Bands of Mercy were apparently under the direct control of the local SPCA, such as the one set up in Auckland in 1892.[60] Others were run by churches and Sunday schools. In Canterbury the Reverend S. Hamilton was the president of the Leeston Band of Mercy, formed in 1885, and Bands of Mercy were initiated at some churches in Dunedin in the early 1890s.[61] The Women's Christian Temperance Union organised some bands,[62] and yet others were established in state schools by enthusiastic staff members in cooperation with the local SPCA.[63]

An adult leader, usually a clergyman or a teacher, directed a band's activities. Members paid a subscription – often a small but significant source of revenue for the local SPCA – and in return received a subscription card with a suitable text, and sometimes a badge (for the Wellington Bands of Mercy it was a primrose-yellow ribbon). They attended meetings where they listened patiently to lectures on kindness to animals, the importance of the pledge and related moral subjects – perhaps enticed by the promise of a show of magic lantern slides at the end. Competitions were popular: there were prizes of books for the best letter or essay on kindness to animals. In 1897 the Wellington SPCA also awarded a special prize for an act of kindness towards an animal. Band of Mercy members would recite poems and sing songs on suitable themes both at meetings and at school and church concerts. In daily life, they were expected to lose no opportunity to show kindness to animals – usually pets. This gave rise to a rather snide adult joke that was published in various newspapers in the 1890s: 'Has my little member of the Band of Mercy been kind to dumb animals to-day?' 'Yes, grandma. I let your canary out of the cage, and when my cat caught it I set Towser [the dog] on her.'[64]

To encourage children to join school bands, from April 1897 the Wellington SPCA produced a monthly children's magazine, the *New Zealand Band of Mercy*. As well as reprinting stories about pets and other animals from overseas publications, this included local features such as 'Clio's Chats with Children', in which SPCA member Mrs Innes described her many childhood pets. It also invited young readers to write letters to 'Captain Kindheart'. Like children's letter pages in other newspapers, this column included youngsters' descriptions of their animal companions, but correspondents also recounted their deliberate acts of kindness to animals – rescuing strays, liberating sparrows caught by cats and so on. In addition, they reported on incidents of animals, usually horses, being mistreated in the streets, and sometimes Captain Kindheart urged them to provide names and identifying details so the SPCA inspector could investigate.

Although some of these letters seem to have been written largely to please Captain Kindheart and win the prizes on offer, others showed the sincerity of

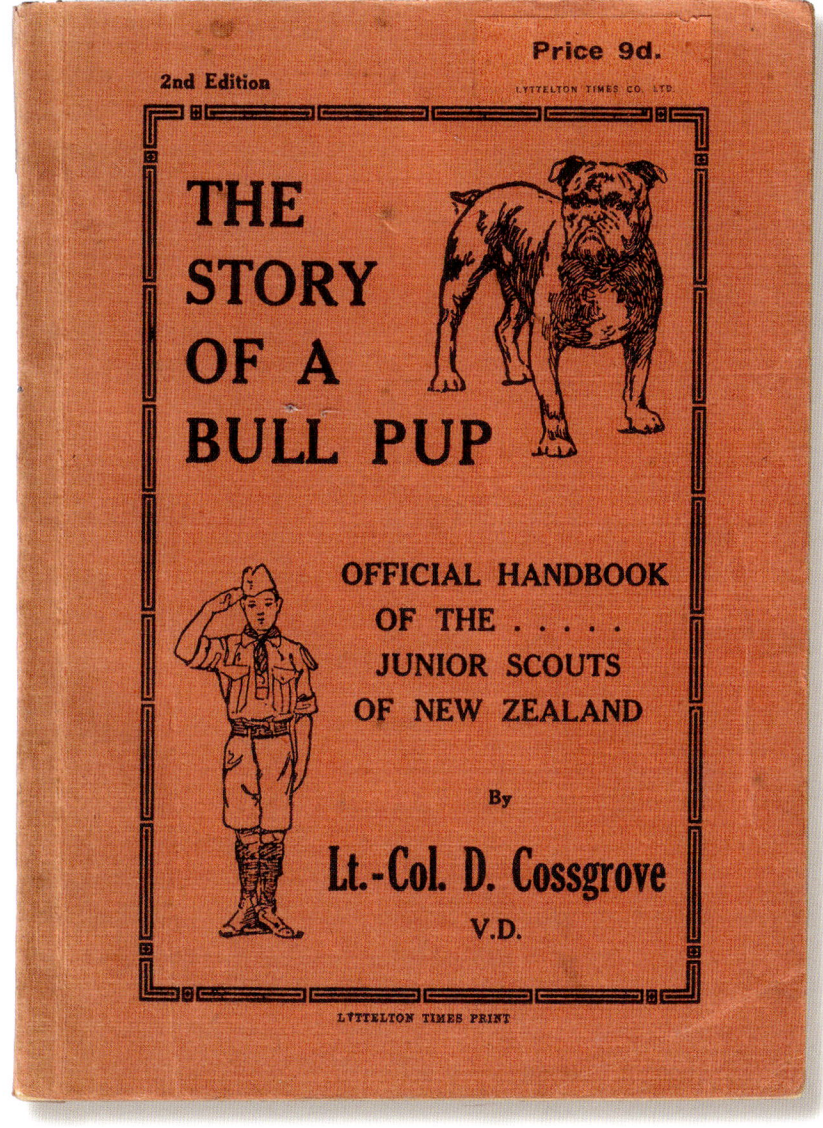

A bulldog and a saluting scout adorn the cover of *The Story of a Bull Pup*, first published by New Zealand scout leader David Cossgrove in 1917. Cossgrove's choice of the bulldog to represent the New Zealand scout was typical of the time, when imperial sentiment in New Zealand was at its height. Bulldogs symbolised 'British' (including colonial) courage and determination in wartime.

Permission of The Scout Association of New Zealand – National Scout Museum

Band of Mercy members and how upset they were by the suffering of abused animals. Eight-year-old Victor Harris commented on a case of two boys who had stoned a cat: 'I have a little kitten named Scottie…and I would be deeply grieved if she received such brutal treatment as that poor cat did.'[65] Another child, on witnessing a cart driver whipping and kicking his horse on Thorndon Esplanade, wrote, 'I felt as though I could go and kick him.'[66]

Unfortunately, it proved too expensive to continue the magazine, and by early 1898 the society had to cease publication and instead import an English paper. This was not a success with the children, and schools stopped taking it. According to one teacher, this was because 'it was written for English children, not for young New Zealanders'.[67] The Wellington Bands of Mercy appear to have died out soon after.[68]

The concept of the Band of Mercy, with its religious and temperance overtones and solemn pledge, was gradually replaced by other SPCA initiatives

Learning to be kind   **121**

The Canterbury SPCA used the occasion of the 1906–07 Christchurch International Exhibition to extend its humane education to a wider group of children. It ran a hugely successful pet show in Wonderland, and some of the photographs taken on that occasion were later published in the Canterbury Times. *According to one newspaper report, 'The exhibits were mostly contained in two large marquees, one of which was given up almost entirely to dogs of every size and breed, while the other was a veritable Noah's ark of birds and animals, ranging from a four-legged hen to hedgehogs.' The SPCA also ran an essay competition on the topic 'Kindness to animals', and entries were received from all parts of New Zealand.*

Christchurch City Libraries. Reference: CCL-Disc20-IMG0029

aimed at children, and by the end of World War I, it seems that the bands had all but disappeared in New Zealand. One of the last newspaper accounts was a *Wanganui Chronicle* report of the Band of Mercy meeting organised by the Aramoho Loyal Temperance Legion in June 1919. The gathering opened with singing and prayer, followed by 'a lesson on the pledge, command, promise and memory gem'. Recitations and a reading followed, and nine new members signed the Band of Mercy pledge.[69]

~

Although Bands of Mercy faded away, they were influential in their day. The principle of kindness to animals, and in particular the notion of making an anti-cruelty pledge or promise, became entrenched in other children's organisations of the late nineteenth and early twentieth centuries. The Salvation Army, active in New Zealand from 1883, started a children's organisation called the Band of Love, which had branches at Nelson and Wanganui by the late 1890s. Although the main aim of the Band of Love was to impart religious teachings, part of the pledge taken by young members was: 'I will try to love all, and be kind to animals.'[70]

The same ideal was part of the early New Zealand Boy Scout and Girl Guide movements, which were introduced to New Zealand in 1908 by David Cossgrove, who had met founder Sir Robert Baden Powell while serving in the South African War. A promise to be kind to animals was part of scout and guide 'law', and children could work towards the Friend to Animals badge, which, among other things, encouraged the proper treatment of pets.[71] One of Cossgrove's most interesting innovations was a junior scout movement called Bull Pups, which preceded the English Wolf Cub movement by a few years. In a 1917 handbook called *The Story of a Bull Pup*, Cossgrove described the training of some bulldog pups that eventually became disciplined enough to become part of a pack of bulldogs. The stories or 'Kennel Yelps' were obviously designed to appeal to young boys, drawing on their familiarity with and fondness for pet dogs and puppies. This book was a huge success, earning the approval of the Minister of Education, and was used as a supplementary reader in schools.[72]

Schools, meanwhile, had continued to cooperate with SPCAs to promote humane ideals. Essay competitions, long a favourite tactic, became even more popular after the turn of the century. In 1905 the Otago SPCA offered prizes for the best essays on kindness to animals written by pupils of Otago Girls' High School, and George Street and Albany Street district schools. Describing the numerous entries as 'evidently thoughtful', the president expressed the hope that

The Pet Show at "Wonderland," N.Z. International Exhibition

SNAPSHOTS OF THE GREAT SHOW.

'the interest aroused upon the subject throughout the schools will induce many of the pupils to study the welfare of the Society and become juvenile members of it'.[73]

Each year from 1910 the Auckland SPCA's school essay competition attracted more and more entries, and in 1914, when Maori schools were invited to participate, two of the winners were Maori children. After 1920, essay subjects began to include pet care: 'How we treat our cats', 'The proper treatment of a dog', 'The care and feeding of a horse' and 'The proper treatment of household pets' as well as the more usual 'Our behaviour to our fellow men and our treatment of animals'.[74]

It was natural for children to see the familiar, affectionate bond between humans and pets as the most compelling reason for being kind to animals. The winning entry in the Wellington SPCA's 1920 competition, written by Constance Moss of Eketahuna School, drew on examples of the loyalty of dogs to explain why people should treat animals considerately:

> *A dog is a faithful friend and companion, perhaps the most loyal friend a man could have. If treated humanely by his master he will stand by him, even if his master should lose his good name and all his friends desert him. A dog has been proved to be the most faithful guardian of little children, and will save them from harm at the risk of his own life.*[75]

As well as working with the SPCAs in the essay competitions, schools began to incorporate more humane teaching in the curriculum. 'Kindness to animals' was an occasional composition topic before 1900, but as an issue it received more attention after that date. In 1904 'Moral training' became a cornerstone of the new primary school curriculum introduced by George Hogben, Inspector General of Schools and Secretary of Education. Moral training covered a broad range of issues, including duty to parents and country, formation of good habits such as tidiness and punctuality, respect for others – and, of course, kindness to animals. Teachers in both state and Maori schools were expected to introduce and reinforce these principles during regular lessons in reading, writing, and other subjects.[76] To assist them, the *School Journal*, established in 1907, published articles promoting care for animals, particularly pets.[77]

~

The new century also saw important changes in animal welfare work. Once, SPCA prosecutions were mainly for cruelty to horses and occasionally mistreatment of stock or poultry in public places.[78] Pets were generally a minor concern for the early Auckland, Wellington, Christchurch and Dunedin SPCA inspectors, possibly because abuse of them occurred mostly in private. Horses remained the focus of SPCA attention until the 1920s, but cruelty to other animals was remarked on more often from the early 1900s. For example, more cases involving abandoned, neglected, diseased or injured cats, dogs, monkeys, songbirds and other pets began to appear in the Auckland SPCA annual reports.

There was an obvious reason for this shift in emphasis. In the first two decades of the twentieth century, electric trams increasingly replaced horse-drawn vehicles. In Dunedin in 1905, for instance, an electric tram service made redundant 500 horses then working in the tram and drag traffic.[79] Horses, although they continued to be used on farms, were beginning to be supplanted by motor vehicles – cars, buses and lorries – on city streets.

But there was another possible contributing factor. One outcome of the spread of humane education from the 1880s was that by the early 1900s adults were more likely to have learnt about the importance of kindness to animals in their youth. Presenting prizes to the winners of the SPCA essay competition in 1917, the Auckland mayoress, Jessie Gunson, 'recalled how the essays she had written in her childhood on this subject had left a lasting impression on her mind'.[80] In 1920 Wellington SPCA president F.W. Meadowcroft also observed how education had led to a change in attitudes. Noting the way soldiers had cared for their horses during the recent war, he commented, 'I think that education is undoubtedly going on and growing at the present time and is surely having its effect on the youth now reaching adult age.'[81]

Because this teaching had often used children's enthusiasm for pets as a way of making its point, rising generations were, it seems, more keen to protect companion animals from neglect and cruelty. The connection was made explicitly in SPCA fund-raising appeals. An *Evening Post* editorial on 27 October 1919 stated, 'The society needs further financial help for its work, which commends itself to every man, woman and child who has loved and been greatly loved in return by some horse, dog, or other pet.'[82]

A noticeable change in SPCA operations was the growth of animal rescue initiatives that benefited pets. SPCA inspectors attempted to relieve the suffering of the growing number of injured and diseased cats and dogs in cities. In the 1920s the harm caused to pets by motor vehicles was also a major preoccupation. 'It is astonishing the number of dogs that are run down by motorists and left to suffer on the Public Highways,' remarked the Canterbury SPCA inspector in 1927.[83]

The Bands of Mercy of the nineteenth and early twentieth centuries were soon succeeded by SPCA Junior Leagues. Their aims were similar: to encourage children to be kind to and protect animals. This badge belonged to a young member of the Canterbury League.

Author's collection. Photograph by Melanie Lovell-Smith

Learning to be kind 125

In Christchurch the SPCA opened its first Animals Home in 1912. Located at the inspector's residence, this cared mainly for stray dogs and cats, and provided veterinary treatment for ailing animals.[84] In the first two decades of the century the Auckland SPCA attempted to raise funds, first for a horse ambulance, then for a dogs' home. It finally succeeded in establishing a Blue Cross Hospital – the blue cross was the SPCA symbol – in New Lynn in December 1928. Managed by vet H.W. Carbury, it provided treatment for sick and injured animals. At first there was a charge for its services, but the SPCA aimed to offer free treatment for animals whose owners could not afford to pay. In its first year the hospital admitted 237 dogs, 87 cats and five other animals as 'boarders'. There was also an 'Infectious Ward' for dogs suffering from distemper, and 33 cases were treated during the year.[85] For financial reasons the Wellington society was slower to follow this example, but it had an ambulance service for small animals by 1940 and a clinic by 1945.[86]

Other animal welfare organisations intent on rescue work emerged during this period. In 1913 a group of Christchurch people founded the Animal Protection Society; one of its aims was to provide an animals' 'Home of Rest' outside the city boundaries. It later established a dog shelter in Colombo Street.[87] Another branch of the society was set up in Auckland in 1938. Among its objects was the establishment of a shelter for homeless animals and a clinic 'where rich and poor may bring their animals for free treatment and free advice'.[88]

SPCAs also revived and expanded their education programmes between the wars. These were not just for children: a receptive adult audience was now taken for granted. In the 1920s an Oamaru man, J.A. Forbes, initiated an annual Animal Welfare Week, which was later run by SPCAs. Although this involved school lectures and other events especially for children, church sermons and radio programmes also targeted their parents. During the 1926 Animal Week, for example, a radio broadcast by the Wellington SPCA featured a humorous roll-call of pet dogs' names, which apparently went down very well with listeners. Churches cooperated with such SPCA initiatives as Animal Sunday. In 1938 the Anglican Bishop of Wellington sent a circular letter to clergy, urging them to participate and recommending a form of prayer and some suitable hymns, including, of course, 'All Things Bright and Beautiful'.[89]

Nineteenth-century initiatives that trained children to be kind to animals by first thinking of their companion animals had a lasting impact. SPCA educational efforts, especially, influenced later generations of their adult supporters, who made connections between animal welfare and caring for pets as a matter of course. This in turn helped to bring about a change in the nature of SPCA work. In the twentieth century it began to focus increasingly on pets.

Pet rescue

A NEW ASPECT of twentieth-century SPCA rescue work in New Zealand was providing for the welfare of pet animals in natural disasters. Earthquakes were a topical concern in the late 1920s and early 1930s, when there was a spate of disasters. The spectacle of human loss was particularly distressing, but some people were also conscious of the suffering of animals. After an earthquake devastated the Murchison area on the South Island's West Coast on 17 June 1929, the Wellington SPCA sent a veterinarian to help injured animals, and some townspeople arranged to feed stray dogs that were left homeless.[90]

Again, after the massive Hawke's Bay earthquake of 3 February 1931, the local SPCA inspector, Mr Davis, organised house-to-house visits to check for any pets that might have been left behind when Napier and Hastings residents were evacuated. The Wellington SPCA also sent its inspector, Captain James Henry, to help in the animal relief effort. According to a report given at the 1931 annual general meeting, 'he spent several weeks in the earthquake area, arranged for the systematic feeding of animals and birds left behind and, in cases where animals were suffering through injury, humanely destroyed them'.[91] Captain Henry's son accompanied him on this mission of mercy, using his own motor lorry to bring in food and to transport animals. Their efforts were apparently greatly appreciated by Hawke's Bay residents: the society received many grateful letters and public tributes.

This disaster raised the question of preparing for future emergencies. The Wellington SPCA was keen to initiate discussions with other SPCAs about a cooperative scheme so that, 'in the event of an earthquake at any time or place in the future, the Societies in other districts will immediately take over the responsibility of caring for the animals in the stricken area'.[92]

Eighty years later, following the Canterbury earthquakes of 4 September 2010 and 22 February 2011, many pet animals went missing or suffered severe trauma because of aftershocks. Desperate pet owners breached police cordons to search for their animal companions. In 2011 a Wellington SPCA Animal Rescue Unit and a Massey University Veterinary Emergency Response Team went to the aid of trapped and injured animals in Christchurch. Some of the many lost and abandoned pet animals were sent to SPCAs and other animal shelters in the North Island to be cared for and rehomed.[93]

Dr Oxnam and others feed stray dogs after the Murchison earthquake in June 1929. Public concern for the plight of companion animals after natural disasters emerged following the major earthquakes at Murchison in 1929 and Hawke's Bay in 1931, and SPCA relief efforts were organised in both cases.

Alexander Turnbull Library, F.N. Jones Collection. Reference: G-26357-1/2. Photograph by Frederick Nelson Jones

Members of the local Calf Club form a semi-circle around the mayor of Morrinsville, Mr Osborne, as he prepares to present the championship trophies on Calf Club Day, about 1937. Interested parents hover in the background. From the beginning, Calf Club Day was a family and community occasion.

Alexander Turnbull Library, New Zealand Free Lance Collection. Reference: F-151271-1/2

Chapter 6
Feels like Calf Club Day

'Summer days, and making hay/feels like Calf Club Day.' For many New Zealanders, this nostalgic refrain from a 1990s Topp Twins song brings back one of the happiest memories of childhood. Calf Club Day – alternatively Calf and Lamb Day; Calf, Lamb and Kid Day or simply 'Ag' Day – was the special occasion in early summer when normal lessons were suspended at country schools. Pupils would rise early to groom their calf or lamb for the competitions ahead. Often the whole family would head to the school to see club members parade their pets, coax them through handling tests and answer questions about their care. It was a day of excitement and laughter, tears and triumph.

Calf clubs developed from the Boys' and Girls' Agricultural Clubs for animal rearing and crop growing that were established in the 1920s and that became a quintessential part of New Zealand rural life. One reason for their success was the immense importance of pets to country children. As Helen Wilson wrote, remembering her childhood on a Mackenzie Country sheep run in the 1870s, 'Nature, especially animal life, plays a large part in the life of the country child.'[1] Growing up, she had a number of 'special pets', including kittens and puppies, lambs, ponies, a piglet, a pigeon and a turkey hen. Her experience was shared by most children who lived in the backblocks. From 1888 many of them wrote to the *New Zealand Farmer*'s Uncle Ned, and favourite pets often featured in their letters. In 1928 the Correspondence School, which had started six years before to provide distance education for children beyond the reach of a school, began producing an annual magazine of pupils' schoolwork, *The Postman*. This, too, was filled with pet poems, stories, sketches and photographs.

In rural areas children were surrounded by animals, so caring for pets was natural, but it was also a way of dealing with isolation and boredom. Until well into the twentieth century most children in farming families had to help with such chores as milking and harvesting crops. Some of them were so far from a school that they had to be educated at home, while others walked or rode many miles over rough roads to and from classes. In an uneventful and often hard life, pleasures were few and simple – reading, games and sports with siblings and neighbouring children, perhaps an annual school picnic. Animals, particularly pet animals, were a major source of entertainment.

Country children often had more pets than their town cousins, and they had different pets. Along with the usual cats, dogs, rabbits and guinea pigs, they owned larger animals such as ponies, and also cared for baby farm animals such as lambs and calves. But there was a catch – the lambs and calves were usually temporary pets, reclaimed by the farmer once they were mature. This went against one of the unquestioned beliefs about pets – that they belonged to their owners for life – yet the children seemed to accept it.

~

Hand-rearing of baby animals was, and is, a seasonal farm job. Every year on sheep runs, farmers collected weak, orphan or twin lambs from the paddocks and brought them back to the farmhouse to feed until they were weaned or strong enough to return to their mothers. In dairying regions, farmers routinely slaughtered male calves, but some females were needed to replenish the herd, so they were hand-reared. It was more profitable to sell the cow's milk and give the calves a cheaper food substitute such as skim milk blended with oatmeal and linseed; lambs were fed a similar mixture.[2] Often a farmer's wife cared for young animals as part of her household duties.

The job was labour intensive, and to begin with, it was a hit-or-miss affair. In the 1870s Lady Mary Anne Barker declared that raising lambs was nearly impossible. Every year she succumbed to the temptation of rearing orphan merino lambs. If she came across one during her 'rambles' she would always want to take it home: 'Now who could turn away from a little helpless thing like that, who positively leaped into your arms and cuddled itself up in delight, sucking vigorously away at your glove, or anything handy?' She experimented with various feeding regimes, involving different combinations of cow's milk, oatmeal and sugar dispensed through a teapot. 'It must have been very ridiculous to a visitor, to see my dear little snowy pets going down on their front knees

It may be faded, but this snapshot is a marvel of composition. The photographer has managed to get two little boys and all their animal friends — pony, puppy, pet lamb, sheep dog and a rather long-suffering cat — into the frame. The boys are Cecil and Eric Elliot, and the setting is rural Waipukurau in August 1905. *Alexander Turnbull Library, Watt Collection. Reference: F-80446-1/2*

before me, and wagging their long tails furiously the moment the tea-pot was brought out.'³ Despite her efforts, all these lambs eventually died.

As knowledge of animal-rearing methods grew, however, there were some outstanding success stories. In the 1880s the shepherd's wife and female domestic servant on a Gisborne sheep run together raised 13 orphan lambs one season, feeding them through rubber tubing leading from a pail of milk. One of the lambs 'attached himself strongly to his new friends, and, not content with visiting them at regulation hours, he haunted the house, asking … "for luncheon, afternoon tea, or some meal or other at every hour of the day."' Toby the lamb came to be seen as 'a household pet' and would come into the parlour to greet visitors.⁴

Possibly because the task of caring for baby animals was so time consuming, it was often delegated to children. For some youngsters, the main incentive was the promise of money when the calf or lamb was ready for slaughter or incorporation in the herd. In the 1890s, in Lorna Monckton's family, the children got 2s and 6d for rearing an ordinary lamb, and 5s for a stud.⁵ Sarah Gadsby of Whenuakura reported to Uncle Ned in 1891 that she and her siblings had raised 22 lambs in the previous season, and sold them for a total of £20.⁶ Alice, of Springston in Canterbury, who raised a lamb in 1890, complained:

This photograph of a girl feeding two pet lambs was taken around 1907. The typically wagging tail of the front lamb is a blur.

Alexander Turnbull Library. Reference: F-151041-1/2

'Father is going to give me ten shillings for it, but I don't think it enough for the trouble I have taken with it. I don't think I shall ever rear any more.'[7] But for most children, animal rearing was not a chore. They thought of their charges as pets, giving them names, caring for them devotedly and playing with them.

Pet lambs became very tame, often following their owners around and butting them in play. They could be trained to do various tricks such as jumping hurdles and 'bull-fighting'. Parents were not always tolerant of these games, as Dorothy complained in 1892: 'I want my father to let me have a pet lamb, but he says they get too tame and come in the house.'[8] One such lamb was named Postman 'because he is always knocking at the door with his nose'.[9] Young children often looked after one or more pet lambs. In 1889, eight-year-old Maggie Burr, of Lismore in Canterbury, had four lambs: 'I reared them quite by myself. They are very tame, and like oats very much, and are always following me about hoping to get some.'[10] The following year she hand-reared seven lambs.[11] Calves also made rewarding pets. In 1891 Maggie wrote again, this time about her calf, Friska:

> I am very fond of her: I make her carry bundles of straw on her back. She is so tame that I could ride her if I wanted to. I have taught her to 'step foot,' and I pretended to milk her; she is very good and stands still. She will, I hope, be a nice, quiet cow, and perhaps I shall be able to really milk her some day – I can milk a little.[12]

By the early twentieth century, competitions for the best pet lambs and sheep had been introduced at some local A&P shows.[13] These were not the only, nor the first, junior events – before this time children could enter horse riding and jumping contests – but they were the first directly related to farm work and recognised the important role that children played in the rearing of young animals. In this respect they foreshadowed boys' and girls' agricultural clubs.

~

Mabel Smith of Taranaki milks a cow, with a pet lamb standing by. The wry title for this 1907 photograph, 'The pet lamb awaiting its turn', suggests how the antics of these appealing creatures provided endless amusement for farming families.

Alexander Turnbull Library, W.A. Collis Collection. Reference: G-6528-1/1. Photograph by William Andrews Collis

During the first two decades of the twentieth century, country children were still heavily involved in day-to-day farm tasks, but not as much as they had once been, thanks to such new labour-saving devices as milking machines. With better access to education they had more employment choices, and some began to leave for the towns. New Zealand's shift from a mainly rural to an urban society, which had begun in the 1890s and started to accelerate after World War I, was a source of anxiety for people in farming communities, who saw their settled way of life being disrupted.

Agricultural education was promoted as a way to interest children in farming. The editorial columns of the *New Zealand Farmer* and the *Farmers' Union Advocate* regularly asserted that that it was vital to recruit more farmers, arguing that primary industries were the source of the country's wealth.[14] In 1900 training in agriculture was introduced into the primary school curriculum. As few teachers in country schools were qualified to teach the subject, from 1908 Education Boards employed itinerant instructors to go around all the schools in their districts teaching agriculture and basic science. The arrangement was unsatisfactory because the areas involved were large and the numbers of instructors were few. Teaching of agriculture was, therefore, patchy.[15]

The time was ripe for the rise of children's agricultural clubs. The idea, which originated in North America, was proposed in New Zealand as early as 1912. That year George Buckeridge, an energetic Taranaki stock and station agent, travelled through the United States and Canada on his way back to New Zealand from England. On this trip he learned about the highly successful 4-H agricultural clubs: the four Hs stood for Head, Heart, Hands and Health. From the early 1900s farmer organisations first in the United States and later in Canada had established these clubs to teach children the basics of animal and crop farming, and to improve standards for the breeding and rearing of cattle. In the United States breed associations distributed heifer calves to boys and girls to rear, and when the animals were judged, the child who had raised the best calf received the prize of a loving cup.[16]

Back in New Zealand, Buckeridge became secretary and organiser to the Taranaki provincial executive of the Farmers' Union, and began pushing for the establishment of clubs through that forum and in the farming columns of the *Hawera and Normanby Star*.[17] The concept also gained supporters in other regions. In 1918 the Otago Expansion League ran a successful crop-growing competition for local boys which became an annual event.[18]

A selling point for agricultural clubs was that they fostered progressive ideas and techniques. The United States Department of Agriculture supported the 4-H clubs because its officials realised that, unlike many adults, children were prepared to experiment with farming innovations. When their parents saw how successful the new methods were, they would accept them. George Buckeridge echoed this reasoning, and also claimed that the clubs would encourage young country people to stay on the land by showing them how interesting and enjoyable farming work could be.[19]

The clubs may have promised fun for children, but for adults they were a serious matter. One earnest advocate was former member of the Otago Expansion League, W. Stuart Wilson, who in 1920 published *An Appeal to the Prince of Wales*, seeking royal endorsement for the idea of boys' and girls' agricultural clubs. These, he claimed, would not only promote 'national health as well as national wealth' and 'raise the standard of citizenship' but act as 'an insurance policy against slackness, haphazardness, drift and social unrest'. As if this was not ambitious enough, he suggested an even higher purpose:

> *This nation-building movement does deserve the whole-hearted encouragement of the Heir-Apparent to the Throne. His words during his great tour here have proved that he does wish to do everything within his power to strengthen the Empire. Here, then, is one great means to help him in this ideal, for which all classes of all countries of the Empire should strive in a mighty fellowship.*[20]

Wilson backed up his appeal with a petition to parliament, seeking a grant to support agricultural clubs, and in 1920 the government duly set aside a sum of £5000.[21]

~

Agricultural clubs were, however, very much the product of local enthusiasm. In South Taranaki, Buckeridge made converts and the Farmers' Union undertook to set up agricultural clubs in 1920. That year the Taranaki Education Board, teacher representatives and Department of Agriculture officials helped to organise clubs for the growing of root crops. In 1921 calf clubs began and soon spread to North Taranaki. Other dairy farming communities showed strong interest in the idea – the Tautari Boys' and Girls' Calf Club was established at Pukeatua, Waikato, in July 1921[22] – and the clubs quickly caught on in other districts.[23]

Although calf clubs operated out of school hours, they were usually based at local schools, sometimes the only meeting places in country districts, and often set up by school committees, whose members were mainly farmers. In some cases the initiative was taken by the teacher: one of the earliest calf clubs was established around 1921 by J.F. Crocker, schoolmaster at the Pipiroa School near Thames.[24] For teachers, the benefits of the clubs were obvious. Not only did they solve the problem of how best to teach agriculture, but they helped children to master other subjects such as reading, writing and arithmetic. Animal-rearing projects fostered observation and reporting skills by requiring children to keep careful records. On the judging day, club members had to be able to talk confidently and answer questions about their assignment. The clubs also secured crucial local support for the schools by involving the farming community. Parents or a pool of local farmers provided calf club members with newborn heifer calves.

The organisation of calf clubs evolved, and varied from district to district, but some features remained constant. Club members were usually primary school children aged nine or over, and they raised their animals over a period of three or four months. They had to note how often and what they fed their calf, and its general health and behaviour. In early days they also had to keep track of the cost of feed, and calves that were uneconomic to rear were disqualified from the competition.[25] Often there were different competition classes for pedigrees as well as ordinary 'grade' calves, and 'light' breeds such as Jerseys and Ayrshires were judged separately from 'heavy' breeds such as Friesians, Shorthorns and Red Polls.[26] The animals were carefully groomed and paraded on the competition day. Later, children were also supposed to train their calves, so that they could be led around a course – a challenge, as these animals could be quite difficult to handle and did not easily submit to being led by a strap or rope attached to a halter.

Some people had proposed that the clubs should be for boys only, but from the start girls could also join. This led to some interesting situations in the days when it was assumed that only boys could become farmers. In 1923, 15-year-old Una Scadden of Kokatau won the Wairarapa Calf-rearing Club's top prize – 'First competition won by girl' gasped a headline in one farming journal.[27]

The secret to the runaway success of the clubs was the eager support given by children themselves. The informal, self-directed learning of animal-rearing projects was probably a welcome novelty in the 1920s, when educational methods were still rigid, involving a lot of rote learning. The farming skills and knowledge taught by the clubs had an obvious practical application that country children could readily understand. Many club members clearly relished the element of competition. And the clubs tapped into, and deliberately exploited, a long tradition among country children of pet keeping and caring for baby farm animals. In 1922 Department of Agriculture official T.H. Patterson described the clubs' main goals: to stimulate and maintain the interest of children in calf rearing, to give them first-hand experience of the work and to foster a love of young farm animals. 'This is not difficult,' he concluded, 'because the instinct for pets is normally very strong in boys and girls.'[28]

~

At first, government support for agricultural clubs was low key. By 1924–25, however, the Department of Agriculture was actively promoting the clubs, providing money towards the cost of running them and helping to organise them in association with local farmers' groups and schools. There were now clubs in the Auckland, Taranaki, Wellington-West Coast, Wairarapa and Otago districts. In 1929–30, as the number of clubs and entries continued to grow, additional money was granted to fund prizes.[29]

Meanwhile, the Department of Education was warming to the idea. In his 1922 report the Minister of Education, C.J. Parr, noted that the clubs, which were supported by the department's travelling agricultural instructors, were of great assistance in teaching 'rural science'. By the end of the decade, school inspectors were commenting very favourably on the clubs and their educational uses.[30] In 1931 the Superintendent of Technical Education observed, 'The work has a very definite value in connection with the school courses, and forms a valuable link between the schools and the farming community.'[31]

In the late 1920s the Department of Agriculture began to find the running of the clubs burdensome, taking staff away from other vital work. The Depression led to funding cuts in 1930–31, forcing the department to withdraw most of its financial support to clubs.[32] In 1935, however, the Department of Education took over responsibility for the funding and organisation of the clubs, and a Labour government was elected. The idealistic new Minister of Education, Peter Fraser, and his like-minded Director of Education, Clarence Beeby, wanted to make schooling more appropriate to each child's abilities and circumstances, and as a result the needs of country children came under scrutiny. Agricultural clubs benefited from this. In 1936 the Education Department received additional money to develop them and it was not long before the Labour government was taking credit for their success.

After the Education Department became responsible for fostering Boys' and Girls' Agricultural Clubs, it began issuing certificates for all children who completed projects, with special ones for winners. In 1941 Peter Hodsell of Waipu District High School won this 'certificate of special merit' for coming third in the 'dairy type' competition.

Permission of Shirley Williams

Agricultural clubs really took hold from the mid-1930s, and more children began to participate, mainly because of vigorous promotion by the Department of Education.[33] In sheep and mixed farming districts, lamb competitions began, but at first the animals were judged simply as pets.[34] Later, similar rules to those for calf rearing applied to lamb-rearing assignments.[35] The range of projects expanded to include chickens, bees and pigs, and urban schools were given the opportunity to participate through home garden projects. In 1938 there was a total of 19,558 entries for club competitions.[36]

Club meetings were restructured so that members could also learn leadership skills and teamwork. Under the guidance of a teacher, children began to run the clubs themselves, electing a president, secretary, treasurer and committee. They organised meetings, which involved discussions about feeding, demonstrations of how to make halters, talks from experienced farmers and so on.[37] From this time, too, the handling and leading aspects of calf competitions, already well established, were given more emphasis. Sometimes children brought calves along to club meetings, proudly displaying their pets' leading abilities to admiring friends.[38]

In the early 1930s the clubs had been extended to 'Native Schools' – a separate educational system run for Maori children in rural areas with high Maori populations, such as the North Island's East Coast.[39] In one such district in 1932, 200 pupils in 13 schools were 'actively engaged in calf clubs or home plots' with the help of parents and teachers.[40] Forging strong links between school and home was an aspect of Native School policy, which sought to influence the opinions and habits of Maori adults so they would adopt Pakeha ways. Another aim was to encourage Maori boys to become farmers.[41] The clubs became as popular as they were in Pakeha farming communities, and in 1936, in a move that signalled the beginnings of wider changes, Native and European schools joined together in the Mangonui District Calf Club organisation in Northland.[42]

Calf Club Day soon became a hugely popular annual fixture at country schools. It was a festive social occasion, attended by everyone in the district. In addition to the animal events there were often other competitions, fund-raising stalls and displays of woodwork, handcrafts, flower arranging and school work. Judges often came from other farming areas, and since many of them also adjudicated for A&P shows, local farmers were keen to listen in to their comments and advice. A 1947 report on calf club days in the Wanganui–Main Trunk Division remarked:

> *Despite the wet and unfavourable season, most of the calves were produced in splendid condition – a credit to their owners and a proof of the interest and effort expended in their rearing. It is indeed satisfying to see the quiet pride and confidence of the youthful owners as they parade their charges as well as to note the increasing interest of the parents in the whole movement.*[43]

Taranaki had a three-tier system of competition. The first stage was the school Calf Club Day, where entrants vied for first prize in categories such as 'best reared', 'best led' and 'dairy type' (an assessment of a calf's suitability to be part of a dairy herd). The next stage was the group or interschool competition, where school winners in an area competed against each other. Finally, the best of the bunch were judged in a district-wide championship. These competitions took place over several months, usually October through to early December.[44] From 1926 until 1950 schools throughout the country battled it out for the coveted Henry A. Lane Challenge Shield, awarded to the school with the most points from group and district competitions and the pet lamb and calf events at A&P shows.[45]

~

When describing agricultural clubs, public servants and politicians often talked grandly of 'the movement' – an expression that suggests both moral and educational purpose. They frequently claimed that the clubs would promote good citizenship and occasionally mentioned their role in encouraging kindness to animals. According to one agricultural instructor, 'The child who rears a calf properly, who cares for it almost from its birth, and who sees how the animal responds to good and kindly treatment, is not likely to look upon the cow as

East Coast Maori children were enthusiastic participants in school agricultural clubs. These children and their calves lined up in the grounds of Tikitiki School, north of Gisborne, on Calf Club Day around 1948. *Alexander Turnbull Library, J. Kaa Collection. Reference: PAColl-3417-1*

a mere money-making machine and the work connected with it as irksome drudgery.'[46]

This emphasis on kindness to animals may have owed something to developments in urban schools in the 1920s and 1930s. SPCAs revitalised and expanded their education programmes between the world wars, in partnership with mainly town and city schools. F.W. Meadowcroft emphasised the importance of school anti-cruelty education in his presidential address to the 1920 annual general meeting of the Wellington SPCA: 'It is at school that children get their first impression of life and of what is right and good, and these form the basis of character. The vitally important work for us is the humane education of the boys and girls who are to be future citizens of this Dominion.'[47]

In the Wellington provincial district, SPCA 'junior leagues' were established in primary schools from 1920, and the idea was also taken up in Auckland. The Wellington SPCA provided local leagues with monthly parcels of pamphlets on the care and treatment of animals, and copies of an English publication called *Little Animals' Friend*.[48] In 1928 several Auckland schools held a pet day – an idea that began to grow in popularity around this time.[49] Teachers were further encouraged to promote humane education when, in 1925, the *School Journal*

The Wellington SPCA drew on its long-established vice-regal connections when it enlisted the help of Mary Monckton, a daughter of Governor-General Viscount Galway, in 1939. She provided a signed photograph of herself with her horse and dog for distribution to members of the Wellington SPCA junior leagues, and it was also used in an edition of *Pets: Their care in sickness and health*, an SPCA-produced pet care manual.

Alexander Turnbull Library, SPCA Wellington Inc. Records. Reference: 89-238-1/08

published articles on kindness to animals. As well as emphasising how wrong cruelty was, these gave detailed instructions for children on how to care properly for their pets. SPCAs were delighted: the Otago society made a point of writing to thank the *Journal* editor.[50]

Economic depression led to the demise of Wellington's SPCA junior leagues in the early 1930s, but they were revived in 1935. This time they targeted secondary rather than primary age children, because 'while in their teens girls and boys are able to take a wider view and to feel an interest in the welfare of animals quite outside the domestic circle'.[51] Pets, however, remained an important teaching aid for the leagues. A booklet produced for members, entitled *Pets: Their care in sickness and health*, was so popular it went through three editions.[52] An annual essay competition started in the early 1930s, and within a few years set topics included 'Day from a dog's diary' and 'An animal I have known'.[53]

Older children often took an intelligent interest in the SPCA's welfare and rescue activities. In 1940, for instance, the Wellington East Girls' College league wrote to the Wellington SPCA expressing concern at a recent case when two injured dogs had not been treated because they were unregistered, and offering to pay for the treatment of such animals in future. Another junior league wrote to the secretary of the New York SPCA in 1939, enquiring about a scheme to license cats in some American cities.[54] The Wellington leagues also contributed a significant amount of money towards the fund for building a city clinic to treat sick and injured animals. At Wellington Girls' College, league fund-raising ideas for 1939 included a competition between school houses, a Deanna Durbin contest, a garden party in association with the Red Cross, an amateur pet photography contest, a staff vs sixth form basketball match, drawing and poetry competitions, a poster drawing competition, a pet show, a competition for the best collection of native plants, and a competition for the best entertainer (time allowed: five minutes).[55]

The Wellington SPCA junior leagues made some inroads into country districts. In the early 1920s there were leagues at Pleckville School at Eketahuna, Hihitahi School at Taihape, Levin School, Carnarvon, Waiata and Kiwitea Schools at Feilding, and Rakaunui School at Pahiatua.[56] In fact the teacher responsible for the league at the Hihitahi School, Miss A.M. Orr, was the driving force behind establishment of junior leagues in Auckland, and made special trips there to organise distribution of leaflets to schools.[57]

When the secondary school leagues started in the late 1930s, the Wellington-based Correspondence School also set up a branch that soon became known as the Animal Welfare Club. Hugely popular with isolated country children, it continued until the early 1970s. Initially, its aim was to drive home 'the realization that our animal friends are worthy of all the care and consideration we can give them'.[58] A few of the children who joined the club won prizes in SPCA essay competitions, and in 1939 one member, James Mossman, was so keen he started an animal welfare club in his district. 'These young folk are going to do all they can to look after the animals they see around them,' *The Postman* announced proudly.[59] Summaries of the club's activities show, however, that it was mainly a forum for swapping stories about pets and information about pet care. Children could borrow magazines and books from an extensive library, and made up scrapbooks about animals, including their own pets, which were circulated to other members. *The Postman* published numerous extracts and photographs from members' correspondence, and these were almost all about pets.

~

This focus on pets and pet keeping rather than the prevention of cruelty was understandable. Many aspects of urban animal welfare work were irrelevant to country children, and in any case, school teachings on kindness to animals conflicted with some of the farming practices children witnessed at home. One of these provided a stark contrast to the calf clubs. The glory days of the animal-rearing projects, the 1930s, coincided with a boom in the 'bobby calf' trade, which had become a major export industry in the late 1920s. Bobby calves were the calves, usually male, surplus to requirements on the dairy farm, that were sent to the freezing works to be slaughtered soon after birth. SPCAs in New Zealand were united in their opposition to the trade, particularly once the Federation of SPCAs was established in 1933.[60] According to one SPCA pamphlet, 'An English visitor, after travelling through Auckland and Taranaki during the "bobby calf" season, declared that New Zealand was surely the cruellest country in the world.'[61]

In June 1935 John Howell, a leading light in the Wellington SPCA and the SPCA Federation, gave a radio talk about the society's work, in which he described the treatment of bobby calves:

> *The facts are – that calves are taken from their mothers at birth; they may or may not be handfed for a few days; are often tied up at a fence and left without any food or shelter in the worst of our winter and spring weather; are then despatched, generally by two means of transport, – first, lorry, and then railway truck, to a distant freezing works, it may be spending over 24 hours in transit and again without food or shelter; are then slaughtered as soon as the works can do so with convenience though this may mean hours of waiting in the yard, and perhaps through the night or even over the week end. It needs little imagination to realise the immense volume of suffering caused to the half million newly born calves treated in this way in our dairying districts; while those who live near, or have cause to travel on our railway lines on certain days of the week during the calving season all the way from Otaki to North Taranaki, and all through the Waikato, have heard the piteous crying of these suffering animals all day long.*[62]

No doubt, in many farming households the radio was snapped off at this point. But children growing up on dairy farms must have been well aware of the difference in treatment of those calves that had a future use on the farm and those that did not.

The claim that sympathy for animals was a desirable trait in those who intended to become farmers was, for some observers, rather unconvincing. Also, it seemed to sit uneasily with another aim of the animal-rearing clubs – to improve farming and in particular calf-raising methods.[63] From the start, the clubs demanded a scientific, objective and detached attitude from their members. Children had to absorb and understand facts about the breed of the animal they were rearing. They were assessed on their ability to answer questions about animal science, and on the quality of their record-keeping. The calves and lambs they reared were judged as farm animals.

Yet the clubs deliberately fostered the development of a close bond between child and the calf or lamb. Children were expected to name their animal and, as well as feeding it, were advised to groom it often. They had to tame it so it would come when called, obey commands and follow when led. Although the term 'pet' was rarely used in official files in the 1920s, 1930s and 1940s, children were tacitly encouraged to view their calf or lamb in this way.[64] By the 1960s club instructions were more explicit about the need to gain the animal's trust: 'Be kind to your calf. Be wise, be firm when necessary, but above all be gentle. You want your calf to be your friend.'[65] In the early 1980s the word 'pet'

Competitions for lamb rearing were held at A&P shows from the early twentieth century, and soon novelty events were introduced. These youngsters won places in a lamb competition at a 1947 show. Their lambs are dressed in costume — one, unawares, carries the sign 'Food for Britain'. *Alexander Turnbull Library. Reference: C-14060-1/2*

appeared in a Waikato Education Board guide to rearing calves and lambs.[66]

There is no doubt that many children formed a strong attachment to their lamb or calf. Those who took part in the clubs over the years regularly used the word 'pet' when reflecting on the experience, and recalled how they loved and cared for their lamb or calf.[67] In 1939 *The Postman* published 'My Calf', an essay by Ian Lawson of Pukeoware about his pet calf Monica, a roan grade Shorthorn. Ian explained in detail how diligently he looked after Monica: he built her a sleeping house of sacking close to home and hand-fed her several times a day on a mixture of new milk, skimmed milk and a stock food called Moose Meal. He oiled her hooves, washed, brushed and combed her, and covered her to keep her clean and warm. As a result of this treatment, he claimed, 'She soon learnt to obey me and I love her, and can tell she loves me better than anyone.'

Feels Like Calf Club Day

By the late 1950s, when Graeme Wright received his certificate for completing his calf-rearing project (and coming first in handling and leading), Department of Education project certificates had been redesigned to depict the various activities of the clubs.

Permission of Graeme Wright

Monica went on to win first prize for Grade Heavy Breed and first prize for Condition Class at the Pukeoware Calf Club Parade in 1938, and second place in both categories at the area finals. 'I was very proud of her,' wrote Ian. 'She was so good.'[68]

Officially, the emphasis on developing rapport with the animal and taming it was presented as a means to an economic end: as one Department of Agriculture organiser put it, a calf 'well looked after and handled as a youngster will grow into an animal which will be a source of profit and a pride to its owner'.[69] Docile animals were easier to milk and manage. But for many children, caring for their animal was an end in itself. Perhaps the grooming and training aspects of club competitions were retained and developed because children responded so well to them — because, in the words of T.H. Patterson, they had 'the instinct for pets'.

~

'The highlight of the school year' is a phrase often used by those remembering Calf Club Day in the post-war decades. Excitement mounted as the day of competition drew near. Ross Matheson, who had pet calves

144 *Creature Comforts*

A warm calf made a comfortable pillow to lie on, as many children discovered. This boy is relaxing with his calf, probably in the 1950s or 1960s.

Permission of Horowhenua Historical Society Inc.

in the 1950s, recalled, 'The grooming, feeding and leading were no longer a chore. On the Saturday before the big day we took our calves to the cowshed for a shampoo. They smelt so nice afterwards. We brushed the halters with sandshoe whitener, hoping that would give our calves an edge over the opposition.'[70] Lambs, too, were shampooed, and sometimes laundry blue was put in their coats to make them totally white – a practice later frowned on.

The day itself was a mixture of serious purpose and fun, as overawed calves refused to be led despite efforts at persuasion, or pet lambs bolted and had to be caught by athletic stewards. There was the sense of accomplishment and pride in competing, and for some, the joy of winning. The memory was still vivid for Shirley Campbell half a century later:

> *I had several calves over the years, the last year at primary school I was in luck winning the champion ribbon with my calf Trixie. I was so thrilled when the purple and white ribbon was draped around her neck, I ran to get my mother to come and admire her and when we arrived back, the calf tied up next to mine was happily chewing the ribbon to bits!*[71]

From early on, prizes were important. At first some schools offered cash prizes or sacks of calf feed.[72] Once the Education Department became involved, it issued certificates to all competitors, with special certificates for winners, and from the late 1940s awarded badges of achievement for three and five years' work.[73] Some schools had their own challenge trophies and ribbons, and others went even further, offering a range of desirable items as prizes. Ivy Hunter, describing the Waiau Pa School Calf Club in the years following World War II, recalled: 'The 1st, 2nd and 3rd place getters at Calf Club could select their prizes. A table was set out with pocket-knives, torches, beautiful bone china and glassware.'[74]

During the 1930s and 1940s, when the agricultural club system reached heights of popularity, children (and their parents) were highly competitive, since winning prizes reflected well on the family and its farming know-how. From the late 1940s and 1950s the clubs focused more on learning and having fun.[75] When children of non-farming families began attending rural schools on the outskirts of towns and cities, pet parades were introduced in addition to animal-rearing competitions at some Calf Club Days.[76] Events such as 'best dressed lamb', where lambs competed wearing fanciful costumes, became crowd-pleasers. These events brought the club competition days closer in feeling to the pet days that were keenly anticipated annual events at some urban schools.

In the post-war years a steady decline in the rural population also led to a decrease in the numbers of country schools. Developments in educational administration, including the abolition of Education Boards and the Education Department from 1989, spelled the end of government support for agricultural clubs.[77] During the 1990s more isolated rural schools closed. Through this period of change, a few long-established calf clubs survived, sometimes funded by a local A&P association or sponsored by businesses.[78] But as more people bought 'lifestyle' blocks near towns and cities there was a revival of Calf Club Day – often billed as Lamb, Calf and Kid Day to include the offspring of goats, which were more likely to be kept on such properties. Poultry-raising competitions were included for the same reason.[79]

The day's events remained much the same. For lambs and calves there were three sections to compete in: 'leading', 'calling' and 'care and attention'. At some schools, lambs competed in the 'high jump' – a test of their ability to walk on a ramp. Kids went through the 'obstacle course', where they showed off their aptitude for climbing hills and negotiating slaloms. Lambs were judged on the quality of their wool and calves on their suitability as beef or dairy cattle. Children answered questions on the care of their animal. And 'care' was defined broadly – for example in 2005 at Wainui School, South Kaipara, an award was made for 'most obvious pet'.[80]

~

Codie White of Waikato is pictured with her calf Buddie and most but not all of the prize ribbons and trophies they won during calf club season in 2011. Their highest achievement that year was winning the Champion Calf Rearing Cup and the Champion Child and Calf Effort Shield at the Waikato Royal Show. Codie competed with a different calf each year from the age of five until she turned 12. Typically the season began in August when Codie chose her calf, about a week after it was born. She would then spend around two hours with it each day, feeding, grooming and training it to lead. Competitions would begin at Matamata in October and finish at Te Kauwhata in December. Once the season was over, the calf would be returned to the herd but Codie would visit it regularly to check on its progress and pet it.

Permission of Codie and Kim White

So what happened to all the carefully groomed calves and lambs after the big day of competition? Some lambs were kept on as pet sheep – a practice that stretched back to the nineteenth century.[81] Calves, too, could remain pets. Sometimes the same animals were paraded at calf club competitions repeatedly, in the yearling, two-year heifer and mature cow classes.[82] Most animals, however, joined the ordinary farm stock. Usually, once the competition was over, the calf was returned to the farmer or the parent who donated it, for inclusion in their herd. When calf clubs started in Taranaki, the calves were auctioned at the end of the competition and each child received the difference between their calf's original price and the auction price.[83] Pigs had a more unfortunate fate if the terms used to describe stages in pig-rearing competitions of the early 1950s are anything to go by: the animal was to be reared to 'porker' weight for judging in December or as a 'baconer' for judging in February.[84]

For some children, having to give up their pet, or, worse, seeing it sent off to the freezing works by an unsympathetic parent, resulted in a lasting sense of betrayal. Trena Marshall's calf, Lindy, joined the dairy herd after winning a ribbon at the Tatuanui Calf Club Day in the mid-1960s, but remained her special pet for years. Her memories of the day she found out Lindy had been 'culled' from the herd remained traumatic: 'I still think of her going in the truck to the works. I hate the idea of that.'[85] Other children, served roast pet lamb, went off eating meat. In 2011 fashion designer Holly McQuillan recalled, 'I ate my pet lamb Pinky, who I won calf and lamb day with, but I didn't know it till afterwards. I wasn't happy about that so I went vegetarian.'[86]

Other children, however, were more reconciled to the situation. Many raised a number of animals while at primary school, cheerfully taking on a new one each year. Some of the names they gave them showed a down-to-earth awareness of the animal's role on the farm. Calling a calf Milkyway, a lamb Roast or a chicken Kentucky was a light-hearted way for children to acknowledge their pet's probable destiny.[87] If the daily chore of feeding and grooming

Not so easily led

'THE CALF should be trained to lead freely and stylishly,' proclaimed some 1946 guidelines for calf-rearing competitions in Taranaki. 'If the calf is trained regularly from the start it should not require pushing, pulling or hitting on judging day.'[94] But this was easier said than done, as many children discovered. Attempting to lead a calf was quite a problem if the calf had other ideas.

To insure against problems under pressure, children practised determinedly. Shirley Campbell of Whananaki, a coastal settlement in Northland, recalled how in the 1940s she and her friends would lead their calves 'up and down the beach and over the dunes'.[95] Jenny James of Waiau Pa, south of Auckland, remembered her cold red hands and nose and the crunching of icy grass under her gumboots as she trained her calf on frosty mornings in the 1960s.[96]

Even after careful preparations, things could go badly wrong on the day. Jenny James described one girl leading her calf round the ring 'when it decided enough and sat down. Everyone thought it very funny when her very physical persuasion would not make it get up at all!' Grace Hamilton had a similar memory of a competition in 1944: 'The leading of the calves was entertaining to viewers, with a calf running away, then others had to be pushed and pulled round the parade area.'[97]

Lynda Hallinan experienced the ultimate disaster when her prize calf, Flac, was within sight of winning the leading trophy at the Onewhero Area School's Calf Club Day in 1987:

> We zigzagged through the line of fencing standards, trotted over the bridge and executed a perfect 360-degree turn at the gate. Victory was so close I could smell it, but Flac could smell something else: the fresh mown school athletics field. We were on the home stretch when, without warning, she went down … rolled in the cut grass and rolled out of contention.[98]

had become a burden, the departure of the animal might be greeted with a mixture of regret and relief. Alex McEwing, who reared calves as a member of the Northern Wairoa Boys' and Girls' Agricultural Club in the 1960s, 'was both happy (don't have that to do any more) and sad because we had become mates'.[88] And if the animal became more aggressive as it aged, as did happen with some sheep and cattle, children might not object to eating it for dinner.

Whatever their feelings, country children generally understood that the lambs and calves they raised were herd animals and would be ultimately returned to the paddocks. In 1920, for instance, one little girl called Tui told the *New Zealand Farmer*, 'I saw my last year's pet lamb some weeks ago for the first time since I turned her out: she had grown a lot, and she still knew me.'[89] Beverley Hodder, who with her siblings raised eight pet lambs in 1939, expressed similar acceptance in *The Postman*: 'About a week after Christmas they went back to the farm. When we go riding round the sheep with Daddy or go for walks we sometimes see them.'[90] Grace Hamilton, who reared a Jersey calf named Mary for Waiau Pa Calf Club in the 1940s, stated matter-of-factly, 'Soon the day was over, the excitement had ceased, and Mary was returned to her paddock to live a normal life.'[91] And Margaret O'Connor, who entered lambs and calves in Waimea Boys' and Girls' Agricultural Club competitions in the 1960s, remarked, 'Our animals, because we lived on a farm, simply became part of the stock … [it] seemed to me that's just what happened. Pragmatic I guess.'[92]

These attitudes were probably learned at home rather than at school, but in some ways animal-rearing clubs reinforced them. Club structures and rules, while encouraging a close bond with the animal, also helped young members to recognise that the relationship was to be a short-term one. The set pattern of the rearing projects, culminating in a final ceremonial day, prepared children to say goodbye to their pets.

For country children animal rearing was an early lesson in the reality of farming life, a reminder that lambs and calves were not 'forever friends' but pets for just one season. One child, writing for *The Postman* in 1933, summed this up in a wistful poem:

I named my pet lamb, Cuthbert Tim
He loves me and I love him,
But in the paddock all the day
He loves to frisk, and jump, and play.

Cuthbert Tim will have to go
Away from here, he's growing so;
But how I'll miss my Cuthbert Tim
For he loves me, and I love him.[93]

This painting of a New Zealand mounted soldier of the South African War, entitled *A Tight Corner*, depicts the heroic horse in action. Such horses were rarely used in fighting, but rather to get troops close to the battlefield and away again swiftly. One man, designated a horse-holder, would stand out of the line of fire, ready to bring the horses forward when they were needed. They could then be used for a speedy – and sometimes nerve-wracking – escape.

Alexander Turnbull Library. Reference: A-256-002.
Chromolithograph by G. Montbard

Chapter 7
From *helpers* to *heroes*

As life returned to normal after the devastation of World War I, British Prime Minister David Lloyd George famously promised to create 'a land fit for heroes'. It was an inspirational slogan that echoed in the furthest corners of the empire. F.W. Meadowcroft, president of the Wellington SPCA, borrowed it when he addressed the society's annual general meeting in 1920, but there may have been a slight stir when he continued: 'If only because of the enormous debt we owe to the animals for their help in the recent war, we must recognise them also as among the heroes, and see to it that this country is more fit for them to live in the future.'[1]

Mr Meadowcroft's provocative speech was a sign of things to come. Wars of the twentieth century prompted a fundamental shift in people's understanding of what animals could offer. In time of war, animals were needed for various practical tasks, both familiar and new, but the comfort they gave was even more essential. As historian Hilda Kean has observed, they were 'ciphers of sanity in an insane world'.[2]

~

In traditional warfare animals, especially horses, were regarded as an expendable resource. Throughout the British Empire horses were used in military operations and law enforcement for transport, patrolling and crowd control. In New Zealand they played a limited part in wars between Pakeha and Maori from the 1840s to the 1860s, and Armed Constabulary forces and police later relied on them, but they were not truly put to the test.³ This changed when, from the end of the nineteenth century, large numbers of horses were sent to overseas wars.

At the outset of the 1899–1902 South African War, Premier Richard Seddon offered to send a mounted contingent to support the British. Before the war's end, a further nine contingents were raised, the third and fourth of which were known as the Rough Riders because they comprised accomplished horsemen. Over 8000 horses were sent to South Africa during this first major overseas war in which New Zealanders took part. Some were gifts from patriotic citizens, others were supplied by the government and many were owned by the volunteers themselves.⁴ After their long journey these horses had little time to acclimatise and suffered in the harsh conditions, especially during long treks. Many were killed, died of disease or had to be destroyed. Only one was permitted by military authorities to return home.⁵

The prominent role of horses in the war, however, changed the way many people thought about them. These faithful steeds carried their riders across dusty miles of veldt, into battle, and away to safety. They helped to shape the national image of New Zealanders as both skilled horsemen and natural soldiers.⁶ They also earned the respect and affection of the mounted soldiers: bonds forged in battle were strong. One man, forced to hand over his 'trusty mare' to a new owner at the conclusion of the war, confessed he 'felt like shedding tears'.⁷

In 1914 New Zealand again responded to the call of empire by sending troops of civilian volunteers – and later conscripts – to fight alongside Britain and its allies in campaigns at Gallipoli, in France, Belgium and Germany, and in Sinai–Palestine. And once again, at the outbreak of hostilities, more than 1400 horses were donated by New Zealand citizens. Another 9300 were purchased, while mounted troopers usually supplied their own horses. Some of these animals went to the Western Front in Europe, where they often suffered from mange in the cold conditions, or were injured by shards of metal concealed in the mud. Most, however, were sent to the Middle East where they had to endure extreme desert heat, disease and the terrors of being shelled and bombed from the air.⁸

During and after the war it was a common boast that New Zealand horses were the hardiest and most suited to desert warfare.⁹ They were also, according to one writer, the best loved. In *The New Zealanders in Sinai and Palestine*, published in 1922, Lieutenant-Colonel C. Guy Powles described the joyful reunion of the New Zealand men with their horses in Egypt after the Gallipoli campaign:

Our Main Body men were horse-lovers by nature, for had they not volunteered and in very many cases brought their own horse? And they were now horse-lovers by conviction born of active experience. They had learned that to no man is a horse so essential as to the mounted soldier. His horse is more than a friend, he is part of the soldier's very life.[10]

Many were the stories of New Zealand troops going to great lengths to retain favourite mounts and making sacrifices to water, feed and tend their horses in adverse conditions. The cooperation established between the horses and their riders while under fire became legendary.

Despite their vital contribution, however, most of the New Zealanders' horses met a sad end. Some that had served in the Middle East were given to occupying forces, but others were sold locally or destroyed on military orders. In February 1919 one trooper wrote, 'The day has come. I lose my horse tonight at 12 midnight. He goes to Moascar into a general remount depot … My very best friend in this land he has been … May he strike a soft job or die soon, for I love him very much.'[11] Often horses did not in fact strike a soft job, but were sold to Egyptians who starved and worked them to death. Aware of this possibility, some New Zealand soldiers preferred to see their horses shot along with those deemed too old or unfit. But helping to destroy their trusted mounts was a bitter experience:

> *It seemed awfully sad that these poor old faithful creatures, after suffering from thirst, hunger and fatigue and carrying heavy loads for hundreds of miles, should have to end their days by being shot down by the very people they had so faithfully served … I can tell you, it made some of us very miserable for some time afterwards, the memory of those lines of bodies lying stark in the desert, faithful unto death.*[12]

Just four horses were shipped back to New Zealand.[13] Powles's Bess was the only horse to leave with the main body of troops and return home. Born in Martinborough in 1910, she was given to Powles when he embarked on overseas service in 1914. She remained with him for the next six years, in Egypt, Sinai, Palestine and France, and after the war in Germany and England. Bess lived out her days at Flock House, Manawatu, where Powles became headmaster. After she died in 1934 he erected a plinth in her honour, which came to be seen as a memorial to all horses that had served in the war. In later years Anzac Day services were held there, with riders on horseback in attendance, and it is now registered as a Category 1 Historic Place by the New Zealand Historic Places Trust.[14]

New Zealand soldiers were not alone in regarding their horses as comrades in arms. The British often depicted the faithful war horse in paintings and poems, and New Zealand publications reproduced some of these. For example, in August 1917 the *School Journal*, which was especially active in informing its young readers of the contributions of animals to the war effort, printed 'The Soldier's Kiss', a poem by Henry Chappell that described, in highly emotive terms, a soldier's farewell to his dying horse. According to a note preceding the poem, it was based on an actual incident in southern Flanders.[15] Such portrayals were used to encourage donations to organisations like the London-based Blue Cross, which raised money to care for sick and wounded horses. In New Zealand, several local SPCAs donated or collected money for this and similar causes during the war.[16]

~

Other working animals served in the war, often, like horses, providing both practical help and companionship. And they too were used in propaganda intended to boost the morale of both soldiers and civilians. Military forces relied on local donkeys, pack mules and camels to carry equipment and supplies and to transport casualties. Such animals could also become the focus of affectionate attention. For example, the donkeys used for carting water and food and carrying injured men down Shrapnel Gully to Anzac Cove at Gallipoli under heavy fire were petted by the men, who gave them names and fed them biscuits when they could.[17] Accounts of the ambulance work were published in Australian and New Zealand newspapers, and soon the faithful little donkey carrying a wounded soldier on its back came to symbolise dutiful sacrifice.

Homing pigeons that carried messages on the battlefield also helped to bolster spirits – they were characterised as 'brave', 'gallant' and even 'heroic'. In 1918 the *School Journal* reported that 350 New Zealand pigeons had been sent to the Western Front in France, and published a photograph of an army truck with an attached pigeon loft. 'When a bird returns, it steps on a board as it enters the loft. Its weight rings a bell, which is heard by the soldier guarding the loft. Thus he knows a little messenger has returned, and at once sends the paper roll to headquarters.'[18]

Dogs also assisted the war effort in various ways. In trench warfare, Red Cross ambulance dogs located wounded men. Wearing bells around their necks so their progress could be traced, they were sent out into no man's land after a battle. When they found a fallen soldier they whined to summon a stretcher bearer.[19] Large dogs transported food and munitions, carried messages and acted as scouts and trench sentries. They won great admiration: as the *School Journal* remarked, 'The dog, the "friend of man" in peace, has proved his faithful ally in war.'[20] A New Zealand bulldog named Caesar was trained as a Red Cross dog and helped to locate wounded soldiers during the Battle of the Somme in 1916. A favourite with both the men and the nurses, he died after being shot in the chest.[21]

~

In a few war memorials, family pets symbolise both the freedoms being fought for and the sacrifice of servicemen and women. This relief sculpture by Richard Gross on the Wellington Cenotaph, unveiled in 1932, depicts the wrench of farewell as soldiers leave their homes to go to war. Sorrowing parents, wives and children cling to their departing loved ones. A dog and a cat also wordlessly entreat them to stay, their presence suggesting the familiar domestic comforts that are being left behind.
Photograph by Jock Phillips

Caesar's role was at first ceremonial. A soldier's pet, he became official mascot of the 4th Battalion (A Company) of the New Zealand Rifle Brigade, and led the battalion's parade down Queen Street in Auckland before its departure overseas. Military mascots were nothing new. Units of the British army had always kept them: some regiments that came to New Zealand to suppress Maori resistance to colonial rule from the 1840s onward adopted animal mascots.[22] So did New Zealand troops in the South African war: Bushie, a dog from Auckland, accompanied men into battle.[23]

During World War I, however, mascots became even more popular. New Zealand and Australian troops were particularly keen on them: a London reporter in Egypt commented, 'One could almost stack a menagerie with the numerous animals that are treasured as mascots by the New Zealanders and Australians.'[24] A cat, a goat, a donkey and many dogs were adopted by New Zealand troops. Some, like Caesar, travelled with soldiers from New Zealand. Others were simply strays picked up in the course of campaigns. After winning over the men, they gradually gained official acceptance.[25]

Traditionally, mascots embodied the spirit of a unit. They were thought to bring good luck, and featured in the superstitions that soldiers relied on to give themselves a sense of control in situations where sudden death was a constant possibility.[26] For many New Zealanders, and Australians, used to working alongside animals, mascots were no doubt a reminder of a familiar way of life. But mascots also helped to create a sense of normality in abnormal situations:

providing company, entertaining the men with tricks and giving comfort through their physical presence. In effect, they were communal pets, and pets were strongly associated with home and family. New Zealand soldiers, thousands of miles from their homes, must have found mascots particularly reassuring.

Because of strict quarantine regulations in both Britain and New Zealand, few animals sent to overseas theatres of war returned.[27] The effort made by one regiment to get its mascot home says much about the sentimental importance of these animals. In 1919 members of the Wellington Regiment, including Lieutenant-Colonel W.H. Cunningham, tried to organise the repatriation of their mascot, an Irish terrier called Paddy. He had been with the regiment right through the war, leaving with the Main Body of the New Zealand Expeditionary Force and accompanying the men in Egypt, at Gallipoli and in France, Belgium and Germany, finally ending up in England after the Armistice.

Paddy's return was thwarted when a rabies outbreak in England forced New Zealand to ban the import of all dogs from there. After high-level negotiations, the Department of Agriculture agreed to make an exception for Paddy, as long as he was given to the Wellington Zoo. Cunningham, who had intended to provide a home for 'the old dog', reluctantly endorsed this plan. In 1921 he wrote, 'I hope we shall see the old chap out here again. He is getting on in years and it would be a pity if he died overseas.'[28] But by late 1922, when arrangements had been finalised, Paddy was getting frail and deaf, and Jennetta Campbell Rogers of Devon, who had been entrusted with his care, appealed against him being sent on a long voyage.

Paddy remained in Devon, and when he finally died in 1929, Mrs Campbell Rogers returned his collar to his old comrades. She wrote:

I should like the Regiment to know that 'Paddy's' last years (he must have been quite 16 when he died a short time ago) were as happy as care and kindness could make them, and when his infirmities of age increased and life was becoming a burden, he was put to sleep, leaving many sad hearts behind. He was a well-known character, and his war service made him an heroic figure.[29]

Paddy, the Wellington Regiment mascot, wears his special coat with sergeant's stripes at a troop inspection by Prime Minister William Massey at Vauchelles, France, on 30 June 1918. Paddy left New Zealand with the regiment and accompanied the men throughout World War I.

Alexander Turnbull Library, Royal New Zealand Returned and Services' Association Collection. Reference: G-13312-1/2. Photograph by Henry Armytage Sanders

~

In a few war memorials, family pets symbolise both the freedoms being fought for and the sacrifice of servicemen and women. This relief sculpture by Richard Gross on the Wellington Cenotaph, unveiled in 1932, depicts the wrench of farewell as soldiers leave their homes to go to war.

Sorrowing parents, wives and children cling to their departing loved ones. A dog and a cat also wordlessly entreat them to stay, their presence suggesting the familiar domestic comforts that are being left behind.

Photograph by Jock Phillips

Caesar's role was at first ceremonial. A soldier's pet, he became official mascot of the 4th Battalion (A Company) of the New Zealand Rifle Brigade, and led the battalion's parade down Queen Street in Auckland before its departure overseas. Military mascots were nothing new. Units of the British army had always kept them: some regiments that came to New Zealand to suppress Maori resistance to colonial rule from the 1840s onward adopted animal mascots.[22] So did New Zealand troops in the South African war: Bushie, a dog from Auckland, accompanied men into battle.[23]

During World War I, however, mascots became even more popular. New Zealand and Australian troops were particularly keen on them: a London reporter in Egypt commented, 'One could almost stack a menagerie with the numerous animals that are treasured as mascots by the New Zealanders and Australians.'[24] A cat, a goat, a donkey and many dogs were adopted by New Zealand troops. Some, like Caesar, travelled with soldiers from New Zealand. Others were simply strays picked up in the course of campaigns. After winning over the men, they gradually gained official acceptance.[25]

Traditionally, mascots embodied the spirit of a unit. They were thought to bring good luck, and featured in the superstitions that soldiers relied on to give themselves a sense of control in situations where sudden death was a constant possibility.[26] For many New Zealanders, and Australians, used to working alongside animals, mascots were no doubt a reminder of a familiar way of life. But mascots also helped to create a sense of normality in abnormal situations:

providing company, entertaining the men with tricks and giving comfort through their physical presence. In effect, they were communal pets, and pets were strongly associated with home and family. New Zealand soldiers, thousands of miles from their homes, must have found mascots particularly reassuring.

Because of strict quarantine regulations in both Britain and New Zealand, few animals sent to overseas theatres of war returned.[27] The effort made by one regiment to get its mascot home says much about the sentimental importance of these animals. In 1919 members of the Wellington Regiment, including Lieutenant-Colonel W.H. Cunningham, tried to organise the repatriation of their mascot, an Irish terrier called Paddy. He had been with the regiment right through the war, leaving with the Main Body of the New Zealand Expeditionary Force and accompanying the men in Egypt, at Gallipoli and in France, Belgium and Germany, finally ending up in England after the Armistice.

Paddy's return was thwarted when a rabies outbreak in England forced New Zealand to ban the import of all dogs from there. After high-level negotiations, the Department of Agriculture agreed to make an exception for Paddy, as long as he was given to the Wellington Zoo. Cunningham, who had intended to provide a home for 'the old dog', reluctantly endorsed this plan. In 1921 he wrote, 'I hope we shall see the old chap out here again. He is getting on in years and it would be a pity if he died overseas.'[28] But by late 1922, when arrangements had been finalised, Paddy was getting frail and deaf, and Jennetta Campbell Rogers of Devon, who had been entrusted with his care, appealed against him being sent on a long voyage.

Paddy remained in Devon, and when he finally died in 1929, Mrs Campbell Rogers returned his collar to his old comrades. She wrote:

I should like the Regiment to know that 'Paddy's' last years (he must have been quite 16 when he died a short time ago) were as happy as care and kindness could make them, and when his infirmities of age increased and life was becoming a burden, he was put to sleep, leaving many sad hearts behind. He was a well-known character, and his war service made him an heroic figure.[29]

Paddy, the Wellington Regiment mascot, wears his special coat with sergeant's stripes at a troop inspection by Prime Minister William Massey at Vauchelles, France, on 30 June 1918. Paddy left New Zealand with the regiment and accompanied the men throughout World War I.

Alexander Turnbull Library, Royal New Zealand Returned and Services' Association Collection. Reference: G-13312-1/2. Photograph by Henry Armytage Sanders

Another world war from 1939 to 1945 provided a reminder of the way animals could support people confronting life-and-death situations. The practical part animals played in military operations was limited compared with the 1914–18 conflict, as new technology had replaced animal power, but the ability of mascots to offer solace was undiminished.

Once again, New Zealand fighting units had official or unofficial mascots, many of which were given mock military rank. They included white Samoyed Sergeant Noodles of 21 Battalion, unfortunately ejected from the transport ship before it left Wellington, and Colonel Ben of A Squadron, Divisional Cavalry, a terrier that saw action in Greece and North Africa.[30] Private Hunt, a parakeet that served with 37 Battalion in the Pacific, learned to 'whisper some very wicked words, mainly in disparagement of members of the intelligence section'.[31]

Perhaps the most beloved mascot of the war, however, was Major, a white bull terrier. His poignant story reveals the profound associations that mascots could acquire. As a pup, Major was given to Errol Williams by his future wife Suzanne Crookston while Williams was training at the Royal Military College at Duntroon in Australia in the late 1930s. The dog accompanied his owner, by then adjutant of 19 Infantry Battalion, to Egypt in 1940. Officially known as No. 1 Dog, 2 New Zealand Division, Major was promoted to second lieutenant by 1941 and major in 1942, thus becoming Major Major. In Egypt he got into a scrap with local dogs and afterwards his left ear flopped down, making him instantly recognisable.[32]

When Williams was killed in action on 28 November 1941, Major was inconsolable for a time. Other members of the battalion cared for him, and he was present during battles in Libya and Egypt, receiving shrapnel wounds at El Alamein. In May 1943 members of the division made a formal application to bring him back to New Zealand at the end of the war, as import of dogs from the Middle East was then prohibited. In support, Brigadier W.G. Stevens wrote, 'In view of the great esteem in which he is held, it is hoped that any necessary legislation may be passed.'[33]

But it was not to be. At the end of 1943 Major accompanied his unit, by then an armoured regiment, to Italy. There, during a very cold winter, he contracted pneumonia and began to weaken. Despite attempts by the men to keep him alive, Major died on 17 December 1944. He was buried with military honours.

Sergeant Major Dave Rench later wrote, 'When we laid Major to rest at Rimini, I think perhaps some of the later members of the unit found it hard to appreciate the deep sentiment shown by the old hands for the old Dog … it was not only as unit mascot that Major was so affectionately remembered, but as a link with his first fine soldier master … and indeed to many other good men who had followed him.'³⁴ Graham Spencer, author of *The Four-legged Major*, an account of Major's life, added:

> The dog was, indeed, a link with many men and places and experiences, many of them impressed indelibly in their minds, fragments of life they could share only with those who had been with them … There was always a special sadness surrounding the death of those who had gone on and on, apparently indestructible, and who 'bought it' at a time when they knew that shortly those who were left would all be going home … it did not seem to them odd that they should feel it about their dog.³⁵

~

Between the two world wars, the helping role of animals in civilian life was changing. Horses, the animal heroes of the South African War and World War I, were disappearing from city streets by the 1920s as motor vehicles took over, and they were gradually replaced on farms by tractors. Other animals, however, retained their time-honoured jobs. Rodent control remained the speciality of cats, and they were often kept in city warehouses, commercial buildings and food stores for this purpose. And new opportunities opened up for them as they moved from private enterprise to public service.

In 1917 the custodian of the Government Buildings in Christchurch sent an unusual appeal to the Under-Secretary of the Department of Internal Affairs in Wellington:

> On account of a large number of rats and mice being seen in different parts of this Building, traps were set to catch them, but without effect. I have since procured a cat, which has caught a large number of them; in fact, this cat is catching rats and mice nearly every day. I am given to understand that a small amount of cash is allowed by the Post and Telegraph Department for food for cats at the Christchurch Post-Office, and, as our cat is doing good work, I shall be glad if you will recommend that 1/- [shilling] per week be granted to provide him with milk and meat.

The request was approved – and it turned out that a similar allowance had also been provided for cats patrolling the Wellington Government Buildings.³⁶

The Post Office was one of the main employers of cats, which were used to control the rats and mice that nibbled at letters, parcels and mailbags. This problem may have become worse in wartime, when food parcels were being sent overseas. According to one account, in 1942 1s 3d per week was allowed per cat for food, later rising to 2s 6d. In May 1953, however, cats were struck off the payroll, and from that time those that remained in smaller post offices were privately owned.³⁷

Cats continued to work as rat catchers in other parts of the public sector for some time, however. Wellington's *Evening Post* published an article on 18 April 1967 entitled 'Civil servant on the cheap'. This told the story of the 'chief rodent

Major Major, the bull terrier mascot of the Wellington Battalion, was photographed with Lieutenant J.E. May in Egypt in August 1942. The following year, a formal application was made to bring him back to New Zealand at the end of the war. This was accompanied by a tongue-in-cheek 'Regimental History of the Dog' which began: 'With more than five of his slender six years spent in martial atmosphere and over three years on active service, Major "Major" the white bull terrier mascot of 19 NZ Armd Regt has a title to the style of No 1 NZ Dog based on something more secure than the mere accident of priority of registration in the NZ Forces. He has known the smug repose of military academies in a peace time army and the rigours of active service in the foul reek of a country whose desert floor was never more than six inches from his fastidious, aristocratic nose. He has been a familiar figure on parade grounds in three or four countries, and he has travelled thousands of miles by every description and mode of conveyance that the mind of man could devise in this age of mobile warfare. By steamer and train, by truck and Bren Carrier and tank, and on occasions even by aeroplane he has accompanied his Unit everywhere it has wandered, and when such artificial aids to movement have failed he has followed the example of the regiment and resorted to the use of his four padded feet.'

Alexander Turnbull Library, War History Collection. Reference: DA-02608.
Photograph by Harold Gear Paton

Staff of British Office Supplies in Wellington pose for a photograph with two young cats about 1940. The animals might have been kept to deal with rodents, or they might simply have been office pets. Workplace mascots seem to have become more common as the number of working animals declined in the later twentieth century.

Alexander Turnbull Library, Gordon Burt Collection. Reference: F-117774-1/2

Topsy, an official New Zealand Post Office cat, was photographed sitting on a large package at the Wakefield Street Parcels Branch, Wellington, in 1950. Her job was to stop rodents damaging postal items. According to a note with the photograph, she was a working mother, having had 27 kittens in nine months.

Archives New Zealand. Reference: AAME 8106 W5603/103 9/13/2 (R20937102)

control officer' at the workshop of the National Publicity Studios: a cat by the name of Mr Moggs, who had held his position since the mid-1950s. Initially he was awarded 7s a week for food, and this was later raised to 10s 6d, but he was still, according to the report, 'the country's lowest paid civil servant'. By 1967 Mr Moggs's duties were evidently light – no rats had been seen in years – but he was a favourite with the staff and even had his name on the telephone list.[38] He had been transformed into a workplace mascot – something that seems to have become increasingly common in the following decades.

There were also new openings for dogs in the public service. From the 1930s they were increasingly used to help with sheep and cattle work on research stations and farms, eradication of goats and deer in state forests and rabbit control on Crown lands. The State Forest Service, the Ministry of Works and the Lands and Survey, Internal Affairs and Valuation departments were among those state agencies with staff who required the assistance of dogs to do their work. Some government departments had paid their employees a horse or forage allowance since the nineteenth century. Now a dog allowance, gradually increased to cover food, registration, routine veterinary costs and replacement costs, was introduced for public servants who used their own dogs 'on official business'.[39]

~

Most animals employed in the public service did the kind of work for which they had always been used, but some new jobs echoed their wartime roles. Following World War I, European countries, including Britain, set up specialist police dog training centres, and as early as the 1930s it was suggested that German Shepherds (Alsatians) might be used for police work in New Zealand. The idea was not taken up immediately, probably because the breed was then under suspicion for its supposed aggressive tendencies. However, about 1950, Sergeant George Spicer of Masterton got permission to use his dog, a purebred German Shepherd called Smokey, for locating missing people. Over 10 years Smokey amassed an impressive record: he found 19 lost children and one mental patient, and tracked down a thief. By the time Smokey retired, highly trained 'canine cops' were beginning to emerge from a new training school.[40]

British police had begun to train German Shepherds after World War II. They found these dogs more suitable than other breeds because of their weight and majestic carriage, acute sight and hearing, agility, speed, strength and endurance. Crucially, they had the ability to learn quickly, and bonded with only one owner, being wary of strangers. In 1955 New Zealand Prime Minister Sid Holland attended a Commonwealth leaders' conference in Britain, accompanied by the Controller-General of Police, Sam Barnett. Both were very impressed by the police dog demonstrations they saw there, and decided to set up a training unit in New Zealand. The following year this was established at Trentham, Wellington, by British police sergeant S.F. (Frank) Riley, a leading trainer who emigrated to New Zealand with several of his German Shepherds.[41]

The bond between police dog Miska and her handler Senior Sergeant Frank Riley is evident in this photograph, taken in March 1957. Sergeant Riley, a leading British police dog trainer, was recruited to establish the Trentham dog training centre. He brought Miska, a champion police dog, with him when he came to New Zealand and she played an important public relations role, demonstrating her skills and obedience for the media. *Alexander Turnbull Library, Dominion Post Collection. Reference: EP-Legal-Crime, Dogs, Police work-01*

At first there was strong opposition from those who saw police dogs as a heavy-handed method of enforcement. In June 1958, for example, the Minister of Police received a resolution passed by the Wellington Women's Branch of the New Zealand Labour Party, protesting against 'the police using dogs for the hounding of people' and objecting strongly to 'the parading of savage dogs through the streets'.[42] The dogs' successes in finding both criminals and missing people, however, gradually won public admiration and convinced a sceptical police hierarchy.[43]

Dogs were selected carefully to ensure they had the right characteristics, including steady temperament and ideal body structure, scenting powers and hearing. They were then matched with police handlers who had an affinity for animals. A strong bond between dog and police officer was essential – dogs had to be willing to face death to protect their handlers. Officer and dog were trained to operate as a team, and after qualifying continued to receive regular instruction for their entire careers. (The philosophy of 'one man, one dog' did not become gender neutral until the late 1990s, when female police officers were finally accepted as dog handlers.)[44]

A police dog would live with the officer's family, and was usually treated as a pet at home, with some important distinctions. It was not allowed toys or permitted to get friendly with anyone beyond the family. To protect the reputation of the unit, police dogs could never be sold or given away. If a handler resigned, the dog would usually be returned to the training unit and matched with a new man or woman. However, when the handler retired or moved to another police section, he or she could apply to keep the dog as a pet if it was near retirement age. In fact, dog handlers in Christchurch asked for this assurance in 1970 after one dog was put down when it became 'non-operational' through age. The Christchurch superintendent echoed their concerns, warning that if men thought their dog might be destroyed at the end of its working life, they would choose not to join the dog unit, putting its future in jeopardy.[45]

Police dogs were particularly useful for tracking work. They were also fearless in attacking and holding armed criminals who could not be safely apprehended by police. Because dogs, simply by their presence, could quell violence before it happened, they had an important role in preventing crime.[46] But the animal-loving public tended to overlook their intimidating image, focusing instead on their astounding skills. The police cultivated this admiration: dogs and handlers frequently showed off their abilities at events such as school galas and A&P shows. These demonstrations were so impressive that dog obedience training soared in popularity with pet owners.[47]

But the use of police dogs was not without controversy. Although training emphasised total obedience, once released to attack the dogs could sometimes go too far, inflicting serious wounds that required hospital treatment. Dogs could also occasionally bite indiscriminately when riled. A police dog handler of the 1970s and 1980s recalled one instance where his dog bit a man who was laying a complaint about police tactics during a brawl, and another when a colleague's dog attacked a small terrier being walked by its owner.[48]

There was also some criticism of the use of dogs for crowd control. Police found dogs useful to deal with small to medium-sized brawls or riots. However, when dogs were used to control an unruly New Year's Eve crowd at Napier in

1970 and several people were bitten, the police realised the potential for a public backlash.[49] They also had to reconsider the use of dogs in situations where people were exercising their democratic right to protest. After some incidents during anti-apartheid and anti-Vietnam war protests of 1969 and 1970, a general police instruction forbade the use of dogs to control demonstrations, except for guarding essential positions such as command vehicles.[50]

Police dogs were expected to perform in dangerous situations where they could be wounded or killed – that was one of the reasons for using them. If it came down to risking a dog's life rather than a man's, the dog was to be sacrificed. Dogs allowed police to operate mostly without firearms in an increasingly confrontational society. But many members of the public who thought of dogs as pets were shocked and distressed when a police dog was injured or died in the course of duty.

This was the reaction when Luke, the four-year-old police dog partner of Constable Jim Donald, was shot by Joseph Simpson in downtown Auckland on 27 October 1983. Simpson, who had recently been released from prison, stole two double-barrelled shotguns and ammunition from a sports store and went on a shooting spree. Shoppers and workers took cover and streets were cordoned off as police tried unsuccessfully to negotiate with the gunman. The unfolding drama was being filmed by a television crew when three police dogs, including Luke, were sent in to stop Simpson. A large television audience watched in horror as Luke fell, wounded in the shoulder. Simpson, who had used up his ammunition, was soon overwhelmed by police, bringing the stand-off to an end.

Luke, meanwhile, received emergency veterinary treatment and later had a plate and pins inserted to help rebuild his elbow. At one stage his leg became infected and it was feared he would die, but he pulled through. Newspapers carried regular bulletins on his progress, and the outpouring of sympathy for his plight was extraordinary. He received over 720 cards from well-wishers in New Zealand and Australia, along with flowers, packs of meat, a sheepskin, two silver medals and even a bottle of holy water from Lourdes. Such was the indignation at his suffering that the Auckland Police Chief, Assistant Commissioner Bryan Gibson, was forced to defend the police decision to send in dogs rather than allowing the Armed Offenders Squad members to shoot Simpson.

After rehabilitation, Luke returned to work briefly but soon retired and was, until his death in 1991, Constable Donald's pet. Luke continued to make numerous public relations appearances for the police, and was awarded the RNZSPCA Silver Medal of Merit for Bravery by Governor-General Sir David Beattie in August 1984.[51] In 1996 it finally became an offence to obstruct, injure or kill a police dog.[52]

~

Constable Terry Andrews and his dog Torr inspect the gravestones at the police dog cemetery at Trentham in March 1993. The officer in charge of the Police Dog Training Centre, Dave Painter, commented that most handlers built up 'a tremendous rapport and affinity' with their dogs and that the cemetery was 'a mark of respect for the dogs'. Alexander Turnbull Library, Dominion Post Collection. Reference: EP/1993/1062/7

The success of the police dog unit encouraged the training of dogs for other search and enforcement roles, including in the prison service and the New Zealand Air Force. From the 1970s the police, the Customs Department and the Post Office used 'sniffer' dogs – usually Labradors – to locate drugs and explosives.[53] In the late 1990s a black Labrador called Geordie became the first dog trained to sniff out accelerants at fire scenes where arson was suspected. On one occasion he lost three of the special leather boots he wore to glowing embers.[54]

Ministry of Agriculture and Fisheries Biosecurity introduced detector dogs for quarantine work in 1997. Beagles were chosen for airport detection work because of their non-threatening appearance and strong sense of smell. Trained to identify a range of odours, they would sit down beside a passenger if they recognised that the person was carrying a prohibited substance. Larger dogs of mixed breeds worked with unaccompanied baggage and mail. Handlers were not allowed to keep the dogs as pets because they could become desensitised to 'target' smells in a private home. After a detector dog retired, however, it was often adopted by its handler.[55]

Dogs were also well suited for bush and mountain rescue work. One of the first to be used in this way was Roy, a collie who spent 15 years in the 1920s and 1930s accompanying guides on Mt Taranaki. He had an excellent sense of direction and could lead the way home unerringly in blizzards. Credited with saving the lives of three people, he also prevented many others from losing their way: 'When all went well and the weather was clear, Roy would follow the steps of thrill seekers with contemptuously lolling tongue, but when human sense of direction failed neither cajoling nor threat could move Roy from what he knew to be the way.'[56] But it was their sense of smell, not their sense of direction, that qualified dogs for search and rescue work later in the century.

From the 1950s, people involved in bush and mountain searches wanted to enlist the help of police dogs, but because of the few available, and the distances they had to travel to get to the search scene, it was not practical to use them. Police dogs regularly located missing persons, but usually in or near urban areas.[57] In 1988 New Zealand Land Search and Rescue began recruiting pet dogs and their volunteer handlers to help find people lost in the vast New Zealand wilderness. The dogs learned to follow residual human scent left on the ground or sniff it in the air. They were particularly useful because they could work at night and in bad weather, and could trace non-responsive people, including young children or people with dementia who would not normally answer the calls of a stranger.[58]

Dogs capable of detecting the scent of a human beneath snow became invaluable to avalanche rescue teams because of their speed in reaching, pinpointing and digging down to the avalanche victim.[59] By 2003, dogs were also being trained by USAR, the urban search and rescue organisation, to find trapped people in collapsed structures.[60]

Dogs could be used to search for creatures other than humans, as early conservationist Richard Henry discovered. In Fiordland in the 1890s he trained his dog, Lassie, to sniff out hundreds of kiwi and kakapo, which Henry then transferred to the predator-free Resolution Island.[61] Following this example, Olly, a golden Labrador, spent 11 years, until his retirement in 2003, locating kiwi for the Department of Conservation's Kiwi Recovery Programme.[62] He was one of several dogs that did this work.

~

Another type of trained dog that gradually appeared on New Zealand streets in the post-war decades was the guide dog. Guide dogs for the blind had been used in other countries since World War I, but despite periodic urging there was no move to set up a guide dog training scheme in New Zealand. One writer to the *Evening Post* in August 1943 commented, 'I cannot understand why the provision of specially-trained lead dogs for the blind receives so little attention in this country. Overseas magazines and papers frequently mention the success of this scheme and give many stories to prove the sagacity of these animals and the comfort they give to their owners in giving them perfect freedom of movement.'[63] The cost of training the dogs was undoubtedly the main obstacle.

An Australian guide dog association began in 1952, with training centred on Melbourne from 1957. Soon, the Dominion Association of the Blind lobbied successfully for Australian-trained guide dogs to be made available in New Zealand, and the Guide Dogs for the Blind Association of New Zealand was formed in 1962.[64]

In 1964 there were only four recognised guide dogs in the country; by 1970 there were 16.[65] Probably because of these low numbers, the right of blind people to go on transport and into restaurants and other public places with their guide dogs was not legally recognised. In 1962, at the instigation of the prime minister, the Railways Department allowed guide dogs to travel with their owners in train carriages, and by 1965 the national airline, NAC, was letting guide dogs into the passenger compartment. That year the Union Steam Ship Company also permitted guide dogs to accompany their owners. Local bus and taxi companies around the country had a range of policies 'from unreserved acceptance to sympathetic opposition'.[66] But health legislation barred all dogs from entering food premises because of concerns about the spread of hydatids, and the Health Department was unwilling to make exceptions.[67]

Although in practice many blind people and their dogs were welcomed onto buses and into theatres and restaurants, occasionally they were turned away. Legislation to ensure this did not happen was proposed but did not eventuate. In 1971 Lynette Brown of Auckland wrote in protest to her local MP: 'Our dogs are really part of us … with us continuously all day and night. My dog stays in the office with me at work, and sleeps by, or on my bed at night.' She urged a law change to make it legal to take guide dogs anywhere. 'I think a lot of the prejudice is just ignorance on the public's part on just how well our dogs are trained and how well they behave. This is not all done through training as being with their owners constantly, our dogs know just what is expected of them and this is through mutual love and affection.'[68]

Matters came to a head in the late 1960s and early 1970s when New Zealand Railways began operating 'prestige' rail services that offered food and beverages on board the train instead of at stations along the route. To comply with health regulations, guide dogs either had to be excluded from these services, or travel in the guard's van. After a flurry of critical publicity there were renewed efforts to change the law.[69] The Dogs' Registration Amendment Act 1973 allowed guide dogs into eating houses, on public transport and into any place to which the public had access, subject to reasonable conditions imposed by the operator or owner.⁷⁰

Also in 1973, the Foundation for the Blind set up a guide dog training centre at Manurewa. Labradors were the dog of choice because of their medium size – making them easy to handle and economical to feed – and their strong desire to please. Later, other breeds, including boxers and Border collies, were tried and German Shepherds, golden retrievers and poodles were in use by the early 2000s. At first puppies were supplied by a breeding programme organised by the Wellington Labrador Retriever Club, but later Guide Dog Services, as the training centre became known, took over this responsibility.⁷¹

A puppy would be placed with a volunteer known as a 'puppy walker' until it was about 10 months old. During this period it was exposed to all the sights, sounds and experiences of everyday living: adults and children, cars, public transport, radio, television, cats and other dogs. Its behaviour in a range of situations enabled the trainers to assess its suitability to become a guide dog. If it showed any sign of nervousness or aggression, it was rejected for training.

A puppy accepted for training was then schooled over a period of around five months, first by qualified instructors and finally with the blind person to whom it was assigned. As well as learning to avoid obstacles, stop at kerbs and recognise traffic signals, it absorbed commands such as 'Sit', 'Down', 'Forward', 'Find the door' and 'Find the steps'. It was taught obedience but also independent judgement. So, for instance, at a road crossing a properly trained dog would resist an instruction from its handler to go forward if there was traffic coming, waiting until it was clear.⁷²

While working, a guide dog wore a light harness with a curved handle held by the blind person. The dog transmitted movement and direction to the person through this handle. When not wearing its harness and therefore off duty, it could relax and play like any other pet dog. Most dogs had a working life of eight to 10 years, but some had to be retired or replaced. In some cases

Heidi the guide dog leads Margaret Wheeler along a Lower Hutt street in November 1971. Heidi was a Melbourne-trained dog – New Zealand was still without a training centre – and she was then the only guide dog in the Wellington region. 'I just follow what Heidi does,' said Mrs Wheeler. 'She guides me through traffic, sees me safely to my destination and back home. She stops when there is danger, and she keeps away from obstacles. Heidi is a wonderful partner. She is my eyes.'

Alexander Turnbull Library, Dominion Post Collection. Reference: EP/1971/5995

the handler was allowed to keep the dog, but only if he or she did not require another.[73]

Technically, guide dogs were working dogs, but the sense of trust and love established between them and their handlers made them companion animals of a unique kind. They helped blind people to develop life-changing confidence and independence. Aucklander Nadia Clark, who had once been too nervous to go out in public, found new freedom when she was matched with Spirit, a Labrador retriever, in 2007. The bond they established was special: 'He is not just a guide dog who works for me, but my companion. Everything that a dog is to an owner.'[74]

These successes led to the training of dogs to aid people with other disabilities. By 1990 dogs were being taught to help those with conditions such as cerebral palsy, muscular dystrophy, multiple sclerosis, stroke and spinal injury, by picking up dropped items, opening and closing doors, pressing elevator buttons and retrieving phones and remote controls.[75] From 1998 hearing dogs assisted deaf people by listening for significant sounds such as the alarm clock, microwave, doorbell or telephone and then alerting their owners by touching them on the leg.[76] Soon there were assistance dogs for people with all kinds of conditions, ranging from epilepsy to autism.[77]

Because it was so expensive and time-consuming to train these dogs, disabled people often had a long wait. In the early 2000s the Puppies in Prison programme matched puppies with inmates, who provided early socialisation. As well as boosting the numbers of mobility assistance dogs, the programme proved helpful in rehabilitating prisoners.[78]

~

Many trained dogs clearly had a role as companion animals, but sometimes this had to be subordinated to the important work they undertook. There were, however, situations where an animal could perform an important job simply by being a pet.

Pets were kept for therapeutic purposes in some mental institutions in England and Germany from the eighteenth century. At the York Retreat in England, for example, patients were allowed to wander around the grounds, in which there were domestic animals such as rabbits and poultry. The patients were encouraged to care for them as part of their treatment, in the belief that they would learn self-control and esteem by looking after vulnerable creatures.[79]

Early New Zealand psychiatric institutions seem to have adopted this idea. When one of the country's first mental hospitals, Sunnyside, was being set up in Christchurch in 1863–64, the superintendent, Edward Seager, listed among

the equipment and chattels for entertaining patients '1 canary and cage'.[80] In 1879 the Inspector of Lunatic Asylums, Frederick Skae, recommended various furnishings for the Nelson Asylum to bring it up 'to a proper standard of comfort', including 'a few singing birds or other pets in which the patients could take an interest'.[81] And in 1881 Dr Walter Hacon, then superintendent of Sunnyside, advertised in the *Star* that he would 'be glad to receive contributions from the charitable of flowers, newspapers, linen, rags, birds, or other animal pets, &c.'. The value,' he remarked, 'of such aids to the managers of an institution like the Asylum cannot be overestimated.'[82]

For the patients, animals may well have served the same function as mascots in wartime. They were reminders of a former, normal life – truly, 'ciphers of sanity'. Because outdoor employment was seen as beneficial, from the late nineteenth century most New Zealand mental hospitals had farms. Some patients tended the animals, including poultry, pigs and cows, on a daily basis. Contact with animals and involvement in the familiar tasks of caring for them may have helped these people cope with impersonal institutional life. Pets, too, remained important. In the 1920s, for reasons of hygiene and economy, new regulations prohibited the keeping of pet animals other than cats and cage birds by either staff or patients without special permission, but it appears that some patients applied for and were granted leave to keep dogs and rabbits.[83]

One of New Zealand's most notorious mental patients, Lionel Terry, was allowed to keep pets. Terry murdered an elderly Chinese man in Wellington in 1905 to publicise his racial views and opposition to Chinese immigration. Judged insane, he spent the rest of his life in prisons and mental hospitals. He escaped four times, and in 1914 ended up in Seacliff Mental Hospital, north of Dunedin, where he was permitted certain privileges on condition that he would not attempt to escape again. He cared for pet goats and sheep, and these tame animals accompanied him on his daily walks outside the hospital grounds. Terry built his animals outdoor shelters in a garden he created. His privileges were withdrawn after he assaulted a doctor in 1940, and the sheep and goats were sent to a slaughterhouse, to the regret of local residents who had befriended them and Terry on his walks.[84]

The guinea pig house at Seacliff Mental Hospital, built like a miniature cottage and complete with guinea pig tenants, in 1897. The care put into the construction of the house and enclosure suggests that pet keeping was considered therapeutic for patients.

Alexander Turnbull Library, E.R. Williams Collection. Reference: G-140508-1/2. Photograph by William Williams

~

From helpers to heroes

The therapeutic potential of animals reached beyond the confines of mental hospitals and into the wider community in the second half of the twentieth century. Those working with the physically and intellectually disabled increasingly recognised the benefits of pets. For example, in 1969 the Wellington SPCA's bi-monthly journal reported, 'Animals can help IH children.' A young golden cocker spaniel called Rossie had become a regular visitor to the centre for intellectually handicapped children in Hamilton, and this innovation had proved so successful that it was decided that dogs should be more widely used as aids in special education, as an outlet for the uninhibited affection that the children had to give.[85]

Riding for the Disabled, an international movement, started in New Zealand in 1972. Horse riding helped both physically and intellectually disabled people. The complex movement of the horse enabled the development of coordination, balance, fitness and muscular strength, and riding also encouraged self-confidence, trust and communication skills. Volunteers assisted in a range of programmes designed to develop these attributes, and the horses, described as 'four legged therapists', were specially selected for their calm temperament. By the early 2000s there were 55 member groups throughout the country.[86]

Although it was obviously not a new concept, the term 'pet therapy' – now better known as 'animal assisted therapy' – was first coined by an American child psychiatrist, Boris Levinson, in 1969. Noticing that withdrawn children had no difficulty relating to his dog, Jingles, Levinson concluded that humans benefited from the unconditional affection and support offered by animals. He advocated introducing animals to hospital and nursing home patients who were isolated from family and friends. His theory gained scientific credibility after experiments in the United States and Australia.[87]

Outreach Pet Therapy, a joint scheme run by the Auckland SPCA and St John Ambulance, began in Auckland in 1988 after the then SPCA executive director Bob Kerridge and his wife saw pet therapy sessions in rest homes in San Francisco. People who were suffering from Alzheimer's disease, disabled by strokes or socially withdrawn responded positively to animals, often stirred by the memory of a pet. Some would smile and talk for the first time. People with little movement would reach out to pat the animal, getting valuable exercise. The Auckland pet therapy programme started with rest homes, but soon extended to hospices, rehabilitation units, schools, mental health establishments and youth correctional facilities. The animals used were mostly dogs, but came to include cats, rabbits and even donkeys, miniature horses and llamas.[88] Similar programmes were set up elsewhere: for instance a pet therapy scheme

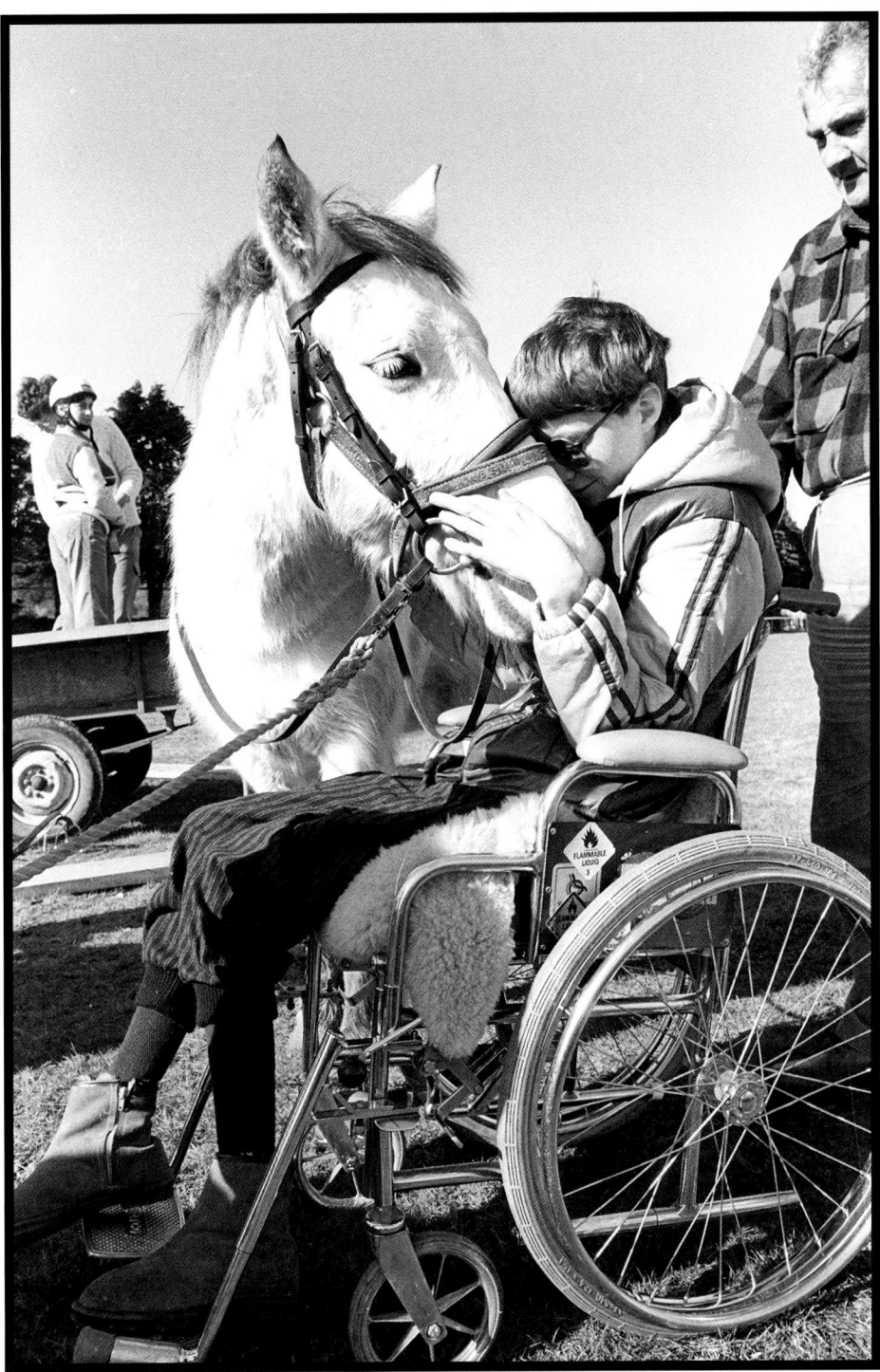

Yvonne Charlton gives her horse, Little Champ, a grateful hug after a Riding for the Disabled session in February 1984. At this time there were three RDA groups in the Wellington region, run by physiotherapists, trained instructors and volunteers. The horses were specially selected for their placid temperament and even gait, and, according to RDA workers, seemed to know instinctively what was expected of them, often shifting their balance to compensate for an awkward rider.

Alexander Turnbull Library, Dominion Post Collection. Reference: EP/1984/0748

'Bring back the cats'

THE LONG-ESTABLISHED role of cats as rat catchers in the workplace became the subject of a national controversy in 1975. The year before, a Labour government had introduced strict new Food Hygiene Regulations, which banned all animals from premises where food was made, packaged or sold. At that time, some owners of small groceries and dairies who lived on the premises kept cats, sometimes as pets, but usually to keep rodents under control. There was an outcry from these people, and from cat lovers, who feared that many cats would have to be put down as a consequence of the ban.[91] One shop owner, Wally Glen of Matakana, started a petition, while another was circulated by the St Francis Assisi Organisation of Dunedin in conjunction with the Upper Hutt Animal Rescue Society and the Anti-Cruelty Society of Palmerston North. Between them, the two petitions are said to have attracted around 12,000 signatures.[92]

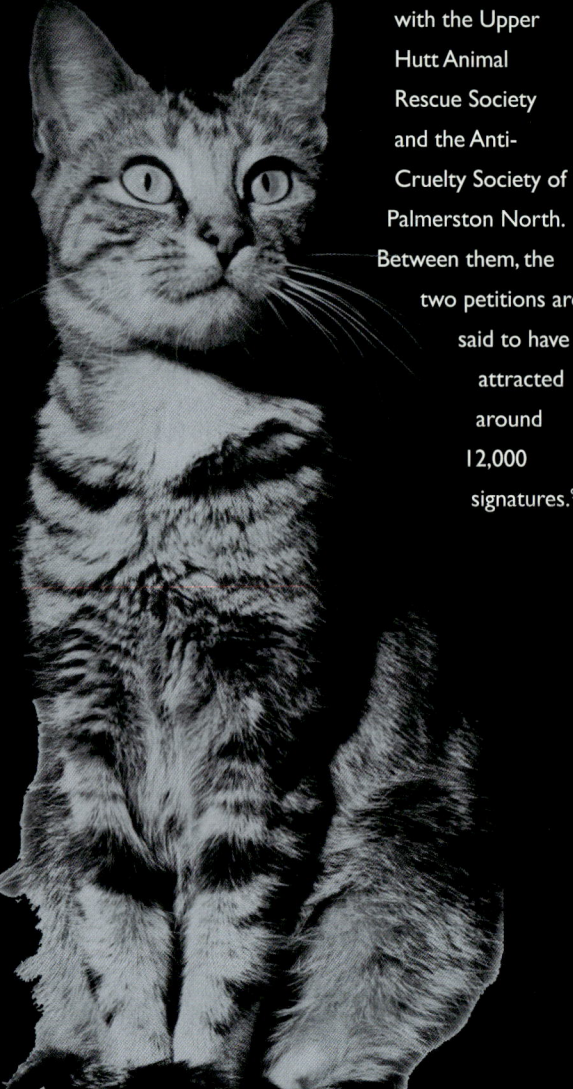

Nineteen seventy-five was an election year, and the National Party seized on the issue. Their campaign stressed the importance of restoring to New Zealanders freedoms that had been lost through government interference, and as part of this they promised to 'bring back the cats'.[93] Once elected, new Prime Minister Robert Muldoon again undertook to repeal the offending clause.[94] Many shopkeepers and cat lovers wrote to congratulate him, but the decision was criticised strongly by other groups, notably the New Zealand Veterinary Association and the Royal Society for the Promotion of Health. They warned of the diseases that could be spread to people by cats, and accused Muldoon of putting politics before people's health. They also claimed that cats were less efficient at rodent control than poison and trapping methods.[95]

Despite these objections, echoed by some within the Department of Health, the regulations were changed in October 1976. The amendment allowed cats owned by the occupiers of food premises to stay, provided the owner took adequate precautions to protect the food from contamination by the cat, which was allowed on the premises 'only to such extent as is reasonably necessary to effect the suppression of rodents'. While the petitioners celebrated, others pointed out that because the conditions of the amendment were so difficult to meet or prove, health inspectors would have no difficulty in prohibiting cats on food premises.[96] The Labour Party also attacked the 'semantic taradiddle' of the amendment in a fiery and sometimes funny parliamentary debate. According to a *New Zealand Herald* report, 'Mr R.W. Prebble (Lab, Auckland Central) said cats were allowed into shops only to chase rodents. That ruled out kittens and elderly cats. What sort of test could be applied to determine whether cats were able to chase rodents? he said. Opposition interjector: "A warrant of kitness".'[97]

Outreach Therapy Pets, a programme run jointly by the Auckland SPCA and St John Ambulance, involves around 250 volunteers and their animals who visit rest homes, hospitals, hospices, special needs schools, mental health and rehabilitation units and correctional facilities. Most of the animals taking part are dogs, but there are also rabbits, guinea pigs, goats, donkeys, ponies, llamas and cats – like the contented Siamese pictured here.

Permission of Auckland SPCA

was trialled at Wellington Hospital's psychiatric ward in 1989, and Canine Friends pet therapy began in Wellington the following year.[89]

Animals could communicate and help in ways that people could not, as a story told by Canine Friends founder Eileen Curry revealed. Visiting a rest home with her dog, she was told by staff not to bother one elderly woman who was blind and deaf, and also rather bad tempered. However, the dog wandered up and lifted the woman's hands with its nose. 'She smiled such a smile. She looked up and said, "It's a dog, isn't it?" … It was absolutely wonderful.'[90]

~

In the course of the twentieth century, distinguishing between working animals and pets became less straightforward, especially as service animals often combined the traits of both. These animals inspired public admiration and, sometimes unexpectedly, affection. And the idea, recognised in early psychiatric institutions, that animals could do important work simply by being companions, took hold during wartime and gained wide recognition with the arrival of 'pet therapy'. For many New Zealanders, animals were now more than just helpers – they were nothing less than heroes.

Two dogs roam the streets of Wanganui in the 1920s. Until more rigorous dog control measures were introduced in cities in the second half of the twentieth century, this would have been a common sight. Dogs had to be wearing registration collars, or they were likely to be picked up and taken to the council pound where they would be destroyed unless claimed within a short period. *Alexander Turnbull Library. Reference: F-22307-1/1*

Chapter 8
Pets or *pests?*

Many a settler farmer would have lain awake at night worrying about wild dogs preying on his flock, but sleep was also elusive for countless inhabitants of colonial towns. People regularly deplored 'the dog nuisance' in letters to local newspapers, complaining that the barking and fighting of packs of dogs disturbed their rest. According to a writer to the *Southland Times* in 1873, 'Nightly do these pests congregate in certain parts of the town, and, for reasons best known to themselves, deliberately bark and wail and howl in concert by the hour together.'[1] There were fewer protests about cats but some people objected to their nocturnal yowling. In 1868 'A Cat Hater' wrote to the editor of the Christchurch *Star*:

> *Unfortunately for me my immediate neighbours are maiden ladies and married couples without incumbrances; consequently, I suppose, their sensibilities tend towards that noble animal – the cat – as a pet. Now, this, I believe, is allowable according to law; but have they any right to loose these unmusical creatures in droves every night, to the annoyance of their less fortunate neighbours with large families?*[2]

A more serious problem was the threat to safety posed by unrestrained dogs. After his son was bitten by one in 1877, a Wellington man signing himself 'A Father' wrote to the *Evening Post*:

> *I should like to draw the attention of the authorities to the danger caused by allowing the streets to be taken possession of by a set of mongrel dogs, which are neither fit for use nor ornament. To go along some of the streets in Te Aro after dark, without a good-sized stick in hand, is simply running into danger … I have no objection to people keeping as many 'pets' as they choose, but let them keep them to themselves.*[3]

Some unfortunate dogs were chained up all the time, but others roamed freely and occasionally went missing. Owners could make strenuous efforts to find their pets. One notice in Wellington's *Evening Post* on 11 November 1901 read: 'Lost, Last Saturday evening in Hobson-street, Black Cocker Spaniel. Finder will be rewarded by returning same to C. B. Izard, 25, Hobson-street.'[4] Another, inserted in the *Ashburton Guardian* on 28 October 1915 by E.E. Bell, appealed to readers' sympathy for servicemen: 'Lost, fortnight ago – A Collie Sheep Pup; tan. Answers to name of Joffre. Soldier's pet.'[5] Occasionally, too, people who found animals attempted to locate their owners. Mr F. Cox advertised in the *Evening Post* on 15 January 1908: 'Found, a Dog at Northland, evidently a pet; owner can obtain same by paying expenses.'[6] However, many wandering dogs were homeless. In Wellington in the early 1900s the SPCA inspector commented on the large number of stray dogs, and other cities and towns had the same problem.[7] Stray cats were also becoming evident in built-up areas by the 1920s.[8]

~

Dogs on the loose had been a worry since the first days of Pakeha settlement, and legislation to control them was soon introduced. In 1844 'An Ordinance to provide a summary mode of abating the Nuisance of Dogs wandering at large in Towns' empowered constables to seize any unaccompanied dogs and keep them in a public place for a day and a night to allow their owners to find and claim them after paying a fine of 5s. Unclaimed dogs were to be destroyed by hanging.

Borough and county councils and road boards administered successive dog control acts and bylaws from the mid-nineteenth century. In many places unregistered dogs found roaming the streets were picked up by the dog collector, taken to the local pound and destroyed by shooting or, worse, by poisoning with prussic acid or drowning.[9] But local authorities did not always collect dogs systematically, and were even less interested in the cat problem. People came to accept homeless animals as part of the city scene. In 1929 well-known Auckland journalist and SPCA stalwart Elsie K. Morton described such cats and dogs haunting the suburbs of Auckland: 'Poor hungry "strays", condemned to a life of vagabondage and thievery, to a precarious diet of scaly rats and mice and odd food scraps of the street; better far a merciful brick and a pail of water ere your young eyes had opened on an unsympathetic world!'[10]

Many of these animals were not just starving but sick with skin and parasitic diseases. Their suffering soon caught the attention of SPCAs. Although the societies did not have the resources to collect and shelter unwanted or lost animals, their city inspection work increasingly involved 'putting down' ailing cats and dogs. Some SPCAs imported 'humane killers' – a type of captive bolt pistol – to despatch old, injured or ill animals. They also tried to persuade local authorities to use kinder methods of destroying stray dogs, promoting gas 'lethal chambers'.

In Auckland in 1915 the city council acquired a lethal chamber using coal gas, which was criticised by the SPCA as inhumane.[11] But when in the early 1920s the council introduced a new, improved chamber, using carbon monoxide, the SPCA committee member present at the first trial pronounced it 'a ghastly failure'.[12] It took a full 20 minutes for the gas to take effect, apparently because the council staff did not understand the correct operating procedure. In the late 1920s the Devonport Borough Council was disposing of stray animals by shooting or cyanide (probably hydrogen cyanide gas). Gas – carbon monoxide, carbon dioxide or nitrogen – remained a common method of euthanasia until the 1980s, when barbiturate injections became standard.[13]

~

The underlying reason for the stray animal problem was that cats and dogs could and did breed prolifically. A female cat could have three litters a year. In seven years she and her descendants could be responsible for as many as 420,000 kittens. Similarly, in just six years a female dog and her offspring could produce up to 67,000 puppies.[14] In the nineteenth and early twentieth centuries, regular litters of puppies and kittens were just part of the experience of owning pets. Inevitably, as pets reproduced, the numbers of unwanted animals grew.

The thought of neutering a pet would not have occurred to many people. Dealing with its illnesses and injuries was a more urgent concern. One of the first locally produced pet manuals, *Pets: Their care in sickness and health*, published in 1936, observed, 'The sick pet is … a difficult problem, particularly in New Zealand where skilled veterinary attention is often difficult and sometimes impossible to obtain.'[15] This was an important point. Some chemists offered to treat pet ailments, but urban vets were few and far between until well into the twentieth century. This meant that specialised animal treatments, including neutering, were unavailable to most pet owners. Even in places where there was a vet, some people – children, elderly and the poor – simply could not afford to pay for the service.

One evening during the Depression of the 1930s, Ruth Park's fox terrier, Flash Jack, dragged himself home after being hit by an Auckland tram. In the Park household there was no spare money for a vet. Ruth and her sister had to rearrange the bones in the dog's crushed paw and try to slip his dislocated shoulder back into place: 'Now and then during this process Flash Jack emitted that shrill, birdlike scream of the injured animal, and softly closed his jaws over my hand.'[16] With devoted nursing he eventually recovered, but he had a lopsided shoulder and a limp for the rest of his life.

Dealing with such emergencies was harrowing enough. Disposing of a pet's litters was even more upsetting. Sometimes baby animals could be given away, but many owners were forced to get rid of them as Elsie Morton hinted – in a pail of water. In November 1929, for example, Aucklander Dorothy Monkman wrote to her friend Winifred Walmsley, 'Frank drowned two of our kittens a fortnight ago & we have two left but I'm afraid they'll have to go also. I don't like parting with them because they are so interesting to watch.'[17] Killing an animal's offspring rather than neutering it was unquestioned practice for decades, and in fact responsible pet owners considered it to be their duty. One woman who wrote to the SPCA in 1945 asking for advice on how to put down her cat's soon-to-be-born kittens was told to place them in an airtight biscuit tin lined with cotton wool impregnated with chloroform, available from the chemist: 'Two minutes should be time enough to put them off.'[18]

DIY euthanasia was also a way of ending the misery of sick or elderly pets[19] – except that it was often in itself a cause of suffering. Drowning, a common method, could be an agonising, protracted death, while shooting of dogs was not always carried out efficiently. The Wellington SPCA committee became concerned about the cruel methods used by some people, and in 1929 purchased a lethal box for painless destruction of cats. This device, which probably used chloroform, was operated by SPCA member Miss Mabel Christmas, and in the 1929–30 year she put down 192 animals.[20] Later, members of the public had the option of using the lethal chamber at the Wellington City Corporation Yards, at a charge of 1s shilling for a cat and 2s 6d for a dog. Some people asked the local SPCA inspector to euthanise old or sick pets,[21] but many still had to do the deed themselves, if they could face it.

There was another common way of dealing with an old, ill or unwanted animal, and that was to abandon it. In the early twentieth century, SPCA inspectors observed that dog owners often set their animals free when the registration fee was due.[22] In the mid-1930s in Wellington there was a stray cat 'epidemic', which the SPCA attributed to abandonment: 'People vacate houses and flats and leave their cats behind, and in other cases that have come under the notice of the Society, cats have been taken away in cars and deliberately abandoned.'[23] These animals, if they survived, bred unchecked, swelling the numbers of strays.

~

For conscientious owners, coping with a pet's health and fertility issues could be a heavy burden. The extent of public eagerness for pet care advice was revealed when the Wellington SPCA opened its first animal clinic in Herd Street in 1945. The clinic was soon overwhelmed by owners seeking help for their pets' complaints: many people were 'quite helpless when confronted with a sick dog or cat, but in some cases the SPCA staff can tell at a glance what ails an animal'.[24] The society began publishing a journal with articles on pet care and first aid, 'of the utmost value to owners who, quite often without realising it, have never had a true appreciation of the needs of their animals'.[25]

Clinic staff were unprepared for the demands on their time by the public, including what were described as 'unreasonable' calls in the evenings and weekends. Within a few years the voluntary staff had to be replaced by three full-time paid employees, and after-hours services were being provided. By 1959 the Wellington SPCA was referring anxious owners to private vets because it was experiencing difficulties in carrying out what it saw as its first duty: dealing with emergency cases.[26]

Some pet owners also took the opportunity to get rid of their unwanted animals at the SPCA. In 1951 the Wellington clinic euthanised more than 100 cats and dogs by chloroform each month. Around this time, people often had a pet 'put to sleep' if they became too ill or elderly to care for it, if a landlord objected to animals, or even if they were going on holiday.[27] SPCA staff would have been aware that by offering painless euthanasia they were saving these animals from abandonment or long drawn-out suffering. But the extent to which pet owners availed themselves of convenience euthanasia was to later to become a major concern for SPCAs.

Until veterinary services for small animals became more widespread after World War II, many pet owners relied on advice given in manuals such as this one, *Hints to Cat Lovers*, published in London in 1927 by A.F. Sherley & Co., manufacturers of animal remedies. As well as describing home cures for a range of illnesses and injuries, this booklet, like other pet care manuals of the time, had a section on 'painless death' – instructions on how to humanely euthanise an old or incurably sick cat. *Author's collection*

~

In the post-war years the problem of unwanted animals began to escalate. By May 1945 the secretary of the Auckland SPCA was feeling the pressure, and enquired about the Wellington SPCA's policy on collecting stray cats and dogs, stating, 'My Society never refuses a call to a sick or injured animal, but we do not collect healthy strays.'[28] Wellington agreed, in 1951 lamenting the 'never ending' stray cat problem. 'The Society's first duty is to sick and injured animals, and it cannot hope to cope with the hundreds of waifs and strays which abound in a city. If they are brought to the clinic they will be painlessly destroyed.'[29]

Despite believing that local authorities should take responsibility for strays, SPCAs soon became involved because of the sheer magnitude of the task. By 1953, for example, the Wellington SPCA was collecting stray cats and dogs and delivering them to the city council.[30] Then, to ensure the animals received the best possible care, some SPCAs began to take in strays. By the late 1950s the Christchurch, Auckland and Dunedin SPCAs had reached agreements with local councils to handle stray dogs.[31]

There were continuing tensions between the dispassionate approach of local authorities and the humane philosophy of SPCAs. The condition of some dog pounds led to SPCA complaints in the 1940s. By the late 1960s several councils were reducing the time they held impounded dogs before destroying them, drawing further criticism from SPCAs.[32] But when Wellington's Moa Point pound closed temporarily in 1968 because nearby residents had objected to the noise, the SPCA volunteered to care for the dogs. In Auckland, too, the various local bodies and the SPCA worked together: pounds sent stray dogs to the society to be euthanised.[33]

Local bodies had a legal obligation to deal with dogs, and occasionally intervened when a cat overpopulation problem got out of hand. In an attempt to rid Lower Hutt of stray cats in 1964 the city council made traps available to members of the public, and offered a cut rate for the destruction of trapped cats at the council yard.[34] Increasingly, however, SPCAs stepped in. By the 1960s much of their time was taken up with receiving, collecting and putting down vast numbers of stray and unwanted cats and kittens. In the 1963–64 year, 12 SPCAs between them destroyed 9656 stray and wild cats. Over 2000 were put down at the Wellington clinic alone in 1965.[35] As well as being demoralising for staff and volunteers, this work was expensive. Some local bodies provided occasional grants to SPCAs, but not until the Finance Act was amended in 1967 were they in a position to give more substantial funding aid.[36]

Why had the population of homeless animals spiralled out of control? Previous generations of strays had almost certainly contributed their progeny to the burgeoning numbers, and the post-war expansion of towns and cities no doubt added to the problem. But so did the increased popularity of pet ownership. Pets were, it seems, victims of their own success. As more people

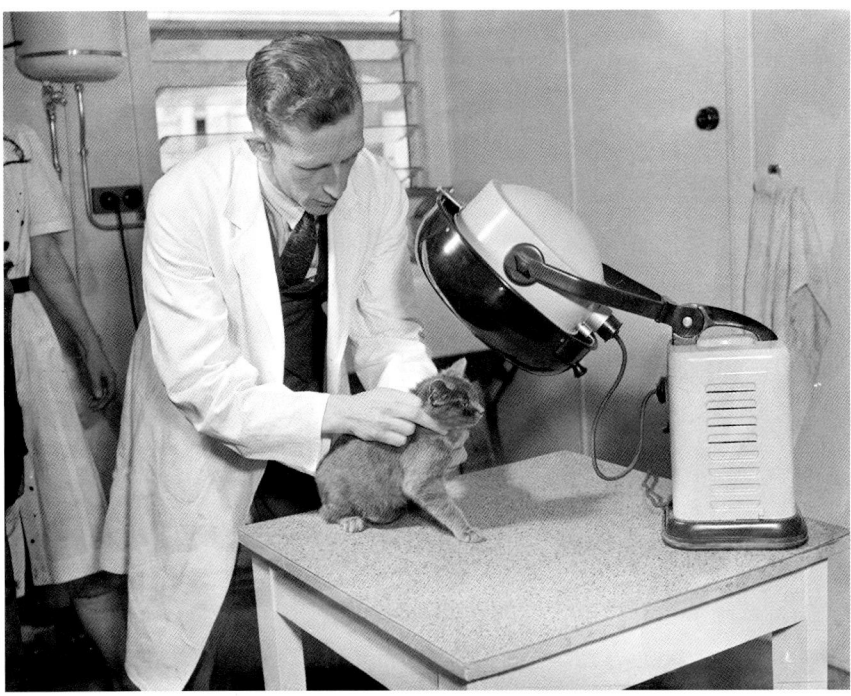

A vet examines a cat at the Wellington SPCA clinic in early October 1951. The clinic, which opened in 1945, initially provided much-needed advice on animal health to the public, and often attended to people's ailing pets. These demands, however, diverted attention from the traditional SPCA anti-cruelty work and owners were increasingly referred on to private vets, while the SPCA put energy into helping homeless animals.

Alexander Turnbull Library, Evening Post Collection. Reference: 114/358/04

acquired pets, there were more unwanted animals – 'surplus' kittens, puppies and other baby animals – and these were abandoned or handed in to the SPCA when they became too much trouble to look after.

The blasé attitudes of many owners did not help. For example, dog owners commonly set their pets free to go for a run unsupervised first thing in the morning and last thing at night.[37] These often unneutered animals congregated and mated with other dogs, fouled the streets, foraged in rubbish and caused traffic accidents. And, of course, they became lost.

The practice of abandoning unwanted pets also continued unabated, even though this was made an offence in the 1960 Animals Protection Act. In 1964 the Wellington SPCA threatened to prosecute people who let dogs go around licence time, and the society made regular appeals to the public not to dump cats and kittens.[38] Many people mistakenly believed that it was kinder to release an unwanted cat into a bush area than to have it put down. In fact it was difficult for domestic cats, accustomed to regular feeding and care, to adapt to the wild.

~

By the early 1970s there was a population explosion of unwanted pet animals in New Zealand, just as there was in other urbanised countries, notably the United States and England.[39] New Zealand SPCAs faced a welfare crisis, with thousands of unwanted animals handed in to them each year. In the 1973–74 year, for example, the Auckland SPCA received 8234 cats, of which 6850 had to be destroyed, and 4880 dogs, of which 2670 had to be put down. Its president commented: 'The Society continues to be a dumping ground for the unwanted animals of Auckland. This is a most unpleasant service that the Society must maintain otherwise there would be an increase in the already growing numbers of animals being abandoned on the outskirts of Auckland.'[40] Pet owning, usually thought of as a wholesome family activity, had, it seems, become the source of an immense amount of animal suffering.

Appalled by the plight of rejected pets, SPCAs began to explore various alternatives to euthanasia. In the early 1950s the Wellington SPCA began advertising for new owners for its animals, initially with success.[41] By the late 1960s it was becoming more difficult to rehome animals because of the huge increase in their numbers, and appeals became more desperate and emotional. On Christmas Eve 1969 the *Dominion* published an article headed 'Death threat today for homeless pets', begging readers to adopt 100 cats and eight dogs languishing at the SPCA.[42] Where possible, SPCAs provided refuges for animals that could not be rehomed. The Upper Hutt SPCA, for example, had a farm at Kaitoke.[43] However, these sanctuaries could cope with only a small proportion of the total. Soon it became evident that there were simply not enough homes for all the unwanted animals.

Animal welfarists became increasingly aware of the need to desex pets in order to reduce future populations of unwanted animals. Auckland and Wellington SPCAs were spaying and neutering some animals in the 1940s.[44] By 1952 the Auckland society was promoting the spaying of female pets, and in 1959 the Wellington society was considering a fund to neuter stray dogs and cats and a public campaign to encourage owners to desex their animals.[45]

By the end of the following decade the need was more pressing. In 1970 the Wellington SPCA was strongly urging owners to spay kittens, and soon the Auckland SPCA was publishing articles with titles such as 'We don't want to kill your pets, please have them spayed'.[46] SPCAs continued to push the message in strongly worded advertisements, including one of 1977 that stated, 'The animal epidemic is here' and 'Responsibility towards Animals begins with YOU'.[47]

These appeals failed to convince sufficient owners. Many actually wanted their pets to breed: a typical reason given was the wish to teach their children the facts of life. Others jibbed at the cost of neutering. SPCAs tried to counter this second objection. Before January 1969 the Wellington SPCA did not charge a fee for people adopting kittens, but after that time staff asked for a dollar, refundable if the kitten was later desexed. In the 1970s people adopting unneutered animals from the Wellington and Auckland SPCAs had to pay the society part of the fee for spaying or neutering. They were then issued with a voucher redeemable with a veterinarian who would perform the operation.[48] (Whether people actually did redeem the voucher was of course up to them.) From the late 1980s, when vets began pre-pubescent neutering, many SPCAs routinely desexed all kittens and puppies, as well as cats and dogs, before rehoming them.[49]

During the 1960s and 1970s SPCA members proposed a range of possible answers to the pet population problem. These included tattooing dogs with an identifying mark so they could be traced back to the owner if lost, charging higher licence fees for unspayed bitches, licensing dog breeders, inspecting properties to ensure they were fully fenced before granting a dog licence to the owner, licensing cats and developing a contraceptive for cats and dogs.[50] Concern about the increase in the urban stray dog population also prompted the New Zealand Veterinary Association to survey 20 local authorities around the country in the mid-1970s: its 1976 report recommended a number of reforms, including improvement of dog ranger and registration services, better procedures for handling strays at pounds, registration of both dogs and their owners, and an education programme.[51] However, euthanasia seemed the only practical short-term solution. Percentages of animals being put down by SPCAs and local bodies were particularly high in the 1970s, but remained elevated through the 1980s.[52]

~

SPCA clinic workers were increasingly troubled at having to euthanise so many animals, and disgusted by those who abandoned them. One wrote, 'I just can't help feeling a sense of uselessness towards those animals – useless because I can do nothing to help them, except give them what little time I can to make them as comfortable as possible.'[53] Another asked, 'Wouldn't it be lovely if everyone had their pets neutered and we no longer had the heartbreak of having to destroy perfectly healthy animals because nobody wants them?'[54] There was frustration, too, that this work was diverting SPCA staff from their original role of dealing with blatant cruelty cases.

Ironically, some members of the public began to criticise SPCAs, claiming that, rather than helping animals in need, they were putting them to death. In 1986 the *Evening Post* published a response, 'Condemned to die – why?', written

'Take me home and love me, those little eyes seem to say' was the caption for this appealing puppy picture, published in Wellington's *Evening Post* in August 1986. That month the local SPCA kennels had reached bursting point and homes were being sought urgently for 14 adult dogs and nine puppies. According to the accompanying article, the SPCA charged $65 per dog, which included spaying or neutering and vaccinations, and checked out a prospective owner's property beforehand to ensure it was suitable for a dog.

Alexander Turnbull Library, Dominion Post Collection. Reference: EP/1986/3997

by Ross McLauchlan of the Wellington SPCA. It counter-attacked with a blunt accusation: 'You have created the situations that cause animals to suffer. When we euthanise, it's your dirty work we're doing.'[55] McLauchlan pointed out that SPCAs could not find homes for the large numbers of animals they were handling, or keep them alive in cages indefinitely. Owners should desex, register, identify and supervise their pets, he insisted, and people should not acquire pets in the first place unless they were prepared to make a long-term commitment to their care.

Most animal advocates would have agreed with this vision but some took a different approach to the immediate problem. In the early 1950s a group of women began feeding stray cats in Wellington, and at the end of that decade Anna Jones set up the Stray Cat Food Trust Fund. By 1969 its members were feeding more than 200 strays in Wellington city, and had arranged to have many neutered.[56] Around the same time, in Christchurch, Ruby Austin was rescuing stray cats, and in 1971 she established a Cats Protection League, based on the

British organisation founded in 1927. Its aims were to provide shelter, food and veterinary assistance for strays, find homes where possible and educate people about caring for and neutering their cats. In 1982 Catherine de la Roche established the Wellington Cats Protection League. She had worked for the British Cats Protection League during World War II and emigrated to New Zealand in 1958. Other leagues were later formed in Hamilton, Upper Hutt and Lower Hutt.[57]

Rather than competing with the SPCAs, the leagues worked alongside them. In Wellington the SPCA provided assistance with neutering of cats, and in Christchurch the SPCA referred cases to the league. Both Christchurch and Wellington leagues attracted an energetic, largely female membership, and following fund-raising and bequests managed to establish permanent shelters. The Wellington league's first shelter was behind the Penthouse Cinema in Brooklyn, and one of the earliest cats taken in, an outgoing male tabby named Floyd, became the resident cinema cat for the next 13 years, often wandering into the theatre during a screening and choosing a lap to sit on.

Unlike the SPCA, the Cats Protection League did not euthanise cats unless they were incurably ill or injured – the animals it took in were either adopted out or kept for life. This encouraged some people to bring unwanted cats to the league rather than the SPCA. As a result, the Wellington league had to make a policy of accepting only emergency cases into its shelters immediately, with a waiting list for others.[58]

Other animal rescue organisations emerged around the country in the 1950s, 1960s and 1970s – often when caring people became aware of a local problem. In 1967, for example, Alan and Kathleen Heathcote White formed the Upper Hutt Animal Rescue Society to rescue and treat stray animals, rehome unwanted pets, provide pet care education and services such as holiday pet feeding, and help needy people with veterinary fees. The society developed an active junior membership through its 'grand pet parades' at

Floyd, the best known of the Wellington Cats Protection League's rescued felines, presides over the box office at the Penthouse Cinema, Brooklyn, in December 1990. By then he was a local celebrity, sauntering around the neighbourhood, sunning himself in the real estate agent's window and occasionally dropping into the deli for a snack. He would also greet cinema patrons in the foyer, and once the lights had gone down would identify a comfortable lap to sit on for the duration of the film.

Alexander Turnbull Library, Dominion Post Collection. Reference: EP/1990/4169

Trentham Park and its educational work. It established branches at Levin and Te Horo, which amalgamated in 1988 as the Horowhenua Animal Rescue Society.[59]

The Humane Society of New Zealand, formed in Auckland in 1975, had a different philosophy. As an article describing its work explained, 'Rather than cope with enormous numbers of unwanted or uncared for animals, they prefer to teach responsible pet ownership, to make the public aware of the undesirable results of pet over-population.'[60] Echoing the first SPCA educational programmes for children, the society ran a Kindness Club for junior members, who had to vow: 'I promise to be kind to animals as well as to people and to speak and act in defence of all living creatures.'[61] Despite its initial stance, the society was eventually drawn into rescuing and rehoming animals.

~

Fashion was partly responsible for the overpopulation problem. Breeders willingly provided pedigree animals for those people who wanted an unusual or exotic pet. As early as 1972, the Waikato SPCA suggested that dog breeders were producing excessive numbers of puppies, many of which ended up on the streets. SPCA members also pointed out that unregulated breeding of animals was resulting in genetic defects, including blindness, deafness, joint deformities and behavioural problems – all possible reasons why owners might abandon pets.[62] The appearance of pedigree dogs among the unwanted animals brought into SPCA shelters in the 1980s was a sign, according to the society, 'that there are far too many dogs being bred'.[63]

Prized breeds of cats, too, were dumped. In 1993 Carol Kisby, long-time president of the Wellington Cats Protection League, recalled a case of two Persians:

> *I couldn't even speak to the woman who brought them to me. I just picked them up and I didn't tell her to go, but my body language said 'Go'. Then I just sat down and howled, they were in such a state. Their fur was so matted they could hardly walk. I rushed them off to the vet to have them shaved. Underneath they were covered in ringworm, running sores.*[64]

Fads for certain breeds were causing problems on another front. In the early 1980s Rottweilers enjoyed a vogue among dog lovers, and a Rottweiler club was set up in Auckland. But because Rottweilers were sometimes chosen by owners who wanted to project a threatening, macho image, many people feared them.[65] Pit bull terriers got the same response, with more reason. In 1987, after much public debate and forceful SPCA opposition, importation of American pit bulls was permitted. The strongest of all dogs by weight, the pit bull was popular

with pig hunters, but soon gained a reputation for savage attacks on other animals and people. It also became associated with sinister activities such as dog fights, often organised by gangs.[66] The uproar over pit bulls was reminiscent of the debate about Alsatians in the 1930s. The recognition that some dog breeds were potentially extremely dangerous swelled a tide of anti-pet and particularly anti-dog sentiment that had been ebbing and flowing for years.

Public concern about dog attacks and dangerous dogs led to increased regulation of dogs and dog owners in the 1980s and 1990s through further dog control acts. It seemed impossible, however, to reach agreement on which dogs were dangerous: many involved in attacks were breeds usually considered to be docile, such as Labradors. The debate began to resemble that for and against guns in the United States. Some people defended dogs, claiming that owners were the problem, while others took the stance that all dogs, in certain circumstances, were capable of attacking.[67]

In the end, a shocking attack on a child was the spur for radical legal changes. In 2003, seven-year-old Carolina Anderson was savaged by a previously well-behaved Staffordshire terrier in an Auckland park. The dog ripped the skin from her face down to the bone and badly damaged her right eye. The owners were imprisoned for two months and ordered to pay compensation to the Andersons; the dog was promptly put down.[68] Politicians, viewing photographs of Carolina's horrific injuries, vowed to review the law.

Subsequently several breeds, including American pit bull terriers, were classified as dangerous and their importation was banned. A new classification of 'menacing' was introduced, and all such dogs had to be muzzled in public. Council powers to seize dogs were strengthened, and penalties for breaches of the law were increased. The most significant change was the introduction of microchipping, in response to a case made by Bob Kerridge of the Auckland SPCA. With the exception of working farm dogs, all dogs first registered from 1 July 2006 and those classified as dangerous or menacing had to have a microchip transponder with a unique number implanted. Details of the dog and its owner were then recorded on a national dog database, making it easier to track problem dogs and reunite stray dogs and owners.[69]

~

Safety was just one reason for tighter dog control. Over the previous four decades, local bodies had increasingly placed restrictions on dogs and their owners for other reasons. In 1969, in an attempt to address the problem of stray and wandering animals, the Wellington City Council introduced zones within the city where dogs were prohibited or allowed only on a lead. Other local

This Health Department poster warning of the dangers of hydatids dates from the early 1960s. Unlike other campaigns, which targeted adults, particularly farmers, this one was clearly aimed at children, who were likely to treat strange dogs as pets. Concern about hydatids was probably one reason why in the twentieth century many country children were forbidden by their parents to play with farm dogs.

Archives New Zealand. Reference: AAFB 24223 W2555/2 (R23461775)

authorities followed suit, banning dogs from many public places. By the 1970s it was becoming more difficult for urban dog owners to find spaces to exercise their dogs.[70] This prompted the introduction of special dog exercise areas in urban parks and on beaches.

From 1959 until 1996, when the disease was finally wiped out, combating hydatids was another important aspect of dog control. Hydatids had been introduced to New Zealand in the mid-nineteenth century with sheep imported from Australia. It was caused by a tapeworm, *Echinococcus granulosus*, which lived in the gut of dogs that had eaten offal from dead sheep containing fertile hydatid cysts. Sheep in turn became infected by grazing on pasture contaminated with the faeces of dogs carrying hydatids. The hydatids eggs excreted by dogs could easily be transferred to humans. Children patting dogs or playing near dog droppings were particularly at risk – in fact hydatids was often described as a children's disease. Hydatids cysts could develop in the lungs, liver, heart and brain, and major surgery was the only treatment. Often the disease was fatal. By the mid-twentieth century New Zealand had the highest rate of hydatids disease in the developed world.[71]

One of the main reasons hydatids was not overcome sooner was that some farmers persisted in feeding their dogs uncooked sheep meat and offal, despite education initiatives. Finally in 1959 a national control programme began, administered by local authorities. This involved inspection of all dogs, including pets, at dog dosing strips around the country – a routine immortalised in Ken Avery's comic song 'By the Dog Dosing Strip at Dunsandel'. The reality was less amusing: the dogs were purged and their faeces examined for signs of infection, and those affected were treated. The process was unpleasant for both dogs and their owners: 'On purging day at the hydatid dosing strip, dogs did not behave like man's best friend. On seeing the threatening pellet dosing gun nozzle – and the anticipatory shovel – many put on a Disney cartoon performance. Legs braced, leash taut, they braked and skidded their way towards the dreaded Hydatid Control Officer.'[72] Sometimes the officers made house calls, getting the same reaction from dogs that knew what was coming.

Then there were the health and pollution problems caused by dogs fouling city streets and public places. By the 1980s some councils had introduced 'pooper scooper' bylaws requiring owners to clean up after their dogs.[73] Taking the dog for a walk now meant carrying a plastic 'poo bag'.

Increased regulation provoked complaints from dog owners. In 2008 newspaper columnist and dog owner Linley Boniface claimed that Wellington was 'the least dog-friendly city in New Zealand', and observed that 'in recent years dog owners have been put in the same category as other types of weirdos who hang around trees in parks'. She maintained that the city's designated dog exercise areas were 'on sections of wasteland so remote and uninhabitable that I doubt crack dealers would be prepared to set up operations there'. She pointed out that these areas lacked facilities such as dog waste bins, and alleged that council staff were overzealous in patrolling and fining owners.[74]

Wellington city councillor Stephanie Cook demonstrates how to use an 'Absolutely Poo-sitively Wellington doggie-doo bag' in April 1998, while her dogs Roxy (front) and Pup look on with interest. That year the council distributed 50,000 of the bags free in an attempt to persuade dog owners to pick up after their dogs. Those caught not doing so were liable for a $200 instant fine.

Alexander Turnbull Library, Dominion Post Collection. Reference: EP/1998/1248

But it was clear that some citizens were less than enthusiastic about other people's canine companions: they were annoyed by dogs barking incessantly when left chained or penned while owners were at work, startled by large or exuberant dogs rushing up to them or their children when they were out walking, and disgusted by dog excrement in streets and parks. Responding to Linley Boniface's column, Wellington City Council Public Health Officer, Alison Box, commented, 'We know thousands of Wellingtonians, like Linley, love dogs. Thousands more Wellingtonians, however, are either not interested in dogs or, in fact, do not like them. Many are frightened by them.'[75]

~

Another challenge to New Zealand pet owners came from conservationists, who by the 1970s were more outspoken about the threat posed by certain animals to New Zealand's native flora and fauna. The Australian brush-tailed possum, introduced in the nineteenth century for the fur trade, was one such animal. Originally regarded with favour – a writer to the *Otago Witness* in 1894 claimed 'they are perfectly harmless and make excellent pets'[76] – by the 1970s possums were widely acknowledged to be serious pests. They bred rapidly, eating their way through bush and preying on native birds and their eggs. Also, as carriers of bovine tuberculosis they were a concern to the farming industry. Some people, however, still found them very appealing: in 1976 it was estimated that, north of Taumarunui, over 90 permits had been issued under the Noxious Animals Act 1967 for pet possums. One of the conditions of the permit was that owners had to take all practical steps to stop them breeding. But some people kept possums without a permit, and others allowed them to range freely.[77]

Environmental problems were also created by the demand for unusual pets, which often led to illegal import of some species. By the late 1970s the Ministry of Agriculture and Fisheries was forced to tighten up import regulations for tropical fish because of the arrival of undesirable species, including koi carp. When cleaning aquariums, some owners released fish and invasive aquatic weeds into waterways, where they competed with native species. In February 1982 the Noxious Plants Council banned the sale and distribution of aquatic plants that were beginning to infest rivers and lakes.[78]

Ferrets, the pet of choice for the young and trendy from the 1970s, were also seen as a potential menace to New Zealand's native wildlife. Under Wildlife Regulations of 1985 people could own up to two ferrets but needed a licence to breed or sell them. Conservationists worried that escaped pet ferrets would swell the population of those that had been introduced in the 1880s to control rabbits. Wild ferrets had multiplied and were extremely efficient predators of native birds. Dismissing protests by owners, in 2002 the Department of Conservation declared ferrets unwanted organisms under the Biosecurity Act, and subsequently there was a ban on selling, distributing and breeding them.[79] These measures were intended to phase out all pet ferrets in New Zealand, but some owners continued to resist through a 'ferret underground': 'They are my children. Why should I let the government take them away?' said one owner in 2008.[80]

Environmental concerns led to a backlash against more common pets, such as cats and dogs. As early as the mid-nineteenth century some people recognised that cats could threaten native bird populations. Charles Hursthouse observed in 1857 the tendency of settlers' cats to 'prowl about the near woods' and breed generations of wild cats that did not depend on humans.[81] A few decades later

An eight-year-old Hawke's Bay farm boy, referred to simply as 'Davy Crockett', was pictured with his pet, Percy the possum, in the *Evening Post* in 1973. Percy apparently went everywhere with his young owner, often attached to the front of his jumper or on top of his head. The accompanying article cautioned readers who wanted to keep a pet possum that they would need to obtain a permit under the Noxious Animals Act 1967 first.

Alexander Turnbull Library, Dominion Post Collection. Reference: EP/1973/4951

Westland explorer Charlie Douglas confirmed the suspicion that there were wild cats in the bush: 'Before we left the Copland we saw the Tracks of a Cat … a few more months and pussy will extend operations and the small birds will vanish forever.'[82] Feral cats on island bird sanctuaries, the first of which were established in the late nineteenth century, had to hunt to survive and soon wreaked havoc on indigenous species. Efforts to eradicate them began in the 1890s, and were redoubled by the Wildlife Service after World War

II, using increasingly harsh measures: gin traps, biological control through the introduction of feline enteritis and 1080 poison.[83]

Because of their formidable reputation for catching rodents and other small animals, cats were deliberately introduced to control rabbits on farmland. The Amuri Rabbit Board, for example, liberated 400 cats, along with 1000 stoats and 1000 ferrets, in 1888. Large numbers of cats were also released in Wairarapa and Kaikoura in the 1880s to deal with rabbit infestations. In the 1890s cats were released on Mangere Island, in the Chathams group, to combat the rabbit problem there, and there were proposals to use cats for rabbit control in Canterbury as late as the 1960s.[84] These cats were not only unable to control the extraordinary numbers of rabbits but they also bred and turned their attention to other prey, notably birds, with devastating effect.

By the 1960s some conservationists became concerned that abandoned cats in and near urban areas were killing off native birds. In 1966 the Wildlife Service of the Department of Internal Affairs prepared a pamphlet for all New Zealand households, urging people not to dump unwanted cats on the outskirts of towns and in bush areas. 'If you have to dispose of cats or kittens, have it done humanely. Don't abandon them. Think first of the hardships they will endure when deprived of your care, then consider the birds that will be threatened.'[85] By presenting both the conservation and cruelty aspects of the problem, this initiative gained wide support: SPCAs, acclimatisation societies and all Royal Forest and Bird Protection Society branches helped to distribute the pamphlet, which went through several printings.[86]

As environmental awareness grew, even perfectly tame household cats were looked at askance. One of New Zealand's most distressing conservation disasters had been the loss of the country's only flightless perching bird, the Stephens Island wren. Discovered in 1894, it became extinct in 1895 and the prime suspect was Tibbles, the lighthouse keeper's cat.[87] A century later scientists began to suggest that even well-fed suburban cats were capable of killing large numbers of native birds, insects and lizards each year. In one study, even a collar with a bell did not prevent cats from killing – it just lowered their strike rate.[88] The suggestion that this carnage was outweighed by the feline propensity to hunt that other great enemy of native birds, rats, did not convince some conservationists. According to them, keeping cats indoors all the time was the only way to stop them laying waste to indigenous wildlife. Pet dogs, too, came under suspicion: when let loose in bush areas they were known to kill birds, particularly the threatened kiwi.[89]

In 1997 Forest and Bird began to advocate pet-free subdivisions in ecologically sensitive areas. The first such subdivision was Mahakirau Forest

A pamphlet, *Problem Cats*, was first produced in 1966 by the Wildlife Service and distributed to all New Zealand households. It went through several printings. As the cover suggests, the main purpose of this campaign was to limit the threat to native wildlife by cats living in forested areas.

Archives New Zealand. Reference: AANS W3546/20 WIL 13/10/6 (R1433359)

The Wildlife Service pamphlet also drew attention to the cruelty of people dumping domestic cats and kittens in bush reserves where they either starved or learned painfully to fend for themselves. It was far-sighted in acknowledging both the humane and conservation sides of the story.

Archives New Zealand. Reference: AANS W3546/20 WIL 13/10/6 (R1433359)

Estate, adjoining the Manaia Forest Sanctuary on the Coromandel Peninsula. After hearing the Forest and Bird case, the developers recognised the potential market for eco-subdivisions and gained regional council endorsement for a condition of sale that new owners could not bring with them any introduced species of animals or fish, including pets. While acknowledging that one of the attractions of pet ownership was the way it allowed people to forge an empathetic link with the animal world, eco-advocates suggested, 'It is a bold new mind set to suggest that, in some communities, people might live in greater harmony with nature without the ubiquitous cat and dog.'[90] Within five years similar 'wildlife friendly' subdivisions had been established on the Coromandel Peninsula and the Hauraki Islands, and in Northland and the Kapiti Coast and Wellington regions.[91]

In 2009 fears about global warming and the slowing of world oil production generated yet another environmental argument against pets. *Time to Eat the Dog*:

The real guide to sustainable living, by New Zealand academics Robert and Brenda Vale, compared the ecological footprints (or pawprints) of various common pets, by calculating what they ate and how much land it took to produce their food. The Vales found that the 'pawprint' of a large dog was about twice that of a Land Cruiser driven 10,000 kilometres a year, based on the land required to produce the car's fuel. A cat's impact was nearly equivalent to that of a Volkswagen Golf. Controversial solutions they suggested included keeping edible or food-producing animals such as chickens, pigs and rabbits, or avoiding pet keeping altogether.

> *If we accept that we need to take steps, we can metaphorically 'eat the dog' by not replacing our pet, as part of our plan to reduce our personal impact on the planet. If we do not take heed, we may find ourselves in an unplanned future of resource shortages and high prices when we may be forced to eat the dog to keep the family going. Either way, it may not be a good time to be a dog.*[92]

Needless to say, the more radical solutions proposed by environmentalists did not go down well with many pet owners. The Vales' book provoked an outcry. A suggestion by Raewyn Empson, Conservation Manager for Wellington's Karori Sanctuary, that neighbouring property owners should not replace a pet cat if it died, was roundly opposed by the majority of respondents to a 2012 newspaper survey.[93] A similar campaign by entrepreneur Gareth Morgan in 2013 generated passionate opposition from cat lovers.[94]

Clashing views hampered efforts to find humane answers to the problem of 'excess' animals, illustrated in the debate over supported cat colonies. Some people saw this concept, which had been implemented with some success in France, Britain, the United States and Scandinavia from the 1970s, as a solution to the urban stray cat problem. The cats were trapped, neutered and if necessary provided with veterinary treatment, then returned to the colony. Volunteers fed them and monitored the colony to ensure that sick cats were treated and new arrivals trapped and neutered. From the 1990s New Zealand advocates of cat colonies established organisations such as Forgotten Felines, the Lonely Miaow Association and the SPCA Auckland Cat Coalition. Opponents, however, portrayed colony cats as vicious, carriers of disease and a threat to wildlife.[95]

In the early twenty-first century animal overpopulation was still a major concern. Despite the efforts of an even more diverse range of shelters, refuges and rescue organisations, in 2010 the Royal New Zealand SPCA estimated that as many as 50,000 animals were being euthanised at New Zealand shelters each year.[96] Strays continued to create headaches in and near urban areas. And the urge of some people to rescue and care for these animals contrasted with the desire of others to get rid of them. Clearly, one person's pet was another person's pest.

Fur furore

IN MID-1969 panic spread among cat lovers around New Zealand, especially in Wellington. Home-loving cats were disappearing without trace, and owners feared that they had been stolen. This suspicion grew with media reports that a British company was making enquiries in Lower Hutt about the possibility of importing cat skins from New Zealand. At that time fur coats were still the rage, and cat skins were allegedly worth $6.50 each on the British market, compared with $1.50 for possum skins.

Anna Jones, the organiser of Wellington's Stray Cat Food Trust Fund, started a petition to parliament, which rapidly obtained 4841 signatures. Briefly it laid out the case:

1. That proposals have been made for the exporting of domestic cat skins.
2. That such proposals, if proceeded with, would be objected to by animal lovers throughout New Zealand.
3. That such proposals would lead to domestic pets being at risk of being seized, stolen and killed for the obtaining of skins.

   Your petitioners therefore humbly pray that your Honourable House will pass legislation prohibiting the exporting of skins of all cats or the use of such skins for commercial purposes in New Zealand.[97]

In the publicity that followed, at least one observer saw a possible answer to the cat overpopulation problem. A writer to the *Dominion* using the pseudonym 'Poor Pussy' commented, 'If the proposed commercial enterprise to trade in cat skins were set up it would be a simple matter for owners of unwanted felines to notify the organisation, which could collect the animals for painless disposal.'[98] But many people feared that the prospect of commercial gain would encourage unscrupulous people to 'catnap' pets, and some, such as Anna Jones, believed that even unwanted cats deserved protection from such a fate.

Messages of support for the petition flowed in. 'Why should we have to live in constant fear of losing our treasured friends who have been companions to us through the years?' asked Mrs D. Sherley of Seatoun, Wellington. 'The idea of the skinning of domestic cats is absolutely horrifying to the animal lover and on behalf of all the poor strays and neglected cats I say a Mighty big Thankyou,' wrote 'Ann of Otaki'. 'This is a practice which I feel must be halted at all costs before people start breeding cats for this specific purpose, as is already done with so many unfortunate animals,' added Mrs E. McNeill of Christchurch. And Mrs F.E. Smith of Wanganui no doubt summed up the thoughts of many when she said, 'Good luck to Miss Jones for the stand she is taking on behalf of poor old puss and poor young puss alike who have the misfortune to be born with a fur coat, apparently now considered highly profitable for commercial interests, may it continue to be worn by its rightful owner. God Bless Puss.'[99]

Arnold Nordmeyer, MP for Island Bay, presented the petition to parliament in June, and it got a favourable reception. There was then a flurry of official activity as the departments of Internal Affairs, Agriculture and Customs examined their legislation to see if it could be amended. Customs pointed out that no cat skins had in fact been exported, and there was no evidence of any processing of skins in New Zealand.[100] But in late July, a Canterbury SPCA inspector found 10 cat carcasses at the Methven dump, and in his opinion they had been skinned by an expert: 'There was not one bit of hair left on them right down to the nose.'[101] The Minister of Customs was forced to concede that there could be a problem. In a *New Zealand Gazette* notice dated 21 August 1969, he made the export of cat skins illegal.[102]

Not for the first time, New Zealand pet owners proved to be a powerful pressure group.

North Egmont Hostelry

We the undersigned verify the fact that the cat ("Ginger") from the Mountain House followed us right into the Crater of Mount Egmont on Tuesday January 16th 1917. A photo was taken in the crater of the said cat.

Signed H. McCallum Rundle
A. Wells
W. M. Clemance
B. Pigott
P. S. Clemance
A. E. Clemance

Chapter 9
Local *legends*

Harry Williams holds a blasé Ginger at the summit of Mt Taranaki on 16 January 1917, after the cat's amazing ascent of the mountain.

Puke Ariki, New Plymouth. Reference: PHO2012-0645

A testimonial certifying that Ginger conquered Mt Taranaki was signed by Harry Williams and the five women who made the climb. It and other artifacts, including Ginger's collar, are now in New Plymouth's Puke Ariki Museum.

Puke Ariki, New Plymouth. Reference: ARC2002-68

One blustery day in January 1917, five women and their male guide trudged through a fresh fall of snow to the top of Mt Taranaki, or Egmont as it was then known. It was not unusual for intrepid trampers to scale the peak; what made this ascent memorable was that the group was followed by a six-month-old cat named Ginger. 'This kitten, belonging to the hostel,' the *Taranaki Herald* later reported, 'has often followed parties to Humphries' Castle [a crag on the mountain], but on this occasion went right to the top and was photographed there. On account of the party glissading a good way down, thus coming too quick for any cat, Mr Williams carried it back home.'[1]

Ginger was then a well-known identity at North Egmont Mountain House. Rescued from the bush as a kitten by the manager, Harry Williams, he was soon following tramping and walking parties, even through snow. His paws were often frostbitten as a result, and after an expedition he would lie on his back with his legs in the air to ease the pain. His most notable adventure was to conquer the summit, and following this he became quite a star.[2] He was not unique. New Zealand has had plenty of animal celebrities in the past 160 years – some enjoying regional fame, others becoming nationally and even internationally known. While they lived, the public followed their exploits avidly, and when they died, they were often deeply mourned.

~

The concept of celebrity emerged in the western world in the nineteenth century, fostered by the expanding news media. Probably because it coincided with the rise of pet culture, celebrity soon extended from prominent people to outstanding animals.[3] One of the first and best-known animal celebrities was Greyfriars Bobby, a Skye terrier who between 1858 and 1872 faithfully guarded his owner's grave in Greyfriars Churchyard, Edinburgh, and is memorialised there.[4] Another was Balto, canine leader of a sled dog team that in 1925, in sub-zero temperatures, delivered an urgently needed diphtheria anti-toxin to the town of Nome in Alaska. There is a statue to him in New York's Central Park.[5]

Some animals drew special attention for a variety of reasons. Remarkable achievements like Ginger's mountaineering feat quickly attracted notice. An animal might display traits or behaviours that humans admired, such as unusual speed, strength or beauty. It might inhabit or frequent a particular place. It might be owned by a well-known person. But for an animal to achieve genuine celebrity status, people had to relate to it – and they did this by interpreting its behaviour in human terms. This anthropomorphic way of thinking came naturally to pet owners.[6] If people thought an animal was brave or self-sacrificing they regarded it with respect and admiration. If they detected endearing traits such as playfulness, loyalty or friendliness, they were won over. People projected their feelings about their pets onto such animals, which became, in a sense, public pets.[7]

Animal celebrity was a human invention and it served human ends. Animal stars had commercial potential. They could be used to sell products and promote brands. They could attract support for public causes such as prevention of cruelty towards animals, and conservation. They could be used for political purposes. And they could be central to national mythologies.

~

A classic New Zealand example of such mythologising is the story of James Mackenzie and his dog. For Pakeha, it became a compelling pioneering legend.

Born in Scotland, James Mackenzie emigrated to Australia about 1849. He came to New Zealand in the 1850s, working as a drover in the hope of acquiring his own land. In 1855 pursuers tracked him to the basin of the upper Waitaki River, South Canterbury, where he was found with a mob of around 1000 sheep that had recently gone missing from the huge Levels Station, north of Timaru. It appeared that, with the help of his dog, he had driven the sheep south, fording rivers and traversing a difficult pass through the Southern Alps to the plains beyond.[8] Mackenzie fled the scene, leaving the dog faithfully guarding the sheep. After evading capture for some days, he was arrested and tried at Lyttelton for theft. Remaining silent during the proceedings, he was found guilty and jailed for five years with hard labour.

All accounts emphasise Mackenzie's special understanding with his dog. One contemporary told how the dog was brought into the courtroom during the trial. She immediately recognised her master, wagging her tail and whining. On seeing her, Mackenzie broke down and tearfully begged the judge to allow her to accompany him to jail.[9] Another eyewitness later wrote a heart-rending description of the scene:

> *When the judge called out, 'Bring in the dog' I saw McKenzie [sic] start and gnaw his fingers a moment as the crowd stared at the slim timid black beast that had outwitted grey old shepherds with the dumb tricks McKenzie had taught her. She slipped her chain coming in and in another minute the slim, sad-eyed thing was scratching and whining at the woodwork trying to get to McKenzie. And McKenzie – the dog's eyes had made a baby of him, six-footer though he was – the tears ran down and lost themselves in his red beard as he said, 'Aye Lassie, poor Lassie, they've got you too.'*[10]

Unable to tolerate imprisonment, Mackenzie escaped twice, was recaptured and finally placed in irons. Henry Tancred, Sheriff and Commissioner of Police for Canterbury, intervened to have his case reconsidered and it was decided that his trial had been flawed, partly because as a native Gaelic speaker with poor English Mackenzie understood little of the proceedings and was unable to defend himself. In 1856 he was pardoned and it is believed he returned to Australia.

People marvelled at the unusual skill and loyalty of Mackenzie's dog, a black and tan Border collie called Friday. Her exceptional ability to mesmerise such a large flock of sheep into going in the right direction allowed Mackenzie to achieve his stupendous feat. Said to be one of the first 'strong-eyed' sheep dogs in New Zealand,[11] she came to be revered by shepherds.

Friday's fate is unknown. One story says that the magistrate ordered her to be destroyed.[12] Another claims she was taken south 'where for years her progeny was much sought after'.[13] Yet another maintains she was kept by a police inspector in Christchurch for a while and then given to a runholder: although several shepherds tried to work her in the Gaelic language she was used to, she would not answer to commands

This old photograph from the Alexander Turnbull Library collections is filed under 'Mackenzie' and labelled simply 'The famous dog'. Could it be Friday, the legendary accomplice of South Canterbury sheep rustler James Mackenzie? *Alexander Turnbull Library. Reference: F-7818-1/2*

given by anyone other than Mackenzie.[14] There are even suggestions she may have ended up as a working dog at The Levels, the station from which the sheep disappeared.[15] This mystery probably accounts for some of the story's lasting grip on the public imagination.

Within just a few years of Mackenzie's trial, the region where he was discovered was being referred to as the Mackenzie Country,[16] and the pass he crossed to get there was named the Mackenzie Pass. However, the legend really began to flourish when Canterbury celebrated its fiftieth jubilee in 1900. A commemorative book recounted it, newspaper articles gave it further publicity and it was repeated and elaborated in subsequent local and national histories. Mackenzie's physical fortitude, daring and initiative were among the reasons he became a folk hero. But the close bond between him and his dog was the key to the story's continuing appeal.

~

Friday did not achieve national renown until many years after her death. Another nineteenth-century animal icon, however, was feted in the media in his lifetime. He became not just locally but internationally famous, helping to create New Zealand's image overseas as a natural wonderland.

Around 1888 a dolphin began meeting steamers travelling between Wellington and Nelson near the entrance to Pelorus Sound. Soon people were calling him Pelorus Jack (although his gender was never confirmed – he could have been Pelorus Jill). He would accompany a vessel across Admiralty Bay as far as Collinet Point adjacent to the turbulent French Pass, where he would meet ships travelling in the opposite direction. He would often stay with a ship as long as 20 minutes, and locals who were familiar with his habits claimed that he preferred faster steamers. To the amazement and pleasure of all who witnessed his appearances, he would play about the bow and rub against the vessel. Some said he was feeding off the cuttlefish that were collected by the ship as it moved through the water, others that he was ridding himself of barnacles. A more recent theory is that he enjoyed being carried along by the bow wave.[17]

Most people knew little about dolphins at this time – Pelorus Jack was often referred to as 'the fish'. Those who saw him were astonished by his intelligence: he would avoid certain vessels if their passengers had tried to harm him in the past, and he seemed to know when a ship was approaching. Aside from his unusual habits, the big dolphin – he was about 14 ft (4.2 m) long – was a striking colour: bluish-white, with dark flippers. This pallor made his appearances after dark particularly memorable: 'At night, when the sea is

Pelorus Jack's international fame was confirmed when he featured on the front page of the Illustrated London News *on 24 December 1910. This artist's impression was accompanied by a somewhat inaccurate caption: 'The fish that is under special government protection: Pelorus Jack escorting a steamer.'*

National Library of New Zealand, General Lending Collection – copy provided by Alexander Turnbull Library. Reference: S-L-242-COVER

The Illustrated London News

REGISTERED AT THE GENERAL POST OFFICE AS A NEWSPAPER.

No. 3740.—VOL. CXXXVII.   SATURDAY, DECEMBER 24, 1910.   With Supplement in Colours, In Christmas Mood.   SIXPENCE.

THE FISH THAT IS UNDER SPECIAL GOVERNMENT PROTECTION: PELORUS JACK ESCORTING A STEAMER.

As we note under the photographs of the fish which appear elsewhere in this number, Pelorus Jack, a Risso's Dolphin, is in the habit of escorting steamers, by day and night, on the Nelson-Wellington run. He is specially protected by Clause 4e of the Fisheries Regulations of the New Zealand Government. Many stories are told of him. One is that there dwells in him the spirit of a brave Frenchman who was drowned while attempting to rescue a countryman. Pelorus Jack is said to take his name from this man, who was called Jacques Trégoulet. It may also be noted that it is said that on one occasion a vessel bumped into the fish, with the result that it now avoids this particular ship as a plague.

DRAWING BY OUR SPECIAL ARTIST, CECIL KING—SEE PHOTOGRAPHS ON ANOTHER PAGE.

phosphorescent, he presents a magnificent and weird spectacle – darting about the bows like a fiery torpedo, followed by an ever-widening trail of greenish light.'[18] Many tried to photograph him but he was too fast for most camera shutters; a short film and a few blurred snapshots are all that survive.

After hearing reports of some people trying to shoot or harpoon Pelorus Jack, the Reverend D.C. Bates lobbied for him to be legally protected, working through the Department of Tourist and Health Resorts, which had been established in 1901. Bates's identification of Pelorus Jack as a rare Risso's dolphin (*Grampus griseus*) helped the case for his protection, and the Tourist Department was beginning to see him as a valuable visitor attraction, but it was also obvious that the public regarded him with affection. In a memo to his minister, department head T.E. Donne noted, 'There is a good deal of sentiment regarding Pelorus Jack, and I think it would be a popular act if the Government were to extend protection to it, besides being a very good advertisement.'[19]

In 1904 an Order-in-Council under the Sea Fisheries Act protected Pelorus Jack – a world first. The order, which prohibited the taking of Risso's dolphins in Cook Strait and adjacent bays, sounds and estuaries for five years, was renewed in 1906 and again in 1911. The regulation was necessary, as Cook Strait was then a centre for the whaling industry.

It was not just Pakeha seafarers and travellers who looked out for Pelorus Jack. Whales and dolphins had always had great significance for Maori, who regarded them as guardians. Maori tribes living around Cook Strait immediately recognised and revered Pelorus Jack as a taniwha: a spiritual creature. In his 1911 booklet, *Pelorus Jack: The white dolphin of French Pass*, James Cowan recounted an interview with Kipa Hemi Whiro, an elder of the Ngati Huia tribe, who identified the dolphin as Kaikai-a-waro, a taniwha who had accompanied his ancestor Matua-hautere when he came to the Sounds. Kipa told how Kaikai-a-waro was the embodiment of tribal mana and the protector of those who ventured out to sea in their canoes.[20] Other Maori saw the dolphin as the taniwha Tuhirangi, who was said to have guided the great explorer Kupe to New Zealand. Tuhirangi was left by Kupe at in the Sounds to guide canoes across the treacherous waters of the strait between the North and South islands.[21]

The story of Pelorus Jack spread by word of mouth among visitors to New Zealand, and through articles published in New Zealand, American and British newspapers. He was also the subject of several booklets. His publicity included front-page coverage in the *London Illustrated News* in December 1910. The Tourist Department, eager to capitalise on the interest, supplied information for journalists and other curious individuals, and distributed postcards of Pelorus Jack. Many overseas visitors, including writers Mark Twain and Frank Bullen, travelled to Nelson especially to see him, impressed by the fact that he was the first dolphin in the world to be legally protected. Pelorus Jack helped to reinforce the image of New Zealand as an awe-inspiring tourist destination, and his special status suggested also that New Zealanders as a people were far-sighted and humane: an idea that appealed to national pride.

Pelorus Jack was last seen in late 1912. There were theories that he was harpooned by Swedish whalers or killed by the twin propellers of the steamer *Arahura*. It is probable, however, that he simply died of old age.

~

Some of the animal celebrities that came after Pelorus Jack were working or wild animals, given the status of honorary pets,[22] but many were actually pets. Although their special standing was the outcome of media promotion, they often came to public notice in the first place through the efforts of their owners. The eagerness of some people to publicise their animal's attributes suggests they were confident of a receptive audience of like-minded pet owners.

Jack, a rough-haired collie, became well known in the Auckland region in the mid-1930s, and his fame outlasted him because he was the subject of a book. Perhaps it is more correct to say he was the author of the book, for in a triumph of anthropomorphism it was written by his owner, George Parker, as if Jack himself had narrated it. *'Jack': A true story of a clever New Zealand farm dog* was published by the Auckland Sunday School Union in 1945 after Jack's death. As well as Jack's 'autobiography', the book contained extracts from stories about him in the *New Zealand Herald* between 1933 and 1935, and letters from W.J. Jordan, the High Commissioner in London, former Governor-General Lord Bledisloe and others, testifying to his amazing skills.

Parker was a poultry farmer at Mangere, then a rural district on the outskirts of Auckland, and he trained Jack to do a range of tasks on the farm. Jack proved to be extremely clever and quick to learn. Among other things, he could 'bring in' individual cows and horses when Parker called their names, divide a flock of hens by their colour and feed them from a grain box that he carried in his mouth and deliberately shook out, fetch named tools out of a shed, carry notes to and from the house, and climb ladders. He could also

'Jack the wonder dog' was photographed some time in the mid-1930s, having just fed the chickens on the Mangere poultry farm where he lived. He did this by carrying a box in his mouth and shaking out the grain.

G.H. Parker (1945), 'Jack': A true story of a clever New Zealand farm dog, Auckland Sunday School Union, Auckland, opposite p. 27

open gates by walking on his hind legs, so that the pony and sledge driven by Parker could pass through. This trick was filmed by Fox Films for a newsreel, *Clever Dogs of the World*, which was shown throughout New Zealand and Australia in the 1930s.[23]

As well as mastering these tasks, Jack had to overcome one vice that was unforgivable on a poultry farm – as a puppy he loved eating raw eggs. Not only did he learn to refrain from eating eggs, he would actually help to gather them, bringing them out one by one in his mouth. According to a 1935 *Herald* report entitled 'Jack the wonder dog',

> at one time a pullet that had been reared near the house used to lay in Jack's kennel, and as the bucket they collect the eggs in came past, he would dart into the kennel and bring the egg out without being told to do so. This action was all the more praiseworthy and reflected great credit on the training, when it is remembered that, in all probability, the egg had been laid some time, and with his former reputation as an egg-eater, it would not have been safe for a minute, much less several hours.[24]

'Jack' was firmly in the tradition of nineteenth-century educational children's literature about animals. It explained how useful dogs were when well trained, and confirmed how remarkably intelligent some could be. It also provided a moral example for children to follow. Describing his early training, Jack emphasised the importance of obedience: 'Oh boys and girls, readers of this little book, how much brighter and happier life will be for you if you learn early in life to obey your parents and guardians. I will go further and say life will be fuller and richer and freer if you will submit your will to theirs.'[25] And finally, it reinforced the importance of kindness to animals. Jack let it be known that he was trained without harsh treatment – George Parker evidently supported the SPCA. Jack gave a demonstration of his skills at the opening of the Penrose Blue Cross Hospital in 1934,[26] and the organiser of the SPCA Junior League endorsed the book.

When Jack died of old age in the late 1930s George Parker had his skin cured and made into a rug. Parker considered this a fitting tribute to the memory of a special animal. So did the owner of Sutherland's Tannery in Onehunga, who wrote a touching letter of condolence:

> *Dear Mr Parker,*
>
> *When reaching the works this morning I was very surprised and shocked to see the skin of your celebrated dog Jack brought for us to cure. I am sorry you have had to separate with your friend, for you must feel parting with him very much. I write this to convey my sympathy (feeble though it be) at your loss. The man who is curing the hide has my instructions to do the very best he can to make a good job of it. Several of the staff add their sympathy as well.*

Believe me,
Yours faithfully,
J. Lawry
PS: We feel it a privilege to dress the skin of such a wonderful dog — without charge.[27]

~

The story of another exceptional animal that rose to fame 60 years later has much in common with that of Jack, showing the continuing popularity of pet celebrities. In the mid-1990s, when Taranaki resident Max Corkill set off on his motorcycle, his black cat Rastus eagerly went along for the ride, either in a special bag or with front paws on the handlebars. Rastus was a character with some very non-feline quirks: he growled like a dog, ate a vegetarian diet and even refrained from stalking birds. He was allegedly friendly with dogs, merely tolerating other cats.

Like Jack, Rastus had unusual abilities, but was transformed with the help of his owner into a media star through a carefully crafted image that appealed to people's love of pets. With his specially made helmet (a converted ice cream sundae dish), goggles and red bandana, 'the motorcycling moggy' was a press photographer's dream, and also attracted television cameras. He soon had a high profile and was used for promotional and charity purposes. With his owner he starred in a television advertisement for a brand of tea, visited schools and made appearances at events to raise money for the SPCA.

Sadly Rastus, along with Max Corkill and his partner Gaynor Martin, died in a head-on crash with a car in January 1998. Their funeral procession was a solemn event, with over 1000 bikers following the hearses from Inglewood to New Plymouth crematorium.[28] After their deaths, the memory of Rastus and Max was kept fresh with an internet tribute site, and a series of children's books was written about their adventures.[29]

~

The prevalence of strays in cities, particularly from the twentieth century, was a moral challenge to the thinking animal lover. A lost or suffering animal often brought forth expressions of sympathy and protectiveness. Acts of kindness towards homeless or abandoned animals made people feel they were doing something to ease the apparently insoluble problem. One stray that

This poster, 'signed' by Rastus, shows him in his helmet and kerchief riding on the motorbike driven by Max Corkill, in 1998. It was used for fund-raising by the North Taranaki SPCA. *Puke Ariki, New Plymouth. Reference: ARC2008-433. Photograph by Derek Hughes*

was rescued from a dire fate — Wellington's Paddy the Wanderer — seems to have reinforced the popular idea of New Zealanders as a generous, caring people. This was almost certainly a factor in his celebrity.

Paddy, a brown and ginger Airedale terrier, frequented Wellington wharves in the 1930s. It was said that he had once belonged to a little girl, and after her death he strayed from his home, searching the city for her. Groups of workers around the waterfront — sailors, wharfies, harbour board employees and taxi drivers — fed and cared for him, and paid his registration, thus saving him from being taken to the pound. His distinctive appearance, friendly nature and habit of accepting lifts from sympathetic taxi drivers made him a local identity. With the appearance of newspaper advertisements that announced, 'I beg to thank the Greens, Greys, Diamonds, ATC and KKK Taxis for registering me this year — Paddy the Wanderer',[30] and regular humorous accounts of his adventures in the *Evening Post* and the *Dominion*, he was soon known to many Wellingtonians.

Paddy's fame spread abroad because he liked to get on the interisland ferry, coastal ships or larger vessels and travel to places such as Nelson, Greymouth, Auckland and even Sydney. On one occasion when he went missing for three months, there were reported sightings the length of the North Island. When he returned to Wellington he was granted the freedom of the city. In late 1935 he was in the news again when he went for a flight in a Gipsy Moth aeroplane. Such was the public affection for him that when it became clear he was dying, in 1939, the news was broadcast on radio and in the newspapers, and many people called at the wharves to enquire after him. After his death in July that year, obituary notices appeared in local newspapers and a fleet of taxis formed a funeral cortège.

Paddy's legend lived on. The public gave money for a memorial to him, and finally in late 1945 one was erected on Queen's Wharf. Consisting of a drinking fountain for humans, with water basins at the foot of the pedestal for dogs, it had a brass plate with a relief sculpture of a dog's head, and the inscription 'To the memory of Paddy the Wanderer'. His story was also the subject of a best-selling book by Diane Haworth, published in 2007, which implied that during the

In 1939, not long before his death, Wellington's famous stray dog, Paddy the Wanderer, was photographed sitting on his favourite vantage point — the tally clerk's stand at the entrance to Queen's Wharf. By this stage he had the freedom of the city, and was officially the Honorary Assistant Nightwatchman of the Wellington Harbour Board, 'responsible for hunting out pirates, smugglers and rodents'.

Alexander Turnbull Library, Evening Post Collection. Reference: F-122301-1/2 harsh days of the Depression Paddy provided a much-needed 'good news' story. Haworth also suggested that he had enduring appeal because he embodied the spirit of a place – its physical environment and the character of its inhabitants. One woman who knew him remarked, 'Whenever I think of my early years, I think of Wellington's winds and the hills of Wellington and I think of Paddy the Wanderer.' But, as well, Paddy made a community feel good for extending him special protection during his life. As a writer for the *San Francisco Chronicle* asked in 2004: 'How can you not love a city that treats its strays this way?'[31]

~

Another animal rescued in his hour of need was Hector, the famous sulphur-crested cockatoo that lived at Farmers Trading Company department store in Hobson Street, Auckland. In 1936 Hector was donated to the store by an elderly Grey Lynn woman who could no longer care for him. She claimed he was 90, and had been a family pet since before she was born. Hector's subsequent story illustrates a new and growing trend: the use of animal celebrities for commercial purposes. Hector took up residence in the pet department, where he would squawk loudly and greet his admirers with a cheerful 'Hello'. Because children loved to visit Hector, and also stop by the children's playground on the top floor,

Cockatoo Hector looks on from his cage during a sales event at Farmers Department store in Auckland in the 1960s. In October, known as 'Hector's month', associated promotions and competitions were run to attract shoppers. *Auckland War Memorial Museum Tamaki Paenga Hira. Reference: Farmers' Trading Company records, 1909–1987, ms 1400, box 4, folder 1, image 002*

parents found it convenient to shop at Farmers – making the bird a valuable asset to the store.

In 1946, when Hector turned 100, he was made the focus of a storewide sale. A three-tier birthday cake was baked in his honour, with customers receiving a slice on the last night of the sale. Every year after that, October was 'Hector's month' at Farmers, celebrated with sales and promotions. There were competitions to write limericks and songs about him, and one year he was even taken to visit other Farmers stores in Auckland, travelling in style in a pink limousine. The big event of 1959 was Hector's Harbour Race, a competition where people vied to travel across the harbour from the Farmers store in Devonport to the Hobson Street store by the fastest or most novel means.

Hector was famous for his sociability. In 1973 he became ill and was taken to see the vet. In the waiting room, an Alsatian began growling and leaping at his cage. To the great amusement of those present, Hector chirped 'Hello' and the dog recoiled, terrified. Hector's very long association with Farmers made him known well beyond Auckland, and he figured in the happy memories of childhood for many New Zealanders. He lived on as the store's mascot until his death in 1977, when he would have been an extraordinary 131 years old.[32]

Colin's, the famous feline stowaway, was also a much-loved workplace pet at Port Taranaki. The announcement of her death in 2007 read: 'We will all miss our little friend who had become a permanent feature at Newton King Tanker Terminal. How can we forget the sight of that little figure waiting at the door for the next shift to come on duty. Colin's was a bright and noisy little soul who will be greatly missed. The place will not be the same.' *Permission of Port Taranaki*

~

Years later, yet another animal became the recipient of human benevolence, in more ways than one. A friendly stray tortoiseshell cat took up residence at Port Taranaki in the 1990s. She was named Colin's after Colin Butler, the tanker terminal manager who adopted her. Colin's shot to international fame in 2001 as a stowaway on a methanol tanker heading from New Plymouth to South Korea. A Korean sailor, assuming from her loud miaows that she was hungry, had taken her on board the *Tomiwaka* to feed her. They both fell asleep, waking when the tanker was well out to sea. The local newspaper heard about the cat's plight and carried daily bulletins about her, with the *Tomiwaka* crew passing on details by email. There was also extensive television coverage of the strenuous attempts to get her back to New Zealand.

At first it was planned to retrieve Colin's by passing her to a New Plymouth-bound tanker, but a transfer at sea was deemed too dangerous, and instead a pet-food company

paid for the port superintendent to fly to Korea to bring her home. On her return she was made an honorary ambassador for her home city 'in recognition of her involvement in the enhancement of international relations, on behalf of the people and felines of New Plymouth'.[33] She lived on at the port until her death in 2007. When the news broke, tributes and condolences flowed in from those who had been touched by her incredible story.[34]

~

Some animals became famous because of the human company they kept and also helped to enhance their owners' public image. At the height of her fame in the 1930s, aviator Jean Batten carried with her a black kitten mascot called Buddy. He was a gift after her epic flight from England to Australia in May 1934, and was soon appearing in newspaper photographs with her. In late 1934, when Batten made a triumphant tour around New Zealand flying from town to town in her Gipsy Moth plane, Buddy accompanied her, stowed in the luggage locker. This was not a happy experience for poor Buddy, who developed such an aversion to planes that he would run and hide at the sight of one.[35]

More relaxed in the limelight was Minstrel, a black and white sheep dog who belonged to 'the people's poet', Sam Hunt. From the late 1960s Hunt journeyed around the country performing his own poems and those of others. Minstrel was his constant travelling companion and the subject of some of his best-known poems. So well loved and recognised was Minstrel that his death in 1988 overshadowed news of the resignation of Labour Party finance minister Roger Douglas the same day.[36]

New Zealand politicians have not used pets as a way of ingratiating themselves with the electorate, as presidents of the United States have since the early twentieth century.[37] This, however, may be changing: John Key's cat, Moonbeam, became a darling of the media during the 2011 election campaign.[38]

Minstrel listens attentively to his master's voice in this photograph illustrating a 1976 newspaper article about poet Sam Hunt. Travelling the country with Hunt, and inspiring his 'Bow Wow' poems, Minstrel became a public figure in his own right.

Alexander Turnbull Library, Dominion Post Collection. Reference: EP/1976/0034. Photograph by Ron Fox

~

While domestic animals and household pets dominated the celebrity stakes, more wild animals were elevated to this status in the late twentieth century. Their stories reflect the rise of environmental consciousness in New Zealand, which was, in many ways, inconsistent with aspects of pet culture. However, the tendency of pet owners to view animals as individuals could be extended to wild creatures as well as companion animals, and sometimes even assisted conservation efforts.

That dolphins had special appeal for New Zealanders is suggested by the way Pelorus Jack's story endured long after his disappearance. It was revived regularly in the *School Journal*, newspapers and books. Two World War I dog mascots were named after him, as was a brand of chocolate fish, and several poems and popular songs were composed about him.[39] The Tourist Department was still receiving enquiries about him in the 1950s.[40] And people were, it seems, on the lookout for a successor.

In 1944 a white porpoise called Pelorus Jack II began following launches in Pelorus Sound and, like its famous namesake, was soon protected.[41] But the more widely acknowledged heir to Pelorus Jack was a dolphin from the Far North. In 1955 a young female bottlenose dolphin (*Tursiops truncatus*) began appearing in the waters of Hokianga Harbour near Opononi. Named Opononi Jack, once her gender was established she was simply known as Opo. At first she followed boats of local fishermen, evidently attracted by the sound of outboard motors. She consented to be touched, and was soon enjoying a rub with oars or mops. Then she began venturing closer to the shore, and delighted swimmers by playing with rubber balls and empty beer bottles, throwing them into the air and balancing them on her nose. She was particularly gentle with children, allowing some to ride on her back.

Opo attracted huge crowds over the summer of 1955–56 – thousands of people travelled to Opononi especially to see her. Traffic officers had to be brought in to deal with the numbers of cars; the motor camp was packed out, and the hotel and tearooms could barely cope with the demand for food and drink. The press loved her, her antics were captured on film and in photographs, and she inspired a song, 'Opo the Friendly Dolphin'. Fearing that she could become the target of ill-intentioned people, locals set up a society to watch over her. Like Pelorus Jack, she was to have been protected officially by an Order-in-Council in early March 1956, which would have prohibited the taking of dolphins in Hokianga Harbour for five years. But on 8 March she was found dead, trapped between rocks near the harbour entrance. Locals believed that she had been stunned by a blast when someone was fishing illegally with gelignite.

Soon after Opo's death in 1956, children's author Avis Acres wrote and illustrated Opo the Gay Dolphin *– one of a number of memorials and now an item of Kiwiana. It concluded: 'She had brought fun and laughter to so many. No wonder everyone had loved her. Dear, gay, gentle Opo.'*

Permission of Penguin Group, New Zealand

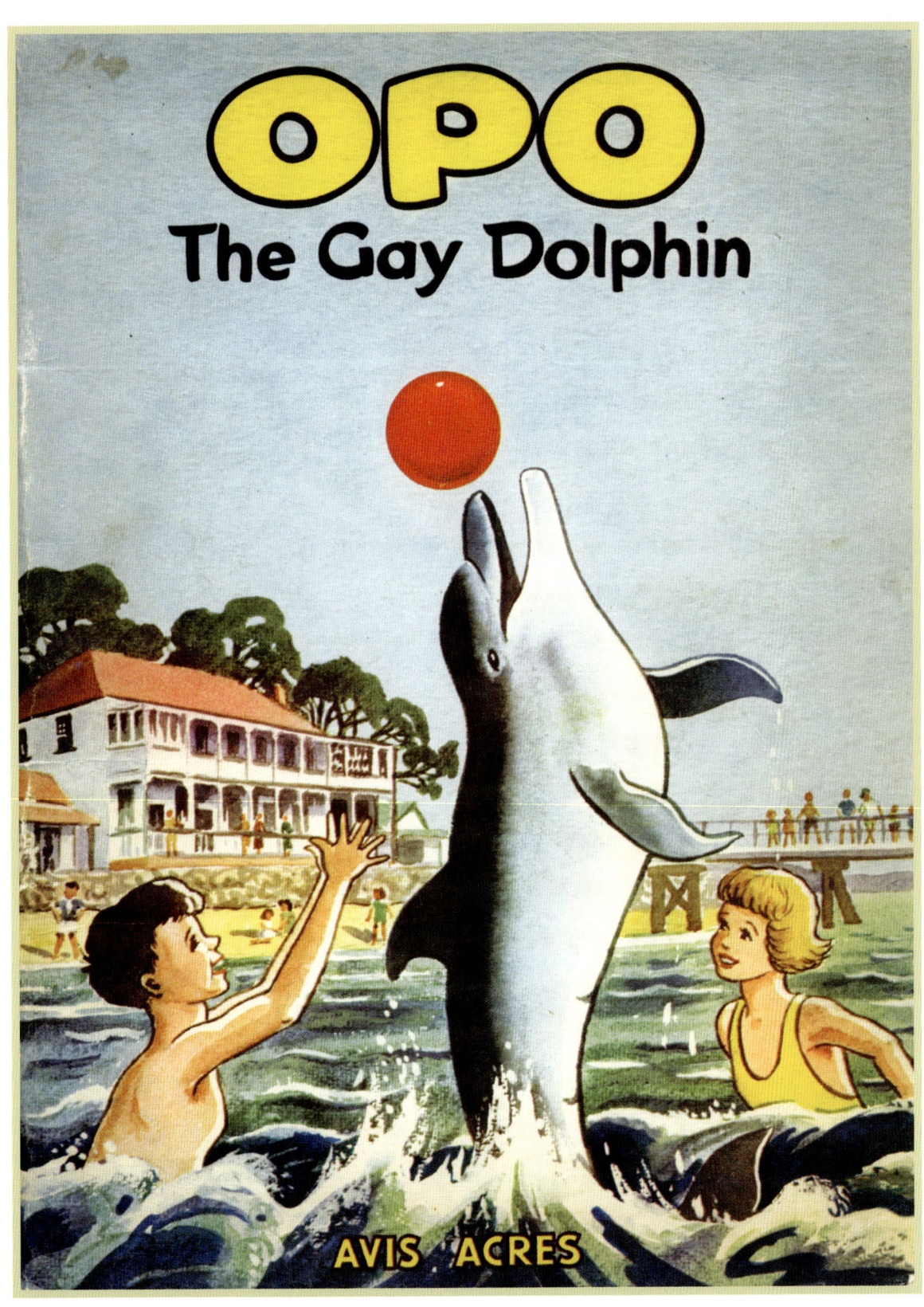

Sorrow was widespread because of the close relationship that Opo had established with people, especially children. Governor-General Sir Willoughby Norrie sent a telegraph of sympathy to the children of Opononi, and on 10 May a girls' hockey team at Whangarei wore black armbands on the field. Opo was buried at Opononi, where the New Zealand flag was flown at half mast, and sculptor and illustrator Russell Clark created a statue of her there.[42]

~

The growing interest of New Zealanders in marine mammals was piqued when Blossom, a quaintly named male sea elephant, began appearing periodically at Wellington beaches between 1962 and 1967.[43] Soon public fascination with such creatures was being exploited commercially: in 1965 Napier's Marineland opened and its main attraction, performances by trained dolphins, drew large crowds.[44] But some years passed before a wild star to rival Opo appeared.

Between 2007 and 2010 a cheeky adolescent bottlenose dolphin called Moko frolicked with surfers and swimmers at Mahia Peninsula, Gisborne, Whakatane and Mt Maunganui beaches, and crowds flocked to these places to see him. Some speculated that he may have lost his mother and become attached to humans instead. He often stole beach balls and boogie boards, and enjoyed playing fetch with pieces of driftwood.

Unlike former dolphin celebrities, Moko was automatically protected under the Marine Mammals Protection Act 1978, a law that reflected growing environmental awareness. But while public respect for dolphins, whales and seals had developed considerably, understanding of their behaviour had not. Many people regarded Moko as pet-like, and the Department of Conservation's warnings that he was potentially dangerous did not stop them from trying to play with him. Moko's behaviour was sometimes a little frightening: for instance he attempted to push one female swimmer out to sea when she tried to return to shore after a game with him. There were echoes of the behaviour of Wellington's Blossom, who initially tolerated people getting close and even chasing him or throwing things at him, but eventually began showing aggression in return.

Like Pelorus Jack, Moko had special significance for Maori. When he died unexpectedly in July 2010 there were debates about which tribe should have the right to bury him. Ngati Rongomaiwahine of Mahia and Ngati Kahungunu of Hawke's Bay wanted him to be buried at Mahia, but Ngati Awa of Whakatane and Ngai Te Rangi of Matakana Island, where his body was found, prevailed. After a public ceremony at Whakatane he was buried at Matakana, but sands from his grave were sent back to Mahia, symbolically returning his spirit there.[45]

There were disputes between East Coast and Bay of Plenty iwi over who should be allowed to bury Moko the dolphin. Eventually Ngai Te Rangi of Matakana Island, where his corpse washed up, gained that right and a tangi was held for Moko at Panepane Point on 17 July 2010. Here, his coffin, decorated with messages, is lowered into the grave.

Permission of Department of Conservation. Photograph by Pete Huggins

Moko's celebrity was of a different order to Pelorus Jack's and Opo's. Like them, he became the subject of a song and books, and there were plans to erect a statue in his honour. However, the internet catapulted him to world attention, especially after an incident when he apparently guided two pygmy sperm whales to open sea when it seemed certain they would become beached at Mahia.[46] Film of him was posted on the web, and he was the subject of international news coverage. People from many countries were moved by his story. In 2011, in recognition of the whale rescue, *Time* magazine named him one of the top 10 heroic animals in the world.[47]

~

Moko's spectacular rise to international fame showed the immense power of digital media. This was also an important factor in the emergence of two other wild animal celebrities, and was harnessed to win support for conservation initiatives. In 2009 a native endangered parrot became an internet sensation. Sirocco was a kakapo who had been hand-reared at a special sanctuary on Codfish Island near the west coast of Stewart Island. Having already developed an unusual predilection for the company of human beings, he came to world

Most people do not have an opportunity to see kakapo because the birds are so rare. The Department of Conservation has used Sirocco as an ambassador for his species, and he has travelled from his home on Maud Island in the Marlborough Sounds to various places around New Zealand, including Auckland Zoo in 2009; Orokonui Ecosanctuary, Dunedin, and Zealandia, Wellington, in 2011; and Maungatautari Sanctuary, Waikato, in 2012. The nocturnal superstar is shown with his minder, Alisha Sherriff, at Zealandia in 2011. *Permission of Kakapo Recovery. Photograph by Kevin Stent*

attention in 2009 when he was filmed attempting to mate with the head of zoologist Mark Cawardine during the making of the BBC television series *Last Chance to See*, featuring Stephen Fry. A YouTube clip of this got over 700,000 hits in one week and transformed Sirocco into an unlikely star. The Department of Conservation made the most of the chance to get more publicity for its efforts to save the kakapo. Sirocco soon had his own Facebook page, Twitter account and website, and in January 2010 was appointed Official Spokesbird for Conservation by Prime Minister John Key.[48]

In June 2011 a woman walking her dog on Peka Peka Beach, north of Wellington, came across an Emperor penguin. The disoriented bird, more than 3000 kilometres off course from Antarctica, was dubbed Happy Feet, after the popular cartoon penguin, and public and media interest in him quickly became intense. When Happy Feet began eating sand and driftwood, mistaking it for snow, he fell ill. Responding to mounting public concern, Department of Conservation staff intervened. Wellington Zoo vets operated on him to remove around 3 kg of sand from his digestive system and he soon recovered. For the next two and a half months he lived in a temperature-controlled room at the zoo, dining on salmon and frolicking in party ice. His expensive stay was sponsored by philanthropist Gareth Morgan, various commercial companies and generous donations from his many admirers, who were able to watch his activities on the internet via a webcam set up in his enclosure.⁴⁹

Eventually Happy Feet was taken back to the Southern Ocean and released with a tracking device, but as this stopped transmitting after a week, his fate is unknown. One conservationist argued that the money and resources spent on him should have been used to save critically endangered New Zealand bird species such as the kiwi.⁵⁰ Others defended his treatment. The zoo experienced a spike in visitor numbers during his stay, and staff claimed that the publicity he attracted helped with their bird conservation programmes.⁵¹ Columnist Sean Plunkett further suggested that he was an ideal ambassador for the 2011 Rugby World Cup, remarking that his story 'portrays us as a country that cares about nature, visitors, the environment and the world around it'.⁵² But the woman who found him and who wrote a book about him, Christine Wilton, probably got to the heart of his wide appeal: 'Even if we never know what happened to him, he certainly brought a lot of joy and love to the world and a one-in-a-lifetime experience for many people.'⁵³

A disoriented and sick Emperor penguin – soon to be dubbed 'Happy Feet' – is pictured on Peka Peka Beach north of Wellington in June 2011 with Department of Conservation ranger Clint Purches. Images like this were soon being published by newspapers around the world.

Photograph by Richard Gill

~

Time-honoured ideas about national character and identity were implicit in the stories of many animal celebrities. One animal star of the 2000s, a very woolly merino sheep, presented a challenge to one of these beliefs. Shrek was a 'hermit' sheep – that is, a sheep that had escaped from the flock to live a solitary life. Having managed to avoid muster for six years by living high in the hills on Bendigo Station in Central Otago, he was discovered in April 2004. By then his wool was so long that he was 'wool blind' and only a small part of his face was visible. He was named after the popular animated film character because he looked like an ogre but was gentle by nature.

Shrek's story, which first appeared in a local newspaper, was seized on by the international media, and for a time was the top item on CNN and BBC television. The owner of Bendigo Station, John Perriam, quickly saw the

When Shrek the sheep died in June 2011, this cartoon by Malcolm Evans was among the affectionate tributes. *Alexander Turnbull Library. Reference: DCDL-0018018. Permission of Malcolm Evans*

opportunity to use Shrek as a 'celebrity ambassador' for a children's medical research charity, Cure Kids. A natural entrepreneur, Perriam masterminded a succession of publicity stunts that kept Shrek in the news. First, Shrek was shorn of his huge 27 kg fleece on live television and the sale of the wool was donated to charity. In May 2004 he was taken to meet the Prime Minister, Helen Clark, and in 2006 he was shorn again on an iceberg floating off the coast of Dunedin. In 2008 he was shorn at the top of the Sky Tower in Auckland, and in 2010, aged 14, he went on a tour of Auckland and Northland.[54] Shrek's public appearances raised thousands of dollars for Cure Kids, and he became a particular favourite with children and elderly people because of his placid temperament.

Perriam himself was initially baffled by the international appeal of Shrek's story. Like other farmers, he saw sheep primarily as an economic resource. But he recognised that people loved the idea of an animal outwitting humans and surviving alone. He also shrewdly realised that overseas, New Zealand was strongly associated with sheep, which vastly outnumbered the human population. He therefore promoted the idea that Shrek was representative of New Zealand and New Zealanders. In a book about Shrek, published in 2010, he drew parallels between the Pakeha settler history of immigration and adaptation and that of Shrek's sheep ancestors: 'The story of Shrek very much mirrors the story of New Zealand, the new-world country in which we live and of which we are so proud.'[55] This was a radically new take on a strand of national mythology that eulogised rural virtues. In this version the farmed animal, rather than the farmer or the working animal, was the hero.

Perriam emphasised that Shrek was no ordinary sheep, ensuring that he always made his carefully choreographed public appearances wearing a custom-made red coat, and creating special quarters for him, known as The House of Shrek, at Bendigo Station. Shrek was treated like a special pet; indeed, one of his public appearances was at an Auckland Pet Expo.[56] Perriam stressed that Shrek was an 'icon', bringing together country and city people by providing a unique focus for national pride. He seems to have succeeded. When Shrek died in 2011, television reviewer Jane Clifton observed that he had many of the virtues New Zealanders admired in their heroes: endurance, stoicism, independence of spirit and generosity. 'Shrek's life was an important New Zealand story – a gentle parody of what we look for in a great New Zealander, and a reminder that, even while our farm animals are generally thought of in amorphous terms, in bulk, as collective items, they are all also individuals.'[57]

~

Loved during their lifetimes, many animal celebrities were remembered long after their deaths. The last decades of the twentieth century saw the appearance of more memorials to notable animals – poems, songs, paintings, children's books – and statues, the most public and accessible form of tribute. And as well as commemorating well-known animal celebrities, these monuments created even more.

Some recalled an entire class of animals. In the late 1960s two memorials honouring generations of farm dogs were erected in the Mackenzie District. In March 1968 Governor-General Sir Arthur Porritt unveiled a statue of a collie sheep dog at Lake Tekapo, South Canterbury. Funded by the people of the Mackenzie Country, it remembered with gratitude the dogs that made possible the development of the high-country sheep runs.[58] The figure of a dog looking out over the lake and towards the mountains stood on a huge greywacke boulder with a base of stones and rocks taken from the Jollie River. On this was inscribed 'Honour to the sheep dog' in Gaelic. This statue soon became a favourite with visitors: as Sir Arthur remarked, 'There is something magnificent and mystical about it.'[59] Later the same year a plaque to boundary dogs was placed at Dog Kennel Corner, the intersection of State Highway 8 and Haldon Road, near Burkes Pass in South Canterbury.[60]

In the following decades many more monuments to working dogs appeared. These included a statue to the huntaway sheep dog erected at Hunterville in the

The 'magnificent and mystical' statue to South Canterbury sheep dogs was unveiled at Lake Tekapo in 1968. It was the first of many memorials to the dogs that were co-workers with humans in developing New Zealand's farms.

Permission of Te Ara, the Encyclopedia of New Zealand, © Crown Copyright 2005–2011 Ministry for Culture and Heritage, New Zealand. Photograph by Melanie Lovell-Smith

Right: This statue of well-known nineteenth-century Wellington businessman John Plimmer and his equally well-known dog Fritz is a popular city landmark at the foot of Plimmer Steps. *Photograph by Nancy Swarbrick*

Rangitikei region in 1999.[61] As well as recognising the role of the huntaway in developing the surrounding sheep farms, the statue helped to establish Hunterville's claim to be 'the huntaway capital of the world', with more huntaways than any other place in New Zealand. This bit of local boosterism was reinforced by an annual Huntaway Festival, which included an event called the 'Shepherds' Shemozzle', an obstacle race for shepherds and their huntaway dogs.[62]

In addition, there were new memorials to individual animals. Some revived local stories. A statue of pioneer Wellington businessman John Plimmer (1812–1905) and his faithful dog Fritz was placed at the foot of Plimmer Steps, Wellington, in 1996. In later life Plimmer often walked around town with Fritz at his heels, hence the decision to depict their affectionate bond.[63]

Sam Mahon's sculpture of James Mackenzie and his faithful dog Friday at Fairlie gives new life to a potent pioneering legend. *Permission of Te Ara, the Encyclopedia of New Zealand, © Crown Copyright 2005–2011 Ministry for Culture and Heritage, New Zealand. Photograph by Shirley Williams*

Left: The statue to Richard Henderson and his donkey at the National War Memorial in Wellington pays tribute to the role played by stretcher bearers and their donkeys in evacuating wounded men at Gallipoli in World War I.

Photograph by Andy Palmer

Other monuments commemorated unusual stories that were not widely known: for instance the adventurous life of Mrs Chippy, pet tabby cat of explorer Harry McNeish. Mrs Chippy, who was in fact a male, travelled on the *Endurance* during the 1914–16 trans-Antarctic expedition. When the ship was crushed in sea ice and sank, expedition leader Ernest Shackleton ordered all the animals, including Mrs Chippy, to be shot. McNeish, who performed acts of heroism on the expedition, never quite forgave him. In 2004 Mrs Chippy was immortalised in a bronze statue placed on McNeish's grave in Karori Cemetery, Wellington, by the New Zealand Antarctic Society.[64]

Growing interest in New Zealand's war history gave rise to a memorial that provided a new angle on a very influential Australasian legend. In 1915 during the Gallipoli campaign an Australian soldier, Private John Simpson, brought wounded men down from the battlefields to the beaches, often

Animal heroes

SOME ANIMALS have become celebrities through acts of heroism in saving human life. Formal recognition of such animals began in 1943, when Maria Dickin instituted the Dickin Medal in Britain as an award for any animal displaying conspicuous gallantry or devotion to duty in war. It was awarded 64 times between 1943 and 2013 to pigeons, dogs, cats and horses.[71]

Animal welfare organisations used incidents of animal heroism to raise their profile and gain supporters. For eight years from 1960 the Wellington SPCA ran a national competition for Most Heroic Dog of the Year. Winners included a sheep dog called Top who stopped an enraged bull that was charging his owner; corgi Tammy who saved her owner from a blazing bedroom; and a French poodle called Andre, who raised the alarm when a Thames general store caught fire in the middle of the night, threatening the lives of nine people.[72]

From the 1950s the national federation of SPCAs also awarded a medal for bravery in some cases where animals saved human lives or vice versa.[73] One posthumous recipient was George, a 14-year-old Jack Russell terrier from the Taranaki township of Manaia. In 2007 he defended five children from attacking pit bull terriers. After suffering massive injuries during the ordeal, George had to be euthanised.[74] In addition to his New Zealand honour he was awarded the PDSA gold medal,[75] instituted in 2002 by the People's Dispensary for Sick Animals in Britain, for animals that assisted in saving animal or human life or showed exceptional devotion to duty in the face of danger.[76] A bronze statue of George now stands in the centre of Manaia.

Some animals have been given awards usually reserved for humans. In 2012 Irish wolfhound Guinness received a Local Hero Medal in the Kiwibank New Zealander of the Year awards. The huge dog was recognised for his work in raising morale in Christchurch's eastern suburbs after the destructive earthquake of February 2011. Accompanying his owner, Sean Scully, who helped with the clean-up, Guinness became a well-known sight, giving children rides on his back and providing a welcome diversion for local residents.[77]

Two-legged heroes were also acknowledged by the SPCA and other animal welfare groups. In 1951 the Animal Protection Society of Christchurch placed a memorial plaque in Severn Street, Oamaru, to record the heroism of an 11-year-old girl, Norma Anne Kearns, who died saving her dog from the wheels of an express train in 1950.[78]

through heavy fire, with the help of a donkey. The pair were a symbol of hope to the Australian and New Zealand soldiers at Gallipoli,[65] and after Simpson was killed the story became widely known on both sides of the Tasman. It was for many years fundamental to both nations' understanding of the Gallipoli campaign and the fraternal bond between Australia and New Zealand.[66] A statue of Simpson and his donkey was erected at the National War Memorial in Canberra in 1988. Two years later a similar statue was unveiled at the National War Memorial in Wellington, but this one commemorated a New Zealand soldier and his donkey. Private Richard Henderson, along with others, continued the dangerous rescue work at Gallipoli after Simpson died, using one of Simpson's donkeys, Murphy. Henderson went on to serve in France, and survived the war but never fully recovered from gas poisoning. He died in 1958.[67] The statue to Henderson and Murphy was an assertion of the importance of New Zealand's place in the Anzac tradition.

At least one new memorial was based on a well-recognised story. The legend of James Mackenzie and his dog remained potent: interestingly, many locals believed that the Tekapo sheep dog statue depicted Mackenzie's dog, Friday.[68] In 1970 James McNeish published a much-praised novel, *Mackenzie*, following it in 1973 with *The Mackenzie Affair*, an historical investigation. These books inspired songs, further fiction and more research. In 2003 a statue of Mackenzie and Friday was erected in the centre of Fairlie, in the Mackenzie Country,[69] recognising the pair's local and national significance. If they had not been celebrities during their lives, they were now.

Commercial motives played a part in this enthusiastic memorialising. As well as paying tribute to animals that were important in the economy or culture of a region, some statues were obviously intended as tourist attractions.[70] Those at Fairlie and Hunterville enticed motorists and tourist buses to stop and spend money in otherwise quiet country towns. The city statues, too, were magnets for overseas visitors – many a German backpacker posed for a photograph with John Plimmer and his 'Hund' Fritz.

But animal memorials also revealed the burgeoning interest in New Zealand history and identity. As their numbers continue to grow, they provide a quirky perspective on the past, explaining national values and beliefs. Remembered animals – wild and tame, ordinary and famous – help to tell New Zealand's stories.

Chapter 10
One of the family

In 2010, speaking at the New Zealand Companion Animal Conference in Christchurch, Barry Shields proudly described his two miniature schnauzers, Molly and Jojo, as his 'daughters'. According to him, since his three children had left home, Molly and Jojo had 'filled the gap nicely'.[1] He and his wife took the dogs to a café each day, bought them coffees and allowed them to lick off the froth. On learning this, some people may have been a little bemused. Less than a century earlier they would have been outraged.

In the nineteenth and early twentieth centuries, New Zealand newspapers regularly ran stories about pampered pets in the United States, Europe and Britain. These described how the pets of the rich were fed on chicken livers; washed, dressed and exercised by specially appointed maids; lodged in pet hotels when their owners went on holiday; and, at the end of their lives, buried in elaborate caskets in pet cemeteries.[2] The tone of such accounts was always incredulous horror. According to one apoplectic description of a London dog show, published in Wellington's *Evening Post* in 1913, the spectacle of highly groomed animals, with their specially constructed stalls, revealed 'the degeneracy of part of the governing classes of the Old Country'. The window of a nearby pet store, with its display of cushions, rugs, boots and costumes for cats and dogs, showed how a section of society had 'broken down to the Sybaritic level which preceded the fall of Imperial Rome'.[3]

This hostility may seem strange, given the growing popularity of pet keeping and fancying, and the increasing sympathy towards animals and concern about

Impeccably groomed, Mr Raynes and his dog sit hand in paw, gazing confidently into the camera in this 1910 studio photograph. With its distinctly modern air, it foreshadows new developments in pet culture in the twentieth century.

Sir George Grey Special Collections, Auckland Libraries. Reference: 920 RAY. Photograph by Herman John Schmidt

cruelty to them. But it revealed a deep-seated and widespread belief, held even by pet owners, that it was simply not right to treat animals as if they were human. Those strongly of this view often claimed that obsession with pets was one of the failings of an unjust class system: it was scandalous, they insisted, that animals should have luxuries many people were denied.

How times changed. By the twenty-first century more New Zealanders not only treated their pets like adored children, but they were happy to announce the fact in public. It is tempting to suggest that this was the inevitable outcome of the belief that no home was complete without a pet or two, and the dawning recognition that animals could provide both psychological and physical assistance. These were significant, but there were two more important developments.

~

Evolving philosophies about the status of animals influenced public opinion. In the nineteenth century people generally accepted that, as stewards of all that God had created, they had a religious duty to be kind to animals. But they also believed animals were inferior, and this was reflected in the terms they used to describe them. The most ardent animal lovers repeated expressions such as 'poor dumb animals' and 'brute creation' without any thought that they might be demeaning. In the early twentieth century, for instance, the Auckland SPCA aimed 'To prevent cruelty to animals by enforcing the existing laws, by procuring any further legislation that may be found expedient, and by exciting and sustaining an intelligent public opinion regarding man's duty to the lower animals.'[4]

But some thinkers challenged the assumption that animals were subordinates, created simply for human use. Englishman Henry Salt, author of *Animals' Rights: Considered in relation to social progress*, published in 1894, disagreed that humans should feel entitled to exploit animals. Observing that oppression of animals was often based on the belief that they were totally different creatures, he pointed out 'the significance of their numberless points of kinship with mankind … When once the sense of affinity is awakened, the knell of tyranny is sounded, and the ultimate concession of "rights" is simply a matter of time.'[5] In 1891 Salt formed the Humanitarian League, which campaigned against hunting, the use of fur and feathers for fashionable adornment, and vivisection.[6] Its activities were occasionally reported in New Zealand newspapers.

Press articles also kept New Zealanders informed of the impassioned protests against vivisection in Britain and elsewhere in the second half of the nineteenth century. Vivisection, operating or experimenting on live animals, had been carried out for centuries: until the 1800s, usually on cold-blooded animals such as reptiles. With the development of anaesthesia, scientists began dissecting warm-blooded animals such as cats and dogs – but they often used anaesthetics sparingly or not at all. Anti-vivisectionists were concerned about the use of animals that in other circumstances would be pets: many feared their cats and dogs could be stolen for experiments. Supporters of vivisection argued that medical advances depended on it but opponents claimed that it was not just cruel, but morally wrong. They believed that the interests of animals sometimes could, and indeed should, override those of humans. This was a truly revolutionary idea.[7]

In New Zealand a few individuals such as Jessie Mackay – poet, journalist and champion of unpopular social causes – spoke out against vivisection, as did some organisations with international connections.[8] New Zealand women's groups backed British and American feminists who campaigned against vivisection as part of a wider anti-oppression philosophy.[9] Theosophists, who became established in New Zealand in the 1890s, opposed vivisection on spiritual grounds, arguing that a single life principle united humans and animals, who had an equal right to life and happiness.[10]

This cartoon from an 1899 edition of the *Auckland Weekly News* pokes fun at the hypocrisy of two women who rebuke a little boy for stealing birds' eggs while themselves wearing hats decorated with stuffed birds. It suggests that Humanitarian League campaigns had some impact in New Zealand. One of these concerned 'murderous millinery': the fashion for using birds' bodies, wings and feathers to trim hats. *Sir George Grey Special Collections, Auckland Libraries. Reference: AWNS-18990210-3-3*

At first the debate was theoretical only, but in the 1920s it became apparent that experiments on animals were being carried out in New Zealand teaching hospitals and clinics. Many animal lovers were disturbed by this. By 1930 some had established an Anti-vivisection Society in Auckland.[11] Vivisection was also a hot topic for SPCA members between the wars. In the late 1920s and early 1930s societies investigated local reports of vivisection, and put forward conference remits calling for its abolition.[12] In 1937 a delegation from the SPCA federation asked the Minister of Internal Affairs to legislate against vivisection of the dog, on the grounds that it 'was a highly intelligent animal with a highly-developed nervous system'.[13] But it was difficult to achieve consensus. New Zealand SPCA members, like their English counterparts, had a wide range of opinions on vivisection, from total opposition through to the belief that human needs should always come before those of animals.

The conviction that vivisection was the only way to overcome deadly diseases gave its supporters the moral high ground. In 1927, for example, the Otago SPCA investigated complaints about vivisection at the Otago Medical School. Monkeys were being used there in experiments to find a cure for poliomyelitis, a crippling disease that typically affected children and young people. On being assured that 'every precaution was being taken by the professors to prevent any undue or unnecessary pain to the monkeys', the society decided not to take any action. Backing off was the politic thing to do. Since New Zealand had already suffered three severe child polio epidemics, and was to experience more in the 1930s, 1940s and 1950s, many people would have supported any research 'to combat this dire disease'.[14] Opposing vivisection remained a minority viewpoint.

~

A more widely accepted development that signalled changing ideas about animals was the growing commercialisation of pets and pet products. Once, people with surplus puppies, kittens or baby birds often gave them to friends and family. Some pets, and equipment such as cages, leads and collars, were available in general stores. A few specialist shops sold caged birds and catered for their needs. By the 1930s, however, pet stores selling a broader range of animals and pet accessories had sprung up. Some big stores such as Farmers in Auckland opened pet departments, a great lure for children accompanying their mothers on shopping expeditions.

The pet shop was the setting for some contradictory ideas. The most attractive items for sale were the animals themselves: they were essentially commodities. But the items sold for them – the food, bedding, toys, apparel, medicines and so on – were designed to make their lives more comfortable, stimulating and healthy, so pets also became in a sense consumers.[15] Their needs, real or just invented for the purposes of marketing, were what made pet shops profitable. Pet shops also pandered to the shifting emotions – love, anxiety and pride – that owners felt for their animal companions.

The infant 'pet industry' began to influence owners' expectations – about food, for instance. Traditionally cats and dogs were fed on raw meat or leftovers, but from the late nineteenth century some brands of dog cakes, including Spratt's and Buffalo Meat, were imported. Others were produced locally. In

1880, for example, the Excelsior Steam Biscuit Factory in Invercargill boasted that it was 'Sole Manufacturer for Southland of the Celebrated Dog Biscuits'.[16] Advertisements began to hint that dog owners had an obligation to feed their pets prepared foods. One in 1908 urged owners, 'Care for your dog! Treat him as a friend and feed him on Spratt's dog biscuits.'[17]

Bird seed, often imported from Australia, was another packaged food that became available in the nineteenth century. Advertisements frequently suggested that certain types of seed would assist birds to sing or talk: in February 1891 the *Taranaki Herald* noted 'Messrs White & Carter call the attention of those who keep birds as domestic pets to Carter's Universal Bird Seed, said by those who have tried it to be A1 food for song and talking birds. Our readers will, doubtless, give it a trial.'[18] Advertising also insisted that budgerigars, parrots and canaries required different foods. The number of people keeping caged birds appears to have increased, possibly because these little feathered friends were cheap to feed: by 1939 a local manufacturer of bird foods claimed that 'more than one half of the people in New Zealand' had pet birds.[19] Responding to growing demand, in the late 1930s Auckland firms such as Arthur Yates Ltd and Hutchinson Brothers began making new products including such brands as Defiance and Prize Winner iodine nibbles and Eganbisk bird food.[20]

Slowly, veterinary care for pets began to develop. Before World War II most veterinarians worked with farm animals, but a few also undertook small animal work. One such vet was Wilmot C. Quinnell, who opened the Wellington Animal Hospital and School of Farriery in January 1907. By August he had treated 288 horses, 53 dogs, six cats, six cows, two bulls, one camel and one pigeon. An *Evening Post* article about his surgery in March the following year was mildly mocking, suggesting that it was primarily 'doting lady owners' who took their pets – fashionable pug dogs and cross-bred rough-haired terriers – for treatment. 'It may take a month to restore the "curled darling" to health, much to the regret of the owner's neighbours, who pray for a decease.' But, the article continued, 'even decent dogs may be seen at the institution. The patients include collies, bulldogs, greyhounds and others liable to canine complaints, such as distemper, troubles of the eye and ear.'[21] Mr Quinnell also cared for sick monkeys, cats and birds, treating canaries for broken limbs and parrots for 'tongue-tiedness' – a deformity of the beak that prevented them from speaking.

People were clearly intrigued and attracted by the idea of veterinary care for pets. One very popular silent film that did the rounds of provincial towns in 1911 was *Animal Hospital*: scenes from an institution for the treatment of sick cats, dogs and horses in a French city. When Fullers' Pictures screened it at the Wanganui Opera House in February the *Wanganui Chronicle* reported enthusiastically, 'Skilled surgeons are seen dressing wounds, bandaging limbs, operating, and applying lotions on the same lines as human beings are treated when incapacitated … Altogether it is said to be a remarkable picture, and one which appeals especially to all lovers of dumb animals.'[22]

Boarding kennels where owners could leave their cats and dogs when they went on holiday emerged by the 1920s. In 1928 London-qualified 'canine nurse' Miss Mabel Christmas advertised her move to Regent Street, Wellington, giving as the reason 'increase of business requiring more spacious premises'. As well as treating sick dogs and cats she ran the Tip-Top Boarding Kennels with special accommodation for toy dogs and cats. Even more astonishing, she operated an Animals' Beauty Parlour, where animals could be washed, groomed and have their claws cut.[23]

Such services remained few in number, however, and were available to a very small group of pet owners. And there was still outspoken opposition to the idea of cosseting pet animals. In 1924 *New Zealand Truth* published a savagely satirical account of a toy terrier and cat show in Auckland, alleging that it 'brought joy to those who love four-legged things to pamper, in preference to the tiny little things with only two legs'. The reporter, who described himself as a 'plain domesticated man', clearly believed that the animals on display were baby substitutes for their female owners, for whom he felt pity mixed with 'a certain amount of disgust and indignation'. Hearing one gushing woman tell another how she fed her dog only the best of foods, he was struck by the contrast with his own home, where the humans made do with a plain diet.[24]

But the emerging attitude that pets were entitled to consideration was highlighted by a fascinating campaign during World War II. When meat rationing was introduced, no provision was made for domestic animals. In Auckland the SPCA asked daily papers to publish a recipe for alternative food for dogs, and shops there and in Christchurch distributed horse and goat meat for pets. In Wellington, however, shortages were such a concern that over 2000 people signed a petition 'protesting against the present inadequate arrangements for animal food'. A deputation led by Labour MP Mabel Howard, including representatives of the Ladies' Auxiliary of the Wellington SPCA, the Wellington Kennel Club and a group called the Wellington Domestic Animal Owners' Organisation, went to see the Minister of Supply in 1944. As a result, a Manawatu meat company was asked to deliver meat to butchers' shops in Wellington, and by mid-1945 the Domestic Animal Owners' Organisation had a shop selling pets' meat.[25]

~

Interestingly, the dog is the centre of attention in this happy family group on the cover of a National Party 1949 election campaign booklet (National became the government that year). The role of pets in family life was to become even more important in the post-war years.

Alexander Turnbull Library. Reference: Eph-A-NZ-NATIONAL-1949-01-cover

World War II marked the beginning of major social and political changes that affected the way people viewed animals in general, and pets in particular. In the 1940s opposition to vivisection in New Zealand gathered momentum. This was partly a response to events overseas: vivisection had increased steadily in Britain in the 1930s, and the war gave further impetus to animal experiments.[26] It may also have been a reaction to the recent establishment of government animal research stations in New Zealand. In 1946 a Wellington branch of the British Union for the Abolition of Vivisection was set up, and a conference hosted by the long-established Auckland branch attracted delegates from the four main centres.[27] There was also an active anti-vivisection group in Gisborne. In 1947 the Wellington BUAV distributed a tract, *The Case for the Abolition of Vivisection*, written by leading Auckland Theosophist Geoffrey Hodson. This described vivisection as ineffective for combating disease,

The Animals' Bill of Rights

Mabel Howard feeds cats at the Canterbury SPCA shelter in 1964. The parliamentary champion of animals used to walk around the cattery with tears in her eyes, saying she wished she could take them home with her.

Permission of Fairfax Media/Christchurch Press

BEST REMEMBERED for waving two pairs of oversized women's bloomers in the House of Representatives during a 1954 debate to illustrate the need for standardised clothing sizes, Mabel Howard was also famous for her work on behalf of animals.

A Christchurch Labour MP who became the first woman cabinet minister in New Zealand, Howard had a flamboyant, fearless style. She made no secret of her great love for animals. Especially fond of cats, at one stage she housed seven former strays at her Christchurch home. She lavished attention on them, feeding them the best meat and fish, and would sit up all night if necessary waiting for a cat to come home. Parliamentary colleagues noted that she preferred not to go on long trips because of worry about her cats, and she would become agitated if the House sat late on Fridays. She once got leave of absence 'to attend a bereavement in Christchurch' when one of her cats, Tumbles, died, and at such times she cried for days. Her cats were her children: shrugging off open mockery of her devotion to them, she told the House, 'I've had more love from animals than humans.'[28]

In the late 1940s, when there was a danger that the animal home run by the Canterbury SPCA would close down, Howard, then a vice-president of the society, was instrumental in keeping it open. She soon became president, and for nearly two decades worked tirelessly to revive the society and improve its financial position. During her time as president the Canterbury SPCA began to collect stray dogs in Christchurch streets, and she helped to establish a new animal home.[29] She therefore had a detailed knowledge of the challenges of SPCA work and was well acquainted with the cases of gross cruelty encountered by its inspectors. She also knew how hard the society found it to obtain prosecutions. Outrage at this injustice gave her the energy and zeal to go into battle on behalf of animals.

It has been suggested that Mabel Howard probably put more effort into her Prevention of Cruelty to Animals bill than any other political project. She gathered information from overseas, basing her bill heavily on a similar piece of legislation recently passed in New South Wales. She made it clear that she alone, rather than any SPCA, had drawn up the bill, but pointed out that the SPCA federation endorsed it.[30] Howard focused on ensuring that the law would clearly define various common types of cruelty and make prosecutions easier to obtain. Although the act that resulted from her initiative did not fully achieve these goals, it was a huge step forward.

Before the bill was introduced, and as it made its way through various readings, Mabel received numerous letters of support from animal lovers throughout New Zealand. She was especially proud of a poem written by a Christchurch friend when the Animals Protection Act passed in 1960. It concluded:

> For justice for all dumb creatures
> She launched a ceaseless fight
> Of her effort she can be justly proud
> In the Animals' Bill of Rights.[31]

The Federation of New Zealand Societies for the Prevention of Cruelty to Animals agreed with this assessment, and in 1965 presented her with a gold medal of merit for her work.[32]

and 'an evil thing, a dark stain on human character and conduct and a blot upon modern civilisation'. Referring to recent revelations of Nazi concentration camp atrocities, it argued that vivisection of animals inevitably led on to experimentation on humans.[33]

Hodson was, among other roles, president of the Council of Combined Animal Welfare Organisations, which began in Auckland in 1944 as an alliance of the Auckland Animal Protection Society, the BUAV, the New Zealand Vegetarian Society and the Animal Welfare Group of the Theosophical Order of Service in New Zealand. CAWO promoted animal welfare causes and was particularly opposed to vivisection. Although many of its members were radical, CAWO wooed ordinary pet owners, running children's animal painting competitions and a 'kindness to animals' campaign. By the early 1950s CAWO had branches in Wellington, Christchurch and Dunedin.[34] Once, the SPCA had been the only organisation lobbying for the interests of animals in New Zealand; the emergence of other animal welfare groups during the 1930s and 1940s suggested some people felt that it was not effective enough. CAWO in particular challenged the SPCA's methods.

In the 1940s the SPCA federation prepared a clutch of animal protection bills to improve on existing inadequate legislation. These included a new Prevention of Cruelty to Animals bill, a Dogs' Registration (Amendment) bill, a Protection of Birds bill and an Animals (Anaesthetics) bill.[35] The federation also drafted a Slaughter of Animals bill, to make stunning an animal before slaughter mandatory. It failed to get political support for any of these measures.

Frustrated at the SPCA's lack of progress on enforcing humane killing in abattoirs, from 1947 CAWO organised a nationwide petition. Geoffrey Hodson led a deputation to the Minister of Agriculture and CAWO later claimed responsibility for the amendment to the regulations governing slaughter of stock in 1951.[36] CAWO also led a campaign to outlaw the use of live hares as quarry in coursing and the recreational shooting of captive birds; some of its members asserted, rather unfairly, that the SPCA was apathetic about these issues. Mabel Howard decried the cruelties of these sports in parliament in 1953, and in 1954 they were outlawed.[37]

Howard, a stalwart of the Canterbury SPCA and a devoted cat lover, became the much-needed parliamentary champion for animal welfare. In 1957 she introduced a private member's bill to consolidate and add to existing animal welfare legislation, then spread across a number of separate acts.[38] Howard's Prevention of Cruelty to Animals Bill attracted support from both sides of the House. It was, however, referred to the Agricultural and Pastoral Committee for further consideration, and when it was revived in 1959 as the Animals

Protection Bill, the Department of Agriculture took the lead in redrafting it. Reintroduced as a government measure in September 1960, it passed that year.[39]

CAWO may have been the ginger group for legislative change, but one of its chief hopes was dashed by the Animals Protection Act 1960. Far from outlawing vivisection, the revised act stated that 'any research or experimental work carried out on any animal by any bona fide research worker' was excluded from its provisions. This clause, introduced by the Department of Agriculture, allowed investigations at animal research stations to continue unimpeded.[40] Vivisection, not even mentioned in previous animal welfare legislation, now had legal standing in New Zealand. SPCA supporters, on the other hand, hailed the act as a great leap forward. There had not been a law solely concerned with preventing cruelty to animals since 1880, so in their eyes the issue was once again given the prominence it deserved. Although not perfect, the act was more comprehensive than previous legislation, identifying new cruelty offences including abandonment, restricting some farming and animal transport practices, and increasing the powers of inspectors.[41]

The act stated that any inspectors appointed were to be Department of Agriculture staff, but after urgent submissions to the Minister of Agriculture SPCA inspectors regained their former status. This reaffirmed the SPCA's position as New Zealand's leading animal welfare group. From the 1960s many more branches were set up and the organisation became more visible. It continued to campaign on behalf of all animals, but with Department of Agriculture inspectors now involved in matters relating to treatment of farm animals, SPCAs increasingly promoted responsible pet ownership.

Post-war SPCA publicity suggested that pet owning was a worthy undertaking, and that cruelty to pets was particularly heinous. The term 'animal lover' became synonymous with 'pet owner'. It is telling that the Wellington SPCA's journal, published between 1968 and 1988, was called *Pet Pride*. SPCAs endorsed the privileged place of pets in the home: from the 1970s the slogan 'one of the family' was often used to remind people of the special claims of their companion animals. The family metaphor extended to the language of rehoming unwanted animals: they were now 'adopted'.

~

Law changes put care of animals in the spotlight, but other important developments affected views on how they should be treated. In 1936 there were 50 vets in New Zealand, 30 of whom were employed by the Department of Agriculture. By 1954 there were 236. The occupation became professionalised under the Veterinary Surgeons Act 1956, which had a clause

When this graphic reminder appeared in the Wellington SPCA magazine *Pet Pride* in 1968, the organisation was using the well-tested tactic of teaching children empathy for animals by

to phase out practitioners without university degrees.⁴² Before the 1960s New Zealanders wanting to become vets had to go to Australia or further afield to get qualifications. Training became more accessible to New Zealanders when the Massey University Veterinary School opened in 1962, and the number of vets increased.

During the 1950s and 1960s veterinary practices in cities changed. Once, many of these had provided services for both large farm animals and household pets. Now, many vets found the two specialties incompatible and began providing services exclusively for small animals. More women entered the profession, and they often found it easier to combine work with family responsibilities if they joined urban small animal practices.

Important research discoveries improved the quality of treatment for small animals. New Zealand vets, for example, devised orthopaedic surgical techniques to deal with fractures and joint conditions in dogs and cats in the 1960s. Vets working alongside surgeons at Green Lane Hospital in the 1960s and 1970s helped to develop heart valve replacement techniques that could be used in both humans and animals. Interested vets established the Companion Animal Society of the New Zealand Veterinary Association in 1972.⁴³

More vets were available to do the unwelcome jobs of neutering and euthanising animals, and they could do so without causing pain. By the 1960s it became standard to neuter cats under anaesthetic – before then it had not always been used. Painless barbiturate injection was the preferred method of euthanasia by the late 1970s, replacing less satisfactory methods. A bigger range of vaccines and medications became available.⁴⁴

These developments made pet owning more enjoyable and attractive by making it less stressful. People did not have to worry about treating seriously sick animals themselves. Reliable and easily administered home treatments for fleas and worms, widely available by the 1970s, also helped people to overcome longstanding fears about the possibility of catching diseases from their pets. Animals and humans could live together more comfortably. It is likely that these changes also affected people's sense of obligation to their pets. Not only could they obtain veterinary care for their animals more readily, but they began to recognise that they should do so.

~

The behaviour of pet owners was also influenced by a post-war boom in the pet-food industry throughout the western world. In New Zealand around 1955 J. Watties Canneries began making tinned pet food – Fido for dogs and Felix for cats. J.R. Butland Pty of Auckland was also producing tinned pet food by

1956, and another Auckland company, Holmes Pet Food, entered the market in 1959.[45] Around the same time local manufacturing of dog biscuits expanded, and well-established brands such as Tomoana and Bonny were joined by others. By 1965 Watties was selling 10 million cans of cat and dog food in New Zealand each year, and expected this total to grow by 15 per cent annually.[46]

The rise of supermarkets and the trend towards processed goods affected the way people bought, prepared and ate their food, and it has been suggested that this changed their views on what and how they should feed their pets. Convenience was one attraction: prepared pet foods made the daily chore of feeding cats and dogs less irksome. But in addition, persuasive advertisements appealed to owners' sense of duty, promising that a 'scientific' and 'balanced' diet would allow pets to live longer, healthier lives.[47]

In New Zealand, human health issues hastened the move towards prepared pet foods. One of the ironies of the pet-food industry was that it used 'unwanted' animals to feed 'wanted' animals. Old horses, sheep and cattle, and 'pest' animals like goats and possums were slaughtered for pet food. During the 1960s the Department of Agriculture began to regard outlets that sold this meat with suspicion. Officials feared that some animals killed for pet meat were diseased, and were being slaughtered in the open, in unhygienic conditions, creating health risks for both pets and their owners. Regulations of 1969 listed the species of animals that could be used for raw pet meat, and made it compulsory to kill them in slaughterhouses under hygienic conditions. Consumers protested that this would push up the price of raw pet meat, and in 1970, 975 Christchurch pet owners petitioned the Minister of Agriculture – to no avail. By the late 1970s the higher cost of raw meat had indeed driven more people to buy canned and dry pet food;[48] from the 1980s this was increasingly imported or manufactured locally by overseas companies such as Nestle Purina.

Concern about hydatids also encouraged people to buy prepared foods. The Hydatids Act 1959 made it an offence to feed dogs diseased meat or raw offal from sheep, which often carried hydatids cysts. Traditionally, farmers butchered sheep as food for their dogs and many were slow to change their habits. However, as the campaign against hydatids intensified, prepared foods for farm dogs became more widely accepted.

A local success story was the Tux dog biscuit. Its inventor, Cyril Ralph (Tiny) Moore of Marlborough, was concerned that local farm dogs were not well fed. In 1954 he developed a recipe for a dog biscuit containing nutritious ingredients, including meat and bone meal, fish oil and molasses. The product's name was derived from the well-known New Zealand expression 'dog tucker'. Farmers recognised its convenience and cleanliness (it was advertised as 'hydatid-free'), and appreciated not having to kill stock to provide meat for dogs at the end of a tiring day. From 1967 Tux biscuits became available in supermarkets, along with Tuxettes for pet dogs and puppies.[49]

~

The pet industry thrived in the post-war consumer society. New Zealand in the 1950s and 1960s was prosperous and stable. Rising incomes and a higher standard of living were accompanied by greater emphasis on leisure activities and hobbies. People now had more money to spend on their pets.

Masterpet, established in 1961 in Wellington, was a pioneering pet-supply company,[50] and by the 1970s there were many more, selling animals, pet food, diet supplements, remedies, accessories such as aquariums, cages and kennels, toys, and equipment from cat doors to dog leashes. Innovative pet products supported the growing view that companion animals played an important part in people's lives and deserved special care. This was reinforced by the development of more pet services. By the late 1950s both the number and standards of boarding kennels were climbing.[51] Commercial home feeding services for pets whose owners were on holiday had emerged by the 1970s.[52] In that decade pet cemeteries were established[53] and pet cremation became popular, as did urns, caskets and grave markers. In the 1980s pet grooming salons began to multiply.[54]

In 1979 the Pet Industry Joint Advisory Council was formed in Auckland,[55] and *New Zealand Pet Trade News*, a news sheet for retailers, wholesalers, manufacturers and importers of pets and pet products and veterinary supplies, began. In an early issue Mr D. Lawler commented that the industry had

> *expanded markedly in the last decade ... there seems little dispute that more people are keeping animals as pets. Companies have been established to supply the market, a wider range of products is being imported and there are more pet shops than ever before. Advertisements for a variety of pet products are now being seen both in national magazines and on television, an indication of the size of the market.*[56]

This explanation of cause and effect could be turned the other way around: the flourishing industry was not just a symptom but a cause of the growth in pet owning.

Statistics on pet ownership are scarce, but it is clear that there was a significant upward trend after the war. A 1965 survey revealed that 37 per cent of New Zealand homes had a pet cat, and 11 per cent a dog. By 2007, according to a similar poll, 52 per cent of New Zealand households had a cat (18 per cent had more than one), and nearly 30 per cent had a dog.[57] Not only the number but the range of pets was increasing. Alongside the predictable pets – cats, dogs, birds, horses, ponies, guinea pigs, rats and mice – there were more unusual ones,

Ten-year-old Alison Campbell grooms her New Zealand Peruvian guinea pig, Matahara Teepee, in preparation for the New Zealand Cavy Club Show held in Wellington in February 1979. The show attracted over 300 guinea pigs and their owners from as far north as Whangarei and as far south as Dunedin – evidence of renewed interest in this long-popular pet.

Alexander Turnbull Library, Dominion Post Collection. Reference: EP/1979/0537

including ferrets, turtles and tortoises, and tropical fish.[58] There was considerable variety within many of these species because of the spread of fanciers' groups – encouraged and catered for by the pet industry.

Guinea pigs had always been popular, but in the 1970s and 1980s they became positively fashionable: angoras and other exotic types were imported and cavy clubs were set up.[59] Rabbits were also favourite pets in the mid-nineteenth century, but after they were recognised as an agricultural pest they fell from favour and from 1886 only licensed 'professors of biology' could keep them in captivity. This prohibition was finally relaxed in 1979 to allow New Zealand White, Angora, Flemish Giant, Rex, Chinchilla and California breeds to be kept under strict conditions. Farms breeding and selling the rabbits emerged, and clubs were formed.[60]

Pet-related societies were in transition. In 1975 there were 41 cage bird societies throughout New Zealand and around 16 organisations for people interested in bantams and ornamental fowls and pigeons, but the hobby was declining in urban areas. By the 1960s many towns had prohibited the keeping of roosters in built-up areas because of the noise they made.[61] On the other hand, some pet organisations were experiencing an upsurge. In the mid-1970s there were three herpetological societies for people who bred mainly native skinks and geckos. There were also numerous fish and aquaria clubs with a total

What's in a name?

THE NAMES of pets provide a fascinating insight into relationships between humans and animals. Names can reveal the nature of the bond or the attitude of the owner towards the pet. They can be chosen to show off a person's knowledge, sense of humour or social aspirations. It is interesting to consider what has and has not changed down the years.

In the early nineteenth century the lowly place of pets was reflected in their names, which were often generic rather than personal. Dog and Puss (and variations on these references to the species of animal) were commonly used, as were traditional non-human names, such as Dobbin for a horse, Towser for a dog and Topsy for a cat. Interestingly, in 2010 Dog and Bitch remained highly ranked names for dogs in New Zealand.[62]

It became popular to choose names to suit the animal's appearance or behaviour, for instance Spot, Patch, Ginger and Rover. When children's letter pages started up in the *New Zealand Farmer* and the *Otago Witness*, both Uncle Ned and Dot began providing names for children's pets in response to regular requests, and they often matched these to the animal's characteristics. When asked to provide a name for a rabbit in 1889, Uncle Ned replied, 'What colour is your rabbit? If white Snowflake would be a nice name, but its name should suit its colour.'[63] Many people still go along with this approach.

Sheep dogs and other working animals usually had short names that could be easily called. Many dogs were, and still are, given names such as Lad, Girl, Fly and Gyp, which could be said repeatedly without difficulty.[64] In contrast, names for pedigree animals were lengthy. These incorporated the breeder's unique 'prefix' name and a show name. The result, for example Suncrest Princess Rangatira, could be a mouthful and seem slightly absurd to those not in the know.[65]

Some Victorian owners could not resist flaunting their superior education or patriotism. Pet names referring to classical heroes, such as Hector or Caesar, or to social or military rank, for example Duke or Major, were common. Nowadays, 'show off' names tend to refer to popular culture: examples include Darth Vader, Snoop Dog or Spock.[66] Maori names were used for pets from the nineteenth century by both Maori and Pakeha. Canterbury runholder John Enys called his favourite cat Taipo, meaning goblin or devil, and sheep dogs were sometimes given short, easily pronounced Maori names such as Tika, Mana, Rua and Poi.[67]

Gradually, names for companion animals became similar to those given to children, underlining the new emotional closeness of the human–animal relationship. Dog registration records of the 1850s and 1860s illustrate this development. Although most dogs listed had traditional names such as Rover, Lady, Prince and Gipsy, there were a few called Bob, Carlo and Rose.[68] In the early twenty-first century the most popular New Zealand dog names were Max, Molly and Bella – and they were also among the favourite names for babies at that time.[69]

One modern development seems to be a greater sense of humour and originality in naming pets. This contrasts with the more serious, less imaginative approach of our forebears: just as a name might be passed from father to son or mother to daughter, and even from sibling to sibling if an older child died before the next baby was born, so generations of nineteenth-century pets might inherit the same name. One settler of the 1850s, apparently stumped for ideas, called all his pets – a kaka, a cat and later a dog – Jerry.[70] Sometimes, though, the same name was used for successive pets for sentimental reasons. Charlie Douglas, who explored much of the West Coast from the late 1860s to the early 1900s, clearly valued his dogs greatly, and called at least two of them Betsey Jane.[71] And Mr A. Hansen, lighthouse keeper at Puysegur Point, was particularly fond of his dog Hector, 'the wisest and gentlest dog that ever breathed'.[72] As a result he used the name for all his later dogs – Hector II, Hector III and Hector IV – though, sadly, none of them lived up to the standard set by Hector I.

Champion blue Persian Natasha, wearing regal tiara and robes, was photographed with her proud owner, Patricia Mackenzie, in July 1980, soon after winning the title of best neuter spay at a national show for pedigree Persian cats. Following dissension within the membership and legal disputes during the 1960s, the cat fancy revived from the 1970s.

Alexander Turnbull Library, Dominion Post Collection. Reference: EP/1980/2442/16A. Photograph by Philip John Reid.

membership of over 9000 – one of the largest hobby groups in New Zealand at that time.[73]

In the country, pony clubs were immensely popular. They had been established in the 1940s to give formal riding instruction for children and to instill values of teamwork and sportsmanship through mounted games, races and treks. Dorothy Campbell set up the Heretaunga Pony Club in 1944, other clubs followed and in 1946 the New Zealand Pony Clubs' Association began. By 1969 the clubs had a nationwide membership of 14,473, with more than two-thirds of the members aged under 17.[74]

The cat and dog fancies also underwent a post-war resurgence. As well as local shows, there were now huge national cat and dog shows. These events became popular, with members of the public queuing to see the splendid and unusual animals and, in the case of dogs, to marvel at their skills.

One of the family **239**

Dog groomer Kylie Gilbert, pictured with Jake (left), Max (in van) and Clyde (right), was profiled in a feature about unusual jobs in Wellington's *Evening Post* in February 1998. The grooming business, Dogworkz, was run by a veterinary clinic. Food delivery, administering of medication and general nursing were offered, along with washing, blow-drying and nail clipping. At this time mobile grooming vans were still something of a novelty, but they were soon a common sight in cities.

Alexander Turnbull Library, Dominion Post Collection. Reference: EP/1998/0585

In 1955 the Kennel Club held its first national dog show. It gradually became more inclusive of the broad range of dog enthusiasts, adopting rules for obedience trials in 1956 and allowing non-pedigree dogs to participate in them from 1966. Agility competitions, where a handler and dog ran through a course of hurdles and obstacles, began after they first were introduced in Britain in the late 1970s. The Kennel Club also allowed novelty events such as fancy costume competitions. Pooches paraded in a variety of home-made costumes, impersonating brides, All Blacks, hula girls, surfers and a range of other characters.[75]

Cat fancying, too, gained in strength, despite some setbacks. The New Zealand Governing Council of the Cat Fancy had gone into recess during World War II, but was revived in 1949. It held its first national cat show at Hastings in 1963. After disputes within the council in the 1960s, culminating in a Supreme Court case, a new constitution was drawn up and the organisation was renamed NZ Cat Fancy (Inc.) in 1972. New Zealand's first international cat show took place in Auckland in 1982.[76]

Fanciers' events now had a noticeable commercial side. Often pet-food companies sponsored major cat and dog shows. And from 1960, television publicised pet hobbies while advertising related products. One extremely popular local programme of the 1990s was *Tux Wonder Dogs*, in which teams of dogs and handlers competed in obedience, agility and other fun events. 'Co-presenter' Dexter, a Labrador, became a widely recognised animal celebrity.[77]

~

Just as the pet industry was expanding, anti-vivisection campaigns were reinvigorated. The worldwide animal liberation movement of the 1970s had its roots close to home: its most prominent leader, Peter Singer, was an Australian. Singer's highly influential book, *Animal Liberation*, first published in 1975, argued that because animals – or rather, 'nonhuman animals' – felt pain just as humans did, and chose to avoid it if they could, their interests should be given equal consideration to those of people. Singer offered modern examples of vivisection and factory farming to illustrate how plainly they were not. He described the automatic assumption that animals were less important than humans as 'speciesism': a form of prejudice comparable to racism and sexism. By making a connection between the current liberation movements to free black people, homosexuals and women from centuries of oppression, and the struggle of those trying to end exploitation of animals, Singer annexed a powerful revolutionary energy.

Singer's outlook was quite different from that of the stereotypical animal lover. In his introduction to *Animal Liberation* he described a social occasion he attended with his wife, at which a fellow guest took his interest in animals to mean that he was a pet owner, as she was.

> *We tried to explain that we were interested in the prevention of suffering and misery … Neither of us had ever been inordinately fond of dogs, cats, or horses in the way that many people are. We simply wanted them treated as the independent sentient beings that they are, and not as a means to human ends – as the pig whose flesh was now in our hostess's sandwiches had been treated.*[78]

Following Singer's lead, animal liberationists were swift to expose the hypocrisy of conventional pet owners, and they invariably adopted a vegetarian or vegan 'cruelty free' diet.

By the time Singer published a revised edition of his book in 1990 the movement was global, with millions of adherents. Some groups had sparked considerable controversy by their raids on vivisection laboratories and factory farms to free the animals kept there and obtain evidence of animal abuse. By the 1990s, too, other philosophers had explored the status of animals. Some went further than Singer, suggesting that animals had independent rights that went beyond moral claims on humans for fair treatment. Others argued that animals should be citizens with legal rights. In addition, some animal rights advocates rejected pet keeping, believing that it was just another form of human tyranny over other species.[79]

~

In New Zealand renewed interest in the status of animals prompted the formation of a number of animal rights and liberation groups.[80] The two largest organisations opposing experiments on animals originated as branches of the British Union for the Abolition of Vivisection.

The Wellington BUAV had long since faded away when in 1978 a new branch was formed by English immigrant Bette Overell. After she failed to get support from the parent organisation in London, she reorganised the branch as an autonomous group called the New Zealand Anti-Vivisection Society. The NZAVS demanded total abolition of vivisection on the grounds that it was not only cruel but also scientifically unsound. It drew attention to the research on animals being carried out in New Zealand at universities and animal research stations, and increasingly at commercial laboratories. The NZAVS attracted an energetic membership, many of whom were young and anti-establishment – punks were prominent in its ranks. Between 1980 and 1992 the society held flamboyant anti-vivisection marches in Wellington, Christchurch and Dunedin, in which members' pets took part.[81]

The NZAVS clashed with the other major New Zealand anti-vivisection organisation, SAFE (Save Animals from Experiments), accusing it of being too conciliatory. SAFE was the successor of the Auckland Branch of the BUAV. When this folded in the late 1970s the organisation regrouped and changed its name. SAFE's aim was 'To oppose vivisection absolutely and entirely and without attempts to compromise of any kind'.[82] SAFE soon had branches at Rotorua, South Auckland, Hamilton, Tauranga, Christchurch and Dunedin. A visit from Peter Singer in May 1981 gave the organisation a further boost. In July 1982 it presented to parliament a petition against vivisection, with an impressive 120,000 signatures.[83]

Within a short time anti-vivisectionists had managed to rally significant numbers, many from outside the movement, to their cause. Different tactics helped. The new organisations continued to oppose vivisection for medical research but they now revealed, often graphically, how animals were used to test products such as cosmetics and household cleaners. Many animal lovers were horrified at the idea of tormenting mice, guinea pigs, rabbits, cats and dogs merely to serve the convenience and vanity of humans. These people were targeted. For one 1981 fund-raising effort, SAFE organisers suggested, 'If your dog is good with people, how about donating some time to collecting money at the fete, people respond so much better to the big brown eyes of a collecting dog than the big brown eyes of a member!' Pointers on how to interest people in the cause included the hint 'Chat up dog-walkers, they are invariably interested'.[84] Such comments identified important common ground – for despite the ambivalence of some animal rights activists about pet keeping, many had companion animals.

New Zealand scientists reacted swiftly to the anti-vivisection campaigns, recommending legislative change to safeguard research involving animals.[85] During the 1980s the Animals Protection Act was amended to set up codes of ethics and an ethics advisory council for research. Naturally, these changes were stridently opposed by anti-vivisectionists on the grounds that they simply regulated experiments on animals instead of abolishing them. The NZAVS scornfully described the law changes as 'the vivisectors' charter' and in 1989 presented a 100,460-signature petition to parliament calling for the abolition of vivisection.[86]

Over the next few years the NZAVS and the scientific community battled to win the hearts and minds of pet owners. In 1990 the Agricultural Chemical and Animal Remedies Manufacturers Association of New Zealand, in association with various medical research foundations and the Ministry of Agriculture and Fisheries, produced a booklet entitled *Animal Research Saves Lives: Humans and animals both benefit*. Clearly aimed at the pet-keeping public, it included such statements as 'just like you, scientists love animals and protect them from cruelty'. Laboratory animals, it explained, were mainly specially bred rats, mice, guinea pigs and hamsters, with a few 'surplus' cats and dogs obtained from breeders or pounds. It appealed to pet owners' interests by pointing out that each batch of distemper, parvovirus and cat flu vaccine needed to be tested on a cat or dog to prove its effectiveness and safety. This, it claimed, 'means that 50,000 loved pets are assured of protection from agonising deaths'.[87]

In the 1980s and 1990s members of the New Zealand Anti-Vivisection Society in Wellington marched to parliament each year on 27 April, World Day for Laboratory Animals. A tortoiseshell kitten called Rain took part with owner Michelle Weakley in 1991.

Alexander Turnbull Library, Dominion Post Collection. Reference: EP/1991/1146

Bette Overell of the NZAVS responded in 1993 with a 368-page book, *Animal Research Takes Lives – Humans and animals both suffer*. Seizing on the admission in *Animal Research Saves Lives* that some unwanted pets were used for experiments, she launched a withering attack on the pet industry. Overell lambasted breeders for supplying the market with thousands of animals which – unwanted, old, lost and dumped – ended up in pounds and in some cases vivisection laboratories. She also asserted that pet-food manufacturers were responsible for the 'indiscriminate slaughter' of wild and intensively farmed animals to create products for 'cute' pet animals. She concluded,

> The claim that vivisection exists to administer the health and well-being of pet cats, dogs and farm animals is emotional blackmail and far from the truth. The vivisection industry and its affiliates promote the pet industry solely for the source of income and availability of animals it represents.[88]

By this time, however, parliament had shelved the anti-vivisection petition of 1989, and official mechanisms for enabling animal experiments were well entrenched. With Overell's retirement in the mid-1990s, the NZAVS became Christchurch-based, shifting its focus from political action to anti-vivisection education.[89]

~

SAFE took a different tack. In 1987 it changed its name again to Save Animals From Exploitation and initiated campaigns against factory farming. In 1995 it presented to parliament a petition calling for a referendum on the phasing out of battery hen cages. With over 200,000 signatures, this fell only slightly short of the number required to force a referendum. SAFE also protested against intensive pig farming, launching a national campaign to ban the sow crate in 1997. In the late 1990s the organisation also began using endorsements from local celebrities to reach out to a wider range of people.[90]

Like the early SPCAs, which encouraged animal lovers to transfer the empathy they had for their pets to other animals, SAFE harnessed people's attachment to companion animals to attract support for its causes. In its publicity it extended the definition of 'pet', profiling hens and pigs – often animals rescued from intensive farming operations – to show how lovable they were. SAFE supporters who provided homes for former battery hens spoke about them as other pet lovers might describe their cats or dogs. One family said of Rusty and Averill: 'They are clever, naughty and have personalities … One even sneaked in through the cat-flap and roosted on the telly!'[91]

The involvement of a revitalised and unified SPCA federation (it became the Royal New Zealand SPCA in 1982) in the anti-factory farming crusade suggested growing co-operation between mainstream animal welfare organisations and more radical animal rights groups.[92] One joint initiative aimed to enhance the status of companion animals – as pets were now often known. In 1996 the New Zealand Companion Animal Council, an alliance of animal welfare and rights organisations, including the RNZSPCA and SAFE, was set up. Its definition of companion animal was very wide: the 'entire spectrum of animals with whom interaction and/or companionship is enjoyed by humans, and where a responsible guardianship is established and accepted for their welfare by humans'.[93]

The subject of companion animals remained contentious among some animal rights activists. Deciding that the terminology used to define relationships between people and animals was part of the problem, in 1999 SAFE joined an international campaign called 'They are not our property, we are not their owners'. This rejected the idea that animals 'belonged' to humans, considering it to be at the root of all animal welfare abuses. Instead of 'oppressive' terms such as 'pet' and 'owner', alternatives such as 'companion', 'friend', 'guardian' and 'caretaker' were suggested.[94] These ways of describing the human–animal bond soon became more widely used.

By the 2000s, with the help of new groups such as New Zealand Open Rescue, animal rights campaigns were to achieve a measure of success: cages for battery hens were increased in size from 2008, and in 2011 the government announced that sow stalls would be phased out by 2016.[95] These victories were undoubtedly assisted by a perceptible shift in public opinion. From the 1980s numbers of New Zealanders signed petitions against animal experimentation and rejected products tested on animals. And from the 1990s consumer unease about factory farming was reflected in increased demand for free-range eggs and meat. Most people who cared about animals would now have agreed that they had 'rights', though what they meant by that probably varied.[96] Not all those who rejected vivisection

This happy hen, modelling the latest in chicken knitwear, is held by Auckland SPCA worker Amy Symes. Concern about factory farming from the 1990s led some people to adopt ex-battery chickens through animal shelters and rehoming organisations. Because of the overcrowded conditions in which the birds had been kept, most had few feathers left. One solution was to knit cosy jumpers for them until the feathers grew back: the RNZSPCA even published a pattern on its website. *Permission of Amy Symes*

A 2010 cartoon by Tom Scott commented humorously on a proposal to extend legal representation to animals in Switzerland. By this time some New Zealanders would have agreed with the idea.

Alexander Turnbull Library. Reference: DCDL-0013597. Permission of Tom Scott

and factory farming went along with every aspect of the animal liberation agenda, but they responded readily to the emotional appeals of the campaigns.

~

In 1999, in response to the impassioned public debates about treatment of animals, parliament passed a new Animal Welfare Act. It introduced stronger penalties for offences (and these were further stiffened after a vigorous campaign by a new welfare organisation, Paw Justice, in 2010). The main focus of the 1999 legislation, however, was the prevention of cruelty and neglect. The owner was now responsible for an animal's suffering, unless it was deliberately inflicted by someone else. According to an expert commentator, this made the act 'one of the most advanced pieces of animal welfare legislation in the Commonwealth'.[97] But although the act was progressive in many ways, it still defined all animals, including pets, as property.[98] This was problematical in a society where a growing number of people no longer thought of their animal companions as possessions.

Now, many New Zealanders referred to their pets as child surrogates – 'fur babies' – sometimes ironically, but often quite seriously. The loosening of family ties and an increase in marriage breakdown have often been cited as reasons for the heightened importance placed on pet animals. By 2001 a quarter of New Zealand households were 'dinky' – double income, no kids – and a further 23 per cent consisted of a single person.[99] In these homes, some suggested, pets received more attention and possibly acquired greater emotional significance. But there is ample evidence that pets also enjoyed higher status in families with children. More people felt able to talk openly about their close relationship with their pets without fear of being accused of sentimentality. They were eager to share their enthusiasm for pets, contributing photos and anecdotes to newspaper features and websites. They often mourned openly when a pet died, expressing their grief publicly in pet obituaries.

These reactions were encouraged and supported by the pet industry. Pet services and products became even more varied, imaginative and specialised. Puppy pre-school and animal psychotherapy helped to resolve animal behaviour problems. Doting 'pet parents' could practise reflexology on their cats, or take their dogs to 'doggie dancing' lessons. Medical treatments for animals were no longer strictly differentiated from those for humans: natural animal health products and procedures, including herbal and homeopathic remedies, hydrotherapy and naturopathy, developed. With the introduction of diagnostic procedures such as MRI scans, and the availability of cardiac and cancer specialists at regional pet hospitals, medical care for pets became increasingly sophisticated — and expensive. And if all else failed, the end was dignified. Pet funeral celebrants emerged, along with pet grief counsellors.

In 2007 *Consumer* magazine made a light-hearted comparison between the costs of raising a puppy and a baby for the first year: the puppy's care came in only $534 cheaper, and its medical costs and food were actually more expensive.[100] Animals once fed on scraps from the dinner table could now expect to be treated like people. Indeed, that is the way they were often regarded by their owners. One did not hesitate to pay the $4000 bill for hip surgery when her cat was hit by a car. She sold her own car to cover the cost, explaining, 'He's human.'[101] Another commented, 'There isn't a "too much" regarding money … would you declare you had spent too much on your child, parent, or grandparent?'[102] Major currents of change — in particular consumerism and the altered status of animals — converged in these perspectives. They were no longer considered shocking or even unusual. For many people, a pet had become a necessary companion, loved and cherished — quite literally, one of the family.

Former All Black Norm Hewitt, pictured with his daughter Elizabeth and cat Huna, fronted the One of the Family campaign initiated by the Royal New Zealand Society for the Prevention of Cruelty to Animals in 2006. Its aim was to teach school children respect for animals as a way of curbing violence towards both animals and humans. This echoed nineteenth-century campaigns but went a crucial step further: the society wanted animals to be 'safe, secure and loved members of the human families whose homes they share'. *Permission of RNZSPCA*

Endnotes

Preface
1. New Zealand Companion Animal Council (2011), *Companion Animals in New Zealand, July 2011*, NZCAC, Auckland, pp. 8, 11–17.

Chapter 1 Making introductions
1. Anne Salmond (1997), *Between Worlds: Early exchanges between Maori and Europeans 1773–1815*, Viking/Penguin Books, Auckland, p. 79.
2. Georg Forster, *A Voyage Round the World*, Nicholas Thomas and Oliver Berghof (eds) (c. 2000), assisted by Jennifer Newell, vol. 1, University of Hawaii Press, Honolulu, p. 125.
3. GC [Geoffrey Clark], 'Family Canidae: Kuri', in Carolyn M. King (ed.) (2005), *Handbook of New Zealand Mammals*, Oxford University Press, Auckland, 2nd edn, pp. 255–60; W. Colenso, 'Notes, chiefly historical, on the ancient dog of the New Zealanders', *Transactions of the New Zealand Institute*, vol. 10, 1877, p. 142; Anne Salmond (1991), *Two Worlds: First meetings between Maori and Europeans, 1642–1772*, Viking, Auckland, p. 407.
4. Katharine Luomala, 'The native dog in the Polynesian system of values', in Stanley Diamond (ed.) (1960), *Culture in History: Essays in honor of Paul Radin*, Columbia University Press, New York, pp. 192–95.
5. Ibid., pp. 200–04, 223; James Serpell, 'From paragon to pariah: some reflections on human attitudes to dogs', pp. 248–50, and Juliet Clutton-Brock, 'Origins of the dog: domestication and early history', p. 15, in James Serpell (ed.) (1995), *The Domestic Dog: Its evolution, behaviour and interactions with people*, Cambridge University Press, Cambridge.
6. Margaret Titcomb (1969), *Dog and Man in the Ancient Pacific*, Bernice P. Bishop Museum Special Publication 59, Honolulu, pp. 45–47.
7. Quoted in Salmond, *Between Worlds*, p. 25.
8. Forster, *A Voyage Round the World*, vol. 1, p. 125.
9. Salmond, *Between Worlds*, pp. 355, 407.
10. Quoted in Salmond, *Two Worlds*, p. 268.
11. Salmond, *Two Worlds*, p. 407.
12. James Serpell (1986), *In the Company of Animals: A study of human-animal relationships*, Basil Blackwell, Oxford, pp. 37–41, 130; Keith Thomas (1984), *Man and the Natural World: Changing attitudes in England 1500–1800*, Penguin, London, pp. 100–20.
13. Anne Salmond (2003), *The Trial of the Cannibal Dog: Captain Cook in the South Seas*, Allen Lane/Penguin Press, London, p. 6.
14. Luomala, 'The native dog and Polynesian values', p. 199.
15. Joan Druett (1983), *Exotic Intruders: The introduction of plants and animals into New Zealand*, Heinemann, Auckland, p. 16.
16. Serpell, *In the Company of Animals*, p. 135.
17. Ibid., pp. 37, 122–24, 130, 137.
18. Salmond, *Between Worlds*, p. 42.
19. This theory is discussed by Serpell, *In the Company of Animals*, pp. 3–5, 174–75.
20. Elsdon Best (1942:1977), *Forest Lore of the Maori*, Dominion Museum Bulletin no. 14 and Polynesian Society Memoir no. 18, Government Print, Wellington [first published Polynesian Society and Dominion Museum, Wellington, 1942], pp. 193, 291; Margaret Orbell (2003), *Birds of Aotearoa: A natural and cultural history*, Reed, Auckland, p. 8.
21. Orbell, *Birds of Aotearoa*, p. 8; Salmond, *Between Worlds*, p. 510; Te Ahukaramu Charles Royal, 'First peoples in Maori tradition', Te Ara: the Encyclopedia of New Zealand, updated 15 March 2013, www.TeAra.govt.nz/en/first-peoples-in-maori-tradition
22. Bradford Haami, 'Te whanau puha – whales', Te Ara: the Encyclopedia of New Zealand, updated 9 November 2012, www.TeAra.govt.nz/en/te-whanau-puha-whales; Royal, 'First peoples in Maori tradition', Te Ara.
23. Basil Keane, 'Kuri – Polynesian dogs', Te Ara: the Encyclopedia of New Zealand, updated 4 December 2012, www.TeAra.govt.nz/en/kuri-polynesian-dogs; Luomala, 'The native dog in the Polynesian system of values', p. 213.
24. Keane, 'Kuri – Polynesian dogs', Te Ara; Luomala, 'The native dog in the Polynesian system of values', pp. 206, 210.
25. Miriam MacGregor Redwood (1980), *A Dog's Life: Working dogs in New Zealand*, Reed, Wellington, p. ix; Luomala, 'The native dog in the Polynesian system of values', pp. 207–08.
26. MacGregor Redwood, *A Dog's Life*, p. x; J.S. Polack (1838:1974), *New Zealand: Being a narrative of travels and adventures during a residence in that country between the years 1831 and 1837*, Capper Press, Christchurch [facsimile of edition published Richard Bentley, London, 1838], vol. 1, pp. 308–10.
27. Luomala, 'The native dog in the Polynesian system of values', pp. 208–09; Best, *Forest Lore of the Maori*, pp. 167–69, 170.
28. A.J. Anderson and G. Clark, 'Advances in New Zealand mammalogy 1990–2000: Polynesian dog or kuri', *Journal of the Royal Society of New Zealand*, vol. 31, no. 1, March 2001, p. 162.
29. Nick Tupara, 'Turanganui-a-Kiwa tribes', Te Ara: the Encyclopedia of New Zealand, updated 4 December 2012, www.TeAra.govt.nz/en/turanganui-a-kiwa-tribes; Rawiri Taonui, 'Nga waewae tapu – Maori exploration', Te Ara: the Encyclopedia of New Zealand, updated 4 December 2012, www.TeAra.govt.nz/en/nga-waewae-tapu-maori-exploration; MacGregor Redwood, *A Dog's Life*, p. ix; Luomala, 'The native dog in the Polynesian system of values', pp. 208, 215.
30. Jay Bay-Petersen, 'Competition for resources: the role of the pig and dog in the Polynesian agricultural economy', *Journal de la Societe des Oceanistes*, vol. 77, 1983, pp. 121–29.
31. Keane, 'Kuri – Polynesian dogs', Te Ara; Kelly Keane, 'Nga manu – birds' in Te Ara: the Encyclopedia of New Zealand, updated 4 December 2012, www.TeAra.govt.nz/en/nga-manu-birds; GC [Geoffrey Clark], 'Family Canidae: Kuri', p. 260; Best, *Forest Lore of the Maori*, pp. 120–23; Luomala, 'The native dog in the Polynesian system of values', pp. 231–32.
32. Patricia Te Arapo Wallace, 'He whatu ariki, he kura, he waero: chiefly threads, red and white', in Bronwyn Labrum, Fiona McKergow and Stephanie Gibson (eds) (2007), *Looking Flash: Clothing in Aotearoa New Zealand*, Auckland University Press, Auckland, p. 16.
33. Best, *Forest Lore of the Maori*, pp. 181, 352; Keane, 'Nga manu – birds', Te Ara; Royal, 'First peoples in Maori tradition', Te Ara.
34. Best, *Forest Lore of the Maori*, p. 197, 202–03; Kelly Keane, 'Nga manu – birds', Te Ara; Basil Keane, 'Te tahere manu – bird

catching', Te Ara: the Encyclopedia of New Zealand, updated 4 December 2012, www.TeAra.govt.nz/en/te-tahere-manu-bird-catching; Basil Keane, 'Pounamu – jade or greenstone', Te Ara: the Encyclopedia of New Zealand, updated 4 December 2012, www.TeAra.govt.nz/en/pounamu-jade-or-greenstone

35 Salmond, *Between Worlds*, p. 472; Best, *Forest Lore of the Maori*, pp. 309–11, 314; Murdoch Riley (2001), *Maori Bird Lore: An introduction*, Viking Sevenseas NZ Ltd, Paraparaumu, p. 201.

36 Best, *Forest Lore of the Maori*, pp. 201–02; Richard Taylor (1855), *Te Ika a Maui, or, New Zealand and its Inhabitants*, Wertheim and Macintosh, London, p. 202; Edward Jerningham Wakefield (1845:1971), *Adventure in New Zealand from 1839 to 1844: With some account of the beginning of the British colonization of the islands*, Wilson and Horton, Auckland [facsimile of edition published John Murray, London, 1845], vol. 1, p. 382.

37 Salmond, *Between Worlds*, pp. 103, 40–43, 85, 118–19.

38 Ibid., p. 119.

39 Salmond, *Two Worlds*, pp. 331, 335, 372.

40 Salmond, *Between Worlds*, p. 58

41 Ibid., pp. 68, 128.

42 Druett, *Exotic Intruders*, p. 13.

43 Salmond, *Between Worlds*, pp. 322, 327, 329–30.

44 Druett, *Exotic Intruders*, p. 13; Salmond, *Between Worlds*, p. 327; Melinda S. Allen, Elizabeth Matisoo-Smith and Ann Horsburgh, 'Pacific "Babes": issues in the origins and dispersal of Pacific pigs and the potential of mitochondrial DNA analysis', *International Journal of Osteoarchaeology*, vol. 11, issue 1–2, 2001, pp. 4–13; C.M.H. Clarke and R.M. Dzieciolowski, 'Feral pigs in the northern South Island, New Zealand: I. Origin, distribution and density', *Journal of the Royal Society of New Zealand*, vol. 21, no. 3, 1991, pp. 237–47.

45 June Starke (ed.) (1986), *The Journal of a Rambler, by John Boultbee*, Oxford University Press, Auckland, pp. 54–56; Jock Phillips, 'Whaling', Te Ara: the Encyclopedia of New Zealand, updated 4 February 2013, www.TeAra.govt.nz/en/whaling; Jock Phillips, 'Sealing', Te Ara: the Encyclopedia of New Zealand, updated 9 November 2012, www.TeAra.govt.nz/en/sealing; Nancy Swarbrick, 'Flax and flax working', Te Ara: the Encyclopedia of New Zealand, updated 9 November 2012, www.TeAra.govt.nz/en/flax-and-flax-working

46 Salmond, *Between Worlds*, p. 489.

47 Polack, *New Zealand*, vol. 1, p. 314 and other early sources use puhihi. For the explanation of ngeru, see Michael King (1986), *Maori: A social and photographic history*, Penguin, Auckland, p. 83.

48 Salmond, *Between Worlds*, pp. 450, 460–61, 487, 507.

49 Wakefield, *Adventure in New Zealand*, vol. 2, p. 17.

50 Salmond, *Between Worlds*, p. 472; Best, *Forest Lore of the Maori*, p. 308

51 W. Colenso, 'Vestiges: reminiscences: memorabilia of works, deeds and sayings of the ancient Maoris', *Transactions of the New Zealand Institute*, vol. 24, 1891, p. 457.

52 GC [Geoffrey Clark], ' Family Canidae: Kuri', pp. 255–60.

53 Colenso, 'Notes, chiefly historical, on the ancient Dog of the New Zealanders', p. 151

54 W.D. Murison, 'Note on the wild dog', *Transactions of the New Zealand Institute*, vol. 10, 1877, pp. 322–24.

55 Taylor White, 'On the wild dogs of New Zealand', *Transactions of the New Zealand Institute*, vol. 22, 1889, pp. 327–30.

56 MacGregor Redwood, *A Dog's Life*, pp. ix–xii; G.M. Thomson (1922), *The Naturalisation of Animals and Plants in New Zealand*, Canterbury University Press, Christchurch, pp. 68–70.

57 Charles Hursthouse (1857), *New Zealand or Zealandia: The Britain of the south*, Edward Standford, London, vol. 1, p. 160; Karl Scherzer (1863), *Narrative of the Circumnavigation of the Globe by the Austrian Frigate, Novara*, Saunders, Otley and Co., London, vol. 3, p. 121.

58 Ernest Dieffenbach (1843:1974), *Travels in New Zealand: With contributions to the geography, botany and natural history of that country*, Capper Press, Christchurch [facsimile of edition published John Murray, London, 1843], vol. 2, pp. 45–46.

59 Salmond, *The Trial of the Cannibal Dog*, p. 8.

60 James Serpell, 'From paragon to pariah', p. 248.

61 In *The Trial of the Cannibal Dog*, pp. 1–9, Salmond argues that the explorers shed their inhibitions about eating dogs after coming under Polynesian influence.

62 Forster, *A Voyage Round the World*, vol. 1, p. 134.

63 J.R. Elder (ed.) (1932), *The Letters and Journals of Samuel Marsden 1765–1838*, Coulls, Somerville Wilkie Ltd and A.H. Reed for the Otago University Council, Dunedin, p. 271; Richard A. Cruise (1824:1974), *Journal of a Ten Months' Residence in New Zealand*, Capper Press, Christchurch [facsimile of edition published Longman, Hurst, Rees, Orme, Brown, and Green, London, 1824], p. 202; Polack, *New Zealand*, vol. 2, p. 60.

64 Cruise, *Journal of a Ten Months' Residence in New Zealand*, p. 202.

65 Elder (ed.), *The Letters and Journals of Samuel Marsden*, p. 271.

66 Polack, *New Zealand*, vol. 2, p. 60.

67 Charles Nordhoff (1857), *Stories of the Island World*, Harper and Brothers, New York, p. 251.

68 Ibid.; Anna K. C. Petersen (2001), *New Zealanders at Home: A cultural history of domestic interiors 1814–1914*, University of Otago Press, Dunedin, p. 25.

69 G.F. Angas (1847), *Savage Life and Scenes in Australia and New Zealand: Being an artist's impression of countries and people in the antipodes*, Elder and Co., London, vol. 1, p. 274.

70 Hursthouse, *New Zealand or Zealandia*, vol. 1, pp. 126–27.

71 Brenda Guthrie Northcroft (1930:1959), *New Zealand Memories*, A.H. and A.W. Reed, Wellington [first published John Lane, London, 1930], pp. 113–14.

72 George Clarke (1903), *Notes on Early Life in New Zealand*, J. Walch and Sons, Hobart, pp. 25–26.

73 Hazel Petrie (2002), 'Colonisation and the involution of the Maori economy', Paper for the World Congress of Economic History, Buenos Aires, July.

74 R.M. McDowall (1994), *Gamekeepers for the Nation: The story of New Zealand's acclimatisation societies*, Canterbury University Press, Christchurch, pp. 303–36, 346.

75 Protection of Animals Act, 1867; Evaan Aramakutu (1997), 'Colonists and colonials: animals' protection legislation in New Zealand 1861–1910', MA thesis (History), Massey University, Appendix 1: Species protected by Animals Protection Statutes, p. 104.

76 Ibid., pp. 75, 76, 103. The Animals Protection Amendment Act, 1895 introduced a closed season for kereru in 1896 and every sixth year thereafter. This ban was a direct threat to an important traditional food. See also Kate Hunter (2009), *Hunting: A New Zealand history*, Random House, Auckland, pp. 62–65.

77 *Te Waka Maori o Nui Tirani*, 23 April 1873, p. 45.

78 Ross Galbreath outlines the development of this attitude in 'Displacement, conservation and customary use of native

plants and animals in New Zealand', *New Zealand Journal of History*, vol. 36, no. 1, 2002, pp. 38–39.
79 Aramakutu, 'Colonists and colonials', p. 77.
80 Ibid., p. 112, Appendix 1.
81 J.A.W. Steedman, 'Te Kahuhiapo, Rahera ?–1910', from *The Dictionary of New Zealand Biography*. Te Ara: the Encyclopedia of New Zealand, updated 30 October 2012, www.TeAra.govt.nz/en/biographies/2t20/te-kahuhiapo-rahera; Best, *Forest Lore of the Maori*, p. 311.
82 Annie R. Butler (1886), *Glimpses of Maoriland*, Religious Tract Society, London, p. 199.
83 *Tikao Talks: Ka taoka o te ao kohatu. Treasures from the ancient world of the Maori*, told by Teone Taare Tikao to Herries Beattie, Penguin Books, Auckland, 1990 [first published A.H. and A.W. Reed, Dunedin, 1939], p. 135; Tipene O'Regan, 'Tikao, Hone Taare, 1850?–1927', from *The Dictionary of New Zealand Biography*, Te Ara: the Encyclopedia of New Zealand, updated 30 October 2012, www.TeAra.govt.nz/en/biographies/2t43/tikao-hone-taare
84 *The Old-time Maori: By Makereti, some-time chieftainess of the Arawa tribe, known in New Zealand as Maggie Papakura; collected and edited with a bibliography by T. K. Penniman*, Gollancz, London, 1938, p. 252.
85 Adrienne Puckey (2011), *Trading Cultures: A history of the far north*, Huia, Wellington, p. 142.
86 James Cowan (1944), 'The worst dog in the world', in *Tales of the Maori Border*, A.H. and A.W. Reed, Wellington, pp. 17–24.
87 See 'kuri' in H.W. Orsman (ed.) (1997), *The Dictionary of New Zealand English*, Oxford University Press, Auckland.
88 An Ordinance to Abate the Dog Nuisance, 1849.
89 See schedule to The Dog Registration Act, 1880.
90 The Injuries by Dogs Act, 1865.
91 The Dog Registration Act, 1880.
92 Richard Hill (1995), *The Iron Hand in the Velvet Glove: The modernisation of policing in New Zealand 1886–1917*, Dunmore Press in association with the New Zealand Police and the Historical Branch, Department of Internal Affairs, Palmerston North, p. 134.
93 R.C. Wilson (1978), *Wairoa County Council: The first hundred years*, Wairoa County Council, Wairoa, pp. 34, 47–48. Featherston County was one local body that did not enforce dog registration until 1926. See John Dunmore (1991), *Around the Shining Waters: A history of Featherston County Council*, Heritage Press Ltd, Waikanae, p. 103.
94 See for example *New Zealand Farmer: Bee and Poultry Journal*, vol. xi, no. 11, November 1891, p. 471.
95 Angela Ballara, 'Toia, Hone Riiwi, 1858–1860?–1933', from *The Dictionary of New Zealand Biography*, Te Ara: the Encyclopedia of New Zealand, updated 30 October 2012, www.TeAra.govt.nz/en/biographies/2t45/toia-hone-riiwi; Puckey, *Trading Cultures*, pp. 143–44.
96 Mark Derby (2009), *The Prophet and the Policeman: The story of Rua Kenana and John Cullen*, Craig Potton Publishing, Nelson, p. 58.

Chapter 2 Happy homes
1 Jock Phillips and Terry Hearn (2008), *Settlers: New Zealand immigrants from England, Ireland and Scotland 1800–1945*, Auckland University Press, Auckland, pp. 21–22.
2 Philip B. Chadfield (1875), *Out at Sea, or, the emigrant afloat: Being a hand book of practical information for the use of passengers on a long sea voyage*, Chadfield, Derby [first published 1862], preface.
3 Katherine C. Grier, 'Childhood socialization and companion animals: United States, 1820–1870', *Society and Animals: Journal of Human-Animal Studies*, vol. 7, no. 2, 1999, Society and Animals Forum, www.societyandanimalsforum.org [accessed 12 July 2009]; Katherine C. Grier (2007), *Pets in America: A history*, Harvest, Orlando, pp. 172–74; Philip Howell, 'A place for the animal dead: pets, pet cemeteries and animal ethics in late Victorian Britain', *Ethics, Place and Environment*, vol. 5, no. 1, 2002, pp. 5–22; James Turner (1980), *Reckoning with the Beast: Animals, pain, and humanity in the Victorian mind*, Johns Hopkins University Press, Baltimore, p. 76.
4 Charles Hursthouse (1857), *New Zealand or Zealandia, the Britain of the South*, Edward Standford, London, vol. 2, pp. 408, 412; Edward Jerningham Wakefield (1848), *The Handbook for New Zealand: Consisting of the most recent information compiled for the use of intending colonists by a late magistrate of the colony*, John W. Parker, London, p. 445.
5 Wakefield, *The Handbook for New Zealand*, p. 166.
6 Carolyn Mincham (2008), 'A Social and Cultural History of the New Zealand Horse', DPhil. thesis (History), Massey University, pp. 43–44.
7 Wakefield, *The Handbook for New Zealand*, p. 445.
8 Alfred Saunders (1927:2003), *Tales of a Pioneer: Episodes in the life of Alfred Saunders*, Cadsonbury Publications, Christchurch [facsimile of edition published L.M. Isitt, Christchurch, 1927], p. 38.
9 *The Journal of Edward Ward 1850–51: Being his account of the voyage to New Zealand in the Charlotte Jane and the first six months of the Canterbury settlement* (1951), Pegasus Press, Christchurch, pp. 26, 40–41, 51.
10 Joan Druett (1983), *Exotic Intruders: The introduction of plants and animals into New Zealand*, Heinemann, Auckland, pp. 170–71.
11 Madeleine Seager (1987), *Edward William Seager: Pioneer of mental health*, Heritage Press, Waikanae, p. 13.
12 Ellen Shephard Tripp (1929), *My Early Days*, Whitcombe and Tombs, Christchurch, pp. 14–15.
13 John R. Godley (ed.) (1951), *Letters from Early New Zealand by Charlotte Godley, 1850–1853*, Whitcombe and Tombs, Christchurch, p. 9.
14 Neill Atkinson (2001), *Crew Culture: New Zealand seafarers under sail and steam*, Te Papa Press, Wellington, p. 75.
15 Quoted in Alison Clarke (2007), *Holiday Seasons: Christmas, New Year and Easter in nineteenth century New Zealand*, Auckland University Press, Auckland, p. 41. See also Frances Porter and Charlotte Macdonald (eds) with Tui Macdonald (1996), *'My Hand Will Write What my Heart Dictates': The unsettled lives of women in nineteenth-century New Zealand as revealed to sisters, family and friends*, Auckland University Press/Bridget Williams Books, Auckland, 'Settling and unsettling', pp. 77–100.
16 *A Year at Hawkswood: The diary of Frances Caverhill for 1865* (1981), Nag's Head Press, Christchurch, vol. 1: January–June. pp. 27, 46; vol. 2: July–December, p. 19
17 Quoted in Kate Hunter (2009), *Hunting: A New Zealand history*, Random House, Auckland, p. 47.
18 Jan Harris (1994), *Tohora: The story of Fyffe House, Kai Koura*, New Zealand Historic Places Trust, Wellington, p. 31.
19 John Bradshaw (1883), *New Zealand As It Is*, Sampson Low, Marston, Searle and Rivington, London, pp. 11–12.
20 Tripp, *My Early Days*, p. 16.

21. Sarah Amelia Courage (1896:1976), *Lights and Shadows of Colonial Life: Twenty-six years in Canterbury*, Whitcoulls, Christchurch [first published Whitcombe and Tombs, Christchurch, 1896], pp. 36, 63.
22. Jemima Martin to her Aunt Bray, 16 July 1854, *'My Hand Will Write What my Heart Dictates'*, p. 162
23. Diana Harris (2007), *Johnny Jones: A colonial saga*, Reed, Auckland, pp. 169–70.
24. Hursthouse, *New Zealand or Zealandia*, vol. 1, p. 120.
25. John Ward (1840:1998), *Information Relative to New Zealand Compiled for the Use of Colonists*, Kiwi Publishers, Christchurch [facsimile of edition published John W. Parker, London, 1840], pp. 52–53.
26. John Deans III (ed.) (1937:1997), *Pioneers of Canterbury: Deans family letters, 1840–1854*, Cadsonbury Publications, Christchurch [first published A. H. and A. W. Reed, Dunedin, 1937], p. 95.
27. Ellen Hewett (1910:1921), *Looking Back or personal reminiscences by the widow of a New Zealand pioneer settler*, Campfield Press, St Albans [first published 1910], p. 9.
28. Brenda Guthrie Northcroft (1930:1959), *New Zealand Memories*, Reed, Wellington [first published John Lane, London, 1930], p. 160.
29. Adela B. Stewart (1908:1995), *My Simple Life in New Zealand*, Southern Reprints, Auckland [facsimile of edition published Robert Banks and Son, London, 1908], p. 31.
30. William Henwood to his parents in Cornwall from Taranaki, 2 March 1842, *Letters from Settlers and Labouring Emigrants in the New Zealand Company's Settlements of Wellington, Nelson and New Plymouth: From February, 1842, to January, 1843*, Smith, Elder and Co., London, 1843, pp. 149–50.
31. Quoted in Alison Drummond and L.R. Drummond (1965), *At Home in New Zealand: An illustrated history of everyday things before 1865*, Blackwood and Janet Paul, Auckland, p. 107.
32. Sarah Stephens to her mother, Motueka, 29 September 1843, *'My Hand Will Write What my Heart Dictates'* p. 158.
33. *A Year at Hawkswood*, vol. 2, p. 25.
34. Ibid., vol. 1, pp. 31–2.
35. Stewart, *My Simple Life in New Zealand*, p. 25.
36. Quoted in Brian Sutton-Smith (1982), *A History of Children's Play in New Zealand, 1840–1950*, New Zealand Council of Educational Research, Wellington, p. 8.
37. Mincham, 'A Social and Cultural History of the New Zealand Horse', pp. 66–93.
38. Alison Drummond (ed.) (1982), *The Waikato Journals of Vicesimus Lush, 1864–8, 1881–2*, Pegasus Press, Christchurch, p. 109.
39. Shirley Tunnicliff (ed.) (1992), *The Selected Letters of Mary Hobhouse*, Daphne Brasell Associates Press, Wellington, p. 96.
40. Carolyn Mincham (2011), *Attitude and Heart: The horse in New Zealand*, David Bateman, Auckland, pp. 138–49.
41. W. K. Howitt (1947), *A Pioneer Looks Back*, Oswald-Sealy Ltd, Auckland, p. 134.
42. This is recounted in many sources: see for instance Courage, *Lights and Shadows of Colonial Life*, p. 24; Hursthouse, *New Zealand or Zealandia*, vol. 2, p. 356; Samuel Butler, *A First Year in Canterbury Settlement*, Kiwi Publishers, Christchurch [facsimile of edition published Longman, London, 1863], p. 84. For an explanation of the different types of rats, see Bob Brockie, 'Rival rat rating explains separate ecological niches', *Dominion Post*, 12 March 2012, B5.
43. Alison Drummond (1960), *Married and Gone to New Zealand: Being extracts from the writings of women pioneers*, Pauls Book Arcade, Hamilton, p. 85.
44. Godley (ed.), *Letters from Early New Zealand*, p. 185.
45. Courage, *Lights and Shadows of Colonial Life*, p. 24.
46. Saunders, *Tales of a Pioneer*, p. 31.
47. John Rochfort (1853:1974), *The Adventures of a Surveyor in New Zealand and the Australian Gold Diggings*, Capper Press, Christchurch [facsimile of edition published David Bogue, London, 1853], p. 26.
48. Stewart, *My Simple Life in New Zealand*, p. 47.
49. Courage, *Lights and Shadows of Colonial Life*, p. 231.
50. Ibid., p. 62.
51. Wakefield, *The Handbook for New Zealand*, p. 445.
52. Hursthouse, *New Zealand or Zealandia*, vol. 2, p. 416.
53. Agnes Jameson (1916), *Old Memories*, Smith and Anthony, Christchurch, p. 40.
54. Edward Jerningham Wakefield (1845:1971), *Adventure in New Zealand from 1839 to 1844: With some account of the beginning of British colonization of the islands*, Wilson and Horton, Auckland [facsimile of edition published John Murray, London, 1845], vol. 2, p. 7.
55. Godley (ed.), *Letters from Early New Zealand*, p. 185.
56. Wakefield, *The Handbook for New Zealand*, p. 167.
57. *Wellington Independent*, 27 June 1868, p. 4.
58. Druett, *Exotic Intruders*, p. 249.
59. Drummond (ed.), *The Waikato Journals of Vicesimus Lush*, pp. 18, 95.
60. Wakefield, *Adventure in New Zealand*, vol. 2, p. 327; Ellen Petre, diary, Wellington, 1843, *'My Hand Will Write What my Heart Dictates'*, p. 81.
61. Druett, *Exotic Intruders*, pp. 245–46.
62. Keith Thomas (1984), *Man and the Natural World: Changing attitudes in England 1500–1800*, Penguin, London, p. 186; Hilda Kean (1998), *Animal Rights: Political and social change in Britain since 1800*, Reaktion Books, London, pp. 46–47; Grier, 'Childhood socialization and companion animals'.
63. Kathleen R. Johnson, 'The ambiguous terrain of pet-keeping in children's realistic animal stories', *Society and Animals: Journal of Human-Animal Studies*, vol. 4, no. 1, 1996, Society and Animals Forum, www.societyandanimalsforum.org [accessed 12 July 2009]
64. Kean, *Animal Rights*, p. 47; list of books in 'Original Juvenile Library' at the back of Mrs J. E. Aylmer (1862), *Distant Homes; Or the Graham family in New Zealand*, Griffith and Farran, London; *Wellington Independent*, 27 June 1871, p. 2; 'Mrs George Cupples', Notes-Books-Authors, Number 3, 1989, Friends of Dorothy Neal White Collection, www.dnwfriends.nzl.org/dnwbooks/nba3.html [accessed 5 April 2013]
65. See for example advertisements in *Wellington Independent*, 27 June 1871, p. 2; *Nelson Evening Mail*, 28 January 1874, p. 2; *North Otago Times*, 12 July 1866, p. 2; *Hawke's Bay Herald*, 7 October 1863, p. 4.
66. *New Zealand Farmer: Bee and Poultry Journal*, vol. vi, no. 9, September 1886, p. 286; vol. iv, no. 3, March 1886, p. 92; vol. iv, no. 7, July 1886, p. 92.
67. Janet McCallum (2009), *Women and their Words: Notable pioneers in New Zealand journalism*, Fraser Books, Masterton, ch. 8: 'For the children'.
68. See Janet McCallum, 'Baker, Louisa Alice 1856–1926' from *The Dictionary of New Zealand Biography*. Te Ara: the

Encyclopedia of New Zealand, updated 30 October 2012, www.TeAra.govt.nz/en/biographies/3b4/baker-louisa-alice; George Griffiths, 'Fenwick, George 1847–1927' from *The Dictionary of New Zealand Biography*. Te Ara: the Encyclopedia of New Zealand, updated 30 October 2012, www.TeAra.govt.nz/en/biographies/2f4/fenwick-george; Dorothy Page, 'Soper, Eileen Louise 1900–1989' from *The Dictionary of New Zealand Biography*. Te Ara: the Encyclopedia of New Zealand, updated 30 October 2012, www.TeAra.govt.nz/en/biographies/4s37/soper-eileen-louise

69 'Our Little Folk' by Dot, *Otago Witness*, 28 January 1887, p. 32.
70 *New Zealand Farmer: Bee and Poultry Journal*, vol. viii, no. 8, August 1888, p. 297.
71 *New Zealand Farmer: Bee and Poultry Journal*, vol. viii, no. 12, December 1888, p. 493.
72 *New Zealand Farmer: Bee and Poultry Journal*, vol. x, no. 2, February 1890, p. 59.
73 *New Zealand Farmer: Bee and Poultry Journal*, vol. xii, no. 12, December 1892, p. 511.
74 Quoted in Keith Scott (2011), *Dear Dot I Must Tell You: A personal history of young New Zealanders*, Activity Press, Auckland, p. 69.
75 Quoted in Scott, *Dear Dot I Must Tell You*, p. 76.
76 *New Zealand Farmer: Bee and Poultry Journal*, vol. xii, no. 10, October 1892, p. 430.
77 'In Touch with Nature: Notes on natural history in New Zealand by James Drummond, FLS, FZS', *Evening Post*, 18 June 1910, p. 13.
78 *New Zealand Farmer: Bee and Poultry Journal*, vol. xi, no. 6, June 1891, p. 261.
79 *New Zealand Farmer: Bee and Poultry Journal*, vol. xii, no. 11, November 1892, p. 469.
80 *New Zealand Farmer: Bee and Poultry Journal*, vol. xii, no. 5, May 1892, p. 230.
81 Dorothea Joblin (1975), *The Colonial One: Lorna Monckton of Newstead*, Whitcombe and Tombs, Christchurch, p. 79.
82 Dorothea Joblin (1970), *Behold the Plains: The story of the old houses of Massey*, Longman Paul, Auckland, p. 38.
83 'Rene Edwin's "Log": a picture of middle-class family life in nineteenth century Wellington', in Sandra Coney (1993), *Standing in the Sunshine: A history of New Zealand women since they won the vote*, Penguin, Auckland, p. 63.
84 Mincham, 'A Social and Cultural History of the New Zealand Horse', pp. 62–63 makes a similar point.
85 David Eggleton (2006), *Into the Light: A history of New Zealand photography*, Craig Potton, Nelson, pp. 8–10, 35–6.
86 Courage, *Lights and Shadows of Colonial Life*, pp. 165–66.
87 Katharine MacDonogh (1999), *Reigning Cats and Dogs: A history of pets at court since the Renaissance*, St Martin's Press, New York, pp. 193–97.
88 *New Zealand Farmer: Bee and Poultry Journal*, vol. viii, no. 12, December 1888, p. 493.
89 'General Information', *Bruce Herald*, 26 April 1898, p. 3.
90 *Timaru Herald*, 2 August 1883, p. 1. See also Hunter, *Hunting: A New Zealand history*, p. 172.
91 *Otago Witness*, 23 June 1909, p. 59.

Chapter 3 A man's best friends?

1 *Extracts from the Letters and Journals Addressed to Members of his Family, by Percy Whitehead*; selected by Elizabeth Malleson (1900), privately printed, p. 20.
2 Jock Phillips explains the different aspects of mateship in *A Man's Country? The image of the Pakeha male – a history*, (1987), Penguin, Auckland, pp. 2–42. They are also discussed in James Belich (1996), *Making Peoples: A history of the New Zealanders from Polynesian settlement to the end of the nineteenth century*, Allen Lane/The Penguin Press, Auckland, pp. 424–36.
3 Jill Herron (2003), *Trials and Dogs of the South: A history of sheep dog trialling in Southland*, Southland Dog Trial Association, Gore, p. 9; Hugh Stringleman and Robert Peden, 'Sheep farming', in Te Ara: the Encyclopedia of New Zealand, updated 14 March 2013, www.TeAra.govt.nz/en/sheep-farming
4 Miriam MacGregor Redwood (1980), *A Dog's Life: Working dogs in New Zealand*, Reed, Wellington, pp. 1–3.
5 MacGregor Redwood, *A Dog's Life*, pp. 45, 54–55, 85; Clive Dalton, 'Farm dogs', in Te Ara: the Encyclopedia of New Zealand, updated 9 November 2012, www.TeAra.govt.nz/en/farm-dogs
6 *The Journal of Edward Ward 1850–5: Being his account of the voyage to New Zealand in the Charlotte Jane and the first six months of the Canterbury settlement* (1951), Pegasus Press, Christchurch, p. 138.
7 M.V. Mueller (ed.) (1958), *My Dear Bannie: Gerhard Mueller's letters from the West Coast 1865–6*, Pegasus Press, Christchurch, pp. 101, 159.
8 Andreas Reischek (1889:1984), *The Story of a Wonderful Dog: With some notes on the training of dogs and horses: also hints on camping, bush and mountain exploration in New Zealand*, Capper Press, Christchurch [facsimile of edition published *Star*, Auckland, 1889], pp. 26–27.
9 Ibid., p. 11.
10 Ibid., p. 4.
11 *Mr Explorer Douglas: John Pascoe's New Zealand classic*, revised by Graham Langton (2000), Canterbury University Press, Christchurch, p. 174.
12 Carolyn Mincham (2008), 'A Social and Cultural history of the New Zealand Horse', DPhil. thesis (History), Massey University, p. 56; John E. Martin (1990), *The Forgotten Worker: The rural wage earner in nineteenth-century New Zealand*, Allen and Unwin/Trade Union History Project, Wellington, p. 129.
13 Mincham, 'A Social and Cultural History of the New Zealand Horse', p. 56; Martin, *The Forgotten Worker*, p. 129; Samuel Butler (1863:1997), *A First Year in Canterbury Settlement*, Kiwi Publishers, Christchurch [facsimile of edition published Longman, London, 1863], p. 32.
14 Laurence J. Kennaway (1874:1996), *Crusts: A settler's fare due south*, Kiwi Publishers, Christchurch [facsimile of edition published Sampson Low, Marston, Low and Searle, London, 1874], p. 122.
15 'Old Nugget' in David McKee Wright (1897), *Station Ballads and Other Verses*, J.G. Sawell, Dunedin, pp. 96–98.
16 Kennaway, *Crusts*, pp. 58–59.
17 Mincham, 'A Social and Cultural History of the New Zealand Horse', pp. 57–58, 114–15.
18 Les Morgan, 'Dolly: Our mine pony', *Ohinemuri Regional History Journal*, vol. 13, 1970, p. 26.
19 *Mr Explorer Douglas*, p. 122.
20 Mary Anne Barker (1873), *Station Amusements in New Zealand*, William Hunt, London, p. 223.
21 'Life on a station', *New Zealand Farmer: Bee and Poultry Journal*, vol. x, no. 8, August 1890, p. 300.
22 MacGregor Redwood, *A Dog's Life*, pp. 33–36.

23 Edward Wakefield (1889), *New Zealand After Fifty Years*, Cassell and Company, New York, p. 166.
24 W.K. Howitt (1947), *A Pioneer Looks Back*, Oswald-Sealy Ltd, Auckland, p. 145.
25 John E. Martin, 'Slattery, Edmond 1839/1840?–1927', from *The Dictionary of New Zealand Biography*. Te Ara: the Encyclopedia of New Zealand, updated 30 October 2012, www.TeAra.govt.nz/en/biographies/2s30/slattery-edmond
26 John A. Lee (1977), *Roughnecks, Rolling Stones and Rouseabouts: With an anthology of early swagger literature*, Whitcoulls, Christchurch, pp. 39, 69–73.
27 See Miles Fairburn (1995), *Nearly out of Heart and Hope: The puzzle of a colonial labourer's diary*, Auckland University Press, Auckland, p. 227.
28 Anna K. C. Petersen (2001), *New Zealanders at Home: A cultural history of domestic interiors 1814–1914*, University of Otago Press, Dunedin, pp. 41, 44, 50, 58.
29 Butler, *A First Year in Canterbury Settlement*, p. 84.
30 Ibid., p. 87.
31 E.C. Richards (comp.) (1951), *Castle Hill*, Simpson and Williams Ltd, Christchurch, p. 41.
32 Reischek, *The Story of a Wonderful Dog*, p. 20.
33 Kennaway, *Crusts*, p. 102.
34 Barker, *Station Amusements*, p. 229.
35 'Life on a station', *New Zealand Farmer: Bee and Poultry Journal*, vol. x, no. 8, August 1890, p. 300.
36 The Christchurch Fire Brigade entered Marco Polo, a grey tabby, in the 1884 cat show held in association with the Christchurch Poultry, Pigeon and Canary Society annual show. See *Catalogue of the Seventeenth Annual Show of the Christchurch Poultry, Pigeon and Canary Society Held in the Oddfellows Hall, Christchurch, July 2 & 3, 1884*, The Society, Christchurch, 1884.
37 Edward Jerningham Wakefield (1845:1971), *Adventure in New Zealand: With some account of the beginning of the British colonization of the islands*, Wilson and Horton, Auckland [facsimile of edition published John Murray, London, 1845], vol. 2, pp. 279-80.
38 MacGregor Redwood, *A Dog's Life*, p. 57.
39 Erik Olssen (1995), *Building the New World: Work, politics and society in Caversham, 1880s–1920s*, Auckland University Press, Auckland, p. 42.
40 David Grant (1994), *On a Roll: A history of gambling and lotteries in New Zealand*, Victoria University Press, Wellington, pp. 26, 28, 31.
41 'Diary of the Rev. Robert Taylor, *Hydaspes*, London to Lyttelton, 1869', entry for Friday 30th July, New Zealand Yesteryears, www.yesteryears.co.nz/shipping/diaries/hydaspes1869.html [accessed 5 April 2013]
42 Kate Hunter (2009), *Hunting: A New Zealand history*, Random House, Auckland, p. 40.
43 Wakefield, *Adventure in New Zealand*, vol. 2, p. 6.
44 Phillips, *A Man's Country?*, p. 35.
45 George Chamier (1891), *Philosopher Dick: Adventures and contemplations of a New Zealand shepherd*, T. Fisher Unwin, London, pp. 170–71.
46 Wakefield, *Adventure in New Zealand*, vol. 2, p. 6.
47 W.H. Koebel (1911), *In the Maoriland Bush*, Stanley Paul and Co., London, p. 155.
48 *Mr Explorer Douglas*, p. 49.
49 Quoted in Emily Host (2006), *Thomas Brunner: His life and great journeys*, Nikau Press, Nelson, p. 137.
50 Philip Temple, 'Thomas Brunner, 1821?–1874', from *The Dictionary of New Zealand Biography*. Te Ara: the Encyclopedia of New Zealand, updated 30 October 2012, www.TeAra.govt.nz/en/biographies/1b41/brunner-thomas; Host, *Thomas Brunner*, pp. 209–11.
51 Wakefield, *New Zealand After Fifty Years*, pp. 149–50.
52 Barker, *Station Amusements*, p. 222.
53 MacGregor Redwood, *A Dog's Life*, p. 66; Koebel, *In the Maoriland Bush*, p. 119.
54 MacGregor Redwood, *A Dog's Life*, pp. 6–7, 53.
55 Francis Bennett (1980), *A Canterbury Tale: The autobiography of Dr Francis Bennett*, Oxford University Press, Wellington, p. 72.
56 Robert Gilkison (1930), *Early Days in Central Otago: Being tales of times gone by*, Otago Daily Times and Witness newspapers, Dunedin, p. 185.
57 E.W. Elkington (1906), *Adrift in New Zealand*, John Murray, London, pp. 146–49; Koebel, *In the Maoriland Bush*, p. 285.
58 James McNeish (1972), *The Mackenzie Affair*, Hodder and Stoughton, Auckland, p. 230; Martin, *The Forgotten Worker*, p. 61.
59 Martin, *The Forgotten Worker*, pp. 40, 75–76.
60 'Mr Donald Reid's address', *Otago Witness*, 23 July 1881, p. 6.
61 Wakefield, *New Zealand After Fifty Years*, p. 153.
62 Sarah Amelia Courage (1896:1976), *Lights and Shadows of Colonial Life: Twenty-six years in Canterbury*, Whitcoulls, Christchurch [first published Whitcombe and Tombs, Christchurch, 1896], p. 233.
63 *New Zealand Farmer: Stock and Station Journal*, vol. xxviii, no. 2, February 1907, p. xvi.
64 Mincham, 'A Social and Cultural History of the New Zealand Horse', pp. 109–10.
65 Reischek, *The Story of a Wonderful Dog*, pp. 6–7.
66 Mincham, 'A Social and Cultural History of the New Zealand Horse', pp. 96–97.
67 Reischek, *The Story of a Wonderful Dog*, pp. 27–28.
68 Fairburn, *Nearly out of Heart and Hope*, p. 17.
69 Elkington, *Adrift in New Zealand*, pp. 149, 148.

Chapter 4 The Fancy

1 The Editor, 'The Crystal Palace of Australasia. Triumphant success of the Christchurch Poultry Show', *New Zealand Poultry Journal*, vol. iii, no. 27, 20 June 1908, p. 18.
2 Harriet Ritvo (1987), *The Animal Estate: The English and other creatures in the Victorian age*, Harvard University Press, Cambridge, Massachusetts, p. 87.
3 'Ought we to cage birds', *Star*, 14 May 1897, p. 3; *Poverty Bay Herald*, 28 July 1900, p. 2.
4 Stewart Lusk (1983), *Dogsbody: The story of the New Zealand Kennel Club*, New Zealand Kennel Club, Wellington, p. 2.
5 Katharine MacDonogh (1999), *Reigning Cats and Dogs: A history of pets at court since the Renaissance*, St Martin's Press, New York, p. 116; Harriet Ritvo, 'The sincerest form of flattery', in Mary J. Henninger-Voss (ed.) (2002), *Animals in Human Histories: The mirror of nature and culture*, University of Rochester Press, New York, p. 296.
6 This theory is put forward by Ritvo in *The Animal Estate*, pp. 84, 104–05.
7 Ritvo, *The Animal Estate*, chs 1 and 2.
8 R.M. McDowall (1994), *Gamekeepers for the Nation: The story of New Zealand's acclimatisation societies 1861–1990*, Canterbury University Press, Christchurch, pp. 14, 18, 19, 21.

9   Jock Phillips, 'Shows and field days', in Te Ara: the Encyclopedia of New Zealand, updated 9 November 2012, www.TeAra.govt.nz/en/shows-and-field-days
10 See for example reports on North Otago A&P Association Show, Whangarei Farmers' Club Agricultural Show, Wairarapa and East Pastoral and Agricultural Society Show and Canterbury A&P Association Show in *New Zealand Farmer: Bee and Poultry Journal*, vol. viii, no. 12, December 1888, pp. 480, 481, 482, 484.
11 *New Zealand Poultry Journal*, vol. ii, no. 27, 20 June 1908, p. 25.
12 A.W. Moss (1961), *Valiant Crusade: The history of the RSPCA*, Cassell, London, p. 49; Keith Thomas (1984), *Man and the Natural World: Changing attitudes in England 1500–1800*, Penguin, London, p. 160.
13 'Omnium Gatherum', *Otago Daily Times*, 6 August 1892, p. 4; 'A New Zealand Poultry Association', *Marlborough Express*, 26 May 1893, p. 2; 'News of the Day', *Press*, 22 February 1898, p. 4; 'Local and General', *Star*, 17 June 1899, p. 5; 'News and Notes', *Hawera and Normanby Star*, 2 March 1901, p. 2
14 *Catalogue of the First Annual Show of the Christchurch Poultry Association, Held in the Town Hall, Christchurch, 1 August 1868*, The Association, Christchurch, 1868.
15 The Editor, 'The Crystal Palace of Australasia. Triumphant success of the Christchurch Poultry Show', *New Zealand Poultry Journal*, vol. iii, no. 27, 20 June 1908, p. 18
16 'Taken In' *Being a Sketch of New Zealand Life by 'Hopeful'* (1887:1974), Capper Press, Christchurch [facsimile of edition published W.H. Allen, London, 1887], p. 109.
17 Report on the Auckland Poultry, Pigeon and Canary Association show in *New Zealand Farmer: Bee and Poultry Journal*, vol. x, no. 9, September 1890, p. 366.
18 See for instance 'Growth of poultry farming', *Hawera and Normanby Star*, 20 March 1913, p. 6.
19 'General Regulations' in *Catalogue of the First Annual Show of the Hawke's Bay Poultry and Canary Association Held in the Protestant Hall, Napier, on 26th and 27th September 1879*, The Association, Napier, 1879.
20 *Catalogue of the First Annual Show of the Christchurch Poultry Association, 1868*.
21 *New Zealand Farmer: Bee and Poultry Journal*, vol. vi, no. 9, September 1886, p. 279; vol. ix, no. 9, September 1889, p. 355; vol. x, no. 9, September 1890, p. 364; vol. xii, no. 7, July 1892, p. 4
22 See for instance 'What others are doing', *New Zealand Poultry Journal*, vol. ii, no. 14, 20 May 1907, pp. 18–19.
23 Julia C. Flewellyn, 'What women can do. Work that is a pleasure and not a task. An excellent employment for the home-loving woman.', *New Zealand Poultry Journal*, vol. ii, no. 14, 20 May 1907, p. 10.
24 Ibid., p. 10.
25 *New Zealand Farmer: Bee and Poultry Journal*, vol. ix, no. 7, July 1889, p. 250; vol. ix, no. 8, August 1889, p. 329; vol. xi, no. 4, April 1891, p. 150.
26 *New Zealand Farmer: Stock and Station Journal*, vol. xxvii, no. 1, January 1907, p. xi.
27 *Evening Post*, 13 August 1897, p. 2.
28 *New Zealand Farmer: Bee and Poultry Journal*, vol. v, no. 9, September 1885, p. 279; vol. vi, no. 9, September 1886, pp. 278–79.
29 *New Zealand Farmer: Bee and Poultry Journal*, vol. viii, no. 1, January 1888, p. 84.
30 *New Zealand Farmer: Bee and Poultry Journal*, vol. ix, no. 9, September 1889, p. 355.
31 'Fanciers' Notes', *West Coast Times*, 23 May 1896, p. 4.
32 Ritvo, *The Animal Estate*, p. 23.
33 Gillian Vine (1978), *Longhaired Cats in New Zealand*, Gillian Vine, Gore, p. 21; MacDonogh, *Reigning Cats and Dogs*, p. 233.
34 Ritvo, *The Animal Estate*, pp. 115–16.
35 *New Zealand Farmer: Bee and Poultry Journal*, vol. vi, no. 9, September 1886, p. 279; vol. viii, no. 9, September 1888, p. 355; *Catalogue of the Seventeenth Annual Show of the Christchurch Poultry, Pigeon and Canary Society Held in the Oddfellows Hall, Christchurch, July 2 & 3, 1884. Also of the Cat Show held in connection with the above*, The Society, Christchurch, 1884.
36 *New Zealand Farmer: Bee and Poultry Journal*, vol. vi, no. 8, August 1886, pp. 245–46; vol. ix, no. 9, September 1889, p. 355; vol. xi, no. 10, October 1891, p. 434; 'Christchurch Poultry, Pigeon and Canary Society 21st annual show', *Star*, 19 July 1888, p. 3.
37 *New Zealand Farmer: Bee and Poultry Journal*, vol. vi, no. 8, August 1886, p. 245.
38 See for example *New Zealand Farmer: Bee and Poultry Journal*, vol. vi, no. 9, September 1886, p. 279; vol. viii, no. 9, September 1888, p. 355; *Catalogue of the Fourth Annual Show of the Sydenham Poultry, Pigeon and Canary Society Held in the Oddfellows Hall, Sydenham, August 5 and 6, 1885*, The Society, Christchurch, 1885.
39 *Catalogue of the Seventeenth Annual Show of the Christchurch Poultry, Pigeon and Canary Society 1884*.
40 Vine, *Longhaired Cats in New Zealand*, p. 21.
41 'Cattery at Mornington and a word about dogs and canaries', *Otago Witness*, 10 February 1904, p. 49.
42 *Taranaki Herald*, 19 April 1909, p. 2.
43 *Evening Post*, 25 January 1910, p. 8 – reports a consignment of Siamese cats arriving on the *Arawa*; Vine, *Longhaired Cats in New Zealand*, foreword.
44 'Local and General', *Star*, 12 August 1909, p. 3; 'Fanciers' show', *Evening Post*, 3 June 1910, p. 3.
45 *Auckland Star*, 28 June 1913, p. 4; *Auckland Star*, 11 March 1914, p. 6; *Evening Post*, 28 November 1917, p. 2.
46 MacDonogh, *Reigning Cats and Dogs*, pp. 116–17; Lusk, *Dogsbody*, p. 7; Ritvo, *The Animal Estate*, p. 102.
47 MacDonogh, *Reigning Cats and Dogs*, pp. 91, 100.
48 Ibid., pp. 116–17.
49 Lusk, *Dogsbody*, p. 3.
50 MacDonogh, *Reigning Cats and Dogs*, pp. 116–17.
51 Ibid.; Lusk, *Dogsbody*, p. 6; 'Looking backwards', *New Zealand Kennel Club's Yearbook: Jubilee year 1886–1936*, New Zealand Kennel Club, Wellington, 1936, pp. 17, 21.
52 'Looking backwards', *New Zealand Kennel Club's Yearbook*, pp. 19, 21–22; Lusk, *Dogsbody*, pp. 6, 7, 9, 11.
53 Inspector H. Alder, Auckland SPCA to Minister of Railways, 5 January 1918, in Carriage of dogs 1902–1960, New Zealand Railways (ADQD), series 17422, acc W2478, record group R3W2478, box 18, record no 1902/1168, Archives New Zealand (ANZ).
54 *Evening Post*, 26 August 1911, p. 9.
55 'Looking backwards', *New Zealand Kennel Club's Yearbook*, pp. 18–19.
56 *New Zealand Farmer: Bee and Poultry Journal*, vol. viii, no. 12, December 1888, p. 487.
57 *New Zealand Farmer: Bee and Poultry Journal*, vol. xi, no. 6, June 1891, p. 237.

58 *New Zealand Farmer: Bee and Poultry Journal*, vol. xxvii, no. 1, January 1907, p. xiii.
59 Clipping of letter from 'Lover of Alsatians' to *Auckland Star*, 7 January 1929, and list on file of all Alsatians imported and their origins, 1926–28, in Importation of Alsatian Dogs, 1929–1937, Ministry of Agriculture and Fisheries (AAFZ), series 412, acc W5704, box 191, record Ag 82/2/67, part 1, ANZ.
60 Extract from Australian legislation of 7 June 1929 banning import of Alsatians for five years, and clipping of letter from Thomas Mackenzie to *Dominion*, 9 January 1929, in Importation of Alsatian Dogs, 1929–1937, AAFZ, series 412, acc W5704, box 191, record Ag 82/2/67, part 1, ANZ.
61 See correspondence in Importation of Alsatian Dogs, 1929–1937, AAFZ, series 412, acc W5704, box 191, record Ag 82/2/67, part 1, ANZ; Lusk, *Dogsbody*, p. 18.
62 Clippings from *Dominion*, 12 January 1929 and *Auckland Star*, 13 March 1929 in Importation of Alsatian Dogs, 1929–1937, AAFZ, series 412, acc W5704, box 191, record Ag 82/2/67, part 1, ANZ; National Council for Alsatian Shepherd Dog Control, Registrar of Companies, Wellington (ADSN), series 17632, record group CO-W2, box 2, record 208, ANZ.
63 Notes on file, Importation of Alsatian Dogs, 1929–1937, AAFZ, series 412, acc W5704, box 191, record Ag 82/2/67, part 1, ANZ; Tom Brooking, 'Mackenzie, Thomas Noble 1853–1930' from *The Dictionary of New Zealand Biography*. Te Ara: the Encyclopedia of New Zealand, updated 30 October 2012, www.TeAra.govt.nz/en/biographies/3m18/mackenzie-thomas-noble
64 W.K. Jackson (1972), *The New Zealand Legislative Council: A study of the establishment, failure and abolition of an Upper House*, Otago University Press, Dunedin, p. 92.
65 Lusk, *Dogsbody*, pp. 18, 28, 36.
66 Jackson, *The New Zealand Legislative Council*, p. 92; Notes on file, Importation of Alsatian Dogs, 1929–1937, AAFZ, series 412, acc W5704, box 191, record Ag 82/2/67, part 1, ANZ.
67 Miriam MacGregor Redwood (1980), *A Dog's Life: Working dogs in New Zealand*, Reed, Wellington, pp. 9–10.
68 Ibid., p. 38; Clive Dalton, 'Farm dogs', in Te Ara: the Encyclopedia of New Zealand, updated 9 November 2012, www.TeAra.govt.nz/en/farm-dogs
69 John Gordon (1998), *Three Sheep and a Dog: An insider's view of New Zealand sheep dog trialling*, Reed, Auckland, pp. 61–64.
70 Ibid., pp. 69–86.
71 Ibid., pp. 28–29.
72 Dates vary in different accounts. These are the dates given in 'Dogs, Sheep dog trials', from *An Encyclopaedia of New Zealand*, edited by A.H. McLintock, originally published in 1966. Te Ara: the Encyclopedia of New Zealand, updated 22 April 2009, www.TeAra.govt.nz/en/1966/dogs-sheep-dog-trials
73 MacGregor Redwood, *A Dog's Life*, p. 57; 'Dogs, Sheep-dog trials', *An Encyclopaedia of New Zealand*, 1966.
74 Gordon, *Three Sheep and a Dog*, pp. 7–8.
75 Christine Wright (1996), *Whistles in the Wind: The story of the Methven Collie Club 1896–1996*, Methven Collie Club, Ashburton, p. 22.
76 Gordon, *Three Sheep and a Dog*, pp. 58–59; John Tombleson (2009), *Sheep Dog Trialling in Poverty Bay and Beyond*, Poverty Bay Centre of the New Zealand Sheep Dog Trial Association, Gisborne, p. 38.
77 'Looking backwards', *New Zealand Kennel Club's Yearbook*, p. 20; Lusk, *Dogsbody*, pp. 28–29, 119–20.

78 *New Zealand Poultry Journal*, vol. v, no. 56, 20 November 1910, p. 10.
79 'A fancier's complaint', *New Zealand Poultry Journal*, vol. iv, no. 40, 20 July 1909, p. 20.
80 Margaret Wiseman, 'History of the New Zealand Governing Council of the Cat Fancy 1930–1933' in *New Zealand Cats*, vol. 1, no. 34, August, 1990, pp. 34–38.
81 Lusk, *Dogsbody*, pp. 21–23.
82 Ibid., pp. 10–11.
83 'Women's dispute. Euchre tourney incident. Damages for slander', *Auckland Star*, 21 March 1935, p. 24.
84 See for example *Otago Witness*, 11 November 1897, p. 40.
85 *New Zealand Farmer: Bee and Poultry Journal*, vol. vii, no. 7, July 1887, pp. 207–08; vol. viii, no. 10, October 1888, p. 374; vol. viii, no. 11, November 1888, p. 422; vol. viii, no. 12, December 1888, p. 469.
86 'Looking backwards', *New Zealand Kennel Club's Yearbook*, p. 22.
87 *Marlborough Poultry Pigeon and Cage Bird Association, 1887–1987: Souvenir booklet*, p. 6.
88 'Looking backwards', *New Zealand Kennel Club's Yearbook*, p. 22.
89 Ibid., pp. 19, 22.
90 *New Zealand Farmer*, vol. vii, no. 7, July 1887, p. 207; *New Zealand Cats*, vol. 1, no. 9, May/June 1977, p. 30; *New Zealand Kennel Club's Yearbook*, p. 14.
91 Gavin McLean (2006), *The Governors: New Zealand's Governors and Governors-General*, Otago University Press, Dunedin, p. 154.
92 'Our new Governor and his wife – gossip about the Ranfurlys', *North Otago Times*, 10 August 1897, p. 4.
93 *Observer*, 11 September 1897, p. 6.
94 *Otago Witness*, 2 September 1897, p. 34; 'The fanciers' column. The kennel', *Otago Witness*, 11 August 1898, p. 39.
95 'Annual show of the Wellington Kennel Club', *Evening Post*, 25 August 1900, p. 2.
96 See for example 'Wanganui A&P show', *Wanganui Herald*, 24 November 1899, p. 1; 'Canine champions – awards at the dog show', *Evening Post*, 31 August 1901, p. 2.
97 'Protectors of dumb creatures. Lord Ranfurly on the Society's work.', *Evening Post*, 21 October 1897, p. 2; 'Animals Protection Society. Suggestions by the Governor.', *Evening Post*, 28 October 1898, p. 5.

Chapter 5   Learning to be kind

1 James Serpell (1986), *In the Company of Animals: A study of human–animal relationships*, Basil Blackwell, Oxford, p. 122; Keith Thomas (1983), *Man and the Natural World: Changing attitudes in England 1500–1800*, Penguin, London, pp. 151, 159; Harriet Ritvo (1987), *The Animal Estate: The English and other creatures in the Victorian age*, Harvard University Press, Cambridge, Massachusetts, p. 131.
2 Thomas, *Man and the Natural World*, pp. 154, 166–68, 176; Charles D. Niven (1967), *History of the Humane Movement*, Transatlantic Arts Inc., New York, pp. 51, 53; Hilda Kean (1998), *Animal Rights: Political and social change in Britain since 1800*, Reaktion Books, London, pp. 18–19.
3 Serpell, *In the Company of Animals*, pp. 130, 135; Thomas, *Man and the Natural World*, p. 119.
4 Katharine MacDonogh (1999), *Reigning Cats and Dogs: A history of pets at court since the Renaissance*, St Martin's Press, New York, p. 232.
5 A.W. Moss (1961), *Valiant Crusade: The history of the RSPCA*, Cassell, London, pp. 16, 22–28, 49; Ritvo, *The Animal Estate*,

pp. 127–28; Lyle Munro (2005), *Confronting Cruelty: Moral orthodoxy and the challenge of the animal rights movement*, Brill, Leiden, Boston, pp. 49–50.
6   Moss, *Valiant Crusade*, pp. 29, 156–57, 202; Ritvo, *The Animal Estate*, pp. 125–26, 129; 'Cruelty prosecution: the Royal Society' [letter to the editor], *Nelson Evening Mail*, 2 August 1898, p. 2.
7   See English Laws Act, 1858, which confirmed the application of English law in New Zealand from 1840, and Prevention of Cruelty to Animals Ordinance, 1861, Province of Otago, Session XIV, No. 65.
8   'Cruelty to a horse', *Daily Southern Cross*, 4 February 1871, p. 2.
9   *Daily Southern Cross*, 6 September 1865, p. 4.
10 *Thames Advertiser*, 9 September 1875, p. 2.
11 'Cruelty to animals', *Nelson Examiner and New Zealand Chronicle*, 13 October 1873, p. 3.
12 *Wanganui Chronicle*, 1 January 1878, p. 2.
13 Prevention of Cruelty to Animals Ordinance, 1861, Province of Otago, Session XIV, No. 65; and Prevention of Cruelty to Animals Ordinance Amendment Ordinance, 1862, Province of Otago, Session XV, No. 78; Cruelty to Animals Act, Province of Nelson, Session XXV, No. 5, 1874.
14 Cruelty to Animals Act, 1878, s. 3; Cruelty to Animals Act, 1880.
15 Michael King (2003), *Te Puea: A Life*, Reed, Auckland, pp. 24–25.
16 Richard S. Hill, 'Broham, Thomas 1840–1900', from *The Dictionary of New Zealand Biography*. Te Ara: the Encyclopedia of New Zealand, updated 30 October 2012, www.TeAra.govt.nz/en/biographies/1b34/broham-thomas
17 'Society for the Prevention of Cruelty to Animals', *Star*, 9 June 1882, p. 3.
18 'Society for the Prevention of Cruelty to Animals', *Otago Witness*, 4 August 1882, p. 13; Notes for 1883, Morrie Jalfon and Bob Kerridge (1996), *The History of the SPCA Auckland*, Auckland SPCA, Auckland [np]; 'Society for the Prevention of Cruelty to Animals', *Star*, 2 August 1883, p. 2; 'Society for the Prevention of Cruelty to Animals', *Evening Post*, 7 October 1884, p. 2.
19 David Thorns and Ben Schrader, 'City history and people', in Te Ara: the Encyclopedia of New Zealand, updated 9 November 2012, www.TeAra.govt.nz/en/city-history-and-people; Jane Tolerton, 'Taxis and cabs', in Te Ara: the Encyclopedia of New Zealand, updated 9 November 2012, www.TeAra.govt.nz/en/taxis-and-cabs; Adrian Humphris, 'Public transport', in Te Ara: the Encyclopedia of New Zealand, updated 9 November 2012, www.TeAra.govt.nz/en/public-transport
20 Notes for 1884, Jalfon and Kerridge, *The History of the SPCA Auckland*; S.F. Jackson, 'A little bit of history', *Pet Pride*, vol. 5, no. 2, February–March 1973, p. 11; 'Society for the Prevention of Cruelty to Animals', *Star*, 4 July 1882, p. 3; 'Society for the Prevention of Cruelty to Animals', *Otago Witness*, 4 August 1883, p. 13.
21 'The Society for the Prevention of Cruelty to Animals', *Mercury* [Tasmania], 26 December 1881, Supplement, p. 1, 2 August 1882, Supplement, p. 1; Jalfon and Kerridge, *The History of the SPCA Auckland*; 'Society for the Prevention of Cruelty to Animals', *Otago Witness*, 4 August 1883, p. 13; 'Society for the Prevention of Cruelty to Animals', *Star*, 9 June 1882, p. 3.

22 Kean, *Animal Rights*, pp. 50, 77–78.
23 *New Zealand Farmer: Bee and Poultry Journal*, vol. vi, no. 10, October 1886, pp. 294–95.
24 'Ladies' Column edited by "Clio"', *Evening Post*, 4 November 1893, p. 1.
25 'Society for the Prevention of Cruelty to Animals', *Star*, 4 July 1882, p. 3; 'Society for the Prevention of Cruelty to Animals', *Star*, 15 December 1882, p. 3.
26 *Tuapeka Times*, 19 July 1882, p. 5; 'Society for the Prevention of Cruelty to Animals', *Otago Witness*, 4 August 1883, p. 13; 'Society for the Prevention of Cruelty to Animals', *Star*, 6 September 1883, p. 4; Notes for 1883, Jalfon and Kerridge, *The History of the SPCA Auckland*.
27 *Wellington Society for the Prevention of Cruelty to Animals First Annual Report, 1885*, p. 12 in 'Annual reports 1885–1932', 89-238-6/3, Society for the Prevention of Cruelty to Animals, Wellington, records, MS-Group-89-238, Alexander Turnbull Library (ATL); Jackson, 'A little bit of history', pp. 11–12.
28 'Parliamentary intelligence', *North Otago Times*, 13 October 1884, p. 2; 'Evening sitting', *Southland Times*, 24 October 1884, p. 3; *West Coast Times*, 4 November 1884, p. 2.
29 N.E. Wells (1983), 'The Moral Status of Animals: Reform of animal protection law', LLB dissertation, University of Auckland Faculty of Law, pp. 23–24, 55; Ritvo, *The Animal Estate*, pp. 145–47.
30 'Society for the Prevention of Cruelty to Animals', *Star*, 15 December 1882, p. 3.
31 'Prevention of cruelty to animals', *Evening Post*, 23 February 1894, p. 4; Raewyn Dalziel (1993), *Focus on the Family: The Auckland Home and Family Society 1893–1993*, Home and Family Society, Auckland, p. 29; *Star*, 24 February 1899, p. 4.
32 *Wellington Society for the Prevention of Cruelty to Animals, Sixteenth Annual Report, October 1909*, p. 6 in 'Annual reports 1885–1932', 89-238-6/3, Society for the Prevention of Cruelty to Animals, Wellington, records, MS-Group-89-238, ATL. The balance sheet records for the first time a City Council subsidy of £5. For mention of 'lady collectors' see 'Society for the Prevention of Cruelty to Animals. The annual meeting', *Colonist*, 26 February 1901, p. 1; *New Zealand Society for the Protection of Women and Children and Prevention of Cruelty to Animals, Twenty-first Annual Report and Balance Sheet 1914–15*, The Society, Auckland, 1915, p. 12; *Wellington Society for the Prevention of Cruelty to Animals, Tenth Annual Report, November 1903*, p. 8 in 'Annual reports 1885–1932', 89-238-6/3, Society for the Prevention of Cruelty to Animals, Wellington, records, MS-Group-89-238, ATL.
33 Police Offences Amendment Act 1924 (s. 3); 'Reply to editorial. Fines "earned" by the SPCA', *Evening Post*, 31 October 1964, in 'Scrapbook, 1947–1976', 89-238-6/1, Society for the Prevention of Cruelty to Animals, Wellington, records, MS-Group-89-238, ATL; Veronika Thornburrow (ed.) (1993), *The Compassionate Years: An introduction to the history of the Royal New Zealand Society for the Prevention of Cruelty to Animals*, RNZSPCA, Auckland, pp. 76, 86.
34 See untitled typescript of radio broadcast by John Howell in 'Records', 89-238-2/02; Minutes of meeting of executive council, Wellington SPCA, 4 August 1938, p. 2 in 'Records', 89-238-2/08; and 'Editorial opinion. Tighten the law.', *New Zealand Truth* [nd, c. 1960], in 'Scrapbook 1947–1976', 89-238-6/1, Society for the Prevention of Cruelty to Animals, Wellington, records, MS-Group-89-238, ATL.

35 See 'Society for the Prevention of Cruelty to Animals', *Otago Witness*, 4 August 1883, p. 13; 'Society for the Prevention of Cruelty to Animals', *Star*, 6 September 1883, p. 4.
36 *New Zealand Society for the Protection of Women and Children and Prevention of Cruelty to Animals: Seventeenth annual report and balance sheet 1910–11*, The Society, Auckland, 1911, p. 10.
37 *New Zealand Society for the Protection of Women and Children and Prevention of Cruelty to Animals: Eighteenth annual report and balance sheet 1911–12*, The Society, Auckland, 1912, p. 8.
38 Neil Wells, 'A century of achievement', *Pet Pride*, vol. 2, no. 2, September 1984, pp. 10–11; Thornburrow, *The Compassionate Years*, pp. 44–53.
39 'The passing show', *The Budget: A popular family magazine*, 26 August 1910, p. 13.
40 *Wellington Society for the Prevention of Cruelty to Animals, Twenty-second Annual Report, 1915*, p. 2 in 'Annual reports 1885–1932', 89-238-6/3, Society for the Prevention of Cruelty to Animals, Wellington, records, MS-Group-89-238, ATL.
41 Moss, *Valiant Crusade*, pp. 30–31, 186, 205; Brian Harrison (1982), *Peaceable Kingdom: Stability and change in modern Britain*, Clarendon Press, Oxford, p. 421; Ritvo, *The Animal Estate*, p. 133; William J. Schultz (1924:1968), *The Humane Movement in the United States, 1910–1922*, AMS Press, New York [first published by Columbia University Press, New York, 1924], pp. 11, 52; 'History of the NSPCC', National Society for the Prevention of Cruelty to Children, www.nspcc.org.uk [accessed 3 April 2012]; 'Who we are – history', American Humane Association, www.americanhumane.org [accessed 3 April 2012]
42 *Auckland Star*, 28 November 1873, p. 2.
43 *Daybreak*, 9 February 1895, p. 2; 30 March 1895, p. 6; 13 April 1895, p. 7; 4 May 1895, p. 4; 21 December 1895, p. 3; 28 December 1895, p. 3; 28 December 1895, p. 23. See also Brigid Pike, 'Tasker, Marianne Allen 1852–1911' from *The Dictionary of New Zealand Biography*. Te Ara: the Encyclopedia of New Zealand, updated 30 October 2012, www.TeAra.govt.nz/en/biographies/2t10/tasker-marianne-allen and Julia Millen 'Player, Mary Josephine 1857/1858?–1924' from *The Dictionary of New Zealand Biography*. Te Ara: the Encyclopedia of New Zealand, updated 30 October 2012, www.TeAra.govt.nz/en/biographies/2p21/player-mary-josephine
44 'Local and General' *Evening Post*, 9 March 1897, p. 4; Frances Porter, 'Atkinson, Lily May 1866–1921', from *The Dictionary of New Zealand Biography*. Te Ara: the Encyclopedia of New Zealand, updated 30 October 2012, www.TeAra.govt.nz/en/biographies/2a17/atkinson-lily-may; 'Animals' Protection Society. Suggestions by the Governor.', *Evening Post*, 28 October 1898, p. 5. This report on the fifth annual meeting of the Wellington SPCA notes that an entertainment was soon to be given on behalf of the Wellington SPCA and the Society for the Protection of Women and Children.
45 Notes for 1899, Jalfon and Kerridge, *The History of the SPCA Auckland*; *Eleventh Annual Report and Balance Sheet of the New Zealand Society for the Protection of Women and Children and Prevention of Cruelty to Animals (incorporated and registered 1899), Auckland 1904–5*, in 'Annual reports 1885–1932', 89-238-6/3, Society for the Prevention of Cruelty to Animals, Wellington, records, MS-Group-89-238, ATL. These two sources suggest that the amalgamation was made official in 1899, but Dalziel, *Focus on the Family*, p. 30 makes it clear that the decision was made at a general meeting in February 1898.
46 'Animals' Protection Society. Suggestions by the Governor.', *Evening Post*, 28 October 1898, p. 5.
47 'Society for the Prevention of Cruelty to Animals', *Star*, 9 June 1882, p. 3; Kathleen Kete, 'Pets' in Paula S. Fass (ed.) (2004), *Encyclopedia of Children and Childhood in History and Society*, Macmillan Reference USA, New York, vol. 2, pp. 668–72.
48 See for example *Hawke's Bay Herald*, 19 October 1887, p. 2; *New Zealand Farmer: Bee and Poultry Journal*, vol. x, no. 1, January 1890, p. 24 and vol. xii, no. 5, May 1892, p. 230; Brian Sutton-Smith (1982), *A History of Children's Play in New Zealand, 1840–1950*, New Zealand Council of Educational Research, Wellington, pp. 93, 119–20, 127–28.
49 *Wanganui Chronicle*, 7 November 1888, p. 2.
50 *Clutha Leader*, 13 August 1897, p. 7.
51 'Ill-treating a kitten', *Evening Star*, 4 March 1897, reproduced in Thornburrow, *The Compassionate Years*, p. 65.
52 'How to take care of your pets', *New Zealand Farmer: Bee and Poultry Journal*, vol. v, no. 3, March 1885, p. 93.
53 *The New Zealand Schoolmaster: A monthly educational journal and review*, vol. 1, no. 3, Napier, October 1881, p. 41.
54 *The New Zealand Schoolmaster: A monthly educational journal and review*, vol. 1, no. 12, Napier, July 1882, p. 193.
55 'Society for the Prevention of Cruelty to Animals', *Star*, 9 June 1882, p. 3; 'Society for the Prevention of Cruelty to Animals', *Evening Post*, 7 October 1884, p. 2; Jackson 'A little bit of history', p. 11; Thornburrow, *The Compassionate Years*, p. 72.
56 'Society for the Prevention of Cruelty to Animals', *Star*, 15 December 1882, p. 3; Thornburrow, *The Compassionate Years*, p. 68.
57 'Ladies' Column', *Evening Post*, 21 April 1894, p. 1.
58 Moss, *Valiant Crusade*, pp. 198, 201–02; Frederick S. Milton (2008), 'Taking the Pledge: A study of children's societies for the prevention of cruelty to birds and animals in Britain, c. 1870-1914', PhD thesis, Newcastle University, pp. 81–82; Dalziel, *Focus on the Family*, p. 32.
59 *Star*, 27 May 1885, p. 2. See also Thornburrow, *The Compassionate Years*, p. 68; Peter Lineham, 'Interdenominational Christianity', in Te Ara: the Encyclopedia of New Zealand, updated 9 November 2012, www.TeAra.govt.nz/en/interdenominational-christianity
60 'Telegrams', *Otago Daily Times*, 16 February 1892, p. 2.
61 For example, the Auckland SPCA was planning to circularise Sunday schools to ask them to assist in Bands of Mercy in the early 1890s, according to its eighth annual meeting, 1 October 1891, in 'Minutes AGM October 1883–November 1895', item 1, Society for the Prevention of Cruelty to Animals, Auckland, records, MS 2010/13, AWMM. See also 'Special telegrams', *Otago Daily Times*, 19 July 1892, p. 2; 'Societies, clubs etc', *Star*, 19 July 1886, p. 3; 'Hanover Street Baptist Church', *Otago Daily Times*, 31 May 1893, p. 3.
62 Call for annual reports of unions in *White Ribbon*, 19 November 1917, p. 2, with list of New Zealand superintendents of departments including 'LTL, Cradle Roll, and Band of Mercy', Mrs Clara Neal, Pahiatua.
63 'Rural: Dicky Bird Society', *Clutha Leader*, 25 July 1884, p. 3; *Evening Post*, 13 April 1894, p. 2; *Evening Post*, 11 May 1894, p. 2; 'Local and General', *Evening Post*, 27 October 1896, p. 6; *Evening Post*, 17 May 1895, p. 2; *Wellington Society for the Prevention of Cruelty to Animals, Fourth Annual Report, September 1897*, p. 6, in 'Annual reports 1885–1932', 89-238-6/3, Society for the Prevention of Cruelty to Animals, Wellington,

records, MS-Group-89-238, ATL; 'Education Board', *Taranaki Herald*, 10 September 1896, p. 2; 'Society for the Prevention of Cruelty to Animals: the annual meeting', *Colonist*, 26 February 1901, p. 1.
64 *Bruce Herald*, 5 January 1894, p. 1.
65 Letter from Victor Harris, aged eight, in *The New Zealand Band of Mercy*, 1 December 1897, p. 75.
66 Letter from C. C. [name withheld by the editor], aged 13, in *The New Zealand Band of Mercy*, 1 October 1897, p. 56.
67 *Star*, 24 February 1899, p. 4.
68 'Local and General', *Evening Post*, 9 March 1897, p. 4; *North Otago Times*, 3 May 1897, p. 2; *Marlborough Express*, 30 April 1897, p. 2; 'Local and General', *Evening Post*, 18 January 1898, p. 4; *Evening Post*, 6 September 1898, p. 4. There is no mention of bands of mercy in Wellington SPCA annual reports from 1901.
69 'Band of Mercy', *Wanganui Chronicle*, 10 June 1919, p. 6.
70 *Southland Times*, 9 January 1899, p. 2.
71 S.G. Culliford (1958), *New Zealand Scouting: The first fifty years 1908–1958*, Boy Scouts Association of New Zealand, Wellington, pp. 53, 56, 60; Marie Iles (1976), *65 Years of Guiding 1908–1973: The official history of the Girl Guides Association NZ (Inc.)*, Girl Guides Association New Zealand (Inc.), Christchurch, p. 7; D. Cossgrove (1918), *The Empire Sentinel's Handbook and Ritual*, Andrews, Batty and Co., Christchurch, [np].
72 Culliford, *New Zealand Scouting*, p. 38.
73 *Twenty-fourth Annual Report of the Otago Society for the Prevention of Cruelty to Animals for the Year Ending December 31, 1905*, Otago Daily Times and Witness Newspapers Company Ltd, Dunedin, 1905, pp. 6, 10.
74 *Seventeenth Annual Report and Balance Sheet of the New Zealand Society for the Protection of Women and Children and Prevention of Cruelty to Animals, Auckland, 1910–11*, Wilson and Horton, Auckland, 1911, p. 12; *Eighteenth Annual Report and Balance Sheet of the New Zealand Society for the Protection of Women and Children and Prevention of Cruelty to Animals, Auckland, 1911–12*, Wilson and Horton, Auckland, 1912, pp. 12–13; *Twentieth Annual Report and Balance Sheet of the New Zealand Society for the Protection of Women and Children and Prevention of Cruelty to Animals, Auckland, 1913–14*, Wilson and Horton, Auckland, 1914, pp. 12–13; *Twenty-seventh Annual Report and Balance Sheet of the New Zealand Society for the Protection of Women and Children and Prevention of Cruelty to Animals, Auckland, 1920–21*, Wilson and Horton, Auckland, 1921, p. 9.
75 'Essay. Written by Constance Moss, Eketahuna School, and awarded first prize in 1920 competition', *Twenty-eighth Annual Report of the Wellington Society for the Prevention of Cruelty to Animals, 1921*, in 'Annual reports 1894–1978', 89-238-6/3, Society for the Prevention of Cruelty to Animals, Wellington, records, MS-Group-89-238, ATL.
76 John L. Ewing (1970), *Development of the New Zealand Primary School Curriculum 1877–1970*, New Zealand Council for Educational Research, Wellington, pp. 35–37, 107; 'Moral instruction through literature and history' in *New Zealand Schoolmaster and Educational Review*, vol. xxvii, no. 6, Christchurch, 15 June 1908, pp. 92–93; 'Regulations for inspection and examination of schools', *Supplement to the New Zealand Gazette of April 14, 1904*, 20 April 1904, pp. 1055–95; 'The Education Act, 1908 – Regulations relating to Native Schools', *Supplement to the New Zealand Gazette of Thursday September 30, 1909*, Wednesday 6 October 1909, pp. 2491–522.
77 *School Journal*, vol. iv, no. 9, October 1910, part 1, p. 130.
78 For example, see 'Society for the Prevention of Cruelty to Animals', *Otago Witness*, 4 August 1883, p. 13; 'Society for the Prevention of Cruelty to Animals', *Star*, 15 December 1882, p. 3.
79 *Twenty-fourth Annual Report of the Otago Society for the Prevention of Cruelty to Animals for the Year Ending December 31, 1905*, Otago Daily Times and Witness Newspapers Company Ltd, Dunedin, 1905, p. 7.
80 Auckland SPCA general committee meeting, 11 June 1917, in 'Minutes general committee and AGMs February 1912–August 1917', item 2, Society for the Prevention of Cruelty to Animals, Auckland, records, MS 2010/13, AWMM.
81 *Wellington Society for the Prevention of Cruelty to Animals: Twenty-seventh annual report, 1920*, p. 3, in 'Annual reports 1885–1932', 89-238-6/3, Society for the Prevention of Cruelty to Animals, Wellington, records, MS-Group-89-238, ATL.
82 Reprinted in *Wellington SPCA, 26th Annual Report, 1919*, p. 16, in 'Annual reports 1885–1932', 89-238-6/3, Society for the Prevention of Cruelty to Animals, Wellington, records, MS-Group-89-238, ATL.
83 *Canterbury Society for the Prevention of Cruelty to Animals (Incorporated), Forty-fourth Annual Report and Balance Sheet for Year Ended August 31st, 1927*, p. 12, in 'Annual reports 1885–1932', 89-238-6/3, Society for the Prevention of Cruelty to Animals, Wellington, records, MS-Group-89-238, ATL.
84 Auckland SPCA general committee meeting, 8 July 1912 in 'Minutes general committee and AGMs February 1912–August 1917', item 2, Society for the Prevention of Cruelty to Animals, Auckland, records, MS 2010/13, AWMM; *Canterbury Society for the Prevention of Cruelty to Animals (Incorporated), Forty-fourth Annual Report and Balance Sheet for Year Ended August 31st, 1927*, p. 15, in 'Annual reports 1885–1932', 89-238-6/3, Society for the Prevention of Cruelty to Animals, Wellington, records, MS-Group-89-238, ATL.
85 General committee meeting 12 August 1912, in 'Minutes general committee and AGMs February 1912–August 1917', item 2; General committee meeting 8 December 1919 in 'Minutes of General Committee and AGM September 1917–October 1926', item 3; Society for the Prevention of Cruelty to Animals, records, MS 2010/13, AWMM; *Auckland Society for the Prevention of Cruelty to Animals, 3rd Annual Report, 1929*, p. 4, in 'Annual reports 1885–1932', 89-238-6/3, Society for the Prevention of Cruelty to Animals, Wellington, records, MS-Group-89-238, ATL.
86 Letter from Wellington SPCA secretary to Joyce Whiteman, Secretary of the Wellington East Girls' College Junior League, 16 September 1940, in 'Correspondence Junior SPCA nd', 89-238-2/03, Society for the Prevention of Cruelty to Animals, Wellington, records, MS-Group-89-238, ATL. There is a suggestion in the 1939 annual report that the ambulance service was actually operating that year, but it may just have been imminent; *52nd Report of the Wellington SPCA*, [typed and cyclostyled], in 'Donation forms, certificates and miscellaneous', 89-238-3/12, Society for the Prevention of Cruelty to Animals, Wellington, records, MS-Group-89-238, ATL.
87 'Protection of animals. New society formed', *Press*, 20 October 1913, p. 2; 'News of the Day', *Evening Post*, 5 November 1937, p. 5; 'News of the Day', *Evening Post*, 3 April 1941, p. 3.

88 'News of the Day. Animal protection in Auckland', *Evening Post*, 19 September 1938, p. 8.
89 *Auckland Society for the Prevention of Cruelty to Animals, 3rd Annual Report, 1929*, p. 11, *Forty-fourth Annual Report of the Otago Society for the Prevention of Cruelty to Animals, for the Year Ending December 31, 1925*, p. 7, *Wellington SPCA, 33rd Annual Report, 1926*, p. 5, *Wellington SPCA 40th annual report, 1933*, p. 2, in 'Annual reports 1885–1932', 89-238-6/3; letter to clergy from the Bishop of Wellington, 5 September 1938, in 'Correspondence Junior SPCA nd', 89-238-2/03, Society for the Prevention of Cruelty to Animals, Wellington, records, MS-Group-89-238, ATL.
90 *Wellington SPCA, 36th Annual Report, 1929*, p. 4, in 'Annual reports 1885–1932', 89-238-6/3, Society for the Prevention of Cruelty to Animals, Wellington, records, MS-Group-89-238, ATL.
91 *Wellington SPCA, 38th Annual Report, 1931*, pp. 4–5, in 'Annual reports 1885–1932', 89-238-6/3, Society for the Prevention of Cruelty to Animals, Wellington, records, MS-Group-89-238, ATL.
92 Ibid.
93 Dave Burgess, 'Owners breach cordons for pets', Stuff.co.nz, 26 February 2011, www.stuff.co.nz/national/christchurch-earthquake/4706624/Owners-breach-cordons-for-pets [accessed 5 April 2013]; 'Quake-affected cats relocated', *New Zealand Herald*, 16 April 2011, www.nzherald.co.nz/nz/news/article.cfm?c_id=1&objectid=10719699 [accessed 5 April 2013]; 'Christchurch shelters sending pets north', *New Zealand Herald*, 25 June 2011, www.nzherald.co.nz/nz/news/article.cfm?c_id=1&objectid=10734474 [accessed 5 April 2013]

Chapter 6 Feels like Calf Club Day

1 Helen Wilson (1950), *My First Eighty Years*, Pauls Book Arcade, Hamilton, p. 16.
2 *New Zealand Farmer: Bee and Poultry Journal*, vol. vii, no. 6, June 1887, p. 165.
3 Mary Anne Barker (1873), *Station Amusements in New Zealand*, William Hunt, London, pp. 238–39.
4 Annie R. Butler (1886), *Glimpses of Maoriland*, Religious Tract Society, London, pp. 203–04.
5 Dorothea Joblin (1975), *The Colonial One: Lorna Monckton of Newstead*, Whitcombe and Tombs, Christchurch, p. 78.
6 *New Zealand Farmer: Bee and Poultry Journal*, vol. xi, no. 9, September 1891, p. 394.
7 *New Zealand Farmer: Bee and Poultry Journal*, vol. x, no. 10, October 1890, p. 425.
8 *New Zealand Farmer: Bee and Poultry Journal*, vol. xii, no. 5, May 1892, p. 230.
9 *New Zealand Farmer: Bee and Poultry Journal*, vol. xii, no. 10, October 1892, p. 430.
10 *New Zealand Farmer: Bee and Poultry Journal*, vol. ix, no. 10, October 1889, p. 423.
11 *New Zealand Farmer: Bee and Poultry Journal*, vol. x, no. 7, July 1890, p. 279.
12 *New Zealand Farmer: Bee and Poultry Journal*, vol. xi, no. 6, June 1891, p. 261.
13 See reports of Marlborough and Taranaki A&P shows held in November 1906, *New Zealand Farmer: Bee and Poultry Journal*, vol. xxxvii, no. 1, January 1907, pp. 50, 53.
14 See for example commentary in 'Calf clubs in Taranaki', *New Zealand Farmer Stock and Station Journal*, 1 September 1922, pp. 1196, 1274, 1275.
15 John L. Ewing (1970), *Development of the New Zealand Primary School Curriculum 1877–1970*, New Zealand Council for Educational Research, Wellington, pp. 100, 123; 'Report of the Minister of Education', *Appendices to the Journals of the House of Representatives (AJHR)*, 1925, E1, p. 17; Robert Peden, 'Agricultural education', in Te Ara: the Encyclopedia of New Zealand, updated 9 November 2012, www.TeAra.govt.nz/en/agricultural-education
16 'The Calf Club', *New Zealand Farmer Stock and Station Journal*, 1 September 1921, p. 1187.
17 George Buckeridge, 'Short history of the origin and establishment of the "Boys' and Girls' Agricultural Club movement" in Taranaki and of the movement to form a "Nature Lovers" or Co-operative Citizenship League', 1944, p. 7, in Series 20-Educational History Publications-Origin and establishment of Boys and Girls Agricultural Club, 1944, Taranaki Education Board, Residual Management Unit (ABDU), acc W3570, box 126, record 21, ANZ.
18 Board of Agriculture, report for year ending 30 April 1920, *AJHR*, 1920, H29A, p. 2; W. Stuart Wilson (1920), *An Appeal to the Prince of Wales*, Whitcombe and Tombs, Auckland, p. 10; *Parliamentary Debates*, October 3–November 5 1919, vol. 185, p. 687; R.L. McNabb (1943), 'An investigation into the development and value of the school club movement in Taranaki primary schools, with special reference to the school agricultural club', thesis presented for teachers' 'A' certificate, Victoria University College, pp. 20–21.
19 Buckeridge, 'Short history', p. 12; 'Boys' and Girls' Club, group formed at St Andrews, enthusiastic meeting', *Timaru Post*, 6 November 1936 [np].
20 Wilson, *An Appeal to the Prince of Wales*, pp. 13–14, 15.
21 Reports of the Agricultural and Pastoral Industries, Stock, and Commerce Committee, *AJHR*, 1920, I10, p. 2; 'Petition of W. Stuart Wilson, of Wellington', *New Zealand Farmers' Advocate*, 26 March 1921, p. 15.
22 T. H. Patterson, 'The Tautari Boys' and Girls' Calf Club', *New Zealand Farmer Stock and Station Journal*, 1 May 1922, p. 658; Buckeridge, 'Short history', p. 7.
23 'Calf clubs in Taranaki', *New Zealand Farmer Stock and Station Journal*, 1 September 1922, p. 1274; 'Taranaki: a general review', *New Zealand Farmer Stock and Station Journal*, 1 November 1921, p. 1380.
24 'The Calf Club', *New Zealand Farmer Stock and Station Journal*, 1 September 1921, p. 1187.
25 Buckeridge, 'Short history', p. 15; 'Wairarapa Calf-rearing Club, first competition won by girl', *New Zealand Farmer Stock and Station Journal*, 1 March 1923, p. 363.
26 McNabb, 'An investigation into the development and value of the school club movement', p. 53.
27 *New Zealand Farmer Stock and Station Journal*, 1 March 1923, p. 363.
28 Patterson, 'The Tautari Boys' and Girls' Calf Club', p. 658.
29 Board of Agriculture, *AJHR*, 1921-22, H29A, p. 9; Boys' Agricultural Clubs, *AJHR*, 1922, H29A, pp. 4–5; Department of Agriculture, *AJHR*, 1925, H29, p. 28; Report of the Board of Agriculture, Agricultural instruction in New Zealand, *AJHR*, 1925, H29, p. 4; Department of Agriculture, Fields Division, *AJHR*, 1930, H29, p. 24.

30 Report of the Minister of Education for the year ending 31 December 1922: Manual instruction, *AJHR*, 1923, E1, pp. 15–16; Report of the Chief Inspector of Primary Schools for the year ending 21 December 1929, *AJHR*, 1930, E2, p. 24.

31 Report of the Superintendent of Technical Education for the year ending 31 December 1931, *AJHR*, 1932, E2, p. 10.

32 Department of Agriculture, Fields Division, *AJHR*, H29, 1928, p. 37; H29, 1931, p. 18; H29, 1932, p.18; H29, 1933, p.19; H29, 1934–35, p. 28; H29, 1935, p. 36.

33 McNabb, 'An investigation into the development and value of the school club movement', p. 23.

34 Boys' and Girls' Agricultural Clubs, Wanganui–Main Trunk Area, Annual report of activities for year ending June 30, 1947, in Miscellaneous-Agricultural Clubs-Wanganui District, 1936–1953, Education Department (ACIG) series 17240, record group E2, box 269, record 29/78/3, part 1, ANZ; South Taranaki Boys' and Girls' Agricultural Club Association annual report and results of projects, Season 1957–58, in Multiple number subject files-Instruction-Boys and Girls Agricultural Clubs etc, 1944–1962, Taranaki Education Board, Residual Management Unit (ABDU), acc W3570, box 141, record 23/23, ANZ.

35 Circular memorandum for head and sole teachers from Canterbury Education Board, 16 September 1937, in Miscellaneous-Agricultural Clubs-Canterbury Districts, 1936–1949, Education Department (ACIG), series 17240, record group 2, box 195, record 29/78/7, ANZ; Wellington Education Board, Agricultural and Science Instruction Section (1952), *Your School Agricultural Club*, Wellington Education Board, Wellington; South Taranaki Boys' and Girls' Agricultural Club Association annual report and results of projects, Season 1956–57, in Multiple number subject files-Instruction-Boys and Girls Agricultural Clubs etc, 1944–1962, ABDU, acc W3570, box 141, record 23/23, ANZ.

36 Director of Education to Dominion Secretary of Farmers' Union, 29 April 1937, in Miscellaneous-Agricultural clubs-general correspondence, 1936–1944, Education Department (ACIG), series 17240, record group E2, box 463, record 29/78, part 1, ANZ; Report of the Minister of Education for the year ending 31 December 1936, *AJHR*, 1937-38, E1, p. 3.

37 Buckeridge, 'Short history', p. 17; Wellington Education Board, Agricultural and Science Instruction Section, *Your School Agricultural Club*; R. Syme, Taranaki Education Board, 'Club work in practice: no 1 – calf-rearing in South Taranaki', *New Zealand Education Gazette*, 1 December 1937, [np], in Miscellaneous-Agricultural clubs-general correspondence, 1936–1944, Education Department (ACIG), series 17240, record group E2, box 463, record 29/78, part 1, ANZ.

38 McNabb, 'An investigation into the development and value of the school club movement', p. 46.

39 Ewing, *Development of the New Zealand Primary School Curriculum*, p. 183 says this started in 1929.

40 Report of the Inspector of Native Schools for 1932: Education of Native Children, *AJHR*, 1933, E3, p. 3.

41 John Barrington (2008), *Separate but Equal: Maori schools and the Crown, 1867–1969*, Victoria University Press, Wellington, pp. 197–98.

42 Education of Native Children, *AJHR*, E3, 1934–35, p. 5; E3, 1935, p. 3; E3, 1936, p. 4; E3, 1937–38, p. 5; E3, 1938, p. 2; Circular memorandum for head teachers of native schools in the North Auckland district from Education Department, 1936, in Miscellaneous-Agricultural clubs-general correspondence, 1936–1944, ACIG, series 17240, record group E2, box 463, record 29/78, part 1, ANZ; E.R. Heal, Native School Panapuria, Kaitaia to Director of Education, 22 June 1936, in Miscellaneous-Agricultural Clubs-Auckland District, 1936–1948, Education Department (ACIG), series 17240, record group E2, box 175, record 29/78/1, ANZ.

43 Boys' and Girls' Agricultural Clubs, Wanganui–Main Trunk Division, Annual report of activities for year ending June 30, 1947, in Miscellaneous-Agricultural Clubs-Wanganui District, 1936–1953, ACIG, series 17240, record group E2, box 269, record 29/78/3, part 1, ANZ.

44 Buckeridge, 'Short history', p. 16; A brief summary of the history, aims and organisation of the Boys' and Girls' Agricultural Clubs in Taranaki Schools, in Multiple number subject files-Instruction-Boys and Girls Agricultural Clubs etc, 1944–1962, ABDU, acc W3570, box 142, record 23/23, ANZ.

45 Circular memorandum for secretaries Education Boards, senior inspectors of schools, instructors in agriculture, secretaries boys' and girls' club groups, boys' and girls' agricultural clubs from Director of Education – Henry A. Lane challenge shield, no 1936/109, in Miscellaneous-Agricultural Clubs-Hawke's Bay, 1936–1949, Education Department (ACIG), series 17240, record group E2, box 195, record 29/78/4, ANZ; Selection of A&P society programmes: Hawke's Bay, Ellesmere, Egmont, Blueskin, Dannevirke, Amuri, Stratford, for 1930s–1970s, in Alexander Turnbull Library Ephemera collection; Rod Syme, 'Boys' and girls' club classes' in C.H. Betts (ed.) (1983), *A Centennial History of Egmont Agricultural and Pastoral Association Inc, 1883–1983*, The Association, Hawera.

46 'Agricultural clubs, progress in Waikato, report from instructor', *Waikato Times*, 23 September 1936, [np], in Miscellaneous-Agricultural Clubs-Auckland District, 1936–1948, Education Department (ACIG), series 17240, record group E2, box 175, record 29/78/1, ANZ.

47 *Wellington Society for the Prevention of Cruelty to Animals Annual Report, 1920*, p. 3, in 'Annual reports 1894–1978', 89-238-6/3, Society for the Prevention of Cruelty to Animals, Wellington, records, MS-Group-89-238, ATL.

48 *Wellington Society for the Prevention of Cruelty to Animals Annual Report, 1920*, pp. 3–4 and *Wellington SPCA annual report, 1927*, p. 4, in 'Annual reports 1894–1978', 89-238-6/3, Society for the Prevention of Cruelty to Animals, Wellington, records, MS-Group-89-238, ATL; Auckland SPCA general committee meetings 14 June 1920, 12 July 1920, 9 May 1921, 13 June 1921, 11 July 1921 in 'Minutes of General Committee and AGM September 1917–October 1926', item 3, Society for the Prevention of Cruelty to Animals, Auckland, records, MS 2010/13, AWMM.

49 *Auckland Society for the Prevention of Cruelty to Animals, 3rd Annual Report, 1929*, p. 5, in 'Annual reports 1894–1978', 89-238-6/3, Society for the Prevention of Cruelty to Animals, Wellington, records, MS-Group-89-238, ATL.

50 *Forty-fourth Annual Report of the Otago Society for the Prevention of Cruelty to Animals, for the year ending December 31, 1925*, p. 7, in 'Annual reports 1894–1978', 89-238-6/3, Society for the Prevention of Cruelty to Animals, Wellington, records, MS-Group-89-238, ATL.

51 First annual report of the Junior League, 1935/36, in 'Correspondence Junior SPCA nd', 89-238-2/03; *Wellington SPCA annual report, 1935*, p. 3, in 'Annual reports 1894–1978',

89-238-6/3, Society for the Prevention of Cruelty to Animals, Wellington, records, MS-Group-89-238, ATL.

52 See *Wellington SPCA Annual Report, 1936*, p. 2; *Wellington SPCA Annual Report, 1937*, p. 1; *Wellington SPCA Annual Report, 1939*, p. 1; in 'Correspondence-Junior SPCA nd', 89-238-1/06, Society for the Prevention of Cruelty to Animals, Wellington, records, MS-Group-89-238, ATL.

53 'Junior League and essay competition, c. 1930s', 89-238-2/04, Society for the Prevention of Cruelty to Animals, Wellington, records, MS-Group-89-238, ATL.

54 'Correspondence Junior SPCA nd', 89-238-2/03, Society for the Prevention of Cruelty to Animals, Wellington, records, MS-Group-89-238, ATL.

55 Junior SPCA Wellington Girls' College Branch report for 1939, 'Correspondence Junior SPCA nd', 89-238-2/03, Society for the Prevention of Cruelty to Animals, Wellington, records, MS-Group-89-238, ATL.

56 *Wellington SPCA Annual Report, 1920*; *Wellington SPCA Annual Report, 1922*; 'Annual reports 1894–1978', 89-238-6/3, Society for the Prevention of Cruelty to Animals, Wellington, records, MS-Group-89-238, ATL.

57 Minutes of General Committee, 9 February 1920, 14 June 1920, 12 July 1920, in 'Minutes of General Committee and Annual General meetings, September 1917–October 1926', item 3, Society for the Prevention of Cruelty to Animals, Auckland, records, MS 2010/13, AWMM.

58 'Society for the Prevention of Cruelty to Animals. Junior Branch', *The Postman*, vol. x, 1937, p. 156.

59 'Animal Welfare Club', *The Postman*, vol. xii, 1939, pp. 159–62.

60 The bobby calf trade is mentioned in annual reports of the Wellington and Auckland SPCAs from the late 1920s, and by 1935 it had become a major export business with half a million calves slaughtered annually so the carcasses and hides could be exported to Britain. Opposition to it became a major campaign of the new federation of SPCAs. See typescript of broadcast by John Howell, 1 June 1935, in 'Records nd', 89-238-2/08, Society for the Prevention of Cruelty to Animals, Wellington, records, MS-Group-89-238, ATL; also Veronika Thornburrow (ed.) (1993), *The Compassionate Years: An introduction to the history of the Royal New Zealand Society for the Prevention of Cruelty to Animals*, RNZSPCA, Auckland, p. 44.

61 'Humane education in the post-primary school' by John H. Howell, nd [1930s], in 'Leaflet – humane education in the post primary school', 89-238-1/12, Society for the Prevention of Cruelty to Animals, Wellington, records, MS-Group-89-238, ATL.

62 Typescript of broadcast by John Howell, 1 June 1935, in 'Records nd', 89-238-2/08, Society for the Prevention of Cruelty to Animals, Wellington, records, MS-Group-89-238, ATL.

63 See for instance 'Agricultural clubs, progress in Waikato, report from instructor', *Waikato Times*, 23 September 1936, [np], in Miscellaneous-Agricultural Clubs-Auckland District, 1936–1948, ACIG, series 17240, record group E2, box 175, record 29/78/1, ANZ; Ross and Sally Matheson, and Anne Jameson (eds) (1994), *Waiau Pa School Calf Club, 1944–1994*, R. and S. Matheson, Waiau Pa, 'Principal's welcome'.

64 Apart from the comment by T.H. Patterson in 1922, the only use of the term 'pet' found on official files was in circular memorandum for head teachers of native schools in the North Auckland district from Education Department regarding Calf Clubs, in Miscellaneous-Agricultural clubs-general correspondence, 1936–1944, ACIG, series 17240, record group E2, box 463, record 29/78, part 1, ANZ.

65 Eyre Group Boys' and Girls' Agricultural Clubs [1963], *Schedule of Project and Programme for Stock Parade*, p. 15.

66 Resource book for teachers, Boys and Girls Agricultural Club, Waikato A&P Association, www.waikatoaandp.co.nz/the-show/boys-and-girls-agricultural-club/ [accessed 5 April 2013]

67 New Zealand Country Women's Institute (1994), *School Days*, NZCWI, Wellington: accounts by Shirley Campbell, pp. 46–47, Anna Harraway, p. 72 and Mabel Robinson, p. 112; various accounts in *Waiau Pa School Calf Club*.

68 Ian Lawson, 'My calf', *The Postman*, vol. xii, 1939, p. 93.

69 J. M. Smith, 'Boys' and Girls' Agricultural Clubs: record of activities in 1929–30 season. 1: Taranaki and Wellington areas', *New Zealand Journal of Agriculture*, vol. 41, no. 5, 20 November 1930, p. 355.

70 *Waiau Pa School Calf Club*, p. 34.

71 *School Days*, pp. 46–47.

72 'Calf clubs in Taranaki', *New Zealand Farmer Stock and Station Journal*, 1 September 1922, p. 1274; Patterson, 'The Tautari Boys' and Girls' Calf Club', p. 658.

73 Certificates: Director of Education to Secretary Canterbury Education Board, 26 August 1937, in Miscellaneous-Agricultural Clubs-Canterbury Districts 1936–1949, ACIG, series 17240, record group E2, box 195, record 29/78/7, ANZ; Badges: Boys' and Girls' Agricultural Club Reports and Results, Wanganui–Main Trunk Division [1947–49], in Miscellaneous–Agricultural Clubs–Wanganui District 1936–1953, ACIG, series 17240, record group E2, box 269, record 29/78/3, part 1, ANZ. Badges are also referred to in Eyre Group Boys' and Girls' Agricultural Clubs [1964], *Schedule of Project and Programme for Stock Parade*, p. 3.

74 *Waiau Pa School Calf Club*, p. 27.

75 Ewing, *Development of the New Zealand Primary School Curriculum*, p. 241–42; Sandra Drake, 'Lambs, calves, kids … and chickens?', *Pet New Zealand*, June–August 2001, issue 15, pp. 38–40.

76 See for instance *Waiau Pa School Calf Club*, pp. 7, 19; Boys' and Girls' Agricultural Clubs, Wanganui–Main Trunk Division, Annual report of activities for year ending June 30, 1947, in Miscellaneous-Agricultural Clubs-Wanganui District, 1936–1953, ACIG, series 17240, record group E2, box 269, record 29/78/3, part 1, ANZ; South Taranaki Boys' and Girls' Agricultural Club Association annual report and results of projects, Season 1957–58, in multiple number subject files-Instruction-Boys and Girls Agricultural Clubs etc, 1944–1962, ABDU, acc W3570, box 142, record 23/23, ANZ.

77 Susan Butterworth (1993), *The Department of Education 1877–1989: A guide to its development*, Ministry of Education, Wellington, p. 51; email from Emily Stott, Ministry of Education, 5 August 2009.

78 Email from Noel Smith, Convenor-Secretary Waikato–King Country Boys and Girls Agricultural Club, 4 August 2009.

79 Drake, 'Lambs, calves, kids … and chickens?', pp. 38–40

80 Ibid.; Rachel Clare, 'Join the club', *Pet*, March–May 2005, issue 30, p. 87.

81 *New Zealand Farmer: Bee and Poultry Journal*, vol. xii, no. 11, November 1892, p. 470.

82 Wellington Education Board, Agricultural and Science

Instruction Section (1952), *Your School Agricultural Club*, Wellington Education Board, Wellington; Boys' and Girls' Agricultural Clubs, Wanganui–Main Trunk Area, Annual Report, 1939, in Miscellaneous-Agricultural Clubs-Wanganui District, 1936–1953, ACIG, series 17240, record group E2, box 269, record 29/78/3, part 1, ANZ.
83 Patterson, 'The Tautari Boys' and Girls' Calf Club' p. 658.
84 Wellington Education Board, *Your School Agricultural Club*.
85 Trena Marshall, response to Calf Club survey, 2011.
86 'My favourite table. Fashion designer Holly McQuillan, at Aunty Mena Vegetarian & Vegan Café, Wellington', *Dominion Post*, 23 March 2011, 'Life' magazine, p. 3.
87 *Waiau Pa School Calf Club*, pp. 24, 56.
88 Alex McEwing, response to Calf Club survey, 2011.
89 *New Zealand Farmer Stock and Station Journal*, 1 March 1920, p. 421
90 'Pet lambs' by Beverley Hodder, S 2, Mataroa, *The Postman*, vol. xiii, 1940, p. 36.
91 Grace Hamilton (nee Cole), 'Waiau Pa School Calf Club – as I remember', *Waiau Pa School Calf Club*, p. 28.
92 Margaret O'Connor, response to Calf Club survey, 2011.
93 'Cuthbert Tim' by Pat Peed, S 2, Waipero, Mataroa, *The Postman*, vol. vi, 1933, p. 20.
94 Taranaki Boys' and Girls' Agricultural Clubs – Calf Rearing Competitions – Season 1946, in Multiple subject files-Instruction-Boys and Girls Agricultural Clubs etc, 1944-1962, ABDU, acc W3570, box 142, record 23/23, ANZ.
95 *School Days*, pp. 46–47.
96 *Waiau Pa School Calf Club*, p. 41.
97 *Waiau Pa School Calf Club*, pp. 41, 28.
98 Lynda Hallinan, 'May the best animal win', *Sunday Star Times*, 14 October 2011, 'Sunday' magazine [np].

Chapter 7 From helpers to heroes

1 *Wellington Society for the Prevention of Cruelty to Animals, Twenty-seventh Annual Report, 1920*, p. 2 in 'Annual reports 1885–1932', 89-238-6/3, Society for the Prevention of Cruelty to Animals, Wellington, records, MS-Group-89-238, ATL.
2 Hilda Kean (1998), *Animal Rights: Political and social change in Britain since 1800*, Reaktion Books, London, p. 165.
3 Richard S. Hill (1995), *The Iron Hand in the Velvet Glove: The modernisation of policing in New Zealand 1886–1917*, Dunmore Press/Historical Branch Department of Internal Affairs, Wellington, pp. 60, 374.
4 John Crawford, 'Boer War' in Ian McGibbon (ed.) (2000), *The Oxford Companion to New Zealand Military History*, Oxford University Press, Auckland, pp. 59–63; John Crawford and Ellen Ellis (1999), *To Fight for the Empire: An illustrated history of New Zealand and the South African war, 1899–1902*, Reed, Auckland, p. 21.
5 Crawford and Ellis, *To Fight for the Empire*, p. 39.
6 This point is made by Crawford, 'Boer War' in *The Oxford Companion to New Zealand Military History*, p. 63.
7 Quoted in Crawford and Ellis, *To Fight for the Empire*, p. 40.
8 'Animals', in *The Oxford Companion to New Zealand Military History*, pp. 18–19; A. Briscoe Moore (1920), *The Mounted Riflemen in Sinai and Palestine: The story of New Zealand's crusaders*, Whitcombe and Tombs, Auckland, p. 116.
9 Marcus J. Wilson (2007), 'A History of New Zealand's Military Horse: The experience of the horse in the Anglo-Boer War and World War One', MA thesis (History), University of Canterbury, pp. 101, 102–03; C.G. Powles, H.G. Alexander and H.A. Lockington (1927), *Official History of the New Zealand Engineers During the Great War 1914–1919*, Evans, Cobb and Sharpe Ltd, Wellington?, pp. 294–95; C.G. Nicol (1921), *The Story of Two Campaigns: Official war history of the Auckland Mounted Rifles Regiment*, Wilson and Horton, Auckland, pp. 242–44.
10 C. Guy Powles (1922), *The New Zealanders in Sinai and Palestine*, Whitcombe and Tombs, Auckland, p. 2.
11 Quoted in Terry Kinloch (2007), *Devils on Horses: In the words of the Anzacs in the Middle East 1916–19*, Exisle Publishing, Auckland, p. 339.
12 Quoted in Kinloch, *Devils on Horses*, pp. 337–38.
13 Kinloch, *Devils on Horses*, p. 339.
14 Susan Brocker (2010), *Brave Bess and the ANZAC Horses*, HarperCollins, Auckland, pp. 135–36; 'Memorial to Bess the horse', www.nzhistory.net.nz/media/photo/memorial-bess-horse, (Ministry for Culture and Heritage), updated 10 May 2010; 'Memorial to Bess', New Zealand Historic Places Trust Register, www.historic.org.nz/TheRegister [accessed 3 January 2013]
15 *School Journal*, vol. xi, no. 7, August 1917, part 3, p. 211.
16 The Wellington SPCA annual report for 1915 mentions a fund administered by the RSPCA for assisting the Army Volunteer Corps in their work among wounded horses: *Wellington SPCA Twenty-second Annual Report, 1915*, p. 4, in 'Annual reports 1885–1932', 89-238-6/3, Society for the Prevention of Cruelty to Animals, Wellington, records, MS-Group-89-238, ATL. The Auckland SPCA general committee meeting of 14 June 1915 agreed to send a donation to the Red Star Society, a French organisation, to help suffering animals on the battlefield. Another general committee meeting of 12 March 1917 decided not to give to the RSPCA Fund for Sick and Wounded Horses because the ladies' committee was already collecting funds for the Blue Cross in aid of sick and wounded horses at the Front: 'Minutes – general committee and AGM, February 1912–August 1917', item 2, Society for the Prevention of Cruelty to Animals, Auckland, records, MS 2010/13, AWMM. Later meetings (26 April 1917 and 29 April 1918) talk of the sums raised for the Blue Cross. See also Kean, *Animal Rights*, pp. 169, 171.
17 'Animals', in *The Oxford Companion to New Zealand Military History*, pp. 18–19; Peter Cochrane (1992), *Simpson and the Donkey: The making of a legend*, Melbourne University Press, Melbourne, pp. 139, 142–47.
18 'Pigeons in war-time', *School Journal*, vol. xii, no. 10, November 1918, part 1, pp. 146–51.
19 'The care of the sick and wounded', *School Journal*, vol. ix, no. 6, July 1915, part 3, p. 175.
20 'The dog in peace and war time', *School Journal*, vol. xi, no. 1, February 1917, part 3, p. 22.
21 'Military mascots', www.nzhistory.net.nz/war/mascots, (Ministry for Culture and Heritage), updated 12 June 2008; Patricia Stroud (2003), *Caesar: The Anzac dog*, HarperCollins, Auckland.
22 Cochrane, *Simpson and the Donkey*, p. 140; Timothy Walker (1985), *Robley: Te Ropere, 1840–1930*, Auckland University Press, Auckland, p. 32.
23 *The Historic Highway*, News Media, Auckland, 1967, p. 39.
24 Quoted in Cochrane, *Simpson and the Donkey*, p. 139.

25 'Military mascots', www.nzhistory.net.nz
26 'Animals', in *The Oxford Companion to New Zealand Military History*, pp. 18–19; Cochrane, *Simpson and the Donkey*, p. 147.
27 Colonel of the NZEF to Lieut-Colonel of Auckland Regiment, 11 July 1919, in NZEF in UK, in Health, Welfare, etc-Mascots-pets, regimental-return of, December 1918–March 1920, War Archives (ACID), series 17590, record group WA1, box 1/3/19, record 10/6, ANZ.
28 W.H. Cunningham to Army Department, 7 April 1921, in Miscellaneous-Mascots-NZEF-Correspondence, Army Department (AAYS), series 8638, record group AD1, box 1045, record 65/242, ANZ.
29 Mrs A.C.C. Rogers to Alexander Crabb, 11 January 1929, in Miscellaneous-Mascots-NZEF-Correspondence, AAYS, series 8638, record group AD1, box 1045, record 65/242, ANZ.
30 'Military mascots', www.nzhistory.net.nz
31 A.H.L. Sugden (1947), *Pacific Saga: The personal chronicle of the 37th battalion and its part in the third divisional campaign*, Reed, Wellington, p. 97.
32 Graham Spencer (1987), *The Four-legged Major*, Grantham House, Wellington, p. 12; D.W. Sinclair (1954), *19 Battalion and Armoured Regiment*, Historical Publications Branch, Wellington, Appendix 1, p. 531.
33 Application for permission to import the 19 NZ Armed Regt dog 'Major' into New Zealand at such time as the Unit returns to NZ, 11 May 1943, in Major Major, 1 New Zealand Dog, NZEF: Biography of 19 New Zealand Armoured Regiments mascot [return to New Zealand of regimental mascot dog], Second World War Archives (ADQZ), series 18886, record group WAII1, box 292, record DA 406/380, ANZ.
34 Sinclair, *19 Battalion and Armoured Regiment*, Appendix 1, p. 536.
35 Spencer, *The Four-legged Major*, pp. 159–60.
36 Correspondence between Under-Secretary Internal Affairs and District Engineer Christchurch, 3 July 1917 and 10 July 1917, in Allowances-To provide food for cats in Government buildings-General file re, 1917–1945, Department of Internal Affairs Head Office [record group] (ACGO), record group IA1, box 3358, record 45/11, ANZ.
37 'Post Office cats now honorary', *Dominion*, 4 November 1965, [np], in 'Scrapbook 1947–1976', 89-238-6/1, Society for the Prevention of Cruelty to Animals, Wellington, records, MS-Group-89-238, ATL.
38 'Civil servant on the cheap', *Evening Post*, 18 April 1967, [np], in Allowances and expenses/general-Horse, Dog and Cat allowances-May 1946–August 1980, State Services Commission (AEKO), series 19171, acc W3005, record group SSC1W3005, box 25, record 6/0/12, part 1, ANZ.
39 See Allowances and expenses-Horse, Cat and Dog allowance, 1981–1985, State Services Commission Head Office (AAFH), series 785, acc W3654, box 5, record 6/0/12, part 2; Allowances and expenses/general-Horse, Dog and Cat allowances-May 1946–August 1980, AEKO, series 19171, acc W3005, record group SSC1W3005, box 25, record 6/0/12, part 1, ANZ. The latter source suggests the dog allowance started in 1949.
40 'Police dogs have proved worth: services may be extended', *Waikato Times*, 4 January 1960, [np], in Police dog unit-policy, 1959–1962, Police Department (ACIS), series 17627, acc W2791, record group P1W2791, box 75, record 26/1/-, part 2, ANZ.
41 Valerie and Colin Salt (1972), *Born to Obey*, Collins, Auckland, pp. 31–33, 39–40.
42 Mrs E. M. Fenton, Secretary, Wellington Women's Branch New Zealand Labour Party to Minister of Police, 12 June 1958, in Police dogs-General file, 1920–1955, Police Department (ACIS), series 17627, acc W2791, record group P1W2791, box 75, record 26/1/-, ANZ.
43 Peter Kitchin, 'Musketeer of police dog work [obituary of Alan Symes], *Dominion Post*, 16 October 2008, B3.
44 Salt, *Born to Obey*, pp. 47, 49, 63, 109; Tracey Mehrtens, 'Working dogs', *New Zealand Pet Magazine*, April/June 1998, issue 3, p. 22.
45 Salt, *Born to Obey*, pp. 36, 45, 50, 63, 101; Superintendent, Christchurch, to Chief Superintendent, 1 May 1970, in Police dogs/Office examination-Police Dog Unit: Policy, 1969–1973, New Zealand Police National Headquarters (AAAJ), series 965, acc W3239, box 136, record 26/1/-, part 4, ANZ.
46 Miriam MacGregor Redwood (1980), *A Dog's Life: Working dogs in New Zealand*, Reed, Wellington, pp. 117–20.
47 Susan Butterworth (2005), *More than Law and Order: Policing a changing society 1945–92*, Otago University Press, Dunedin, p. 90; Stewart Lusk (1983), *Dogsbody: The story of the New Zealand Kennel Club*, New Zealand Kennel Club, Wellington, p. 8; Sergeant Riley to Commandant, Police Training School Trentham, 20 December 1963, in Police Dog Unit-policy, 1962–1969, Police Department (ACIS), series 17627, acc W2791, record group P1W2791, box 75, record 26/1/-, part 3, ANZ.
48 Jim Field (1993), *Backtracking*, Wairarapa Times-Age Co. Ltd, Masterton, pp. 93, 132.
49 Chief Superintendent to Assistant Commissioner of Police, 21 June 1971, in Police dogs/Office examination-Police Dog Unit: Policy, 1969-1973, AAAJ, series 965, acc W3239, box 136, record 26/1/-, part 4, ANZ.
50 Butterworth, *More than Law and Order*, p. 187; Confirmed in Chief Superintendent to Assistant Commissioner of Police, 21 June 1971, in Police dogs/Office examination-Police Dog Unit: Policy, 1969–1973, AAAJ, series 965, acc W3239, box 136, record 26/1/-, part 4, ANZ.
51 Ella Donald (2009), *Luke: The story of a police dog, his remarkable life and the 'Downtown' shooting*, Vision Through Communication Ltd, Auckland, pp. 32–33, 43–44, 47, 54–55, 69, 83, 117–18.
52 Police Amendment Act, 1996.
53 Kelly Hawkins, 'The forgotten heroes of the Vietnam War', *New Zealand Pet Magazine*, May–July 2000, issue 11, p. 26; Butterworth, *More than Law and Order*, p. 90.
54 'Sniffer dog uncovers truth from the ashes', *Dominion Post*, 28 January 2006, A17.
55 Gavin McLean and Tim Shoebridge (2010), *Quarantine! Protecting New Zealand at the border*, Otago University Press, Dunedin, pp. 149–53; Mary Longmore, 'A nose for the job', *Dominion Post*, 30 May 2009, p. 12.
56 'Dog mountaineer. An unerring instinct. Fifteen years on Egmont', *Evening Post*, 9 December 1936, p. 4.
57 See correspondence between L.D. Bridge of Federated Mountain Clubs and Assistant Commissioner of Police, December 1956, in Police dogs-General file, 1920–1955, ACIS, series 17627, acc W2791, record group P1W2791, box 75, record 26/1/-, ANZ.
58 SAR Dogs Otago, www.sar-dog.org.nz [accessed 18 December 2010]

59 Search and Rescue Land SAR Search Dogs, http://searchdogs.co.nz [accessed 18 December 2010]
60 NZ USAR Search Dog Association, www.usardogs.org.nz [accessed 18 December 2010]
61 Gerard Hutching and Carl Walrond, 'Threatened species' in Te Ara: the Encyclopedia of New Zealand, updated 30 January 2013, www.TeAra.govt.nz/en/threatened-species
62 'Famous kiwi dog retires' 16 May 2003, BNZ Save the Kiwi, www.savethekiwi.org.nz [accessed 18 December 2010]
63 'Dogs for the blind' *Evening Post*, 2 August 1943, p. 4.
64 MacGregor Redwood, *A Dog's Life*, pp. 109–10; Esther Irving, 'White, Cyril Charles William 1909–1984', from *The Dictionary of New Zealand Biography*. Te Ara: the Encyclopedia of New Zealand, updated 30 October 2012, www.TeAra.govt.nz/en/biographies/5w22/white-cyril-charles-william
65 Telephone conversation between Mr Christiansen, New Zealand Foundation for the Blind and B.S. Swann, Department of Health, 19 June 1964; Mr Christiansen, New Zealand Foundation for the Blind to Director General of Education, 8 December 1970, in Nuisances-General-Guide dogs for blind persons, 1964–1974, Ministry of Health Head Office (ABQU), series 632, acc W4452, box 757, record 133-42-1, ANZ.
66 Minutes of meeting at Department of Health, Wellington, 23 March 1965 in Nuisances-General-Guide dogs for blind persons, 1964–1974, ABQU, series 632, acc W4452, box 757, record 133-42-1, ANZ.
67 Minutes of meeting at Department of Health, Wellington, 23 March 1965; and K.B. O'Connor for Director General of Health to General Manager, Union Steam Ship Company, 2 July 1965, in Nuisances-General-Guide dogs for blind persons', 1964–1974, ABQU, series 632, acc W4452, box 757, record 133-42-1, ANZ.
68 Lynette Brown to R.O. Douglas MP, 15 April 1971, in Nuisances-General-Guide dogs for blind persons, 1964–1974, ABQU, series 632, acc W4452, box 757, record 133-42-1, ANZ.
69 Neill Atkinson (2007), *Trainland: How railways made New Zealand*, Random House, Auckland, p. 133; Manuals and newspaper clippings on Guide dogs: Blind persons, 1968–1974, New Zealand Government Railways Department, General Manager's Office (AAEB), acc W3293, box 129, record 16/2620/5, part 1, ANZ.
70 Dogs' Registration Amendment Act, 1973.
71 MacGregor Redwood, *A Dog's Life*, pp. 110–11; 'New guide dog breeding centre', *Pupdate*, Summer 2007, [np].
72 Information on training from MacGregor Redwood, *A Dog's Life*, pp. 110–11; publicity material from Australian Guide Dogs for the Blind Association on Nuisances-General-Guide dogs for blind persons', 1964–1974, ABQU, series 632, acc W4452, box 757, record 133-42-1, ANZ.
73 MacGregor Redwood, *A Dog's Life*, pp. 111–12.
74 Rebecca Papprill, 'Training turns puppies into guides', *East & Bays Courier*, 28 December 2007, p. 5.
75 Juliet Jordan, 'Dogsbody helps out', *Evening Post*, 31 October 1994, p. 2. This article talks about the Wellington-based Top Dog Companion Trust, established in 1990.
76 'Our mission', Hearing Dogs for Deaf People New Zealand, www.hearingdogs.org.nz [accessed 18 December 2010]; 'Angus & Peggy', *Pet Magazine,* September/November 2007, p. 28.
77 Margo White, 'Paws for effect', *New Zealand Listener*, 12 November 2011, pp. 48–49.
78 'Prison puppies help twice over', *Correction News*, July/August 2009, p. 4.
79 James Serpell (1986), *In the Company of Animals: A study of human-animal relationships*, Basil Blackwell, Oxford, p. 76.
80 Quoted in Madeline Seager (1987), *Edward William Seager: Pioneer of mental health*, Heritage Press, Waikanae, p. 89.
81 'Annual report on Lunatic Asylums of New Zealand', *AJHR*, 1879, H4, p. 7.
82 'Local and General', *Star*, 29 September 1881, p. 3.
83 See correspondence on: Mental health-Staff-Pets kept by officers, 1924–1976, Department of Health Head Office (AAFB), series 632, acc W2883, box 115, record 30/35/63, ANZ.
84 Frank Tod (1977), *Lionel Terry: The making of a madman*, Otago Foundation Books, Dunedin, pp. 108, 113, 115.
85 'Animals can help IH children', *Pet Pride: The official bi-monthly journal of the Wellington SPCA Inc*, vol. 1, no. 2, February 1969, p. 19.
86 'About us', Dunedin Group Riding for Disabled Assn Inc, www.dunedinrda.co.nz; 'About us' Whangarei Riding Therapy Centre, www.whangareirtc.org.nz; 'Profile', Mid Canterbury RDA, www.mcrda/110mb.com [accessed 11 December 2010]
87 Serpell, *In the Company of Animals*, pp. 73–79.
88 Notes for 1987, Morrie Jalfon and Bob Kerridge (1996), *The History of the SPCA Auckland*, The Society, Auckland [np]; Karen Tay, 'Lend me your ears', *Sunday Star Times*, 4 October 2009, C4.
89 Print 240 under 'Cats', photographic prints relating to Zoology, *Evening Post* illustrations file, PAColl-7327-1-149, ATL; Emily Watt, 'Dogs bring comfort to the elderly', *Dominion Post*, 10 January 2009, A15.
90 Watt, 'Dogs bring comfort to the elderly', A15.
91 Gabriel David, 'Shopkeepers irate over anti-animal proposal', *Evening Post*, 3 January 1974, [np], in 'Scrapbooks, 1947–1976', 89-238-6/1, Society for the Prevention of Cruelty to Animals, Wellington, records, MS-Group-89-238, ATL.
92 Letter to R.D. Muldoon from Pamela M. Dawber, Vice-president of the St Francis Assisi Organisations (Animal Welfare) Inc., Dunedin, 16 March 1976, in Food hygiene-The Food Hygiene Regulations-Administration, 1975–1976, Department of Health Head Office (AAFB), series 632, acc W4914, box 2, record 143/6, part 1, ANZ.
93 'Freedoms, sport and human rights', National Party election material 1975, in Food hygiene-The Food Hygiene Regulations-Administration, 1975–1976, AAFB, series 632, acc W4914, box 2, record 143/6, part 1, ANZ.
94 'Shopped cats get reprieve', *Evening Post*, 9 December 1975, [np], in Food hygiene-The Food Hygiene Regulations-Administration, 1975–1976, AAFB, series 632, acc W4914, box 2, record 143/6, part 1, ANZ.
95 Royal Society for the Promotion of Health to R.D. Muldoon, 26 March 1976, in Food hygiene-The Food Hygiene Regulations-Administration, 1975–1976, AAFB, series 632, acc W4914, box 2, record 143/6, part 1, ANZ; New Zealand Veterinary Association, 'Cats, food shops and society', 25 March 1975, in Food hygiene-The food regulations-Administration, 1975–1977, Department of Health Head Office (AAFB), series 632, acc W4914, box 93, record 143/6, part 2, ANZ.

96 Food Hygiene Regulations, 1974 (with amendments); 'Cats in shops', *Southland Times*, 30 November 1976, [np], in Food hygiene-The food regulations-Administration, 1975–1977, AAFB, series 632, acc W4914, box 93, record 143/6, part 2, ANZ.
97 'Cattish debate in Parliament', *New Zealand Herald*, 20 October 1976, [np], in Food hygiene-The food regulations-Administration, 1975–1977, AAFB, series 632, acc W4914, box 93, record 143/6, part 2, ANZ.

Chapter 8 Pets or pests?

1 'The Dog Nuisance', *Southland Times*, 15 July 1873, p. 3.
2 'The cat nuisance. To the editor of the Star', *Star*, 26 June 1868, p. 3.
3 'Dog nuisance. To the editor of the Evening Post', *Evening Post*, 25 August 1877, p. 1.
4 'Lost and found', *Evening Post*, 11 November 1901, p. 1.
5 'Lost and found', *Ashburton Guardian*, 28 October 1915, p. 1.
6 'Lost and found', *Evening Post*, 15 January 1908, p. 1.
7 *Wellington SPCA Annual Report 1897*, p. 5, *Wellington SPCA Eighteenth Annual Report 1912*, p. 3, and *Wellington SPCA Twentieth Annual Report, 1913*, p. 10, in 'Annual reports 1894–1978', 89-238-6/3, Society for the Prevention of Cruelty to Animals, Wellington, records, MS-Group-89-238, ATL.
8 Auckland SPCA general committee meeting minutes 11 February 1924, in 'Minutes of General Committee and Annual General meetings, September 1917–October 1926', item 3, Society for the Prevention of Cruelty to Animals, Auckland, records, MS 2010/13, AWMM. Members discussed asking the city council to appoint a ranger to collect stray cats and dogs.
9 The lethal chamber [undated], in 'Captain James Henry – information and correspondence', 89-238-9/2, Society for the Prevention of Cruelty to Animals, Wellington, records, MS-Group-89-238, ATL; 'Destruction of stray dogs', *Star*, 11 May 1896, p. 2.
10 Elsie K. Morton (1929), 'Toilers of the morn', in *Joy of the Road*, Wilson and Horton, Auckland, p. 188.
11 Auckland SPCA general committee meeting minutes, 10 May 1915, in 'Minutes of General Committee and Annual General meetings, February 1912–August 1917', item 2; 12 September 1921, 14 August 1922, in 'Minutes of General Committee and Annual General meetings, September 1917–October 1926', item 3; Society for the Prevention of Cruelty to Animals, Auckland, records, MS 2010/13, AWMM.
12 Auckland SPCA general committee minutes, 9 July 1923, in 'Minutes of General Committee and Annual General meetings, September 1917–October 1926', item 3, Society for the Prevention of Cruelty to Animals, Auckland, records, MS 2010/13, AWMM.
13 Notes for 1929, in Morrie Jalfon and Bob Kerridge (1996), *The History of the SPCA Auckland*, Auckland SPCA, Auckland [np]; New Zealand Veterinary Association (1977), *Companion Animal Report, 1976*, New Zealand Veterinary Association, Hamilton, p. 48.
14 'Companion animal overpopulation', from In Defence of Animals USA, www.idausa.org/facts/overpopulation.html [accessed 1 January 2010]
15 Introduction to 'Pets', in 'Miscellaneous correspondence 1930s', 89-238-1/13, Society for the Prevention of Cruelty to Animals, Wellington, records, MS-Group-89-238, ATL.
16 Ruth Park (1993), *A Fence around the Cuckoo*, Penguin, Auckland, pp. 192–93.
17 Dorothy Monkman to Winifred Walmsley, 2 November 1929, MS-Papers-6185-1, ATL.
18 Letter from Secretary Wellington SPCA to Miss F.L. Hawk, Waikanae, 29 September 1945, in 'Records nd', 89-238-2/06, Society for the Prevention of Cruelty to Animals, Wellington, records, MS-Group-89-238, ATL.
19 See 'Pet cats in Victorian New Zealand', posted 21 January 2013 on 'History Geek' blog, historygeek.co.nz/2013/01/21/pet-cats-in-victorian-new-zealand [accessed 27 February 2013]. This discusses and gives examples of drowning cats for behavioural and health problems as well as drowning unwanted litters of kittens in nineteenth-century New Zealand.
20 *Wellington SPCA 36th Annual Report, 1929*, p. 5; *37th Annual Report, 1930*, p. 5; in 'Annual reports 1894–1978', 89-238-6/3, Society for the Prevention of Cruelty to Animals, Wellington, records, MS-Group-89-238, ATL.
21 *Wellington SPCA 38th Annual Report, 1931*, p. 5, in 'Annual reports 1894–1978', 89-238-6/3; various reports in 'Inspectors' reports 1925–1933', 89-238-5/4; Society for the Prevention of Cruelty to Animals, Wellington, records, MS-Group-89-238, ATL.
22 *Wellington SPCA, Eighth Annual Report, September 1901*, p. 7; *Tenth Annual Report, November 1903*, p. 3; *Twenty-seventh Annual Report, 1920*, p. 2; in 'Annual reports 1894–1978', 89-238-6/3, Society for the Prevention of Cruelty to Animals, Wellington, records, MS-Group-89-238, ATL.
23 *Wellington SPCA 42nd Annual Report 1935*, p. 2, in 'Annual reports and general meetings 1930–40', 89-238-1/06, Society for the Prevention of Cruelty to Animals, Wellington, records, MS-Group-89-238, ATL.
24 'The great dane was grateful. X-ray & surgical operations for injured dogs at the modern SPCA clinic', *Freedom*, 14 November 1951, p. 7, in 'Scrapbook, 1947–1976', 89-238-6/1, Society for the Prevention of Cruelty to Animals, Wellington, records, MS-Group-89-238, ATL.
25 *Wellington SPCA, 58th Annual Report Year Ended 20 Sept 1951*, p. 2, in 'Annual reports 1943–1946', 89-238-7/01, Society for the Prevention of Cruelty to Animals, Wellington, records, MS-Group-89-238, ATL.
26 *Wellington SPCA, 54th Annual Report Year Ended 30 Sept 1947*, p. 1, *58th Annual Report Year Ended 20 Sept 1951*, p. 2, *61st Annual Report Year Ended 30 Sept 1954*, p. 1, in 'Annual reports 1943–1946', 89-238-7/01; 'The great dane was grateful', p. 7, and 'Reorganisation of SPCA services. Distressed homeless animals are now to be better cared for' [no source], 22 August 1959, in 'Scrapbook, 1947–1976', 89-238-6/1; Wellington SPCA committee meeting minutes, 15 July 1957, in 'Records nd', 89-238-5/1; Society for the Prevention of Cruelty to Animals, Wellington, records, MS-Group-89-238, ATL.
27 'The great dane was grateful', p. 7; 'SPCA appeal. Care of animals. Wellington lags behind.' [nd, 1947?]; 'Pet destruction thought not due to holiday', [nd, 1959/60?]; in 'Scrapbook, 1947–1976', 89-238-6/1, Society for the Prevention of Cruelty to Animals, Wellington, records, MS-Group-89-238, ATL.
28 Letter from Secretary, Auckland SPCA to Secretary, Wellington SPCA, 17 May 1945, in 'Records nd', 89-238-2/06, Society for the Prevention of Cruelty to Animals, Wellington, records, MS-Group-89-238, ATL.

29 'The great dane was grateful', p. 7.
30 Wellington SPCA committee meetings 16 March 1953, 22 June 1953, in 'Committee minute book 1944–1955', 89-238-5/2, Society for the Prevention of Cruelty to Animals, Wellington, records, MS-Group-89-238, ATL.
31 Draft policy proposals 21 September 1959, Stray dogs control, in 'Draft policy proposals and financial items', 89-238-1/05, Society for the Prevention of Cruelty to Animals, Wellington, records, MS-Group-89-238, ATL. Information on Auckland SPCA pound in 'Minute Book: Monthly meetings of Council and Annual General Meeting minutes, November 1964–August 1974', item 13, Society for the Prevention of Cruelty to Animals, Auckland, records, MS 2010/13, AWMM.
32 Wellington SPCA committee meeting 11 Nov 1946, in 'Committee minute book 1944–1955', 89-238-5/2, Society for the Prevention of Cruelty to Animals, Wellington, records, MS-Group-89-238, ATL; 'SPCA wants better impounding', Pet Pride, vol. 1, no. 3, April 1969, p. 7; Auckland SPCA council meeting, 16 February 1970, in 'Minutes of monthly Council and AGM meetings November 1964–August 1974', item 13, Society for the Prevention of Cruelty to Animals, Auckland, records, MS 2010/13, AWMM.
33 'Lack of dog pound a problem', Evening Post, 5 March 1968, in 'Scrapbook, 1947–1976', 89-238-6/1, Society for the Prevention of Cruelty to Animals, Wellington, records, MS-Group-89-238, ATL; Auckland SPCA council meeting minutes, 13 October 1969, in 'Minutes of monthly council and AGM meetings, November 1964–August 1974', item 13, Society for the Prevention of Cruelty to Animals, Auckland, records, MS 2010/13, AWMM.
34 'Cut rate for destruction. Traps to control Hutt's stray cats', Evening Post, 24 March 1964, in 'Scrapbook, 1947–1976', 89-238-6/1, Society for the Prevention of Cruelty to Animals, Wellington, records, MS-Group-89-238, ATL.
35 W.R. Olliver, Secretary of the Royal Federation of SPCAs, to Secretary, Department of Internal Affairs, 26 March 1965, in Wildlife Service-Cats (wild)-Destruction of, 1937–1969, Department of Internal Affairs Head Office (AAAC), acc W3179, box 29, record 46/40, ANZ; 'These cats just wait and hope', Truth, 14 June 1966, in 'Scrapbook, 1947–1976', 89-238-6/1, Society for the Prevention of Cruelty to Animals, Wellington, records, MS-Group-89-238, ATL.
36 See correspondence between Department of Internal Affairs and Municipal and Counties Associations in Wildlife Service-Cats (wild)-Destruction of, 1937–1969, AAAC, acc W3179, box 29, record 46/40, ANZ; Finance (No. 2) Act, 1967, s. 8.
37 Companion Animal Report 1976, p. 4.
38 'SPCA will prosecute. People who dump dogs are warned', Evening Post, 26 May 1964; 'Public asked to help find homes for city's unwanted kittens', Evening Post, 11 April 1969; in 'Scrapbook, 1947–1976', 89-238-6/1, Society for the Prevention of Cruelty to Animals, Wellington, records, MS-Group-89-238, ATL.
39 E.L. Sincock, 'The stray cat and dog problem', Pet Pride, vol. 7, no. 2, April–June 1975, p. 9.
40 Auckland SPCA Ninety-first Annual Report 1973–74, pp. 4–5 in 'Minute book: executive council and AGM meetings, September 1974–October 1980', item 14, Society for the Prevention of Cruelty to Animals, Auckland, records, MS 2010/13, AWMM.
41 'The great dane was grateful', p. 7; 'Now a waiting list for unwanted pets' [unsourced and undated, 1959?]; 'Homes found for all pets' [unsourced and undated, early 1960s?]; 'SPCA will prosecute. People who dump dogs are warned', Evening Post, 26 May 1964; in 'Scrapbook, 1947–1976', 89-238-6/1, Society for the Prevention of Cruelty to Animals, Wellington, records, MS-Group-89-238, ATL.
42 'Death threat today for homeless pets', Dominion, 24 December 1969, in 'Scrapbook, 1947–1976', 89-238-6/1, Society for the Prevention of Cruelty to Animals, Wellington, records, MS-Group-89-238, ATL.
43 'Rejected animals find new life and sympathy with society', Evening Post, 31 January 1970, in 'Scrapbook, 1947–1976', 89-238-6/1, Society for the Prevention of Cruelty to Animals, Wellington, records, MS-Group-89-238, ATL.
44 Notes for 1947 in Jalfon and Kerridge, The History of the SPCA Auckland; Wellington SPCA committee meetings 17 March 1946, 11 November 1946, 9 December 1946, in 'Committee minute book 1944–1955', 89-238-5/2, Society for the Prevention of Cruelty to Animals, Wellington, records, MS-Group-89-238, ATL.
45 Notes for 1952 in Jalfon and Kerridge, The History of the SPCA Auckland; draft policy proposals, 21 September 1959 and Secretary's report, December 1959 and January 1960, in 'Records, nd', 89-239-4/2, Society for the Prevention of Cruelty to Animals, Wellington, records, MS-Group-89-238, ATL.
46 'We don't want to kill your pets, please have them spayed', [unsourced, undated, c. 1973–74] in 'Scrapbook, 1947–1976', 89-238-6/1, Society for the Prevention of Cruelty to Animals, Wellington, records, MS-Group-89-238, ATL.
47 Animal World, October 1977, back cover, in 'Animal World, Standards magazine July 1977, October 1977, July 1986', 89-238-6/2, Society for the Prevention of Cruelty to Animals, Wellington, records, MS-Group-89-238, ATL.
48 'Kitten charge', letter to the editor by S.F. Jackson, Wellington SPCA, Evening Post, 22 April 1970 in 'Scrapbook, 1947–1976', 89-238-6/1; Minute book January 1978-November 1980, in 'Records, nd', 89-238-4/1, Society for the Prevention of Cruelty to Animals, Wellington, records, MS-Group-89-238, ATL; Auckland SPCA Ninety-second Annual Report 1977–78, p. 2, 'Minute book Executive Council and AGM meetings, September 1974–October 1980', item 14, Society for the Prevention of Cruelty to Animals, Auckland, records, MS 2010/13, AWMM; Dominion Bulletin RNZSPCA, Feilding, RNZSPCA, no. 9, April 1982, pp. 3–4.
49 Email from Bob Kerridge, Auckland SPCA, 10 December 2012.
50 Pet Pride, vol. 2, no. 3, April–May 1970, p. 21; Waikato SPCA, President's Report for year ended 31 March 1973, Inspector's report; Sincock, 'The stray cat and dog problem', p. 9; clipping from Nelson Evening Mail, 31 December 1968, 'Nelson plan for animal control', in Publications-'Problem cats', 1967–1984, Department of Conservation Head Office (AANS), acc W3546, box 20, record WIL 13/10/6, ANZ.
51 Companion Animal Report, 1976, pp. 8–13.
52 See for example statistics from Auckland SPCA annual reports for 1974–75 and 1984–85. The society was forced to euthanise nearly 80 per cent of the thousands of animals it received in 1974–75. A decade later, it still had to put down close to 70 per cent.

53 Marion Gregory, 'Death or rejection – the alternatives to care', *Pet Pride*, vol. 5, no. 4, September–October 1973, p. 18.
54 'News from the Waikato SPCA', Newsletter no. 12, October/December 1977, [np].
55 Ross McLauchlan, 'Condemned to die – why?', *Pet Pride*, vol. 4, no. 3, Spring, 1986, p. 6.
56 *Animal World*, Winter 1958, in 'Records, nd', 89-238-7/02; copies of letters to the editor, early 1960s, unsourced newspaper clippings; 'Cat lovers rally to hit skin trade', *Dominion*, 5 May 1969 in 'Scrapbook, 1947–1976', 89-238-6/1, Society for the Prevention of Cruelty to Animals, Wellington, records, MS-Group-89-238, ATL; letter to the Petitions Committee from A. E. Jones, 7 July 1969, in Feral Cats, 1969–1980, Department of Internal Affairs Head Office (AAAC), acc W3207, box 77, record WIL 33/3/5, part 1, ANZ.
57 Cats Protection League (Canterbury) Inc www.cats.org.nz/about.html [accessed 20 November 2007]; *Cats: Newsletter of the Cats Protection League (Wellington) Inc*, February 1983, November 1983; 'Catherine de la Roche found dead', *Dominion*, 5 May 1997, p. 13.
58 *CPL News: Newsletter of the Cats Protection League (Wellington) Inc*, September 1998, March 2003; *Cats: Newsletter of the Cats Protection League (Wellington) Inc*, December 1990; Ruth Nichol, 'Helping hand for the cats', *Dominion*, Saturday 8 May 1993. p. 14.
59 Upper Hutt Animal Rescue Society, MS-Papers-4953 ATL; 'Society saves 1000 animals', *Dominion*, 25 November 1969, in 'Scrapbook, 1947–1976', 89-238-6/1, Society for the Prevention of Cruelty to Animals, Wellington, records, MS-Group-89-238, ATL.
60 'A caring society', *Pets and Pedigrees: The magazine for people who care about animals*, February 1981, p. 28.
61 'Club news' in *New Zealand Pet News*, February 1983, p. 20.
62 Waikato SPCA, President's Report for year ended 31 March 1972. See also 'SPCA ideas on dog problem in city', *Evening Post*, 25 May 1970, in 'Scrapbook, 1947–1976', 89-238-6/1, Society for the Prevention of Cruelty to Animals, Wellington, records, MS-Group-89-238, ATL; 'Designer animals: built-in cruelty', *Pet Pride*, Autumn/winter, 1987, pp. 5–7.
63 'A disturbing trend', *Pet Pride*, Autumn/winter, 1987, p. 12.
64 Nichol, 'Helping hand for the cats'.
65 Rose Muir, 'Rottweilers' in *New Zealand Pet News*, February 1983, p. 14; Clive Dalton, 'The canine conundrum' *New Zealand Geographic*, no. 12, Oct–Dec 1991, pp. 33–34.
66 Email from Bob Kerridge, Auckland SPCA, 18 December 2012; Tim Hume, 'Pitbulls: unleashing hell', *Sunday Star Times*, 25 July 2010, C1, www.stuff.co.nz/national/3955666/Pitbulls-Unleashing-hell [accessed 30 July 2010]; 'Director's comment – American Pit Bull Terriers', *Pet Pride*, Spring 1987/Summer 1988, p. 2; Dalton, 'The canine conundrum', p. 36.
67 Dalton, 'The canine conundrum', pp. 39–40; Sarah Catherall, 'Once bitten, forever staunch', *Dominion Post*, 6 February 2010, D4.
68 'Hill starts jail term after dog attack' 19 May 2003, http://tvnz.co.nz/content/191301/423466/article.html; 'Dog that attacked girl destroyed', 7 February 2003, http://tvnz.co.nz/content/166754/2591754.xhtml; Hamish Carnachan, 'Who let the dogs out?', *Investigate Magazine*, April 2003 www.thebriefingroom.com/archives/investigate_back_issues/april_03_issue/index.html [accessed 6 April 2013]
69 Email from Bob Kerridge, Auckland SPCA, 18 December 2012; Martin Kay, 'On a tighter leash', *Dominion Post*, 7 October 2009, A3; Dog Control Amendment Act, 2003.
70 'Stricter control of dogs in city decided on', *Evening Post*, 10 December 1969, Scrapbook 1947–1976, 89-238-6/1, Society for the Prevention of Cruelty to Animals, Wellington, records, MS-Group-89-238, ATL; *Pet Pride*, vol. 2, no. 2, Feb–March 1970, p. 1; *Companion Animal Report 1976*, pp. 10–11.
71 J. Ruth Lawson, 'Hydatid disease and sheep measles: the history of their control and the economics of a recent change of control policy', *New Zealand Journal of Zoology*, 1994, vol. 21, pp. 83–89; Honor Anderson (1997), 'Hydatids: A disease of human carelessness. A history of human hydatid disease in New Zealand', MA thesis (History), Otago University, Abstract and pp. 3, 9, 11–12, 19, 34, 35–36, 49, 52, 83–85.
72 Ken Berry (1986), *Scrutiny on the County*, Marlborough County Council, Blenheim, p. 215.
73 For example, Wellington City Council had introduced a regulation by 1988. See 'Picking up after pets', *Evening Post*, 18 March 1988, p. 30.
74 Linley Boniface, 'I've a bone to pick with you', *Dominion Post*, 9 June 2008, B4.
75 Alison Box, 'Doggone it, we're not pooch-haters', *Dominion Post*, 13 June 2008, B5.
76 'The value of opossums', *Otago Witness*, 21 June 1894, p. 21.
77 *Companion Animal Report 1976*, pp. 14–17; 'Nicky' by Ricky Grey Maulder of Titirangi, *New Zealand Pet News*, November 1981, p. 4; Gerard Hutching, 'Possums' in Te Ara: the Encyclopedia of New Zealand, updated 9 November 2012, www.TeAra.govt.nz/en/possums
78 'Illegal turtle importation', *New Zealand Pet Trade News*, vol. 1, no. 6, March 1980, p. 1; B.K. Wiltshier, 'The Greek tortoise in New Zealand', *New Zealand Pet Trade News*, vol. 2, no. 5, January 1981, pp. 5–6; 'Legislation', *New Zealand Pet News*, vol. 2, no. 4, November 1980, pp. 6, 12; 'Danger! NZ waterways threatened', *New Zealand Pet News*, July 1982, pp. 6–9.
79 'Ferrets', Department of Conservation, www.doc.govt.nz/conservation/threats-and-impacts/animal-pests/animal-pests-a-z/ferrets/ [accessed 5 April 2013]; Philippa Jones, 'Friends or foes', *New Zealand Pet Magazine*, May–July 1999, pp. 18–21; 'Pet ferrets to be banned', press release by Sandra Lee, Minister of Conservation, 28 March 2002, www.beehive.govt.nz/release/pet-ferrets-be-banned [accessed 19 March 2011]
80 Bob Church, 'New Zealand ferrets live as outlaws', *Ferret Magazine*, 1 May 2008, www.smallanimalchannel.com/ferrets-magazine/road-with-bob/new-zealand-ferret-owners-live-as-outlaws.aspx [accessed 19 March 2011]
81 Charles Hursthouse (1857), *New Zealand or Zealandia, the Britain of the South*, Edward Standford, London, vol. 1, p. 127.
82 Quoted in Kate Hunter (2009), *Hunting: A New Zealand history*, Random House, Auckland, p. 261.
83 David Young (2004), *Our Islands, Ourselves: A history of conservation in New Zealand*, University of Otago Press, Dunedin, p. 230; Eileen McSaveney, 'Nearshore islands', in Te Ara: the Encyclopedia of New Zealand, updated 29 January 2013, www.TeAra.govt.nz/en/nearshore-islands; Ross Galbreath (1993), *Working for Wildlife: A history of the New Zealand Wildlife Service*, Bridget Williams Books Ltd and Historical Branch, Department of Internal Affairs, Wellington, pp. 196–97.
84 Robert Peden, 'Rabbits', in Te Ara: the Encyclopedia of New Zealand, updated 9 November 2012, www.TeAra.govt.nz/en/

rabbits; *Wanganui Chronicle*, 26 September 1881, p. 2; *Wanganui Chronicle*, 7 November 1888, p. 2; 'The feral cat problem' [internal report, mid 1970s?], in 'Feral cats', 1969–1980, AAAC, acc W3207, box 77, record WIL 33/3/5, part 1, ANZ; 'Cats for rabbit control opposed', clipping from Christchurch *Press*, 22 September 1964, in Wildlife Service-Cats (wild)-Destruction of, 1937–1969, Department of Internal Affairs Head Office (AAAC), acc W3179, box 29, record 46/40, ANZ.
85 'Problem cats' (pamphlet), in Publications-'Problem cats', 1967–1984, AANS, acc W3546, box 20, record WIL 13/10/6, ANZ.
86 Auckland SPCA council meeting minutes, 7 February 1966 and 5 September 1966, in 'Minutes of monthly Council and AGM meetings November 1964–August 1974', item 13, Society for the Prevention of Cruelty to Animals, Auckland, records, MS 2010/13, AWMM; Publications-'Problem cats', 1967–1984, AANS, acc W3546, box 20, record WIL 13/10/6, ANZ.
87 Eileen McSaveney, 'Nearshore islands', Te Ara.
88 Jane Clifton, 'What's dead, pussycat?', *New Zealand Listener*, 28 July–3 August 2001, pp. 19–22.
89 'Pets: New Zealand animal pests and threats', Department of Conservation, www.doc.govt.nz/conservation/threats-and-impacts/animal-pests/animal-pests-a-z/pets/the-threat/ [accessed 6 February 2012]
90 Basil and Ann Graeme, 'Eco-subdivisions: living without cats and dogs', *Forest & Bird*, no. 283, February 1997, pp. 38.
91 'Growing interest in pet-free housing subdivisions', *Forest & Bird*, no. 303, February 2002, p. 5.
92 Robert and Brenda Vale (2009), *Time to Eat the Dog? The real guide to sustainable living*, Thames and Hudson, London, p. 359.
93 'Cats live happily indoors, says vet', *Dominion Post*, 18 July 2012, A5.
94 Karl du Fresne, 'Capitalist with a cause', *New Zealand Listener*, 16–22 February 2013, p. 16.
95 Catherine de la Roche, 'Welfare through population control', *Pet Pride*, vol. 3, no. 3, Spring 1985, pp. 23–24; *CPL News: Newsletter of the Cats Protection League (Wellington) Inc*, April 2000, July 2002; Clifton, 'What's dead, pussycat?', pp. 19–22.
96 'Get your pet neutered now!', RNZSPCA website, http:rnzspca.org.nz [accessed 30 July 2010)]
97 Letter to Petitions Committee from A.E. Jones, 7 July 1969, enclosing a copy of the petition and supporting correspondence, in Feral Cats, 1969–1980, AAAC, acc W3207, box 77, record WIL 33/3/5, part 1, ANZ.
98 Copy of letter from 'Poor Pussy' to *Dominion*, 16 May 1969, in Feral Cats, 1969–1980, AAAC, acc W3207, box 77, record WIL 33/3/5, part 1, ANZ.
99 Supporting correspondence with letter to Petitions Committee from A.E. Jones, 7 July 1969, in Feral Cats, 1969–1980, AAAC, acc W3207, box 77, record WIL 33/3/5, part 1, ANZ.
100 Report of Comptroller of Customs to Clerk of the Petitions Committee, 27 July 1969, in Export Prohibitions & Restrictions Cat Skins Legislation/Applications, 1969–1983, New Zealand Customs Service Head Office (AALN), series 7234, acc W5627, box 44, record 540.022, part 1, ANZ.
101 Newspaper clipping, 'Ten cats skinned, dumped', *Dominion*, 29 July 1969, in Export Prohibitions & Restrictions Cat Skins Legislation/Applications, 1969–1983, AALN, series 7234, acc W5627, box 44, record 540.022, part 1, ANZ.
102 Extract from *New Zealand Gazette*, 21 August 1969, no. 51, page 1569, 'Prohibition on Export of Catskins', in Export Prohibitions & Restrictions Cat Skins Legislation/Applications, 1969–1983, AALN, series 7234, acc W5627, box 44, record 540.022, part 1, ANZ.

Chapter 9 Local legends

1 *Taranaki Herald*, 19 January 1917, p. 2.
2 Virginia Winder, 'Taranaki's famous felines', on Puke Ariki website, www.pukeariki.com/en/stories/naturalWorld/taranakicats.htm [accessed 27 March 2008]
3 The rise of the animal celebrity is discussed in more detail in Helen Pycior, 'The making of the "first dog": President Warren G. Harding and Laddie Boy', *Society and Animals: Journal of Human-Animal Studies*, vol. 13, no. 2, 2005, pp. 110–11, and Katherine C. Grier (2007), *Pets in America: A history*, Harvest, Orlando, p. 290.
4 Hilda Kean, 'An exploration of the sculptures of Greyfriars Bobby, Edinburgh, Scotland, and the Brown Dog, Battersea, South London, England', *Society and Animals: Journal of Human-Animal Studies*, vol. 2, no. 4, 2003, Society and Animals Forum, www.societyandanimalsforum.org [accessed 12 July 2009]
5 Hilda Kean, 'Balto, the Alaskan dog and his statue in New York's Central Park: animal representation and national heritage', *International Journal of Heritage Studies*, vol. 15, no. 5, September 2009, pp. 413–30.
6 James Serpell (1996), *In the Company of Animals: A study of human-animal relationships*, Cambridge University Press, Cambridge, pp. 158, 166–67, 171–85.
7 Harriet Ritvo explains how people could sentimentalise even wild animals, viewing them as 'public pets' in *The Animal Estate: The English and other creatures in the Victorian age*, Harvard University Press, Cambridge, Massachusetts, 1987, p. 228.
8 Cathy Marr, 'Mackenzie, James 1820?–?', from *The Dictionary of New Zealand Biography*. Te Ara: the Encyclopedia of New Zealand, updated 19 February 2013, www.TeAra.govt.nz/en/biographies/1m30/mackenzie-james
9 E.W. Seager (1900), 'The escapades of Mackenzie' in *Canterbury … old and new 1850–1900. A souvenir of the jubilee*, Whitcombe and Tombs, Christchurch, pp. 112–13.
10 Quoted in Miriam MacGregor Redwood (1980), *A Dog's Life: Working dogs in New Zealand*, Reed, Wellington, p. 75.
11 MacGregor Redwood, *A Dog's Life*, p. 4.
12 James McNeish (1972), *The Mackenzie Affair*, Hodder and Stoughton, Auckland, pp. 232–35.
13 Seager, 'The escapades of Mackenzie', p. 113.
14 MacGregor Redwood, *A Dog's Life*, pp. 75–76.
15 McNeish, *The Mackenzie Affair*, pp. 232–35.
16 See for example 'Provincial Council', *Lyttelton Times*, 20 February 1858, p. 3.
17 Gerard Hutching, 'Dolphins' in Te Ara: the Encyclopedia of New Zealand, updated 4 February 2013, www.TeAra.govt.nz/en/dolphins; James Cowan (1911), *Pelorus Jack: The white dolphin of French Pass, New Zealand, with Maori legends*, Whitcombe and Tombs, Christchurch, p. 28; T. Hemfield (T.A.H. Field) (1906), *Pelorus Jack, the mysterious New Zealand fish*; book of ephemera donated to Alexander Turnbull Library by T.A.H. Field, including newspaper clippings, booklets and postcards; Antony Alpers (1963), *Dolphins*, Pauls Book Arcade, pp. 189–205.

18 T.A.H. Field (1910), *The Story of Pelorus Jack* [np].
19 Memo from T.E. Donne to Minister in charge, 25 March 1904, in Acclimatisation – Pelorus Jack, 1903–1950, Tourist and Publicity Department (AECB), series 8615, record group T01, box 153, record 25/7, ANZ.
20 Cowan, *Pelorus Jack*, p. 28.
21 Gerard Hutching, 'Dolphins', and Basil Keane, 'Taniwha' in Te Ara: the Encyclopedia of New Zealand, updated 4 December 2012, www.TeAra.govt.nz/en/taniwha
22 In a variation on the theme of 'public pets', Katherine Grier, in *Pets in America*, p. 285, uses the term 'honorary pets' to describe wild animals that seemed to reflect values humans regarded as important.
23 G.H. Parker (1945), *'Jack': A true story of a clever New Zealand farm dog*, Auckland Sunday School Union, Auckland, p. 27.
24 Parker, *'Jack'*, pp. 41–42.
25 Ibid., p. 11.
26 Ibid., p. 34.
27 Ibid., pp. 45–46.
28 Winder, 'Taranaki's famous felines', Puke Ariki website; Erin MacDonald, 'Biker Rastus rolls into Capital', *Evening Post*, 11 October 1995, p. 1, and 'Mean moggy lives for the road', *Evening Post*, 5 October 1995, p. 1.
29 Max and Rastus Tribute Site, www.petsonthenet.co.nz/commem.htm [accessed 27 March 2008]
30 Dianne Haworth (2008), *Paddy the Wanderer*, HarperCollins, Auckland, p. 121.
31 Haworth, *Paddy the Wanderer*, pp. 214, 215.
32 Ian Hunter (2009), *Farmers: Your store for 100 years*, HarperCollins, Auckland, pp. 134–39.
33 Winder, 'Taranaki's famous felines', Puke Ariki website.
34 'Colin's Cat', Port Taranaki website, www.porttaranaki.co.nz/Colins/colins.htm [accessed 27 March 2008]
35 'Jean Batten and Buddy the cat', www.nzhistory.net.nz/media/interactive/jean-batten-and-buddy, (Ministry for Culture and Heritage), updated 9 February 2010.
36 Jeff Neems, 'The people's poet', *Dominion Post*, 4 June 2011, pp. 12–14.
37 Pycior, 'The making of the "first dog"', pp. 110–11; Grier, *Pets in America*, pp. 290–93.
38 'Campaign diary: Friday, November 4th', 4 November 2011, www.stuff.co.nz/national/politics/campaign-trail/5905720/Campaign-diary-Friday-November-4th [accessed 26 April 2012]
39 Gerard Hutching, 'Dolphins', Te Ara; and Antony Alpers, 'Pelorus Jack', from *An Encyclopaedia of New Zealand* edited by A.H. McLintock, originally published in 1966. Te Ara: the Encyclopedia of New Zealand, updated 22 April 2009, www.TeAra.govt.nz/en/1966/pelorus-jack
40 See correspondence: Acclimatisation – Pelorus Jack, 1903–1950, AECB, series 8615, record group T01, box 153, record 25/7, ANZ.
41 See correspondence: Sea Fisheries – "Pelorus Jack" (Rissus Dolphin) from 4 December 1903 to 7 April 1965, Ministry of Agriculture and Fisheries Head Office (AAFZ), series 7910, acc W1711, box 7, record 2/12/34, part 1, ANZ.
42 Alpers, *Dolphins*, pp. 206–21; Antony Alpers, 'Opo', from *An Encyclopaedia of New Zealand*, edited by A.H. McLintock, originally published in 1966. Te Ara: the Encyclopedia of New Zealand, updated 23 April 2009, www.TeAra.govt.nz/en/1966/opo; Gerard Hutching, 'Dolphins', in Te Ara.
43 Newspaper articles, 1962–1967 in 'Scrapbook 1947–1976', 89-238-6/1, Society for the Prevention of Cruelty to Animals, Wellington, records, MS-Group-89-238, ATL.
44 Maggy Wassilieff, 'Zoos and aquariums', in Te Ara: the Encyclopedia of New Zealand, updated 11 March 2013, www.TeAra.govt.nz/en/zoos-and-aquariums
45 Diane Joyce, 'Decision to bury Moko on island "saddens" Mahia', *Dominion Post*, 15 July 2010, A4; and 'Autopsy fails to reveal what killed Moko', *Dominion Post*, 16 July 2010, A5.
46 Bernard Carpinter and Diane Joyce, 'Competing claims for Moko the dolphin's remains', *Dominion Post*, 9 July 2010, www.stuff.co.nz/national/3900065/Competing-claims-for-Moko-the-dolphins-remains [accessed 4 January 2011]
47 Kayla Webley, 'To the rescue: Moko the dolphin', 21 March 2011, in Time Lists, Top 10 heroic animals, www.time.com/time/specials/packages/article/0,28804,2059858_2059863_2060210,00.html [accessed 31 March 2011]
48 'Sirocco', Kakapo Recovery Programme, www.kakaporecovery.org.nz [accessed 4 February 2012]
49 Kiran Chug, 'What's all the flap about?', *Dominion Post*, 27 August 2011, B1–B2.
50 Dave Hansford, 'Few happy feet in our forests', *Dominion Post*, 25 July 2011, B5.
51 Chug, 'What's all the flap about?'.
52 Sean Plunket, 'Let's not try to be clever when we have a ready-made ambassador', *Dominion Post*, 20 August 2011, A25.
53 Kay Blundell, 'Happy Feet discoverer writes book', *Dominion Post*, 17 September 2011, A17.
54 'Whatever happened to Shrek the Sheep?' Nature of animals, www.natureofanimals.com/ShrektheSheep.html [accessed 18 February 2011]; Students of Tarras School, illustrated by Jenny Chisholm (2004), *Shrek the Famous Hermit Sheep of Tarras*, Tarras School, Dunedin; John Perriam (2010), *Shrek, the Story of a Kiwi Icon*, Random House, Auckland, pp. 7, 13, 58–68.
55 Perriam, *Shrek, the Story of a Kiwi Icon*, p. 17.
56 Ibid., p. 93.
57 Jane Clifton, 'Shrek's independent spirit earned him fame', *Dominion Post*, 8 June 2011, B8.
58 MacGregor Redwood, *A Dog's Life*, pp. 79–80; email from Tony Rippon, Curator, South Canterbury Museum, 15 February 2011.
59 'Governor-General unveils memorial to sheep dogs', *Timaru Herald*, 8 March 1968, p. 14.
60 Email from Tony Rippin, Curator, South Canterbury Museum, 15 February 2011.
61 'Farmers' Best Friend, Hunterville, NZ', Dog statues, on Waymarking.com, www.waymarking.com/waymarks/WM85C0_Farmers_Best_Friend_Hunterville_NZ [accessed 12 February 2011]; email from Shona Jones, Hunterville Huntaway Festival, 12 February 2011.
62 Hunterville Huntaway Festival, www.shemozzle.co.nz [accessed 3 January 2011]
63 'Plimmer for Hall of Fame', *Dominion Post*, 18 June 2009, C2.
64 'Mrs Chippy', Antarctic Society website, www.antarctic.org.nz/pages/projects/mrschippy.php [accessed 13 March 2008]
65 'Simpson and his donkey' Australian War Memorial, www.awm.gov.au/exhibitions/forging/australians/simpson.asp [accessed 25 February 2011]
66 See for instance, '"Murphy" and his mule', *School Journal*, vol. 18, no. 3, April 1924, part 3, pp. 90–95; 'The man with the

donkey', *School Journal*, vol. 19, no. 3, April 1925, part 1, pp. 37–39.
67 Geoff Cumming, 'A picture of bravery', New Zealand Herald, 19 April 2008, www.nzherald.co.nz/nz/news/article.cfm?c_id=1&objectid=10504985 [accessed 12 April 2013]
68 McNeish, *The Mackenzie Affair*, p. 232.
69 'Fairlie', Mt Cook Mackenzie, www.mtcooknz.com/mackenzie/Fairlie/ [accessed 12 February 2011]
70 D.C.M. Burnett, 'Tekapo dog memorial', *Timaru Herald*, 23 March 1968, [np] with email from Tony Rippin, Curator, South Canterbury Museum, 15 February 2011.
71 'PDSA Dickin Medal', PDSA website, www.pdsa.org.uk/about-us/animal-bravery-awards/pdsa-dickin-medal [accessed 12 April 2013]
72 'Award to Top Dog of the year', [no source, 1961], and 'Most heroic dog of '64' [no source, 1964], untitled article, *Dominion*, 3 October 1968, in 'Scrapbook 1947–1976', 89-238-6/1, Society for the Prevention of Cruelty to Animals, Wellington, records, MS-Group-89-238, ATL; 'New Zealand's most heroic dog of the year', *Pet Pride*, vol. 1, no. 1, December 1968, p. 19.
73 Veronika Thornburrow (ed.) (1993), *The Compassionate Years: An introduction to the history of the Royal New Zealand Society for the Prevention of Cruelty to Animals*, RNZSPCA, Auckland, pp. 102–03; 'Valiant George' by Elizabeth Krammer, Smarter than Jack, http://smarterthanjack.com/content/valiant-george-0 [accessed 3 April 2011]
74 'SPCA to award medal to canine hero', media release, 8 May 2007, RNZSPCA, http://rnzspca.org.nz/ [accessed 27 March 2012]
75 'George to get UK bravery gong', *Dominion Post*, 22 January 2009, A3.
76 'PDSA gold medal', PDSA website, www.pdsa.org.uk/about-us/animal-bravery-awards/pdsa-gold-medal [accessed 12 April 2013]
77 Olivia Carville, 'First animal to get Local Hero Medal', 27 March 2012, www.stuff.co.nz/national/6641485/First-animal-to-get-Local-Hero-Medal [accessed 27 March 2012]
78 Email from Chloe Searle, Curator North Otago Museum, 7 March 2011.

Chapter 10 One of the family

1 'Humans turning to pets for love', *Dominion Post*, 6 October 2010, A10.
2 See for example 'The policy of extravagance', *Hawera and Normanby Star*, 17 August 1906, p. 3; *Star*, 15 November 1886, p. 1; *Grey River Argus*, 7 May 1904, p. 4; 'Strange occupations', *Star*, 16 May 1893, p. 1.
3 'Women in print', *Evening Post*, 27 June 1913, p. 9.
4 *Eleventh Annual Report and Balance Sheet of the New Zealand Society for the Protection of Women and Children and Prevention of Cruelty to Animals, Auckland, 1904–5*, Wilson and Horton, Auckland, 1905, p. 4.
5 Henry S. Salt (1892), *Animals' Rights: Considered in relation to social progress*, George Bell and Sons, London, pp. 9, 21.
6 Keith Thomas (1984), *Man and the Natural World: Changing attitudes in England 1500–1800*, Penguin, London, p. 185; Hilda Kean (1998), *Animal Rights: Political and social change in Britain since 1800*, Reaktion Books, London, pp. 111, 118–19, 156–57, 179.
7 Hilda Kean, 'The mood of militancy', *BBC History Magazine*, vol. 8, no. 12, December 2007, pp. 36–38; Kean, *Animal Rights*, pp. 110, 142–43; James Turner (1980), *Reckoning with the Beast: Animals, pain, and humanity in the Victorian mind*, Johns Hopkins University Press, Baltimore, pp. 113–16.
8 Nellie F.H. MacLeod (1955), *A Voice on the Wind: The story of Jessie Mackay*, A.H. and A.W. Reed, Wellington, pp. 82–84.
9 *Daybreak*, 30 March 1895, p. 6; 'Women's Christian Temperance Union', *Otago Daily Times*, 6 April 1896, p. 4; 'Women in print', *Evening Post*, 30 May 1925, p. 14. Internationally, feminist groups were opposed to vivisection. See Turner, *Reckoning with the Beast*, p. 93; Hilda Kean, *Animal Rights*, pp. 133, 140–44.
10 Theosophical Society in New Zealand, history, www.theosophy.org.nz/about_TSinNZ.html [accessed 1 October 2011]; 'Theosophical society', *Evening Post*, 28 July 1926, p. 3.
11 *NZ Truth*, 27 November 1930, p. 1 has an article on the Auckland Anti-vivisection Society's attack on the Auckland Cancer Campaign Committee.
12 Minutes of Wellington SPCA committee meetings, 1 May 1928, 30 October 1928, 4 December 1928, 4 March 1930, 2 April 1930 and 7 May 1930, 'Minutes 1928–1930', 89-238-2/01, Society for the Prevention of Cruelty to Animals, Wellington, records, MS-Group-89-238, ATL; 'The SPCA annual conference' *Evening Post*, 28 February 1929, p. 15; 'Protection of animals. NZ conference', *Evening Post*, 2 March 1933, p. 7.
13 'Animal life. Dogs and birds. Preventing cruelty. SPCA requests.', *Evening Post*, 9 July 1937, p. 10; 'News of the day. No vivisection of dogs.', *Evening Post*, 18 March 1937, p. 8; 'Protection of dogs. A bill to prohibit the vivisection of dogs', in 'Miscellaneous correspondence 1930s', 89-238-1/13, Society for the Prevention of Cruelty to Animals, Wellington, records, MS-Group-89-238, ATL. This campaign mirrored an earlier one in Britain; see Kean, *Animal Rights*, p. 144.
14 *Otago SPCA, 46th Annual Report*, 1927, p. 7, in 'Annual reports 1885–1932', 89-238-6/3, Society for the Prevention of Cruelty to Animals, Wellington, records, MS-Group-89-238, ATL.
15 Katherine C. Grier discusses these ideas at greater length in 'Buying for your best friend', ch. 6 of *Pets in America: A history*, Harvest, Orlando, 2007, pp. 355–409.
16 Advertisement for Excelsior Steam Biscuit Factory, *Southland Times*, 20 November 1880, p. 1.
17 Advertisement for Mason, Struthers & Co, *Star*, 15 August 1908, p. 1.
18 Advertisement for Carter's Universal Birdseed, *Taranaki Herald*, 14 February 1891, p. 2.
19 Letter from Mr E. Poulston, Timaru, to Minister of Department of Industries and Commerce, 6 May 1939, in Propriety lines-animal foods-for dogs, cats, birds and other pets, Department of Industries and Commerce (AEFN), series 19294, record group IC1, box 1384, record 35/14/-, ANZ.
20 Report for Secretary of Industries and Commerce from District Officer Auckland, 5 July 1939; Letter from Secretary for Industries and Commerce to F. Cooper Ltd, 16 October 1940; in Propriety lines-animal foods-for dogs, cats, birds and other pets, AEFN, series 19294, record group IC1, box 1384, record 35/14/-, ANZ.
21 'With the animals', *Evening Post*, 3 March 1908, p. 8.
22 *Wanganui Chronicle*, 23 February 1911, p. 8.
23 Advertisements, *Evening Post*, 16 June 1928, p. 28; 1 September 1928, p. 18.

24. 'Pampered pets on parade', *NZ Truth*, 19 July 1924, p. 5.
25. Letter from Mrs Barbara E. Turner, Secretary of the Wellington Domestic Animal Owners' Organisation to Mr Carter, Managing Director of Manawatu Meat and Cold Storage Co., 9 September 1944, in 'Ladies Auxiliary', 89-238-1/10; Executive meeting of the Wellington SPCA Ladies Auxiliary, 14 June 1945, in 'Minute book 1941–1946', 89-238-5/3, Society for the Prevention of Cruelty to Animals, Wellington, records, MS-Group-89-238, ATL.
26. Kean, *Animal Rights*, pp. 180, 197.
27. British Union for the Abolition of Vivisection, Wellington Branch, Secretary Treasurer's report for the year ending 31 January 1947 by H.G. Lyttle, p. 1, in 'Miscellaneous correspondence 1930s', 89-238-1/13, Society for the Prevention of Cruelty to Animals, Wellington, records, MS-Group-89-238, ATL.
28. Quoted in David Gee (1977), *Our Mabel*, Millwood Press, Wellington, pp. 198–99.
29. Ibid., pp. 202–03, 216–17.
30. Ibid., p. 210; *New Zealand Parliamentary Debates*, 4 July 1957, p. 591 (Prevention of Cruelty to Animals Bill).
31. Quoted in Gee, *Our Mabel*, p. 214.
32. Gee, *Our Mabel*, p. 213.
33. Geoffrey Hodson (1947), *The Case for the Abolition of Vivisection: An examination of the proposition that vivisection is justified by the benefits it confers upon humanity*, Auckland Branch of the British Union for the Abolition of Vivisection, Auckland, pp. 23–24.
34. Brief description of CAWO prefacing Geoffrey Hodson (1953), *Authentic Stories of Intelligence in Animals*, CAWO, Auckland; Winifred E. Miller, Wellington branch CAWO, to Mabel Howard, 15 September 1953, Elsie K. Morton, Auckland, to Mabel Howard, 18 September 1953, R.T. Willan, Christchurch branch CAWO, to Mabel Howard, 17 August 1954, in Mabel Bowden Howard, MS-Papers-3941, ATL.
35. 'Animals Act 1946 and Cruelty to Animals Act 1947', 89-238-3/05, Society for the Prevention of Cruelty to Animals, Wellington, records, MS-Group-89-238, ATL.
36. Winifred Miller, Wellington branch CAWO, to Mabel Howard, 19 September 1953, in Mabel Bowden Howard, MS-Papers-3941, ATL; *New Zealand Parliamentary Debates*, 10 July 1957, p. 741, (Prevention of Cruelty to Animals Bill). The regulations were laid before the House of Representatives in 1951. See schedule of accounts and papers laid upon the table during first session, thirtieth parliament-Meat Act, 1939, order in council making the slaughter of stock regulations 1951, Legislative Department (AEBE), series 18507, record group LE1, box 1373, record 1951/165, ANZ.
37. Elsie K. Morton to Mabel Howard, 18 September 1953, Betty Bisley to Mabel Howard, undated and 19 September [1953], in Mabel Bowden Howard, MS-Papers-3941, ATL; Gee, *Our Mabel*, pp. 205–06; Geoffrey Hodson (1956), *Our Friends the Animals*, Wright and Jacques, Auckland, p. 11.
38. *Parliamentary Debates*, 12 June 1957, p. 10, (Prevention of Cruelty to Animals Bill).
39. Reports of the Agricultural and Pastoral Committee, *AJHR*, 110, 1957, p. 2; Animals Protection Bill, 1959–1960, Ministry of Agriculture and Fisheries (AAFZ), series 7174, acc W1710, box 80, record 2862, ANZ; N.E. Wells (1983), 'The Moral Status of Animals: Reform of animal protection law', LLB Dissertation, University of Auckland Faculty of Law, pp. 29–32.
40. See papers on Animals Protection Bill, 1959-1960, AAFZ, series 7174, acc W1710, box 80, record 2862, ANZ.
41. Wells, 'The Moral Status of Animals', pp. 32–43.
42. A.D.G.M. Laing, 'Notes re official printed sources of veterinary history' and John Lifton, 'Development of companion animal services', pp. 1–2, in 'Historical notes and sources', New Zealand Veterinary Association records, MS-Group-0907, ATL; Veterinary Surgeons Act, 1926; Veterinary Surgeons Act, 1956.
43. Companion Animal Society of the New Zealand Veterinary Association, 'About Us', http://cas.nzva.org.nz/ [accessed 13 April 2013]
44. Notes for 1966 in Morrie Jalfon and Bob Kerridge (1996), *The History of the SPCA Auckland*, The Society, Auckland [np]; Auckland SPCA ninety-third annual report 1976, p. 6 in 'Minute book: Executive Council and Annual General Meetings, September 1974–October 1980', item 14, Society for the Prevention of Cruelty to Animals, Auckland, records, MS 2010/13, AWMM; John Lifton, 'Development of companion animal services', 1–2, 4–5, 7 in 'Historical notes and sources', New Zealand Veterinary Association records, MS-Group-0907, ATL.
45. Memo on letter from Acting Secretary Industries and Commerce to various canning companies, 6 October 1955; Secretary Industries and Commerce to NZ Senior Trade Commissioner, London, 3 October 1956; Secretary Industries and Commerce to Watties, 27 October 1960; J. Watties Cannery to Secretary Industries and Commerce, 28 October 1960; Secretary Industries and Commerce to New Zealand Trade Commissioner, Melbourne, 13 April 1967; in Foodstuffs-Animal food-Pets-Dogs, cats etc, export of, 1954–1967, Department of Industries and Commerce (AEFN), series 19294, record group IC1, box 952, record 15/1/44, ANZ.
46. Secretary Industries and Commerce to Watties, 27 October 1960; Memo from R.J. Gillon to Director of Development Division, Department of Industries and Commerce, 24 November 1965; in Foodstuffs-Pet food-Cats and dogs, 1957–1965, Department of Industries and Commerce (AEFN), series 19294, record group IC1, box 952, record 15/1/43, part 2, ANZ.
47. Copy of article from *Financial Times*, 1957, in Foodstuffs-Pet food-Cats and dogs, 1957–1965, AEFN, series 19294, record group IC1, box 952, record 15/1/43, part 2, ANZ.
48. G.M. Edmonds, Christchurch, to Minister of Agriculture, 20 January 1970 and Minister's reply 24 February 1970, in Pet food manufacture and inspection, 1968–1970, Ministry of Agriculture and Fisheries Head Office (AAFZ), series 7174, acc W1714, box 42, record 21266, part 2, ANZ; *New Zealand Pet Trade News*, vol. 1, no. 3, [nd, but context suggests 1979], p. 6.
49. Lyn Pegram, 'Nestle New Zealand Limited – Marton Factory: historical profile, 1945 to current', typescript, [nd, c. 1994].
50. Catherine Harris, 'Masterpet good company for Ebos', *Dominion Post*, 7 March 2012, C5.
51. See for example 'Pet destruction not thought due to holiday' [unsourced and undated, 1959?] in 'Wellington SPCA Scrapbook, 1947–1976', 89-238-6/1, Society for the Prevention of Cruelty to Animals, Wellington, records, MS-Group-89-238, ATL; 'An "Animotel" with fine facilities', p. 15 and advertisements for 'The Kennels and Kosset Catteries', p. 10, *Pet Pride*, vol. 1, no. 5, August–September 1969.

52 *New Zealand Pet Trade News*, vol. 1, no. 2, August 1979, p. 5.
53 For example, a pet cemetery was established on the outskirts of Christchurch in the late 1970s – see www.bunnylodge.co.nz [accessed 25 February 2011]
54 Rita Thomas, 'Putting on the dog!', *New Zealand Pet News*, February 1983, p. 4.
55 *New Zealand Pet Trade News*, vol. 1, no. 2, August 1979; vol. 1, no. 5, January 1980.
56 D. Lawler, 'A Pet Trade Association for NZ', *New Zealand Pet Trade News*, vol. 1, no. 3, [nd, late 1979?], p. 3.
57 'Special diets for pets', *Pet Pride*, vol. 2, no. 2, February–March 1970, p. 17; Rachael Bowie, 'How much is that cutie in the window? No, really', *Consumer*, July 2007, p. 6.
58 New Zealand Veterinary Association (1977), *Companion Animal Report, 1976*, New Zealand Veterinary Association, Hamilton, pp. 2, 16, 17.
59 *Pets and pedigrees: The magazine for people who care about pets*, May 1981, p. 8.
60 Rabbit Nuisance Act 1882 Amendment Act 1886, s. 5; Agricultural Pests Destruction Amendment Act 1979; 'Bunnies for Easter', *New Zealand Pet Trade News*, vol. 1, no. 6, March 1980, p. 4.
61 *Companion Animal Report 1976*, p. 15; *Marlborough Poultry Pigeon and Cage Bird Association, 1887–1987: Souvenir booklet*, pp. 25, 41.
62 Marianne Gillingham, 'Our best friends get called so many things', *Gisborne Herald*, 16 June 2010, www.gisborneherald.co.nz/article/?id=17810 [accessed 21 May 2011]
63 *New Zealand Farmer: Bee and Poultry Journal*, vol. ix, no. 7, July 1889, p. 273.
64 Clive Dalton, 'The canine conundrum', *New Zealand Geographic*, no. 12, October–December 1991, pp. 43, 46; John Gordon (1998), *Three Sheep and a Dog: An insider's view of New Zealand sheep dog trialling*, Reed, Auckland, pp. 89–90.
65 *New Zealand Kennel Club's Yearbook: Jubilee year 1886–1936* (1936), New Zealand Kennel Club, Wellington, p. 23.
66 Gillingham, 'Our best friends get called so many things'.
67 E.C. Richards (comp.) (1951), *Castle Hill*, Simpson and Williams Ltd, Christchurch, p. 41; Gordon, *Three Sheep and a Dog*, p. 93.
68 Dog Licences–Wanganui, 1858–1868, Wellington Province Government (ACIA), series 16203, record group WP11, box 3/11, ANZ.
69 David Loughrey, 'Top dog names echo world's', *Otago Daily Times*, 7 August 2010, www.odt.co.nz/print/119704 [accessed 21 May 2011]; Kiwi Families website www.kiwifamilies.co.nz/Topics/Babies/Baby-and-You/Baby+Names.html. [accessed 21 May 2011]
70 John Henry Menzies (2003), *Family History to 1877*, Menzies Family History Group, Wellington, pp. 99–100, 117.
71 *Mr Explorer Douglas: John Pascoe's New Zealand classic*, revised by Graham Langton (2000), Canterbury University Press, Christchurch, p. 277.
72 'In touch with nature: notes on natural history in New Zealand by James Drummond, FLS, FZS', *Evening Post*, 18 June 1910, p. 13.
73 *Companion Animal Report 1976*, p. 17.
74 Carolyn Mincham (2008), 'A Social and Cultural History of the New Zealand Horse', PhD thesis (History), Massey University, pp. 221–34; Carolyn Mincham (2011), *Attitude and Heart: The horse in New Zealand*, David Bateman, pp. 149–55.
75 Stewart Lusk (1983), *Dogsbody: The story of the New Zealand Kennel Club*, New Zealand Kennel Club, Wellington, pp. 29, 33, 36, 80–84; 'Agility shows', New Zealand Kennel Club, www.nzkc.org.nz [accessed 26 April 2012]; Dinah Owen, 'The "bride" wore white but had four legs!', *New Zealand Woman's Weekly*, 25 May 1970, pp. 16–18.
76 Gillian Vine (1978), *Longhaired Cats in New Zealand*, Gillian Vine, Gore, p. 47; A.M. Rowlands, 'A history of the Cat Fancy in New Zealand', *New Zealand Cats*, vol. 1, no. 5, January 1984, pp. 9–10; Mrs T. Dixon, 'New Zealand's first international cat show', *Pets and Pedigrees: The magazine for people who care about pets*, November 1981, p. 4.
77 Mark Leishman, 'Death of a pet', www.kiwifamilies.co.nz [accessed 4 February 2011]; Tux Wonderdogs 1999, http://webspace.webring.com [accessed 4 February 2011]
78 Peter Singer (1975:1990), *Animal Liberation*, Avon, New York, p. ii.
79 Tom Regan, 'The case for animal rights', in Peter Singer (ed.) (1985), *In Defense of Animals*, Basil Blackwell, New York, pp. 13–26; Deidre Bourke, 'The use and misuse of 'rights talk' by the animal rights movement', in Peter Sankoff and Steven White (eds) (2009), *Animal Law in Australasia: A new dialogue*, Federation Press, Annandale, NSW, pp. 134–36; Lyle Munro (2005), *Confronting Cruelty: Moral orthodoxy and the challenge of the animal rights movement*, Brill, Leiden, Boston, pp. 2, 6, 16, 18, 55–58; 'Between the species' in *Safeguard*, vol. 1, no. 3, Spring 1992, p. 8.
80 Penelope A. Beynon (2003), 'One Struggle, One Fight! Human Freedom, Animal Rights! Grassroots animal rights activism: incorporating animal liberation and general liberation ideologies', MA thesis (Social Anthropology), Massey University Albany, p. 11.
81 'Founding of society, writings by Bette Overell 1978–1994', 97-267-1/08; *Mobilise for Animals*, no. 2, November 1982, *Mobilise for Animals*, no. 4, May 1983, in 'Mobilise for animals 1982–1986', 97-267-2/10; *Mobilise*, no. 19, September 1987 in 'Mobilise for animals 1987–1993', 97-267-2/11; New Zealand Anti-vivisection Society records, MS-Group-0646, ATL. See also 'Brief history of Anti-vivisection in New Zealand' (written by Bette Overell), www.nzavs.org.nz/about.htm [accessed 20 August 2010]
82 'About SAFE-history', www.safe.org.nz/About-Safe/ [accessed 13 April 2013]; *Newsletter (Save Animals From Experiments)*, November 1981, p. 1.
83 *Newsletter (Save Animals From Experiments)*, February 1981, p. 6; March 1981, p. 1; September 1981, p. 1; September 1982, p. 1.
84 *Newsletter (Save Animals From Experiments)*, March 1981, pp. 6, 11.
85 C.S.W. Reid, 'Ethics, animals, science and the Royal Society', pp. 80–82, and P.J. O'Hara, 'Overview of legislation concerning the use and welfare of experimental animals – New Zealand', p. 9, in *The Use and Welfare of Experimental Animals: Proceedings of the symposium held at the Royal Society of New Zealand*, May 1989, Royal Society of New Zealand, Wellington, 1990. See also Animals Protection Act Amendment Act, 1983 and Animals Protection Act Amendment Act, 1987.
86 'Founding of society, writings by Bette Overell 1978–1994', 97-267-1/08; 'Stop the Vivisectors' Charter', *Mobilise for Animals*, no. 15, July 1986, pp. 6–7, in 'Mobilise for animals 1982–1986', 97-267-2/10; New Zealand Anti-vivisection

Society records, MS-Group-0646, ATL. See also 'Brief history of Anti-vivisection in New Zealand' (written by Bette Overell), www.nzavs.org.nz/about.html [accessed 20 August 2010]

87 *Animal Research Saves Lives: Humans and animals both benefit* (1990), published jointly by the Agricultural Chemical and Animal Remedies Manufacturers Association of New Zealand (AGCARM), the Cancer Society of New Zealand, the New Zealand Heart Foundation, the Medical Research Council of New Zealand and the Ministry of Agriculture and Fisheries, pp. 9, 11.

88 Bette Overell (1993), *Animal Research Takes Lives – Humans and Animals Both Suffer*, NZAVS, Wellington, p. 42.

89 'Obituaries – Bette Overell' and 'About NZAVS', www.nzavs.org.nz/about.html [accessed 20 August 2010]

90 'About SAFE - History', www.safe.org.nz/About-Safe/ [accessed 13 April 2013]; *Safeguard*, vol. 3, no. 1, April–June 1995, p. 11; vol. 3, no. 2, October 1995–January 1996, p. 7; October 1998, p. 3; *SAFE*, March 1999, p. 2.

91 'Rescued hens find freedom', *SAFE*, Autumn/Winter 2003, p. 6.

92 Neil Wells, 'A century of achievement', *Pet Pride*, vol. 2, no. 2, September 1984, p. 10; Veronika Thornburrow (ed.) (1993), *The Compassionate Years: An introduction to the history of the Royal New Zealand Society for the Prevention of Cruelty to Animals*, RNZSPCA, Auckland, pp. 30–31, 37; *Safeguard*, vol. 3, no. 2, October 1995–January 1996, p. 7.

93 New Zealand Companion Animal Council website, http://nzcac.org.nz [accessed 8 October 2010]

94 *SAFE*, October 1999, p. 3.

95 SAFE website, Campaigns, 'Boycott cage eggs', 'Neglected and dying caged hens exposed', www.safe.org.nz/Campaigns/Battery-hens/; 'Pig cruelty factory farming', 'Victory! Sow stalls banned in 5 years!' http://lovepigs.org.nz/Home/ [accessed 24 January 2012]

96 Beynon, 'One Struggle, One Fight!', p. 65.

97 Catriona McLennan, 'Expert evidence crucial under Animal Welfare Act', *New Zealand Lawyer*, 28 June 2001, no. 12, p. 14.

98 Lesley-Anne Petrie, 'Companion animals: Valuation and treatment in human society', in *Animal Law in Australasia*, p. 61.

99 Bowie, 'How much is that cutie in the window?, p. 6.

100 Ibid., p. 8.

101 Lucy Vickers, 'The price of love is high even for pets', *Dominion Post*, 2 January 2009, A7.

102 Bowie, 'How much is that cutie in the window?', p. 6.

Bibliography

Manuscripts and archives

Alexander Turnbull Library (ATL)
Mabel Bowden Howard papers, MS-Papers-3941
New Zealand Anti-Vivisection Society, records, MS-Group-0646
New Zealand Veterinary Association, records, MS-Group-0907
Society for the Prevention of Cruelty to Animals (SPCA), Wellington Inc., records, MS-Group-89-238
Upper Hutt Animal Rescue Society Inc, papers, MS-Papers-4953

Auckland War Memorial Museum (AWMM)
Society for the Prevention of Cruelty to Animals (SPCA), Auckland, records, MS 2010/13

Archives New Zealand, Wellington (ANZ)
Army Department (AAYS)
Department of Conservation Head Office (AANS)
Department of Health Head Office (AAFB)
Department of Industries and Commerce (AEFN)
Department of Internal Affairs Head Office [record group] (ACGO)
Department of Internal Affairs Head Office (AAAC)
Education Department (ACIG)
Legislative Department (AEBE)
Ministry of Agriculture and Fisheries (AAFZ)
Ministry of Health Head Office (ABQU)
New Zealand Customs Service Head Office (AALN)
New Zealand Government Railways Department, General Manager's Office (AAEB)
New Zealand Police National Headquarters (AAAJ)
New Zealand Railways (ADQD)
Police Department (ACIS)
Registrar of Companies, Wellington (ADSN)
Second World War Archives (ADQZ)
State Services Commission (AEKO)
State Services Commission Head Office (AAFH)
Taranaki Education Board, Residual Management Unit (ABDU)
Tourist and Publicity Department (AECB)
War Archives (ACID)
Wellington Province Government (ACIA)

Official publications
Appendices to the Journals of the House of Representatives (AJHR)
New Zealand Parliamentary Debates
New Zealand Gazette

Research websites
Te Ara: the Encyclopedia of New Zealand (including the Dictionary of New Zealand Biography) www.teara.govt.nz
New Zealand History online www.nzhistory.net.nz
New Zealand Acts As Enacted (New Zealand Legal Information Institute) http://www.nzlii.org.nz/nz/legis/hist_act/
Papers Past (National Library of New Zealand) http://paperspast.natlib.govt.nz/cgi-bin/paperspast
Trove (National Library of Australia) http://trove.nla.gov.au

Periodicals and annual reports
Annual reports, Auckland Society for the Prevention of Cruelty to Animals, 1883–2010
Annual report, Canterbury Society for the Prevention of Cruelty to Animals, 1927
Annual reports, Otago Society for the Prevention of Cruelty to Animals, 1905, 1925
Annual report, Palmerston North Society for the Prevention of Cruelty to Animals, 1927
Annual reports, New Zealand Society for the Protection of Women and Children and Prevention of Cruelty to Animals, 1905, 1911, 1912, 1914, 1915, 1921, 1922, 1925
Annual reports, Wellington Society for the Prevention of Cruelty to Animals, 1894–1982
Cats: Newsletter of the Cats Protection League (Wellington) Inc, 1983–1988 (*CPL News: Newsletter of the Cats Protection League (Wellington) Inc*, 1998–2009)
Dominion Bulletin (RNZSPCA), 1980–83
New Zealand Band of Mercy, 1897
New Zealand Cats: The official publication of the New Zealand Cat Fancy Inc, 1976–1979 (*New Zealand Cats: Official magazine of the New Zealand Cat Fancy Inc*, 1982–98)
New Zealand Farmer: Bee and Poultry Journal (*New Zealand Farmer Stock and Station Journal*), 1885–1936
New Zealand Pet Trade News, 1978–80 (*New Zealand Pet News*, 1980–83)
New Zealand Poultry Journal, 1906–28
New Zealand Schoolmaster: A monthly educational journal and review, 1881–89 (*New Zealand Schoolmaster and educational review*, 1905–08)
News from the Waikato SPCA: Newsletter, 1974–80
Newsletter (Save Animals From Experiments), 1981-82 (*Safeguard: Newsletter of Save Animals From Experiments*, 1983-1998)
Pet New Zealand: The magazine for all animal lovers, 1997–2005 (*Pet: The magazine for all animal lovers*, 2005–12)
Pet Pride (Wellington SPCA), 1968–88
Pets and Pedigrees: The magazine for people who care about animals, 1981
Postman: Annual magazine of the Correspondence School, 1928–2002
SAFE: New Zealand's leading animal rights journal, 1999–2010
School Journal, 1907–18 (*NZ School Journal*, 1919–36)
Waikato SPCA President's Report, 1973, 1975

Books and pamphlets
Human–animal studies
Coetzee, J. M. (1999), *The Lives of Animals*, Princeton University Press, Princeton, New Jersey
Fudge, Erica (2002), *Animal*, Reaktion Books, London
Fudge, Erica (2008), *Pets*, Acumen, Stocksfield
Grier, Katherine C. (2007), *Pets in America: A history*, Harvest, Orlando, Florida
Harrison, Brian (1982), *Peaceable Kingdom: Stability and change in modern Britain*, Clarendon Press, Oxford
Henninger-Voss, Mary J. (ed.) (2002), *Animals in Human Histories: The mirror of nature and culture*, University of Rochester Press, New York

Kete, Kathleen (1994), *The Beast in the Boudoir: Petkeeping in nineteenth-century Paris*, University of California Press, Berkeley

MacDonogh, Katharine (1999), *Reigning Cats and Dogs: A history of pets at court since the Renaissance*, St Martin's Press, New York

Pierce, Jessica (2012), *The Last Walk: Reflections on our pets at the end of their lives*, University of Chicago Press, Chicago

Podberscek, Anthony L., Elizabeth S. Paul and James A. Serpell (eds) (2000), *Exploring the Relationships Between People and Pets*, Cambridge University Press, Cambridge

Ritvo, Harriet (1987), *The Animal Estate: The English and other creatures in the Victorian age*, Harvard University Press, Cambridge, Massachusetts

Sankoff, Peter J. and Steven William White (eds) (2009), *Animal Law in Australasia: A new dialogue*, Federation Press, Sydney

Serpell, James (1986), *In the Company of Animals: A study of human–animal relationships*, Basil Blackwell, Oxford

Serpell, James (ed.) (1995), *The Domestic Dog: Its evolution, behaviour and interactions with people*, Cambridge University Press, Cambridge

Simmons, Laurence and Philip Armstrong (eds) (2007), *Knowing Animals*, Brill, Leiden, Boston

Thomas, Keith (1984), *Man and the Natural World: Changing attitudes in England 1500–1800*, Penguin, London

Titcomb, Margaret (1969), *Dog and Man in the Ancient Pacific*, Bernice P. Bishop Museum Special Publication 59, Honolulu, Hawaii

Turner, James (1980), *Reckoning with the Beast: Animals, pain and humanity in the Victorian mind*, Johns Hopkins University Press, Baltimore

Animal welfare and rights

Amey, Catherine (2008), *Clean, Green, and Cruelty Free: The true story of animals in New Zealand*, Rebel Press, Wellington

Animal Research Saves Lives: Humans and animals both benefit (1990), published jointly by the Agricultural Chemical and Animal Remedies Manufacturers Association of New Zealand (AGCARM), the Cancer Society of New Zealand, the New Zealand Heart Foundation, the Medical Research Council of New Zealand and the Ministry of Agriculture and Fisheries

Hodson, Geoffrey (1946:1963), *The Humanitarian Cause: Its extreme urgency*, CAWO, Auckland

Hodson, Geoffrey (1947), *The Case for the Abolition of Vivisection: An examination of the proposition that vivisection is justified by the benefits it confers upon humanity*, Auckland Branch of the British Union for the Abolition of Vivisection, Auckland

Hodson, Geoffrey (1956), *Our Friends the Animals*, Wright and Jacques, Auckland

Jalfon, Morrie and Bob Kerridge (April 1996), *The History of the SPCA Auckland*, The Society, Auckland

Kean, Hilda (1998), *Animal Rights: Political and social change in Britain since 1800*, Reaktion Books, London

Moss, A.W. (1961), *Valiant Crusade: The history of the RSPCA*, Cassell, London

Munro, Lyle (2005), *Confronting Cruelty: Moral orthodoxy and the challenge of the animal rights movement*, Brill, Leiden, Boston

New Zealand Companion Animal Council (2011), *Companion Animals in New Zealand, July 2011*, NZCAC, Auckland

New Zealand Veterinary Association (1977), *Companion Animal Report, 1976*, New Zealand Veterinary Association, Hamilton

Niven, Charles D. (1967), *History of the Humane Movement*, Transatlantic Arts Inc., New York

Overell, Bette (1993), *Animal Research Takes Lives – Humans and Animals Both Suffer*, NZAVS, Wellington

Salt, Henry S. (1892), *Animals' Rights: Considered in relation to social progress*, George Bell and Sons, London

Schultz, William J. (1924:1968), *The Humane Movement in the United States, 1910–1922*, AMS Press, New York [first published by Columbia University Press, New York, 1924]

Singer, Peter (1975:1990), *Animal Liberation*, Avon Books, New York (new revised edition)

Singer, Peter (ed.) (1985), *In Defense of Animals*, Basil Blackwell, New York

Thornburrow, Veronika (ed.) (1993), *The Compassionate Years: An introduction to the history of the Royal New Zealand Society for the Prevention of Cruelty to Animals*, RNZSPCA, Auckland

The Use and Welfare of Experimental Animals: Proceedings of the symposium held at the Royal Society of New Zealand, May 1989 (1990), Royal Society of New Zealand, Wellington

Accounts of animals

Alpers, Antony (1960), *Dolphins*, Paul's Book Arcade, Auckland

Cowan, James (1911), *Pelorus Jack: The white dolphin of French Pass, New Zealand, with Maori legends*, Whitcombe and Tombs, Christchurch

Donald, Ella (2009), *Luke: The story of a police dog, his remarkable life and the 'Downtown' shooting*, Vision Through Communication Ltd, Auckland

Field, Jim (1993), *Backtracking*, Wairarapa Times-Age Co. Ltd, Masterton

Field, T.A.H. (1910), *The Story of Pelorus Jack: The famous white dolphin which meets and pilots steamers in Cook's Strait, New Zealand*, A.G. Betts, Nelson

Gordon, John (1998), *Three Sheep and a Dog: An insider's view of New Zealand sheep dog trialling*, Reed, Auckland

Hemfield, T. [T.A.H. Field] (1906), *Wonders of the World: Pelorus Jack, the mysterious New Zealand fish*

MacGregor Redwood, Miriam (1980), *A Dog's Life: Working dogs in New Zealand*, Reed, Wellington

Mincham, Carolyn (2011), *Attitude and Heart: The horse in New Zealand*, David Bateman, Auckland

Orbell, Margaret (2003), *Birds of Aotearoa: A natural and cultural history*, Reed, Auckland

Perriam, John (2010), *Shrek, the Story of a Kiwi Icon*, Random House, Auckland

Potts, Annie (2012), *Chicken*, Reaktion Books, London

Reischek, Andreas (1889:1984), *The Story of a Wonderful Dog: With some notes on the training of dogs and horses: also hints on camping, bush and mountain exploration in New Zealand*, Capper Press, Christchurch [facsimile of edition published *Star*, Auckland, 1889]

Riley, Murdoch (2001), *Maori Bird Lore: An introduction*, Viking Sevenseas NZ Ltd, Paraparaumu

Salt, Valerie and Colin (1972), *Born to Obey*, Collins, Auckland

Spencer, Graham (1987), *The Four-legged Major*, Grantham House, Wellington

Vine, Gillian (1978), *Longhaired Cats in New Zealand*, Gillian Vine, Gore

Whyte, William (192–), *The Sheep-dog: Judging and conduct of trials and the art of breaking-in*, Whitcombe and Tombs, Auckland

New Zealand animal-related clubs and organisations

Catalogue of the First Annual Show of the Christchurch Poultry Association, held in the Town Hall, Christchurch, 1 August 1868, (1868), The Association, Christchurch

Catalogue of the First Annual Show of the Hawkes Bay Poultry and Canary Association held in the Protestant Hall, Napier, on 26th & 27th September 1879 (1879), The Association, Napier

Catalogue of the Fourth Annual Show of the Sydenham Poultry, Pigeon and Canary Society held in the Oddfellows Hall, Sydenham, August 5 & 6, 1885, (1885), The Society, Christchurch

Catalogue of the Seventeenth Annual Show of the Christchurch Poultry, Pigeon and Canary Society held in the Oddfellows Hall, Christchurch, July 2 & 3, 1884. Also of the Cat Show held in connection with the above (1884), The Society, Christchurch

Eyre Group Boys' and Girls' Agricultural Clubs [1963], *Schedule of project and programme for stock parade*

Grigg, Joanna (1999), *Sheepdogs on Dry Hills: A history of the Marlborough Collie Dog Trial Club 1899–1999*, Marlborough Collie Dog Trial Club, Blenheim

Herron, Jill (2003), *Trials and Dogs of the South: A history of sheep dog trialling in Southland*, Southland Dog Trial Association, Gore

Lusk, Stewart (1983), *Dogsbody: The story of the New Zealand Kennel Club*, New Zealand Kennel Club, Wellington

Marlborough Poultry Pigeon and Cage Bird Association, 1887–1987: Souvenir booklet (1987), The Association, Blenheim

Matheson, Ross and Sally, and Anne Jameson (eds) (1994), *Waiau Pa School Calf Club, 1944–1994*, R. and S. Matheson, Waiau Pa

New Zealand Kennel Club's Yearbook: Jubilee year 1886–1936 (1936), New Zealand Kennel Club, Wellington

Ries, Rex (1996), *A History of the Northland Sheep Dog Trial Movement*, Northland Sheep Dog Trial Centre Archives, Kaiwaka

Tombleson, John (2009), *Sheep Dog Trialling in Poverty Bay and Beyond*, Poverty Bay Centre of the New Zealand Sheep Dog Trial Association, Gisborne

Wellington Education Board, Agricultural and Science Instruction Section (1952), *Your School Agricultural Club*, Wellington Education Board, Wellington

Wright, Christine (1996), *Whistles in the Wind: The story of the Methven Collie Club 1896–1996*, Methven Collie Club, Ashburton

Children's books

Acres, Avis (1956), *Opo the Gay Dolphin*, A.H. and A.W. Reed, Wellington

Anderson, Mona (1975), *Mary-Lou: The story of a high-country lamb*, A.H. and A.W. Reed, Wellington

Aylmer, Mrs J.E. (1862), *Distant Homes; Or the Graham family in New Zealand*, Griffith and Farran, London

Brocker, Susan (2010), *Brave Bess and the ANZAC Horses*, HarperCollins, Auckland

Cossgrove, D. (1917), *The Story of a Bull Pup: Official handbook of the junior scouts of New Zealand*, Lyttelton Times Co., Christchurch

Cossgrove, D. (1918), *The Empire Sentinel's Handbook and Ritual*, Andrews, Batty and Co., Christchurch

Haworth, Dianne (2008), *Paddy the Wanderer*, HarperCollins, Auckland

Hibberd, Shirley [nd, c. 1867], *Clever Dogs, Horses, etc: With anecdotes of other animals*, S.W. Partridge and Co., London

Parker, G.H. (1945), *'Jack': A true story of a clever New Zealand farm dog*, Auckland Sunday School Union, Auckland

Stroud, Patricia (2003), *Caesar: The Anzac dog*, HarperCollins, Auckland

The students of Tarras School; illustrated by Jenny Chisholm (2004), *Shrek the Famous Hermit Sheep of Tarras*, Tarras School, Tarras

Diaries, letters, chronicles and memoirs

A Year at Hawkswood: The diary of Frances Caverhill for 1865 (1981), vol. 1: January–June, Nag's Head Press, Christchurch

A Year at Hawkswood: The diary of Frances Caverhill for 1865 (1981), vol. 2: July–December, Nag's Head Press, Christchurch

Angas, George French (1847), *Savage Life and Scenes in Australia and New Zealand; Being an artist's impression of countries and people in the antipodes; with numerous illustrations*, 2 vols, Smith, Elder and Co., London

Barker, Mary Anne (1873), *Station Amusements in New Zealand*, William Hunt, London

Bennett, Francis (1980), *A Canterbury Tale: The autobiography of Dr Francis Bennett*, Oxford University Press, Wellington

Bradshaw, John (1883), *New Zealand As It Is*, Sampson Low, Marston, Searle and Rivington, London

Buller, James (1878), *Forty Years in New Zealand: Including a personal narrative, an account of Maoridom, and of the Christianization and colonization of the country*, Hodder and Stoughton, London

Butler, Annie R. (1886), *Glimpses of Maoriland*, The Religious Tract Society, London

Butler, Samuel (1863:1997), *A First Year in Canterbury Settlement*, Kiwi Publishers, Christchurch [facsimile of edition published Longman, London, 1863]

Chadfield, Philip B. (1862:1875), *Out at Sea, or, the Emigrant Afloat: Being a hand book of practical information for the use of passengers on a long sea voyage*, Chadfield, Derby [first published 1862]

Clarke, George (1903), *Notes on Early Life in New Zealand*, J. Walch and Sons, Hobart

Courage, Sarah Amelia (1896:1976), *Lights and Shadows of Colonial Life: Twenty-six years in Canterbury*, Whitcoulls, Christchurch [first published Whitcombe and Tombs, Christchurch, 1896]

Cruise, Richard A. (1824:1974), *Journal of a Ten Months' Residence in New Zealand*, Capper Press, Christchurch [facsimile of edition published Longman, Hurst, Rees, Orme, Brown, and Green, London, 1824]

Deans, John III (ed.) (1937:1997), *Pioneers of Canterbury: Deans family letters, 1840–1854*, Cadsonbury Publications, Christchurch [first published A.H. and A.W. Reed, Dunedin, 1937]

Dieffenbach, Ernest (1843:1974), *Travels in New Zealand: With contributions to the geography, geology, botany and natural history of that country*, 2 vols, Capper Press, Christchurch [facsimile of edition published John Murray, London, 1843]

Drummond, Alison (1960), *Married and Gone to New Zealand: Being extracts from the writings of women pioneers*, Paul's Book Arcade, Hamilton

Drummond, Alison (ed.) (1982), *The Waikato Journals of Vicesimus Lush, 1864–8, 1881–2*, Pegasus Press, Christchurch

Elder, J.R. (ed.) (1932), *The Letters and Journals of Samuel Marsden 1765–1838*, Coulls Somerville Wilkie Ltd and A.H. Reed for the Otago University Council, Dunedin

Elkington, E.W. (1906), *Adrift in New Zealand*, John Murray, London

Extracts from the letters and journals addressed to members of his family, by Percy Whitehead; selected by Elizabeth Malleson (1900), privately printed

Forster, Georg, *A Voyage Round the World*, Nicholas Thomas and Oliver Berghof (eds), assisted by Jennifer Newell (c. 2000), 2 vols. University of Hawaii Press, Honolulu

Gilkison, Robert (1930), *Early Days in Central Otago: Being tales of times gone by*, Otago Daily Times and Witness newspapers, Dunedin

Godley, John R. (ed.) (1951), *Letters from Early New Zealand by Charlotte Godley, 1850–1853*, Whitcombe and Tombs, Christchurch

Hewett, Ellen (1910:1921), *Looking Back or personal reminiscences by the widow of a New Zealand pioneer settler*, Campfield Press, St Albans [first published 1910]

Hochstetter, Ferdinand von (1867), *New Zealand: Its physical geography, geology and natural history with special reference to the results of government expeditions in the provinces of Auckland and Nelson*, J.G. Cotta, Stuttgart

Howitt, W.K. (1947), *A Pioneer Looks Back*, Oswald-Sealy Ltd, Auckland

Hursthouse, Charles (1857), *New Zealand or Zealandia, the Britain of the south*, 2 vols, Edward Standford, London

Jameson, Agnes (1916), *Old Memories*, Smith and Anthony, Christchurch

The Journal of Edward Ward 1850–5: being his account of the voyage to New Zealand in the Charlotte Jane and the first six months of the Canterbury settlement (1951), Pegasus Press, Christchurch

Kennaway, Laurence J. (1874:1996), *Crusts: A settler's fare due south*, Kiwi Publishers, Christchurch [facsimile of edition published Sampson Low, Marston, Low and Searle, London, 1874]

Koebel, W.H. (1911), *In the Maoriland Bush*, Stanley Paul and Co., London

Letters from Settlers and Labouring Emigrants in the New Zealand Company's Settlements of Wellington, Nelson and New Plymouth: from February, 1842, to January, 1843 (1843), Smith, Elder and Co., London

Menzies, John Henry (2003), *Family History to 1877*, Menzies Family History Group, Wellington

Morton, Elsie K. (1929), *Joy of the Road*, Wilson and Horton, Auckland

Mueller, M.V. (ed.) (1958), *My Dear Bannie: Gerhard Mueller's letters from the West Coast 1865–6*, Pegasus Press, Christchurch

Nordhoff, Charles (1857), *Stories of the Island World*, Harper and Brothers, New York

Northcroft, Brenda Guthrie (1930:1959), *New Zealand Memories*, Reed, Wellington [first published John Lane, London, 1930]

The Old-time Maori: by Makereti, some-time chieftainess of the Arawa tribe, known in New Zealand as Maggie Papakura; collected and edited with a bibliography by T. K. Penniman (1938), Victor Gollancz, London

Park, Ruth (1993), *A Fence around the Cuckoo*, Penguin, Auckland

Polack, J.S. (1838:1974), *New Zealand: Being a narrative of travels and adventures during a residence in that country between the years 1831 and 1837*, 2 vols, Capper Press, Christchurch [facsimile of edition published Richard Bentley, London, 1838]

Porter, Frances, Charlotte Macdonald with Tui MacDonald (eds) (1996), *'My Hand Will Write What My Heart Dictates': The unsettled lives of women in nineteenth-century New Zealand as revealed to sisters, family and friends*, Auckland University Press/Bridget Williams Books, Auckland

Rochfort, John (1853:1974), *The Adventures of a Surveyor in New Zealand and the Australian Gold Diggings*, Capper Press, Christchurch [facsimile of edition published David Bogue, London, 1853]

Saunders, Alfred (1927:2003), *Tales of a Pioneer: Episodes in the life of Alfred Saunders*, Cadsonbury Publications, Christchurch [facsimile of edition published L.M. Isitt, Christchurch, 1927]

Scherzer, Karl (1863), *Narrative of the Circumnavigation of the Globe by the Austrian Frigate, Novara*, 3 vols, Saunders, Otley and Co., London

Starke, June (ed.) (1986), *The Journal of a Rambler, by John Boultbee*, Oxford University Press, Auckland

Stewart, Adela B. (1908:1995), *My Simple Life in New Zealand*, Southern Reprints, Auckland [facsimile of edition published Robert Banks and Son, London, 1908]

'Taken in' being a sketch of New Zealand life by 'Hopeful' (1887:1974), Capper Press, Christchurch [facsimile of edition published W.H. Allen, London, 1887]

Taylor, Richard (1855), *Ika a Maui, or, New Zealand and its inhabitants*, Wertheim and Macintosh, London

Tikao Talks: Ka taoka o te ao kohatu. Treasures from the ancient world of the Maori. Told by Teone Taare Tikao to Herries Beattie (1939:1990), Penguin Books, Auckland [first published A.H. and A.W. Reed, Dunedin, 1939]

Tripp, Ellen Shepard (1929), *My Early Days*, Whitcombe and Tombs, Christchurch

Tunnicliff, Shirley (ed.) (1992), *The Selected Letters of Mary Hobhouse*, Daphne Brasell Associates Press, Wellington

Wakefield, Edward (1889), *New Zealand After Fifty Years*, Cassell and Company, New York

Wakefield, Edward Jerningham (1845:1971), *Adventure in New Zealand from 1839 to 1844: With some account of the beginning of the British colonization of the islands*, 2 vols, Wilson and Horton, Auckland [facsimile of edition published John Murray, London, 1845]

Wakefield, Edward Jerningham (1848), *The Handbook for New Zealand: Consisting of the most recent information compiled for the use of intending colonists by a late magistrate of the colony*, John W. Parker, London

Ward, John (1840:1988), *Information Relative to New Zealand Compiled for the Use of Colonists*, Kiwi Publishers, Christchurch [facsimile of edition published John W. Parker, London, 1840]

Wilson, Helen (1950), *My First Eighty Years*, Paul's Book Arcade, Hamilton

Wilson, W. Stuart (1920), *An Appeal to the Prince of Wales*, Whitcombe and Tombs, Auckland

Wright, David McKee (1897), *Station Ballads and Other Verses*, J.G. Sawell, Dunedin

General, local and military histories

Andrews, John (2009), *No Other Home than This: A history of European New Zealanders*, Craig Potton Publishing, Nelson

Atkinson, Neill (2001), *Crew Culture: New Zealand seafarers under sail and steam*, Te Papa Press, Wellington

Atkinson, Neill (2007), *Trainland: How railways made New Zealand*, Random House, Auckland

Barrington, John (2008), *Separate but Equal: Maori schools and the Crown, 1867–1969*, Victoria University Press, Wellington

Belich, James (1996), *Making Peoples: A history of the New Zealanders from Polynesian settlement to the end of the nineteenth century*, Allen Lane/The Penguin Press, Auckland

Belich, James (2001), *Paradise Reforged: A history of the New Zealanders from the 1880s to the year 2000*, Allen Lane/The Penguin Press, Auckland

Berry, Ken (1986), *Scrutiny on the County*, Marlborough County Council, Blenheim

Best, Elsdon (1942:1977), *Forest Lore of the Maori*, Dominion Museum Bulletin no. 14 and Polynesian Society Memoir no. 18, Government Print, Wellington [first published Polynesian Society and Dominion Museum, Wellington, 1942]

Betts, C.H. (ed.) (1983), *A Centennial History of Egmont Agricultural and Pastoral Association Inc, 1883–1983*, The Association, Hawera

Butterworth, Susan (1993), *The Department of Education 1877–1989: A guide to its development*, Ministry of Education, Wellington

Butterworth, Susan (2005), *More than Law and Order: Policing a changing society 1945–92*, Otago University Press, Dunedin

Clarke, Alison (2007), *Holiday Seasons: Christmas, New Year and Easter in nineteenth century New Zealand*, Auckland University Press, Auckland

Cochrane, Peter (1992), *Simpson and the Donkey: The making of a legend*, Melbourne University Press, Melbourne

Coney, Sandra (1993), *Standing in the Sunshine: A history of New Zealand women since they won the vote*, Penguin, Auckland

Crawford, John and Ellen Ellis (1999), *To Fight for the Empire: An illustrated history of New Zealand and the South African war, 1899–1902*, Reed, Auckland

Culliford, S.G. (1958), *New Zealand Scouting: The first fifty years 1908–1958*, Boy Scouts Association of New Zealand, Wellington

Dalziel, Raewyn (1993), *Focus on the Family: The Auckland Home and Family Society 1893–1993*, Home and Family Society, Auckland

Derby, Mark (2009), *The Prophet and the Policeman: The story of Rua Kenana and John Cullen*, Craig Potton Publishing, Nelson

Druett, Joan (1983), *Exotic Intruders: The introduction of plants and animals into New Zealand*, Heinemann, Auckland

Drummond, Alison and L.R. Drummond (1965), *At Home in New Zealand: An illustrated history of everyday things before 1865*, Blackwood and Janet Paul, Auckland

Dunmore, John (1991), *Around the Shining Waters: A history of Featherston County Council*, Heritage Press Ltd, Waikanae

Eggleton, David (2006), *Into the Light: A history of New Zealand photography*, Craig Potton Publishing, Nelson

Ewing, John L. (1970), *Development of the New Zealand Primary School Curriculum 1877–1970*, New Zealand Council for Educational Research, Wellington

Fairburn, Miles (1995), *Nearly out of Heart and Hope: The puzzle of a colonial labourer's diary*, Auckland University Press, Auckland

Galbreath, Ross (1993), *Working for Wildlife: A history of the New Zealand Wildlife Service*, Bridget Williams Books and Historical Branch, Department of Internal Affairs, Wellington

Gee, David (1977), *Our Mabel*, Millwood Press, Wellington

Grant, David (1994), *On a Roll: A history of gambling and lotteries in New Zealand*, Victoria University Press, Wellington

Harris, Diana (2007), *Johnny Jones: A colonial saga*, Reed, Auckland

Harris, Jan (1994), *Tōhora: The story of Fyffe House, Kai Koura*, New Zealand Historic Places Trust, Wellington

Hill, Richard S. (1989), *The Colonial Frontier Tamed: New Zealand policing in transition, 1867–1886*, Historical Branch, Department of Internal Affairs/GP Books, Wellington

Hill, Richard (1995), *The Iron Hand in the Velvet Glove: The modernisation of policing in New Zealand 1886–1917*, Dunmore Press in association with the New Zealand Police and the Historical Branch, Department of Internal Affairs, Palmerston North

Host, Emily (2006), *Thomas Brunner: His life and great journeys*, Nikau Press, Nelson

Hunter, Ian (2009), *Farmers: Your store for 100 years*, HarperCollins, Auckland

Hunter, Kate (2009), *Hunting: A New Zealand history*, Random House, Auckland

Iles, Marie (1976), *65 Years of Guiding 1908–1973: The official history of the Girl Guides Association NZ (Inc)*, Girl Guides Association New Zealand (Inc.), Christchurch

Jackson, W.K. (1972), *The New Zealand Legislative Council: A study of the establishment, failure and abolition of an Upper House*, Otago University Press, Dunedin

Joblin, Dorothea (1970), *Behold the Plains: The story of the old houses of Massey*, Longman Paul, Auckland

Joblin, Dorothea (1975), *The Colonial One: Lorna Monckton of Newstead*, Whitcombe and Tombs, Christchurch

King, Michael (1986), *Maori: A social and photographic history*, Penguin, Auckland

King, Michael (2003), *Te Puea: A life*, Reed, Auckland

Kinloch, Terry (2007), *Devils on Horses: In the words of the Anzacs in the Middle East 1916–19*, Exisle Publishing, Auckland

Lee, John A. (1977), *Roughnecks, Rolling Stones and Rouseabouts: With an anthology of early swagger literature*, Whitcoulls, Christchurch

Maclean, Chris and Jock Phillips (1990), *The Sorrow and the Pride: New Zealand war memorials*, Historical Branch, Department of Internal Affairs/GP Books, Wellington

MacLeod, Nellie F.H. (1955), *A Voice on the Wind: The story of Jessie Mackay*, A.H. and A.W. Reed, Wellington

Martin, John E. (1990), *The Forgotten Worker: The rural wage earner in nineteenth-century New Zealand*, Allen and Unwin/Trade Union History Project, Wellington

McCallum, Janet (2009), *Women and Their Words: Notable pioneers in New Zealand journalism*, Fraser Books, Masterton

McCormick, E.H. (1981), *Portrait of Frances Hodgkins*, Auckland University Press, Auckland

McDowall, R.M. (1994), *Gamekeepers for the Nation: The story of New Zealand's acclimatisation societies 1861–1990*, Canterbury University Press, Christchurch

McGibbon, Ian (ed.) (2000), *The Oxford Companion to New Zealand Military History*, Oxford University Press, Auckland

McLean, Gavin (2006), *The Governors: New Zealand's Governors and Governors-General*, Otago University Press, Dunedin

McLean, Gavin and Tim Shoebridge (2010), *Quarantine! Protecting New Zealand at the border*, Otago University Press, Dunedin

McNeish, James (1972), *The Mackenzie Affair*, Hodder and Stoughton, Auckland

Moore, A. Briscoe (1920), *The Mounted Riflemen in Sinai and Palestine: The story of New Zealand's crusaders*, Whitcombe and Tombs, Auckland

Mr Explorer Douglas: John Pascoe's New Zealand classic, revised by Graham Langton (2000), Canterbury University Press, Christchurch

New Zealand Country Women's Institute (1994), *School Days*, New Zealand Country Women's Institute, Wellington

Nicol, C.G. (1921), *The Story of Two Campaigns: Official war history of the Auckland Mounted Rifles Regiment*, Wilson and Horton, Auckland

Olssen, Erik (1995), *Building the New World: Work, politics and society in Caversham, 1880s–1920s*, Auckland University Press, Auckland

Petersen, Anna K.C. (2001), *New Zealanders at Home: A cultural history of domestic interiors 1814–1914*, University of Otago Press, Dunedin

Phillips, Jock (1987), *A Man's Country? The image of the Pakeha male – a history*, Penguin, Auckland

Phillips, Jock and Terry Hearn (2008), *Settlers: New Zealand immigrants from England, Ireland and Scotland 1800–1945*, Auckland University Press, Auckland

Powles, C. Guy (1922), *The New Zealanders in Sinai and Palestine*, Whitcombe and Tombs, Auckland

Powles, C.G., H.G. Alexander and H.A. Lockington (1927), *Official History of the New Zealand Engineers During the Great War 1914–1919*, Evans, Cobb and Sharpe Ltd, Wanganui

Puckey, Adrienne (2011), *Trading Cultures: A history of the Far North*, Huia, Wellington

Richards, E.C. (comp.) (1951), *Castle Hill*, Simpson and Williams Ltd, Christchurch

Salmond, Anne (1991), *Two Worlds: First meetings between Maori and Europeans, 1642–1772*, Viking, Auckland

Salmond, Anne (1997), *Between Worlds: Early exchanges between Maori and Europeans 1773–1815*, Viking/Penguin Books, Auckland

Salmond, Anne (2003), *The Trial of the Cannibal Dog: Captain Cook in the South Seas*, Allen Lane/Penguin Press, London

Scott, Keith (2011), *Dear Dot I Must Tell You: A personal history of young New Zealanders*, Activity Press, Auckland

Seager, Madeleine (1987), *Edward William Seager: Pioneer of mental health*, Heritage Press, Waikanae

Simmons, D.R. (1976), *The Great New Zealand Myth: A study of the discovery and origin traditions of the Maori*, A.H. and A.W. Reed, Wellington

Sinclair, D.W. (1954), *19 Battalion and Armoured Regiment*, Historical Publications Branch, Wellington

Sugden, A.H.L. (1947), *Pacific Saga: The personal chronicle of the 37th battalion and its part in the Third Division's campaign*, A.H. and A.W. Reed for the Third Division Histories Committees, Wellington

Sutton-Smith, Brian (1982), *A History of Children's Play in New Zealand, 1840–1950*, New Zealand Council of Educational Research, Wellington

Thomson, G.M. (1922), *The Naturalisation of Animals and Plants in New Zealand*, Canterbury University Press, Christchurch

Tod, Frank (1977), *Lionel Terry: The making of a madman*, Otago Foundation Books, Dunedin

Walker, Timothy (1985), *Robley: Te Ropere, 1840–1930*, Auckland University Press, Auckland

Wilson, R.C. (1978), *Wairoa County Council: The first hundred years*, Wairoa County Council, Wairoa

Wright St-Clair, R.E. (1987), *Caring for People: Wanganui Hospital Board, 1885–1985*, Wanganui Hospital Board Centennial Committee, Wanganui

Young, David (2004), *Our Islands, Ourselves: A history of conservation in New Zealand*, University of Otago Press, Dunedin

Articles and papers

Allen, Melinda S., Elizabeth Matisoo-Smith and Ann Horsburgh, 'Pacific "Babes": issues in the origins and dispersal of Pacific pigs and the potential of mitochondrial DNA analysis', *International Journal of Osteoarchaeology*, vol. 11, issue 1–2, 2001, 4–13

Anderson, A.J. and G. Clark, 'Advances in New Zealand mammalogy 1990–2000: Polynesian dog or kuri', *Journal of the Royal Society of New Zealand*, vol. 31, no. 1, March 2001, 161–63

Bay-Petersen, Jay, 'Competition for resources: the role of the pig and dog in the Polynesian agricultural economy', *Journal de la Societe des Oceanistes*, vol. 77, 1983, 121–29

Clark, Geoffrey, 'Family canidae: kuri', in Carolyn M. King (ed.) (2005), *Handbook of New Zealand Mammals*, Oxford University Press, Auckland, pp. 255–60

Clarke, C.M.H. and R.M. Dzieciolowski, 'Feral pigs in the northern South Island, New Zealand: I. Origin, distribution and density', *Journal of the Royal Society of New Zealand*, vol. 21, no. 3, 1991, 249–60

Colenso, W., 'Notes, chiefly historical, on the ancient dog of the New Zealanders', *Transactions of the New Zealand Institute*, vol. 10, 1877, 135–55

Colenso, W., 'Vestiges: reminiscences: memorabilia of works, deeds and sayings of the ancient Maoris', *Transactions of the New Zealand Institute*, vol. 24, 1891, 445–95

Dalton, Clive, 'The canine conundrum', *New Zealand Geographic*, no. 12, October–December 1991, 28–46

Galbreath, Ross, 'Displacement, conservation and customary use of native plants and animals in New Zealand', *New Zealand Journal of History*, vol. 36, no. 1, 2002, 36–50

Gillies, R., 'Notes on some changes in the fauna of Otago', *Transactions of the New Zealand Institute*, vol. 10, 1877, 306–22

Grier, Katherine C., 'Childhood socialization and companion animals: United States, 1820–1870', *Society and Animals: Journal of human-animal studies*, vol. 7, no. 2, 1999 (Society and Animals Forum, www.societyandanimalsforum.org)

Howell, Philip, 'A place for the animal dead: pets, pet cemeteries and animal ethics in late Victorian Britain', *Ethics, Place & Environment*, vol. 5, no. 1, 2002, 5–22

Johnson, Kathleen R., 'The ambiguous terrain of pet-keeping in children's realistic animal stories', *Society and Animals: Journal of human-animal studies*, vol. 4, no. 1, 1996 (Society and Animals Forum, www.societyandanimalsforum.org)

Kean, Hilda, 'An exploration of the sculptures of Greyfriars Bobby, Edinburgh, Scotland, and the Brown Dog, Battersea, South London, England', *Society and Animals: Journal of human-animal studies*, vol. 11, no. 4, 2003 (Society and Animals Forum, www.societyandanimalsforum.org)

Kean, Hilda, 'The mood of militancy', *BBC History Magazine*, vol. 8, no. 12, December 2007, 36–38

Kean, Hilda, 'Balto, the Alaskan dog and his statue in New York's Central Park: animal representation and national heritage', *International Journal of Heritage Studies*, vol. 15, no. 5, September 2009, 413–30

Kete, Kathleen, 'Pets' in Paula S. Fass (ed.) (2004), *Encyclopedia of Children and Childhood in History and Society*, Macmillan Reference USA, New York, vol. 2, pp. 668–72

Lawson, J. Ruth, 'Hydatid disease and sheep measles: the history of their control and the economics of a recent change of control policy', *New Zealand Journal of Zoology*, 1994, vol. 21, 83–89

Luomala, Katharine, 'The native dog in the Polynesian system of values', in Stanley Diamond (ed.) (1960), *Culture in History: Essays in honor of Paul Radin*, Columbia University Press, New York, pp. 190–240

Mansfield, Amy, 'Teaching old lawyers new tricks', *New Zealand Lawyer*, no. 74, 28 September 2007, pp. 28–29

McLennan, Catriona, 'Expert evidence crucial under Animal Welfare Act', *New Zealand Lawyer*, no. 12, 28 June 2001, p. 14

Murison, W.D., 'Note on the wild dog', *Transactions of the New Zealand Institute*, vol. 10, 1877, pp. 322–24

Pycior, Helen, 'The making of the "first dog": President Warren G. Harding and Laddie Boy', *Society and Animals: Journal of human-animal studies*, vol. 13, no. 2, 2005 (Society and Animals Forum, www.societyandanimalsforum.org)

Seager, E.W., 'The escapades of Mackenzie' in *Canterbury … old and new 1850–1900. A souvenir of the jubilee*, Whitcombe and Tombs, Christchurch, 1900, pp. 107–16

White, Taylor, 'On the wild dogs of New Zealand', *Transactions of the New Zealand Institute*, vol. 22, 1889, pp. 327–30

Wallace, Patricia Te Arapo, 'He whatu ariki, he kura, he waero: chiefly threads, red and white', in Bronwyn Labrum, Fiona McKergow and Stephanie Gibson (eds) (2007), *Looking Flash: Clothing in Aotearoa New Zealand*, Auckland University Press, Auckland, pp. 12–27

Theses and research essays

Anderson, Honor (1997), 'Hydatids: A disease of human carelessness. A history of human hydatid disease in New Zealand', MA thesis (History), University of Otago

Aramakutu, Evaan (1997), 'Colonists and Colonials: Animals' protection legislation in New Zealand 1861–1910', MA thesis (History), Massey University

Beynon, Penelope A. (2003), 'One Struggle, One Fight! Human Freedom, Animal Rights! Grassroots animal rights activism: incorporating animal liberation and general liberation ideologies', MA thesis (Social Anthropology), Massey University Albany

McNabb, R.L. (1943), 'An Investigation into the Development and Value of the School Club Movement in Taranaki Primary Schools, with special reference to the school agricultural club', thesis presented for Teacher's 'A' Certificate, Victoria University College

Milton, Frederick S. (2008), 'Taking the Pledge: A study of children's societies for the prevention of cruelty to birds and animals in Britain, c. 1870–1914', PhD thesis (History), Newcastle University

Mincham, Carolyn Jean (2008), 'A Social and Cultural History of the New Zealand Horse', DPhil. thesis (History), Massey University

Wells, N.E. (1983), 'The Moral Status of Animals: Reform of animal protection law', LLB dissertation, University of Auckland Faculty of Law

Wilson, Marcus J. (2007), 'A History of New Zealand's Military Horse: The experience of the horse in the Anglo-Boer War and World War One', MA thesis (History), University of Canterbury

Index

Page numbers in **bold** refer to illustrations.

abandoned animals 178, 181, 183, 186, 192, 193, **193**, 205, 232
acclimatisation societies 29, 42, 52, 86
Adams, P. 88
Adventure 13, 20
afterlife of animals 17
Agricultural and Pastoral (A&P) Associations 94, 146; shows 86, 93, 100, 132–33, 138, **143,** 162
Agricultural Chemical and Animal Remedies Manufacturers Association of New Zealand 243
agricultural clubs *see* Boys' and Girls' Agricultural Clubs
agricultural education 133, 204
Agriculture and Fisheries Ministry 164, 190, 243
Agriculture Department 97, 134, 136, 156, 195, 231, 232, 235
Alder, Henry 115, **115**
Alexandra, Queen 96
Alsatians (German Shepherds): attempts to ban import of 96–97; guide dogs 167; police dogs 161
American Humane Association 116
American Society for the Prevention of Cruelty to Animals 116
Anderson, Carolina 187
Andrews, Terry **164**
Angas, G.F. 26
animal fights, organised 73, 113
Animal Hospital (silent film) 227–28
animal liberation movement 241, 244–45, 246
Animal Protection Society 126, 220, 231
animal reproduction issues 177, 180, 182–83, 186, 194
Animal Research Saves Lives 243
Animal Research Takes Lives 244
animal rights 10, 224–26, 229–31, 241–46, **243, 246**
Animal Sunday 126
animal testing of products 242, 243, 245
animal welfare 10, 73, 231, 245; English law 108; law enforcement 111, 113; New Zealand law 108–09, 110, 113, 114–15, 224, 231–32, 246; *see also* cruelty to animals; kindness to animals; SPCAs
Animal Welfare Act 1999 246
Animal Welfare Week 126
animal-assisted therapy *see* pet therapy
Animals' Beauty Parlour, Wellington 228
Animals (Anaesthetics) bill 231
Animals Protection Act 1960 230, 231–32, 243
Antarctica 219
anthropomorphism 198, 203
Anti-Cruelty Society of Palmerston North 172
Aramoho Loyal Temperance Legion 122
Arthur Yates Ltd 227
Ashburton Agricultural and Pastoral Association 86
Ashburton Poultry, Pigeon and Canary Society 86
Atkinson, Arthur Richmond 116
Auckland 86, 87, 90, 92, 93, 95, 105, 111–12, **114,** 170, 173, 176, 182, 206, 216, 231, 240
Auckland Acclimatisation Society 52
Auckland Cat Coalition 194

Auckland Pet Expo 217
Auckland Society for the Protection of Women and Children 117
Auckland SPCA 111, 113, 114, 115, 117, 120, 124, 125, 126, 139, 170, 173, 179–80, 182, 183, 187, 224, 245; junior leagues 141
Auckland Sunday School Union 203
Austin, Ruby 184–85
Australia 9, 10, 22, 24, 26, 38, 56, 83, 95, 96, 97, 105, 112, 154, 155, 163, 166, 170, 188, 198, 199, 204, 221, 227, 234
Avery, Ken 188

back country workers, animal companionship 68–69
Baden Powell, Sir Robert 122
baiting of animals 73, 108, 113
Balto (sled dog team leader, Nome, Alaska) 198
Band of Love, Salvation Army 122
Bands of Hope 119
Bands of Mercy 119–22; pledge on kindness to animals 119, 120, 121, 122
Banks, Joseph 15, 20
Barker, Lady Mary Anne 68, 71, 130–31
Barnett, Sam 161
Bates, D.C. 202
Batten, Jean 209
battery hens 244–45, **245**
Bay of Islands 21, 22–23, 26
Beattie, Sir David 163
Beeby, Clarence 136
Bendigo Station, Central Otago 215–16
Bennett, F.O. 77
Bentham, Jeremy 107–08
Bergh, Henry 116
Bernasconi, Ernesto 102
Bess (World War I horse) 153
Betsey Jane (Charles Douglas's dogs) 65, 67, 74, 76, 238
Binns, Oswald **51**
bird seed 227
birds as pets: introduced birds 39, 52–53, 55, 56–57, **104**; New Zealand native birds 18, 20, 32, 45–46, 56
birds, introduced 39, 42, 56–57; as pets 39, 52–53, 55, 56–57, **104,** 227; recreational shooting of captive birds 231; showing 84, 86, 87, 90; *see also* poultry
birds, New Zealand native **31**; and cats 190–93; endangered and extinct 29–30, 56; hunting 29; as pets 18, 20, 32, 45–46, 56; protection 30, 32; showing 88
Bledisloe, Lord 203
Blossom (sea elephant) 212
Blue Cross Hospitals 126, 154, 204
boarding kennels 228, 236
Boniface, Linley 189
Border collies 62, 98, 167, 199
boundary dogs 68, 77, 217
Box, Alison 189
Boy Scout movement 121, **121,** 122
Boys' and Girls' agricultural clubs 129, 133–38, 142–47, 149; certificates **137, 144,** 146
Bradshaw, John 42–43

Braham, Kenneth 102
breeding of animals 83–83, 85, 86, 87, 88; cats 55, 56, 92, 93, 101–02; dogs 93–95, 96, 98, 101, 186
Britain 10, 20, 83, 85, 88, 89, 96, 105, 107, 108, 116, 119, 156, 161, 168, 194, 223, 225, 229
British Office Supplies, Wellington **160**
British Union for the Abolition of Vivisection 229–31, 242
Brown, Lynette 166
Brunner, Thomas 63, 76
Buckeridge, George 133–34
Buddy (Jean Batten's cat) 209
Bullen, Frank 202–03
Burr, Maggie 132
Butler, Annie 32
Butler, Colin 208–09
Butler, Samuel 70–71

Caesar (mascot and Red Cross dog, World War I) 154–55
Caesar (Andreas Reischek's dog) 64–65, **65**, 71, 79
Calf Club Day **128**, 129, 135, 138, **139**, 144–47, **145**, 147
calf clubs *see* Boys' and Girls' Agricultural Clubs
calves 130, 131, 132, 134, 135, 137, 138–39, 142–44, 147, 148; bobby calves 141–42; leading 148
Campbell, Alison **237**
Campbell, Dorothy 239
Campbell Rogers, Jennetta 156
Campbell, Shirley 145, 148
Canada 133–34
Canine Friends pet therapy 173
Canterbury 24, 40, 41, 42–44, 45, 62, 68, 69, 70, 132, 192, 198–200
Canterbury Dog Show 95
Canterbury earthquakes 127, 220
Canterbury SPCA 111, 112, 113, 114, 119, 122, 124, 125, 180, 185, 195, 230, 231; Animals Home 126
Captain Cooker pigs 22, 73–74
Carbury, H.W. 126
Carrington, C.J. 97
Carter's Universal Bird Seed 227
Carterton 70
Castle Hill Station 71, **72**
cat colonies 194
cats: breeds 55, 56, 92, 93, 101–02; celebrities **196**, 197, 205, **205**, **208**, 208–09, 209, 219; children's pets 55, 56, **106**, 121, 129, 130, **131**, **233**, **247**; companions to isolated men 68, **68**, 69, 70–71, **72**; on Cook's voyages 15, 20, 21; ecological footprint 194; environmental concerns 190–93, 194; food 234, 235; in food premises 172; *Hints to Cat Lovers* 179, **179**; introduced to New Zealand by European settlers 22, 23, **23**, **28**, 38, 40, 41, 42, 43–44, 49–50; mascots 73; pets 9, 43–44, 49–50, 55, 56, **106**, 121, 129, 130, **131**, **233**, 236, **247**; predators 29–30, 191–92; proposal for exporting of skins 195; for rabbit control 192; rodent catching 15, 40, 49, 55, 70, 158, 160, 172, 192; showing 89, 90, 92–93, 101–02, 239, **239**, 240; stray and unwanted cats 175, 176, 177, 178, 179, 182, 183, 184–85, 186, 194, 208–09, 230; as teaching aid 118; wild cats 191–92; and women 90, **91**, 92
Cats Protection League 184–85
Caverhill, Frances 42, 47
Cawardine, Mark 214
celebrity animals 197–221, 240
Chamier, George, *Philosopher Dick* 74

Chappell, Henry, 'The Soldier's Kiss' 153
Charlton, Yvonne **171**
chickens *see* poultry
children: abuse of 116, 117; agricultural clubs 129, 133–38; country children's pets 9, 129–30, **131**, 131–32, **132**, **133**, 136, 141, 142–44, 147, 148–49; cruelty to animals 117–18; disabled 170; education about kindness to animals 118–22, **123**, 124, 141, 204, 231, **233**, 247; and hydatids 188, **188**; literature about pets 53–55, 118, 120–21, **121**; newspaper and magazine columns for 55, 56, 58, 120–1, 129, 131–32, 141; and pets 52, 55–56, 90, **106**, 117, 118–22, **123**, 124, 129–32, 135–36, 140–44, 147, 148–49, **233**, 238, 246–47, **247**; poultry rearing 88; socialisation through pets 53–54, 56; SPCA membership and education initiatives 118, 119–22, **123**, 124, 125, **125**, 126, 139–41
Christchurch 42, 49, 50, 53, 58, 70, 86, 87, 89, 111–12, 184–85, 220, 242, 244
Christchurch Cat Club 93, 103
Christchurch Fire Brigade cat mascot 73
Christchurch International Exhibition 1906-07 122, **123**
Christchurch Poultry Club 83, 87, 88–89
Christchurch Poultry, Pigeon, Canary and Cat Society 90, 92
Christchurch Toy Dog and Cat Club 102
Christian views on animals 15–16, 77, 107, 116, 224
Christmas, Mabel 178, 228
churches, cooperation with SPCA initiatives 126
Clark, Helen 216
Clark, Nadia 168
Clark, Russell 212
Clarke, George 26
Clever Dogs of the World (Fox Films) 204
Clifton, Jane 217
cloaks: dog-skin 18, 24, 26; feather 18
clothing materials, animal 15; campaign against use of fur and feathers in fashion 224, **225**; cat skins 25, 195; dog skins 26; feathers 18; kuri skin and fur 14, 18, 24
Cobb and Co. coaches 67
cockatoos 56, 57, 90, **104**, **207**, 207–08
cockfights 73, 86
Codfish Island 213
Colenso, William 24
Colin's (Colin Butler's cat) **208**, 208–09
colonists, European *see* immigrants and pets
Companion Animal Society, New Zealand Veterinary Association 234
companion animals *see* pets
conservation 30, 32, 165, 190–92, 214, 215
Conservation Department 190, 212, 214; Kiwi Recovery Programme 165
Cook, James 13, 14, 15, 16, 20, 25; animals introduced to New Zealand 20–22, 49
Cook, Stephanie **189**
Cook Strait 202
Corkill, Max 205, **205**
Coromandel Peninsula 67, 193
Correspondence School 129–30; Animal Welfare Club 141
Cossgrove, David 122; *The Story of a Bull Pup* 121, **121**, 122
Council of Combined Animal Welfare Organisations (CAWO) 231, 232
Courage, Sarah Amelia 43, 49–50, 58, 78
Cowan, James 33, 202

Cox, James 70
Crocker, J.F. 135
Crookston, Suzanne 157
cruelty to animals 16, 107, 108, 113, 124–25, 231, 232; by children 117–18, **118**; farm animals 77, 111, 112, 115, 141–42; horses 109–10, 111–12, 121, 124; pets 16, 117, 125, 141; *see also* animal welfare; kindness to animals; SPCAs
Cruelty to Animals Act 1874, Nelson Province 110
Cruelty to Animals Act 1878 110
Cruelty to Animals Act 1880 110
Cruise, Richard 25
Cunningham, W.H. 156
Cupples, Mrs George 54
Cure Kids charity 216
Curry, Eileen 173
Customs Department 164, 195

Darwin, Charles 85
Davenport, Emma 54
David, Edith 56
De la Roche, Catherine 185
Deans, John 45
death of, and mourning for, pets 58, **58**, 236, 247
Devonport Borough Council 177
Dexter (*Tux Wonder Dogs* co-presenter) 240
Dickin, Maria, and Dickin Medal 220
Dieffenbach, Ernst 25
disabled people, assistance by dogs 168
Discovery 20
Dog Kennel Corner 217
Dog Registration Act 1880 34
dog tax 34
Dog Tax Rebellion/War 34–35, **35**
dogs: breeding and breeds 93–95, 96–97, 98, 101, 186–87; Canine Friends pet therapy 173; celebrities 198–200, **199**, **203**, 203–05, **206**, 206–07, 209, **209**, 217–18, **218**, **219**, 240; children's pets 55, 56, 124, 129, 130, **131**, **233**; companions to isolated men 68–70, 71, **72**, 73; companions to sawmill workers 80; control measures 32–34, **174**, 175–77, 187–89; on Cook's voyages 15, 20, 21; dangerous 34, 96–97, 175–76, 186–87; ecological footprint 194; environmental concerns 192, 194; farm dogs 62, 77, 78–79, **80**, 86, 160; food 226–27, 228, 234, 235–36; heroes 220; hunting dogs 50, 71, 74, **75**; interbreeding with kuri 24, 25; introduced to New Zealand by European settlers 22, 38, 39–41, 42–43, 50, 52; kangaroo dogs 24; and Maori 26, **27**, 32–34; mascots 73; military mascots 154–55; Pacific Islands 14; pets 9, 42–43, **51**, 52, 55, 56, **109**, 124, 129, 130, **131**, **233**, 236; police dogs **161**, 161–64, **164**, 165; 'pooper scooper' bylaws 189; as predators 30, 192; in public service 160; racing and other sports 73, 95; search and rescue work 164–65; showing 89, 90, 93–95, **94**, **95**, **96**, 104, 239–40; 'sniffer' dogs 164; stray and unwanted dogs 175–77, 178, 179, 182, 183, 186, 187–88, 205–07, 230; in surveying and exploring expeditions **60**, **63**, 64–65, 67–68, 74, 76; training 78–79, 161–68, 242; in war 154, 156, 157–58, 159, **159**; wild 24; working dogs 62, 80, 95; *see also* kuri; sheep dogs
Dogs' Registration Amendment Act 166–67
Dogworkz **240**, 240
dolphins 200, **201**, 202–03, 210, **211**, 212–13, **213**
Donald, Jim 163

donkeys 154, 155, 170, 173, 219, **219**, 221
Donne, T.E. 202
'Dot's Little Folk' page, *Otago Witness* 55, 238
Douglas, Charles 65, 67–68, 74, 76, 191, 238
Douglas, Roger 209
Dunedin 62, 86, 89, 90, 93, **109**, 111–12, 120, 125, 242
Dunedin Homing Pigeon Club 89
Dusky Sound 64
duty to care for animals 107, 224

earthquakes 127, **127**, 220
ecological footprints of pets 193–94
eco-subdivisions 192–93
Education Department 136, 137, 144, 145–46
Edwin family, Wellington 57
Elkington, E.W. 78, 81
Elliot, Cecil and Eric **131**
Elliot, E.A.J. **99**
Elmslie, John 111
Empson, Raewyn 194
Endeavour 20
English Kennel Club 93, 94, 102
Enys, Charles 71, **72**
Enys, John 71, 238
Europe 15, 83, 89, 96, 107, 161, 223
euthanising animals 176, 177, 178, 179, 180, 183–84, 220
Evans, Malcolm 216
Excelsior Steam Biscuit Factory 227
exporting of animals 105; cat skins 195

factory farming 244–45
Fairburn, Miles 70
Fairlie **219**, 221
family life, role of pets **222**, 223–24, **229**, 232, 246–47, **247**
fanciers 83–86, 102–03
fanciers' clubs 83, 84, 86–87, 89–90, 93, 101–02; shows 84, 86, 87–88, 90, 92–94, 101, 105, 239–42; and British royal family 85, 92, 93
farm animals 9, 217; bought and cared for by European settlers 46–47; cruelty to 16, 76–77, 111, 112, 115, 141–42; dogs 62, 77, 78–79, **80**, 86, 160; hand rearing of baby animals 76, 130–33, **132**, 134, 136, 137, 138–39, 142–44, **143**, **144**; handling and evaluating 77–79, 81; horses 66, 67, 71, 77, 78, 79, 81, 86; introduced by European settlers 22–23, 38, 39, 41; introduced by explorers 20–22; as pets 9–10, 47, 130, **131**, 131–32, **132**, **133**, 142–44, 147, 148–49; *see also* calves; food animals; lambs; sheep dogs
Farmers Trading Company store, Auckland **207**, 207–08
Farmers' Union 134
feeding of pets 44, **44**, 226–27, 228, 234, 235–36; home feeding services 236
feminism, and animal rights and welfare 116, 117, 225
ferrets 190, 237
FitzGerald, James and Fanny 50
Flock House, Manawatu 153
Floyd (cinema cat, Wellington) 185, **185**
food animals 10, 16, 46; birds 29, 30, 32; calves and cattle 141–42, 148, 149; cats 25; different views of Maori and European settlers on animals used for food 25; dogs 76; kuri 14–15, 17–18, 25; lambs and sheep 148, 149; Pacific Islands 14–15; pigs 22, 25, 26, 87, 147; poultry 87; on ships 20, 38

food premises: cats in 172; guide dogs in 166–67
Forbes, J.A. 126
Ford, Lucy 58
Forgotten Felines 194
Forster, Georg 14, 15, 21, 25
Forster, Johann 15, 21
Foundation for the Blind 167
4-H (Head, Heart, Hands and Health) agricultural clubs 133–34
Fraser, Peter 136
Fraser, Sir William 77–78
Friday (James Mackenzie's dog) 198–200, **199, 219,** 221
Fritz (John Plimmer's dog) 218, **218,** 221
Fry, Stephen 214
Fyffe, George and Catherine Douglas 42

Gadsby, Sarah 131
Gallagher, Mr **68**
Gallipoli campaign 152, 154, 156, 219, 221
gambling and animals 73
George (Jack Russell terrier, Manaia) 220
German Shepherds *see* Alsatians (German Shepherds)
Gilbert, Kylie **240**
Ginger (cat that climbed Mt Taranaki) **196,** 197
Girl Guide Movement 122
Gisborne 131, 212, 229
Glen, Wally 172
goats 20, 21, 46, 146, 169
Godley, Charlotte 41, 49, 50
Green Lane Hospital 234
Grey, George 53
Greyfriars Bobby (Skye terrier) 198
grooming animals 9, 38, 84, 129, 135, 142, 144, 145, 147, 148, 223, 228, 236, **237,** 240, **240**
Gross, Richard 155
guide dogs 165–68, **167**
guinea pigs 52, 55–56, 83, 90, 130, 169, **169,** 236, **237**
Guinness (Irish wolfhound, Christchurch) 220
Gunson, Jessie 125

Hacon, Walter 169
Hall, Sir John 112
Hallinan, Lynda 148
Hamilton 170, 185, 242
Hamilton, Grace 148, 149
Hamilton, S. 120
Hansen, A. 56, 238
Happy Feet (penguin) 214–15, **215**
hare-coursing 73, 111, 231
Harris, Victor 121
Harvey, H.P. 103
Hastings 127, 240
Hawera 100
Hawke's Bay 62
Hawke's Bay earthquake 127
Hawkes Bay Poultry and Canary Association 84
Haworth, Diane 206–07
Hay, Mary 45–46
heading dogs 62, 98, 100
Health Department 166, 172, 188
Heaphy, Charles 63
hearing dogs 168

Heathcote White, Alan and Kathleen 185–86
Hector (Farmers' cockatoo) **207,** 207–08
Henderson, Richard **219,** 221
Henry A. Lane Challenge Shield 138
Henry, James 127
Henry, Richard 165
hens *see* poultry
Henwood, William 46
Heretaunga Pony Club 239
heroic animals 151, 152–53, 173, 213, 217, 220
Hewett, Ellen 45
Hewitt, Norm and Elizabeth **247**
Hibberd, Shirley, *Clever Dogs, Horses, etc.* 54, **54**
Higgins, Sarah 49
Hill, Woodroffe 112
Hints to Cat Lovers 179, **179**
Hobhouse, Mary 48
Hodder, Beverley 149
Hodsell, Peter 137
Hodson, Geoffrey 229–31
Hogben, George 124
Hokianga 34–35, 210, **211,** 212
Holland, Sid 161
Holmes Pet Food 235
home: idealisation of 38; pets' role in making 37–38, 43–44, 52
Horowhenua Animal Rescue Society 186
horses: cruelty to 109–10, 111–12, 121, 124; farm horses 66, 67, 71, 77, 78, 79, 81, 86; introduced to New Zealand by European settlers 22, 23, 38, 39; as pets and companions 48–49, 70, 71; racing and other sports 48, 73; Riding for the Disabled 170, **171;** training 79; for transport 47–48, **48,** 66, 67, 109, 111–12, **114,** 121, 125, 158; in war 150, **150,** 151–54; work horses 65–67, 71, 158
hospitals and clinics for animals 140, 179, 204, 227–28, 247
Hoturoa (Panapa's pig dog) 33
Howard, Mabel 228, 230, **230,** 231–32
Howell, John 142
Howitt, W.K. 48–49, 69
human–animal connections 10; in hunting cultures 16–17; Maori 16–17, 20, 33; mateship 62; and names of pets 238; terminology 245
Humane Society of New Zealand, Kindness Club 186
Humanitarian League 224
Hunt, Sam 209, **209**
huntaways 62, 98, 100, 217–18, **218**
Hunter, Ivy 146
Hunterville 217–18
hunting: dogs used in 50, 71, 74, **75;** game animals introduced to New Zealand 29; by Maori 16–18, 26, 29, 32–33, 34, 35; of pigs 32–33, 50, 73–74, **75,** 187; restrictions 29, 32; for sport 73, 108, 111
Hursthouse, Charles 24–25, 26, 50, 190
Hutchinson Brothers 227
hydatids 166, 188–89, 235
Hydatids Act 1959 235

Igglesden, Charles Moore 43
Ihenga 12, 17
immigrants and pets 10, **36,** 37–38, 42–44, **43, 44,** 45–46, 52–53, **53;** transport of animals 38–41, **39**
importing of animals 46, 86, 96–97, 105, 190

Injuries by Dogs Act 1865 33
Innes, Mrs C.L. 112
Internal Affairs Department 97, 158, 160, 195
internet 11, 213, 214, 215
Invercargill 90, 227
Irawaru 16–17
isolated workers, animal companionship 68–69

Jack (George Parker's dog) **203,** 203–05
James, Jenny 148
Jameson, Agnes 50
Jervois, Lady Lucy 112
Jervois, Sir William 93, 112
Jones, Anna 184, 195
Jones family, Taranaki **48**
Jordan, W.J. 203
J.R. Butland 234

kahu kuri 18
Kaikoura 42
kaka 18, **30, 31,** 32, 45, 56, **65,** 238
kaka poria 18, **19**
kakapo 17, 18, 29, 30, 56, 64, 76, 165, 213–14, **214**
kakariki **31,** 32, 45–46, 56, 88
kangaroo dogs 24
Karori Sanctuary 194
Katikati 46
Kawau Island 53
Kean, Hilda 151
Kearns, Norma Anne 220
Kehu 76
Kennaway, Laurence 66, 67, 71, 78
The Kennel column, *Otago Witness* 103
kennels, boarding 228, 236
Kerridge, Bob 170, 187
Key, John 209, 214
killing of animals 81, 178, 194, 231; *see also* euthanising animals
kindness to animals 107–08, 112, 224, 231; *see also* animal welfare; Bands of Mercy; cruelty to animals; SPCAs
King, Philip Gidley 22
kiore 16, 49
Kirk, Lily 117
Kisby, Carol 186
kiwi 16, 17, 29, 30, 64, 88, 165, 192, 215
Koebel, W.H. 74, 78
kunekune pigs 22
Kupe 17, 202
kuri 14–15, 17–18; interbreeding with European dogs 24, 25

Lambert, G. 58
lambs 130–32, **131, 132, 133,** 137, 142–44, **143,** 145, 146, 147, 148
Last Chance to See (BBC television series) 214
Lawlor, D. 236
Lawson, Ian 143–44
Leeston Band of Mercy 120
The Levels Station 198, 200
Levinson, Boris 170
Lewin, Monty 100
Lilico, James 98
Lineham, Elizabeth 55

lizard 46
Lloyd George, David 151
London (later National) Society for the Prevention of Cruelty to Children 116
Lonely Miaow Association 194
loners, animal companionship 68–69
Loudon, Jane 54
Lovell-Smith family, Christchurch **53**
Lower Hutt 49, 167, 195
Luke (police dog) 163
Lush, Vicesimus 47, 52
Lyttelton 40, 41, 42, 49, 50, 62

Mackay, Jessie 225
Mackenzie Country 200, 217
Mackenzie, James 198–200, **219,** 221
Mackenzie, Patricia **239**
Mackenzie, Sir Thomas 96–97
Mahakirau Forest Estate 192–93
Mahon, Sam 219
Major (dog mascot, 19 Infantry Battalion) 157–58, 159, **159**
Mangere Island 192
Mangonui District Calf Club 138
Maori: adoption of European dress 24–25; and animals introduced to New Zealand by European settlers 22–23, **23,** 35; and animals introduced to New Zealand by explorers 20–21; and birds as pets 18, 20, 32; childrens' education 124, 137–38, **139;** choice of pets 26; and different views from European settlers on animals used for food 25; and dogs 26, **27,** 32–34 (*see also* kuri); hunting 16–18, 26, 29, 32–33, 34, 35; kuri 14–15, 17–18, **23,** 24–25; and New Zealand wars 26, 29, 151, 155; pet-keeping practices 18, 20, 26; significance of whales and dolphins to 202, 212, **213;** spiritual view of animals 16–17, 20, 202, 212; station hands 78
Maori schools 124, 137–38
Marine Mammals Protection Act 1978 212
Marineland, Napier 212
Marion du Fresne, Marc Joseph 15, 21
Marlborough 24, 61
Marlborough Poultry, Pigeon and Cage Bird Association 105
Marsden, Samuel 22, 23, 25
Marshall, Robert 102
Marshall, Trena 148
Martin, Gaynor 205
Martin, Jemima 41–42, 44
Marton 94
mascots 73; Buddy (Jean Batten's cat) 209; Hector (Farmers' cockatoo) 208; military 155–56, 157–58, 159, **159,** 210; workplace 160, **160**
Massey University Veterinary School 234
Masterpet 236
mastery over animals 77–79, 81
Matakana Island 212, **213**
mateship **60,** 62
Matheson, Ross 144–45
Maui 17
May, J.E. **159**
McEwing, Alex 149
McLauchlan, Ross 184
McNeish, Harry 219
McQuillan, Holly 148

Meadowcroft, F.W. 125, 139, 151
memorials to animals 153, 198, 206–07, 212, 213, 217–19, **218,** 219, **219,** 220, 221
men: companion animals 67–71, **72,** 73; mastery over animals 77–79, 81
menageries 52–53
Mendel, Gregor Johann 85
mental health, and pets 168–69, 170, 173
Mesopotamia sheep run 70
Methven Collie Club 100
mice 49, 52, 69, 158
microchipping of dogs 187
mining, use of ponies 67
Minstrel (Sam Hunt's dog) 209, **209**
missionaries 22–24, 25, 26
mobility assistance dogs 168
Moko (dolphin) 212–13, **213**
Monckton, Lorna 56–57, 131
Monckton, Mary 140, **140**
monkeys 16, **42,** 43, **43,** 52, 90, 125, 226
Monkman, Dorothy 178
Monro family, Palmerston North 57
Moonbeam (John Key's cat) 209
Moore, Cyril Ralph (Tiny) 235–36
Morgan, Gareth 194, 214
Morgan, Les 67
Morrinsville Calf Club **128**
Morton, Elsie K. 176, 178
Moss, Constance 124
Mossman, James 141
Motueka 46–47
Mrs Chippy (Harry McNeish's cat) 219
Mt Maunganui 212
Mt Taranaki 164–65, **196,** 197
Mueller, Gerhard 64, 74, 76
Muldoon, Robert 172
Murchison earthquake 127, **127**
Murison, W.D. 24
Murphy (Richard Henderson's donkey) **219,** 221

names of pets 238
Napier 84, 127, 162
Napier Marineland 212
Napier Poultry and Canary Association 90, 92
National Council for Alsatian Shepherd Dog Control 97
National War Memorial, Canberra 221
National War Memorial, Wellington **219,** 221
Native (Maori) schools 124, 137–38
Nelson 45, 49, 56, 76, 90, 105, 122, 203, 206
Nelson Asylum 169
Nelson Poultry, Bird and Dog Show 88, 90, 92
Nelson Provincial Council 110
neutering pets 177, 178, 182–83, 194, 234
New Plymouth 208–09
New Plymouth Homing Pigeon Club 89
New York Society for the Prevention of Cruelty to Children 116
New Zealand Alliance 116, 117
New Zealand Alsatian Club 97
New Zealand Antarctic Society 219
New Zealand Anti-Vivisection Society (NZAVS) 242, 243, 244
New Zealand Band of Mercy 120–21

New Zealand Cat Club 101–02
New Zealand Cavy Club 237
New Zealand Collie Club 105
New Zealand Companion Animal Council 9, 245
New Zealand Farmer 55, 103, 105, 118, **118,** 129
New Zealand Governing Council of the Cat Fancy 101–02, 240
New Zealand Kennel Club 93, 94, 97, 101, 102, **103,** 105, 240
New Zealand Kennel Council 102
New Zealand Land Search and Rescue 165
New Zealand Open Rescue 245
New Zealand Pekingese and Persian Cat Club 102
New Zealand Pet Trade News 236
New Zealand Pony Clubs' Association 239
New Zealand Rifle Brigade, 4th Battalion (A Company) 155
New Zealand Schoolmaster 118, 119
New Zealand Sheep Dog Trial Association 100
New Zealand Vegetarian Society 231
New Zealand Veterinary Association 183; Companion Animal Society 234
New Zealander of the Year, Local Hero Medal 220
Newton Pigeon and Canary Club 88
Newton Pigeon, Canary and Cage Bird Association 87
Nordhoff, Charles 25
Nordmeyer, Arnold 195
Norrie, Sir Willoughby 212
North Egmont Mountain House **196,** 197
North Island Sheep Dog Trial Association 100, 101
Northern Wairoa Boys' and Girls' Agricultural Club 149
Northland 22, 24, 68, 148, 193, 216
Noxious Animals Act 1967 190, 191
NZ Cat Fancy (Inc.) 240

O'Connor, Margaret 149
Onewhero Area School Calf Club Day 148
Opo (dolphin) 210, **211,** 212
Orari Gorge Station 43
Orbell, John and Catherine 45
Ordinance to Abate the Dog Nuisance 1849 33
Ordinance to provide a summary mode of abating the Nuisance of Dogs wandering at large in Towns 1844 176
Orr, A.M. 141
Otago 24, 45, **60,** 69, 78, 215–16
Otago Expansion League 134
Otago Medical School 226
Otago Provincial Council 109
Otago SPCA 109, 111, 112, 113, 122, 124, 180, 226
Outreach Therapy Pets 170, **173,** 173
Overell, Bette 242, 244

Pacific Islands 13, 14, 15, 20
Paddy (Wellington Regiment dog mascot) 156, **156**
Paddy the Wanderer (Airedale terrier, Wellington) **206,** 206–07
Painter, Dave 164
pampered pets 223–24, 228
Papakura, Makereti 32, **33**
Parihaka 34
Park, Ruth 177–78
Parker, George 203–05
Parr, C.J. 136
Parr, Elizabeth 55
Paterson, A.M. 79, 81

Patterson, T.H. 136, 144
Paw Justice 246
Pease, Joseph 108
pedigree animals 83, 85, 92, 93, **94,** 186, 238
Peka Peka Beach 214–15, **215**
Pelorus Jack (dolphin) 200, **201,** 202–03, 210
Pelorus Jack II 210
penguins 214–15, **215**
People's Dispensary for Sick Animals (PDSA), Britain 220
Perriam, John 215–16
pet food 226–27, 228, 234, 235–36, 244
pet industry 226, 236, 244, 247
Pet Industry Joint Advisory Council 236
pet keeping 10, 245; New Zealand 9, 10, 180–81, 236–37; range of animals 236–37; and scientific discovery 15
Pet Pride 232
pet shops 226
pet shows 90, 122, **123**
pet therapy 168–70, **170,** 173
Petre, Ellen 52–53
Petre, Henry 39, 52–53
pets: costs of care 247; 'cult of pets' 85, 198; definition of 'pet' 10; numbers 9, 237; owners' tenderness towards other animals 108; pet-related societies and organisations 237–39; symbols of success 52; terminology 245
Pets: Their care in sickness and health (SPCA) 140, 177
Phipps, William 89, **89**
photography and pets 57, **57,** 59, **59,** 90; studio portraits; 57, 59, **91, 222**
Pigeon Bay, Banks Peninsula 45–46
pigeons: postal services 89; racing 88–89; rearing 88; shooting 111; in war 154
pigs 22, 26, 41, 47, 147, 194; hunting 32–33, 50, 73–74, **75,** 187; intensive farming 244, 245
Pikewati 76
pit bull terriers 97, 186–87, 220
place names and animals 17
pledges on kindness to animals 119, 120, 121, 122
Plimmer, John 218, **218,** 221
Plunkett, Sean 215
Polack, J.S. 25
police dogs **161,** 161–64, **164,** 165
Police Offences Act 1884 113
ponies 48, 67, 129, **131**
pony clubs 239
'pooper scooper' bylaws 189
Porritt, Sir Arthur 217
possums 190, **191**
Post Office: cats 158, **160**; dogs 164
The Postman 130, 141, 143, 149
Potaka Tawhiti (Houmaitawhiti's kuri) **12**
Potaka Tawhiti (Ihenga's kuri) 17
poultry 20, 21, 26, 38, 46, **82,** 83, 88, 105, 194; battery hens 244–45, **245**; farming 87, **203,** 203–04; showing 82, 83, **84,** 86, 87, 92, 93, 101, 105, 146
pounds 174, 180, 183, 206, 244
Powles, C. Guy 152–53
Pratt, Alfred 118
Prebble, R.W. 172
Prevention of Cruelty to Animals bill 230, 231
Prevention of Cruelty to Animals Ordinance 1861, Otago 108–09

Priest, Mary 102–03
prisoners, and dogs 164, 168
Protection of Birds bill 231
psychiatric hospitals and wards, pets in 168–69, 173
public service, animals employed in 158, 160–64
Puckey, William 24
Puppies in Prison programme 168
Purches, Clint **215**
Puysegur Point, Fiordland 56

quarantine 96, 156, 164

rabbiters 68
rabbits 9, 52, 55, 83, 90, 190, 192, 194, 237
Ranfurly, Constance, Countess of 58, 104, **104**
Ranfurly, Uchter John Mark Knox, Earl of 104
Rastall, Stan 102
Rastus (Max Corkill's cat) 205, **205**
rats 15, 20, 40, 49, 50, 70, 158, 160, 192; 'rat pits' 73
Rawene 35
Raynes, Mr **222**
Reischek, Andreas 64–65, 71, 79, 81
Rench, Dave 157–58
rescue: of animals 125–26, 127, 140, 184–86, 194; dogs used in search and rescue 164–65
Resolution 13–14, 16, 21
Rice, Court 105
Riding for the Disabled 170, **171**
Riley, S.F. (Frank) 161, **161**
Risso's dolphin *(Grampus griseus)* 202
Rochfort, John 49
rodent control 15, 40, 49, 55, 70, 158, 160
Royal Forest and Bird Protection Society 192–93
Royal New Zealand Society for the Prevention of Cruelty to Animals (RNZSPCA) 163, 194, 244, 245; One of the Family campaign 247
Royal Society for the Prevention of Cruelty to Animals (RSPCA) 108, 112, 113, 116, 119
Rua Kenana 34, 35
Ruatoria 23

SAFE (Save Animals from Experiments/Save Animals from Exploitation) 242, 244, 245
Sale, G.S. 56
Salt, Henry 224
Salvation Army 122
sanctuaries and shelters for animals 126, 182, 185
Scadden, Una 135
School Journal 124, 139–40, 153–54
schools: agricultural clubs 136–39, **139,** 142–44; and pet days 139, 146; and SPCA education initiatives 122, 124, 139–41
Scully, Sean 220
Sea Fisheries Act 1904 202
Seacliff Mental Hospital 169, **169**
Seager, Edward 40–41, 168–69
search and rescue, dogs used in 164–65
Seddon, Dick **35**
Seddon, Richard 152
sentience, concept of 107–08, 241
Shackleton, Ernest 219
Sharp, Captain and Mrs 43

Shaw, W.H. 119
sheep 22, 24, 33, 38, 61–62, 76, 78, 98, 100, 147, 215–17
sheep dog trials 73, 98, 100–01
sheep dogs 50, 61, 62, 77, 98, **99, 131,** 198–200, 217–18, 238
Sherriff, Alisha **214**
Shields, Barry 223
Shrek (sheep) 215–17, **216**
Simpson, John 219, 221
Simpson, Joseph 163
Singer, Peter 241–42; *Animal Liberation* 241
Sirocco (kakapo) 213–14, **214**
Skae, Frederick 169
Slattery, Edmond (Ned) 69, **69**
Slaughter of Animals bill 231
Smith, Mabel 133
Smithies, Catharine 119
'sniffer' dogs 164
social class, and animals 15, 85, 88, 93, 112
social function of pets 10, 52, 67–71, **72,** 73; *see also* family life, role of pets; home – pets' role in making; pet therapy
Society for the Prevention of Cruelty to Animals *see* Royal New Zealand Society for the Prevention of Cruelty to Animals (RNZSPCA); Royal Society for the Prevention of Cruelty to Animals (RSPCA); SPCAs
Society for the Protection of Women and Children and Prevention of Cruelty to Animals 117
South African War **149,** 152, 155
South Island Sheep Dog Trial Association 100
Southland 69
SPCAs: and animal welfare legislation 113, 114–15, 224, 231, 232; and animals used in warfare 154; and bobby calf treatment 141–42; bonds with child protection organisations 116; children's membership and education initiatives 118, 119–22, **123,** 124, 125, **125,** 126, 139–41, 204; and euthanising animals 177, 178, 179, 180, 183–84, 194; and factory farming 244–45; and farming communities 115; federation 141, 220, 230, 231, 244–45; finance 114, 117, 120, 125, 140–41, 180; inspectors 94, 113, 114, 115, 124–25, 176–77, 232; ladies' auxiliaries 112, 228; 'lady collectors' 114; rescue initiatives 125–26; solicitors 113; special constables 113; and stray or unwanted animals 176–77, 179–80, 181–84, 186, 192; veterinarians 113; and vivisection 225–26; *see also* Royal New Zealand Society for the Prevention of Cruelty to Animals (RNZSPCA); Royal Society for the Prevention of Cruelty to Animals (RSPCA); and names of branches
Speedy, Rose 52
Spencer, Graham 158
Spicer, George 161
spiritual guardians or guides, animals as 17, 202
St Francis Assisi Organisation, Dunedin 172
St John Ambulance 170, 173
St Matthew's Band of Hope, Christchurch 119
Stephens Island wren 192
Stephens, Sarah 46–47
Stevens, W.G. 157
Stewart, Adela 46, 47, 49
Stewart, Mervyn 46
Stout, Robert 112
stray and unwanted animals: cats 175, 176, 177, 178, 179, 182, 183, 184–85, 186, 194, 208–09, 230; dogs 175–77, 178, 179, 182, 183, 186, 187–88, 205–07, 230; as military mascots 155; and SPCAs 176–77, 179–80, 181–84, 186, 192

Stray Cat Food Trust Fund 184
Strutt, William 26, 27
Sunnyside Hospital 168–69
surveying and exploring expeditions, use of dogs **60, 63,** 64–65, 67–68, 74, 76
Surville, Jean François Marie de 14–15, 21
Sutherland's Tannery 204–05
swaggers 69, **69**
Sydenham Poultry, Pigeon and Canary Society 87
Symes, Amy **245**

Taieri Agricultural Society 78
talking birds: and bird seed 227; galah 57; Hector (Farmers' cockatoo) 208; kaka 18, 32; kakariki 45–46; tui 18, 20, 24, 32, 56
Tancred, Henry 199
Tane 16
Taranaki 23, 46, **48,** 48–49, 69, 133, 134–35, 138, 148, 164–65, 205
Taranaki Education Board 134
Tatuanui Calf Club 148
Tautari Boys' and Girls' Calf Club 135
Tawhiao 110
taxidermy 58
Te Arawa 12
Te Huihuinga 34
Te Urewera 34
Te Whiti 34
Teina 22
temperance movement, and animal protection 116–17, 119, 120, 121, 122
Terry, Lionel 169
Theosophical Order of Service in New Zealand 225; Animal Welfare Group 231
Tikao, Teone Taare 32
Tikitiki School, Calf Club Day **139**
Tip-Top Boarding Kennels 228
Toia, Hone Riiwi 34–35
Tollemache, Algernon Gray 41
Tourist and Health Resorts Department 202
toy dog clubs 94, 102
training animals 78–79, 81, 161–68, 240
transport: of animals 38–41, **39,** 105, 115, 232; animals used for 47–48, **48,** 66, 67, 109–10, 111–12, **114,** 121, 125, 158
Treaty of Waitangi 32
Tripp, Ellen Shephard 41, 43
tui 18, 20, **21,** 23–24, 30, **31,** 32, 45, 56, 88
Tux dog biscuits 235–36
Tux Wonder Dogs (television show) 240
Twain, Mark 202–03

'Uncle Ned,' *New Zealand Farmer* 55, 56, 58, 129, 131–32, 238
United States 10, 83, 86, 105, 116, 119, 133–34, 140, 194, 223, 225
Upper Hutt Animal Rescue Society 172, 185–86
Upper Hutt SPCA 182

Vale, Robert and Brenda 194
veterinary care 177, 179, 183, 227–28, 232–34, 247
Veterinary Surgeons Act 1956 232–34
Victoria Medal 108

Victoria, Queen 58, 85, 90, 92, 93
Vincent, Mrs F. 102–03
vivisection 224–26, 229–31, 232, 241
Von Alzdorf, Baron Charles 49

Wadsworth, Oliver Laking 56
Waiau Pa School Calf Club 146
Waikato 23, 71, 110, 142
Waikato Education Board 143
Waikato Royal Show 147
Waikato SPCA 186
Waimea Boys' and Girls' Agricultural Club 149
Wainui School, South Kaipara 146
Waipara Station 43–44
Wairarapa 62, 87, 192
Wairarapa Calf-rearing Club 135
Waitaki 100
Wakefield, Edward Jerningham 23, 39–40, 50, 52, 69, 78
Walker, Alfred 83
Walmsley, Winifred 178
Wanganui 90, 122, **174,** 227–28
Wanganui Poultry and Dog Show 88
war: New Zealand wars 26, 29, 151, 155; use of animals in 151–58, 159, 219, **219,** 221
Ward, Edward 40, 62
Ward, John 45
Wark, R. 105
watchdogs 17, 50, 52
Waterhouse, G.M. 112
Watson, H.O.M. 111
Watson, William 115
Watties 234, 235
Weakley, Michelle 243
Wellington 40, **43,** 47, 52, 58, **58,** 62, 86, 93, 94, 95, 96, 105, 111–12, 178, 184, 187, 189, 195, 206–07, 212, 218, 228, 242, 243
Wellington Bands of Mercy 120, 121
Wellington Cats Protection League 185, **185,** 186
Wellington Cenotaph relief sculpture **154**
Wellington Domestic Animal Owners' Organisation 228
Wellington East Girls' College 140
Wellington Girls' College 140–41
Wellington Harbour Board 206

Wellington Kennel Club 102, **103,** 104, 228
Wellington Labrador Retriever Club 167
Wellington Poultry Show 88
Wellington Regiment 156, **156**
Wellington Society for the Protection of Women and Children 117
Wellington SPCA 104, 111, 112, 114, 115, 116, 117, 120, 124, 125, 126, 127, 139, 142, 170, 178, 179, 180, 182, 183, 185, 228; junior leagues 140–41; Most Heroic Dog of the Year competition 220; *Pet Pride* 232
Wellington Zoo 214–15
Wells, Benjamin 46
West Coast 64, 65, 73, **75,** 76
Whakatane 17, 212
whales 17, 213
whaling 42, 202
Wheeler, Margaret 167, **167**
Whiro, Kipa Hemi 202
White, Codie 147, **147**
White, Taylor 24
Whitehead, Percy 61, 62
wildlife friendly subdivisions 192–93
Wildlife Regulations 1985 190
Wildlife Service 191–92; *Problem Cats* 192, 193, **193**
Wilford, Elizabeth **59**
Williams, Errol 157
Williams, Harry **196,** 197
Wilson, Helen 129
Wilson, W. Stuart 134
Wilton, Christine 215
Winters, Barney ('Barney Whiterats') 69
women: and animals 46–47, 76, 88, 112, 117, 234; violence to 116, 117, 118
Women's Christian Temperance Union 120
Wood, J.G. 54
working animals 10, 15, 46, 61–62; as pets 48–49; *see also* farm animals; sheep dogs; surveying and exploring expeditions; transport – animals used for
World War I 152–56, **155, 156**
World War II 157–58
Wright, David McKee, 'Old Nugget' 66–67
Wright, Graeme 144